Mission: Concept in Context

Series Preface

Regnum Studies in Mission are born from the lived experience of Christians and Christian communities in mission, especially but not solely in the fast growing churches among the people of the developing world. These churches have more to tell than stories of growth. They are making significant impacts on their cultures in the cause of Christ They are producing 'cultural products' which express the reality of Christian faith, hope and love in their societies.

Regnum Studies in Mission are the fruit often of rigorous research to the highest international standards and always of authentic Christian engagement in the transformation of people and societies. These are for the world. The formation of Christian theology, missiology and practice in the twenty-first century will depend to a great extent on the active participation of growing churches contributing biblical and culturally appropriate expressions of Christian practice to inform World Christianity.

Regnum is supported by the generosity of EMW

Mission: Concept in Context
Post-Communism Religious Revival in Eastern Central Europe as Experienced in the Seventh-Day Adventist Church

László Szabó

First published 2021 by Regnum Books International

Regnum is an imprint of the Oxford Centre for Mission Studies
St. Philip and St. James Church
Woodstock Road
Oxford OX2 6HR, UK
www.ocms.ac.uk/regnum

09 08 07 06 05 04 03 7 6 5 4 3 2 1

British Library Cataloguing in Publication Data
A catalogue record for this book is available from the British Library

ISBN: 978-1-5064-8372-6

eBook ISBN: 978-1-5064-8394-8

Typeset by Words by Design

Cover image: Joseph Sun from www.unsplash.com

Distributed by Fortress Press in the US, Canada, India, and Brazil

Dedication

To God,

Because He always opened another door, when one closed.

To my parents

Because political, economical and social challenges during Communism were for you not a research topic but day-to-day reality. Whatever tried to bring you down to your knees, you always presented courage, creativity, love and genuine Christian attitude. Thanks for never giving up and being an example for us.

Father, you often worked 24 or sometimes even 48 hours shifts at work. Then you came home and continued working in our garden or with your bees, just to make sure our needs were met. As the head of the ambulance station and as a Christian, you presented convincing precision in your work and creativity in emergency situations. You served like Daniel for decades as a leader under very difficult circumstances. Although your directors were against your religious attitude, they acknowledged and affirmed your competence and didn't want to miss your service. Your life was a depiction of the message that quality work is more precious than benefits through compromise.

Mother, you masterfully ensured that we enjoyed family cohesion, care and the best food during the time of Gulas Communism. Regardless of what challenged our family, your versatility, adaptability and creativity had always found a solution and earned admiration in our neighbourhood. Also, in a time of atheism, your life was the best argument for faith in God and Christian values.

To my wife Szilvia:

With love and gratitude. You stood by me through the good times and challenges. You are a very special blessing from God not only for me. Thank you.

To my children Dominik and Zsanna:

You endured years of research and writing with great faithfulness. You are special to me and I wish you to learn from our history: God always opens another door, when one closes.

Contents

Abbreviations

ADRA:	*Adventist Development and Relief Agency*
AFC:	*Alliance of Free Churches*
ATF:	*Adventista Teológiai Főiskola (Adventist Theological Seminary)*
ÁVH:	*Államvédelmi Hatóság*
DET:	*Dunamelléki Egyházterület (Duna Conference)*
EUD:	*Euro-Africa Division of Seventh-day Adventist Church*
EVS:	*European Values Study*
FILEK:	*Fiatal Lelkészek Egyesülete (Young Pastor's Fellowship)*
GC:	*General Conference of Seventh-day Adventist Chruch*
GYICSŐ:	*Gyülekezeti Ifjúsági Csoportok Összejövetele*
HNA:	*Hetednapi Adventista Egyház (Seventh-day Adventist Church)*
HUC:	*Hungarian Union Conference*
ISSP:	*International Social Survey Programme*
LG:	*Lumen Gentium*
MTA:	*Magyar Tudományos Akadémia*
SDA:	*Seventh-day Adventist Church*
SED:	*Sozialistische Einheitspartei Deutschland*
SOCA:	*State Office for Church Affairs*
SPA:	*State Protection Authority*
TB:	*Területi Bizottság (Conference Executive Committee)*
TED:	*Trans-European Division of Seventh-day Adventist Church*
TET	*Tiszavidéki Egyházterület (Tisza Conference)*
UB:	*Unióbizottság (Union Executive Committee)*
WVS:	*World Values Survey*

1. Introduction

From Oppression to Opportunity

The present European trends of growing practical secularisation (a decline in religious activity), the secularisation of ideas (meaning that religious ideas are not central) and desacralization (loss of a sense of the sacred) stand in sharp contrast to a recent decade during which one of the greatest religious opportunities of the century occurred in Eastern Central Europe. The modern mission era has experienced in the former Communist countries an unprecedented religious revival and this study focuses on its historical, religious and social context.

We can see at least two major shifts in the religious attitudes of Eastern European countries in the past forty years: the shift from socialist secularism to unprecedented religious revival, and from that religious revival to practical secularisation.

The political changes that took place in Eastern Central Europe in 1989 transformed the landscape of the Eastern Bloc politically, spiritually and in many other ways. After World War II, Christian churches in Eastern and Central European Communist countries faced on-going oppression from the Communist governments, which were largely determined to eliminate religious activities, with little regard for basic human rights or ethical principles. In 1945 the Seventh-day Adventist Church was a young movement with a solid vision of mission and evangelism. Its focus on fulfilling the 'great commission' made the church one of the fastest-growing religious groups, with increasing influence in various parts of Europe.

For some years, religious observance stagnated in the socialist countries of Eastern Europe, including Hungary. Adventists and other Christians were then met by strong rejection of religion on the part of the public. People turned away from churches during the years between 1958 and 1978 and religion and church attendance virtually became non-issues in public life. From the second half of the 1950s onwards the regime was able to isolate the church and undermine its influence in society. By forcing compromise in many areas of church activity, the government caused inner divisions and organizational splits within the church. As a consequence, church members longed for religious freedom, dreamed about spiritual revival, and desired to have more opportunities for fulfilling their vision and the mission mandate of the church.[1]

Christian churches in Central and Eastern European countries, including the Adventist church, suddenly received what they had dreamed of when the Communist period ended around 1989. Surveys at that time revealed that Christian churches already held a leading position among the most trusted and best-known organizations. According to Greeley, 'One of the great religious opportunities of the last hundred years had started.'[2] The proclamation of the Christian message became possible through the fall of Communism; even many who had never considered it before were now free to listen to it. By and large, society reacted positively and became open and supportive towards Christian churches after 1989. Many denominations and mission-oriented organizations in western countries discovered an increasing opportunity for mission. Case studies reveal an overwhelming interest that local congregations could hardly handle. One example from Hungary may illustrate this. In 1990 a small church in Szeged, with just over 30 members, organized public meetings on Bible topics. After 40,000 invitation cards had been distributed in the town, thousands of people indicated an interest in the programme. The church had to conduct the meetings three times each evening in order to give everybody a chance to participate. The large lecture hall in the university town of Szeged was not able to accommodate so many people. Altogether, around 4,000 people attended the programme. In 1995, a few years after the regime change, Greeley concluded, 'Enough research has been done on religion in Eastern Europe that one can say with considerable confidence that religion is reviving in the former socialist countries.'[3]

Some denominations experienced renewal, others planted new churches, and tens of thousands of interested people joined religious programmes organized by churches or missionary societies. The fact that so many countries suddenly became active in missionary efforts was unprecedented in the modern mission era.

From Opportunity to Disappointment

Christian churches received the right to organize their own religious life and a unique opportunity to start mission activities for the multitudes of people who signalled trust and openness towards religious groups. However, paradoxically, at some point in time within the ten years after the political change, these churches experienced a loss of confidence and an even larger loss of interest in churchgoing on the part of the population in Central and Eastern European

---

[1] See: Miklós Tomka, *Church, state, and society in Eastern Europe* (Washington, DC: Council for Research in Values and Philosophy, 2005), 28: Cultural Heritage and Contemporary Change Series IVA.

[2] Andrew Greeley, 'Religious Revivals in Eastern Europe', *Society*, 1 (2002), 76–77.

[3] Greeley, 'Religious Revivals in Eastern Europe, p. 76.

countries. Many turned away from Christianity. Researchers studying the opinions of the public stated that the time for religious revival appeared to be over: 'The renaissance of religious faith did not take place. Esteem for church and faith did not grow in society.'[4] The Adventist church, together with other denominations, was not able to make significant progress in Hungary; many of those who joined the church later left it altogether.

In the following decades a growing practical secularisation and also a decline in church membership and church attendance characterized the religious landscape of many former Communist countries. The unprecedented religious revival of the modern mission slowly faded out. The trend had changed quickly, and very soon Christian churches had to cope with a disappointing reality.

Christian churches in Eastern and Central Europe went from one crisis to another, from Communism and oppression to the transition period of the exciting years of regime change, and then into a crisis of mission. The changing context of their mission has forced Christian denominations to reflect about the real nature and commission of the church. Some look back nostalgically on the almost unbelievably successful years of the transition period but many Christians and local congregations have crucial questions about the future of their denominations. Among Adventists there is also considerable disappointment at all levels of the church body regarding its mission. Since the church considers mission to be a duty, many different mission activities are still undertaken, but frustration is growing. Members are looking suspiciously at new methods recommended by leaders and talking about their frustration more and more openly.

Deeper Questions of Mission

This current crisis, along with careful consideration of past experiences in Central Eastern Europe, when mission theology and theory faced challenging reality, may be helpful in exposing shortcomings in the theological and theoretical foundation of mission. It may also help to start a clarification process that will allow church leaders and members to become fully alive to the church's nature and mission. It is not enough for congregations in Eastern Central European countries merely to import Western thoughts, methods and ideas, as happened in the early 1990s. The church pays a high price if it works like a trading company dealing in evangelistic methods and tools.

Behind all mission activities is a particular interpretation of the Bible concerning evangelism. The mission theology of a denomination is the source of theories, methods and actions. If the fruits of the mission theology are not satisfying, 'communities are placed in critical tension with the received biblical

---

[4] György Fischer, *A vallásosság és a médiumok világa* (Budapest: Gallup, 2000), p. 6.

and theological resources.'[5] In light of past experiences, it is also necessary to review the foundations of mission theology and mission practices.

David Bosch rightly points out that 'an inadequate foundation of mission and ambiguous missionary motives and aims are bound to lead to an unsatisfactory missionary practice.'[6] Where mission theology and biblical interpretation have borne unpalatable fruit, the church must recognize the need for reflection and re-examination of its own theology and praxis in the light of biblical teachings and of the church's place in society. Without understanding and analysing the past, it is difficult to know what to do in the present and the future. Hendrik Kraemer once argued, 'Strictly speaking, one ought to say that the Church is always in a state of crisis and that its greatest shortcoming is that it is only occasionally aware of it.'[7] He even reasons that failures and sufferings are often needed in order for the church to become 'fully alive to its real nature and mission.'[8]

The Focus of the Present Study

The aim of this study is to analyse factors contributing to what happened to the Adventist church and its mission during the time of regime change in Hungary, in the context of political changes in Central and East European countries, and to understand and benefit from the implications for missiology in the twenty-first century.

Some of these factors are related to the consideration that the Seventh-day Adventist Church is a worldwide body with strong international connections and that it is organized according to a representative form of church government.[9] The General Conference represents the worldwide organization. Its constituent membership is defined in the Constitution of the General Conference. To facilitate its worldwide activity, the General Conference has established regional offices covering areas called Divisions of the General Conference. By action of the General Conference Executive Committee at Annual Councils, these offices have been given general administrative oversight responsibilities for designated groups of unions and other church units within specific geographical areas.

The General Conference has its headquarters in a Western country, but through the special hierarchical structure of the denomination it makes a significant impact on the life and development of other, national, entities of the

---

[5] Daryl M. Balia and Kirsteen Kim, *Edinburgh 2010 Volume II: Witnessing to Christ today* (Oxford: Regnum Books International, 2010), Edinburgh 2010 Series, p. 13.

[6] David J. Bosch, *Transforming Mission: Paradigm shifts in theology of Mission* (Maryknoll, NY.: Orbis Books, 1991), p. 5.

[7] Ibid., p. 2.

[8] Hendrik Kraemer, *The Christian message in a Non-Christian World* (New York: Harper, 1938), p. 24

[9] General Conference of Seventh-day Adventist Church, *World Church Structure and Governance* <http://www.adventist.org/world-church/facts-and-figures/structure/index.html>.

church in many countries. Strategic plans by the General Conference for mission projects and for missionaries to implement them have determined church activities and developments in Eastern European countries and have resulted in very strong similarities among mission activities across the region. After the uniformity among many aspects of the material relevant to this study was recognized, and the international dimensions which the figures appear to have were also noticed, selected areas of this research were extended to cover, not only Hungary but other Central Eastern European countries: Bulgaria, the Czech Republic, Former East-Germany, Poland, Romania, Serbia and the Slovak Republic. However, the findings related to these countries have not been included in this study.

Thus the research question is: How did the mission theology and the global strategy of the Seventh-day Adventist Church impact upon the life and missionary activities of the church in Hungary and to what extent was the SDA church able to meet to the needs of the public in the context of the regime change?

More specifically, the study is intended:

1. To study political, economic, social and religious developments as the context of Adventist life and activities at the time of regime change, and to examine their influence on the denomination and its members;
2. To study and evaluate the denomination's mission theology that formed the raison d'être for its evangelistic activities and to analyse how this mission theology allowed members of the church to recognize, evaluate and use opportunities during a time when changes were taking place in Hungary;
3. To describe and analyse the mission activities of the Adventist church in the context of the regime change.

Structure, Sources and Methodology

The present study is made up of a number of major parts. First, the SDA Church will be examined in its historical, socio-economic and religious context at the time of regime change in Hungary. Publications, archival data, articles in church papers, statistical reports and survey data have been used to provide information about the history and development of the church during the transition time. Historical analysis of the documents offers crucial insights supporting the argument presented in this study.

The questions about the political, socio-economic and religious developments in pre-and post-Communist society open up a wide range of interdisciplinary research areas and involve examining a number of qualitative and quantitative studies about the development of society. A number of national and international surveys[10] provided useful data for various analyses carried out by leading research institutes and sociologists. The literature analysis and the review of selected publications about questions relevant to this study provide a solid basis for understanding processes in society that provided the context of church life and activities in the period of time that is under examination.

The second section presents and discusses the mission theology behind the activities of the Seventh-day Adventist Church. Historical analysis and document analysis are utilized to examine the development of the Seventh-day Adventist Church and its mission theology before and at the time of the regime change. Church publications related to the research period, archival data and official statistics and church reports are analysed.

The third part of the study examines Adventist mission activities after the regime change. Documents about the strategic plans drawn up by the General Conference, the strategies of the Trans European Division and the Hungarian Union Conference, stand-alone publications and articles in church papers, reports by pastors and administrators, along with an abundance of statistical data that has become available, are analysed and provide the basis for insights into the factors sought for as part of the research aim.

The fourth part of this study is an analysis of how the historical context and the situation of the church, the mission theology of the church and its mission activities related to and affected each other. Special attention is paid to an evaluation of how the mission theology of the global Adventist church made an impact on the mission activities of the church in Hungary and of what relationship they had with the recognized needs of the population. This critical analysis leads to conclusions about the mission theology and mission activities of the Seventh-day Adventist Church.

In 1985 the General Conference of the Seventh-day Adventist Church started 'Harvest 90', a worldwide programme for mission. This plan exercised a strong influence on Adventist mission in Hungary and determined the activities of the church at the time of regime change. The year 1985 is the starting point of the main focus of this study.

The involvement of the church in Hungarian history shows that the years 1985–1995 were indeed years of change. After 1995 the regime change had been fully accomplished and in terms of evangelistic/missiological activities, high-profile efforts were reduced.

This research has been carried out in relation to Hungary as part of the Eastern Bloc. The regime change in Hungary took place in 1989 but was part of a longer, on-going process of transition that included many ups and downs and a wide variety of important factors. This study is not aimed at giving an overview or a

---

[10] International Social Survey Program (ISSP), the waves of the Hungarian Household Panel Survey Program conducted by the TÁRKI research institute, the survey data on Social Stratification in Eastern Europe after 1989, surveys by the Central Statistical Office in Hungary, and others.

detailed description of this process. Only general trends and details that are strongly connected to the main questions being posed in the study have been discussed, and it is not claimed that the research has been exhaustive in any one particular area.

The study is not intended to offer a comprehensive presentation of a biblical mission theology or the mission theology of the Seventh-day Adventist Church. The main question essential for this study in the field of mission theology is, 'What theological views and theories were behind the activities of the Adventist church in the period from 1985 to 1995 and how did they influence the practical way of doing mission?' Much work has been done on the mission theology of the Adventist church and it is not my intention to re-enter areas that have been seen as preliminary in relation to this research and that have already been covered by other scholars.

My Position

This study is linked with a major period in my life, which is connected to the Eastern Bloc. I grew up in Hungary before the regime change and I experienced, at first hand, how Communists organized the way of life, how the system affected family life and how Christians were treated in the educational institutions, at work and also in the military service. In order to prevent insurrection under 'Goulash Communism', parents were kept busy with work beyond their normal capacities and the government controlled the schools and job opportunities and limited the freedom of Christians to take advantage of the study, work and social opportunities available at that time.

The most challenging years were those of my childhood and teens, before 1989. I was the only pupil with a Christian background in my elementary school class and became the target for religious criticism by my history teacher. He demonstrated great satisfaction in challenging me without giving me the chance to reply or say anything to support my beliefs. He acted in conformity with the system and just continued on a small scale what the communist regime did on a larger scale. He was also a member of the Communist party and presented his ideology and conviction boldly in the elementary school. The books of Marx, Engels and Lenin used to be part of his standard equipment for teaching in the elementary school classes. Although he carried these quite heavy books regularly to his classes, I cannot remember any occasion when he opened and read any of them during class hours. But I still clearly remember some of his words addressing my Christian background. I was about 11 years old when he once entered the class with his big books. He placed them gently on the lecturer's desk, walked around thoughtfully, giving the impression that he had something important on his mind. After a while he scanned the class with his eyes and finally looked at me. Everybody was watching in silence, wondering what was going to happen next. Breaking the silence, he addressed a question to me: '*Blessed are the poor in spirit, for theirs is the kingdom of heaven.* Do you also think like that, Szabó?' A strange smile on his face accompanied his irritating question. Suddenly I found myself the focus of the situation without knowing how to react to the words of my elderly teacher. The silence following his statement, together with his smile on his face, indicated that all those people following strange, religious ideas must certainly be poor in spirit. I remained silent and felt a growing pressure. Most school conversations about religion were similar to this and during my eight elementary school years I learned that religious content and practices belonged to the category of elements unwanted in public life and in the educational system. I never heard any pupils during my school years leading a conversation connected to any religious idea and none of my teachers ever showed any interest in or positive attitude to Christian topics or church-related issues.

My personal experience provides an example of the methods of the communist modernisation paradigm. Beyond the legal separation of church and state, the goal of the regime was to embrace a 'worldly' or non-religious ideology. Socialist secularism was a core ideological imperative for Eastern European countries and reshaped societies successfully aiming to create the 'modern socialist new man', if necessary by means of force and power. No other options remained available before regime change. In my military service I faced the danger of imprisonment regularly, just because of my Christian faith.

No one expected or foresaw the monumental regime change in many socialist countries but its consequences illustrate well what really happened in society. Is it an irony of fate that some of my former teachers and military officers, who had lost their previous orientation, appeared more and more often in Christian churches, attending special evangelistic programmes and expressing interest?

2. The Seventh-Day Adventist Church in its Historical, Socio-Economic and Religious Context at the Time of the 1989 Regime Change in Hungary

Introduction

For more than forty years the Hungarian Seventh-day Adventist Church had to design the life and ministry of the denomination within the context of the Communist system in Hungary. As was true for all other churches under Soviet domination, the life and activity of the Adventist church were completely changed by the destabilising activities of the regime. All areas of church life were affected and the size and influence of the church in society were radically reduced, resulting in struggles, inner tensions, the death or decline of local congregations, and leadership crises.

Reflection on this process of change in the context of Eastern and Central European developments is crucial if one is to understand the life and mission of the church at the time of the regime change. It is also true that the evaluation of the mission theology of the Adventist church, presented in the next chapter, and the analytical study of the church's mission activities that is also provided, are essential if meaningful consideration is to be given to the very special development of the church in relation to the needs in Hungarian society.

This chapter provides an analysis of how the totalitarian government reshaped the life of the church and how that church approached the new era. The story has involved a number of struggles. There has been hope as well as loss and there are on-going processes engendered by the system. This chapter is intended to explain why Hungarian society turned towards Christian churches, giving them a unique opportunity for mission.

The Seventh-day Adventist Church in Hungary up to 1989

Adventist missionaries started working in Hungary at the beginning of the 1890s. The first church was established in Fogaras[1] in 1898 and this was also the year when the first pastor began his ministry in the country. As a mission territory,

---

[1] Fogaras was in Transylvania at that time. The region used to be part of Hungary, although today it belongs to Romania.

Hungary belonged at that time to the German-Russian Union of the Adventist church. The young church grew to 23 congregations and 400 members within the next nine years. In 1908 the territory was divided into the Transylvanian Conference and the Hungarian Mission Field; later, in 1912, it became the Danube Union together with Croatia, Serbia, Bulgaria and Bosnia.[2] Between the two World Wars, the young Adventist church was not recognized by the state; it had not received any legal rights that would have allowed it to maintain its life as a church. The situation of the church gradually worsened because politics increased the pressure on small Protestant churches. In 1939 the government banned all the activities of the smallest Protestant denominations, including those of the Adventists. Despite its illegal status, the denomination continued to grow throughout the years of WW II.[3]

The Seventh-day Adventist Church regained its strength very quickly after World War II. Although the church had become an illegal organization on 2 December 1939 and remained so until 31 July 1945, it grew constantly as an underground movement.[4] The increasing number of its lay evangelists created an impetus for mission, which resulted in rapid growth that continued after 1945. By 1948 the church had over 400 church members working as lay evangelists across the country. They led over 1,200 adults to baptism and established 62 new local congregations in the next four years.[5] Between 1945 and 1948 the Adventist church in Hungary was able to re-establish connection with the worldwide organization of the church and receive support from Adventists in Western countries. The church members recognized the basic human needs of their fellow citizens, including the need for counselling and hope, following the world war, and Adventists started a need-oriented ministry supported by the General Conference.[6]

In 1948 Communists were able to gain power in Hungary. They established a totalitarian government aimed at eliminating all churches. Nevertheless, despite all challenges and in face of discrimination by the Communist regime, Adventism remained a growing movement until 1955. It then began to lose its strength and slowly entered a period of crisis that reshaped the church and weakened its standing in society. Statistics indicate how intensive the destructive

---

[2] Zoltán Rajki, A H. N. Adventista Egyház története 1945 és 1989 között Magyarországon (Budapest: Advent Kiadó, 2003) p. 12; See more in Szigeti, Fejezetek a H. N. Adventista Egyház magyarországi történetéből.

[3] Ibid., p.12

[4] Adventists had 2,404 church members in 1935 in Hungary and 3,608 in 1945. General Conference of Seventh-day Adventist Church, Office of Archives, Statistics, and Research, http://www.adventiststatistics.org [accessed 21 April 2012].

[5] László Szabó, 'A szocializmus hatása az egyházi misszióra', *ATF Szemle*, 2 (2005), 48–56. <http://atf.adventista.hu/kiadvanyok/atf_szemle/2005_2.pdf> [accessed 15 April 2012] (p. 48).

[6] Rajki, A H. N. Adventista Egyház története, p. 22.

influence was; it made an impact on all areas of the life of the young denomination.

Figure 1. SDA Church membership Development in Hungary from 1920 to 1989

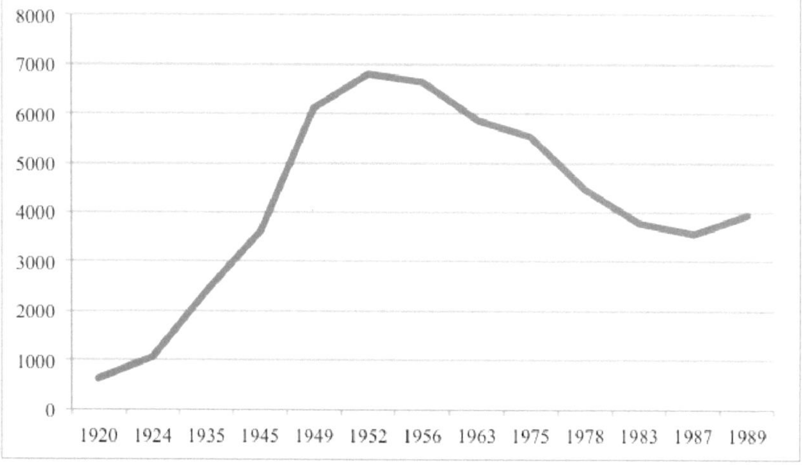

*Source: Archive of the Hungarian Union Conference
of Seventh-day Adventist Church*

After 1955 Adventists had to face an almost fifty-per-cent loss of membership, with local congregations disappearing around the country and the evangelistic and missionary activity dying. The crisis within the church at that time can also be observed in the number of splinter groups that left the church during the Communist period. Three major schisms occurred in the Adventist church before the regime change and no decade remained peaceful in the denomination; there were further defections from the mainstream organization in 1956, 1965-66 and 1975-6. The last one was the most severe crisis in the church and had major consequences for the next decades. About twenty to twenty-five per cent of the estimated number of church members left the denomination, creating on-going tensions that continued to influence the life of the church for decades after the regime change. The very intensive process of the socialist type of secularization also played an important role in the loss of membership. Within 10 to 15 years the membership of churches dropped dramatically. One of the main reasons was that many people moved from rural areas to cities.

The evaluation of what happened is easier today than it was previously because some relevant data has recently become available. In recent years new resources were made searchable when access to data was allowed in The

National Archives of Hungary, in the State Office for Church Affairs (SOCA)[7] and in the Historical Archives of the Hungarian State Security organization. Together with the study of political, socio-economic and religious development of the society, they reveal the destructive influence of the Communist regime, as well as the inner struggle of the Adventist church and how it was shaped by the system.

The Historical and Political Context of Adventist Mission and Its Impact on the Religious Activity of the Church

Strategies used by the Soviet regime to counter religious belief

According to the terms of the agreement negotiated by the victors in WWII, the Soviet Union had received a free hand in Central Europe. Miklós Tomka's comprehensive study on the effects of Communism on Eastern and Central Europe concludes in reference to the Communists' goals:

> It might create arbitrary human conditions, test people and societies, or try means and techniques of social management. The ultimate goal of all these attempts was supposedly the creation of a better and more human society. It required the reformation of the people and the reshaping of cultural and human relationships.[8]

Tomka also describes the new, everyday reality of Eastern Europeans which 'consisted of hard facts: foreign domination, attempts by the ruling group to destroy the existing social structure and the traditional culture, the coercive and manipulative methods of the party-state, oppression and the lack of freedom'.[9]

The Communist system was highly centralized and dependent on the political influence of Moscow. It relied heavily on Marxist ideology, which was anticlerical and anti-religious. It was intended, as a totalitarian system, to completely transform society and de-Christianize Communist countries. Those in authority often tried to carry out de-Christianization but recognized that they could not proceed in too militant a manner if they were to avoid compelling the

---

[7] The Hungarian Parliament established the State Office for Church Affairs in the spring of 1951, in order to set up an institution supervising officially and directing politically the activity of the clergy. The records of the State Office for Church Affairs were transferred to the National Archives of Hungary only after the dissolution of the institution in 1989. The actual transfer took place between 1992 and 1998. See in: *National Archives of Hungary* http://old.mol.gov.hu/index.php?akt_menu=928. [accessed 21 April 2012].

[8] Miklós Tomka, *Church, State and Society in Eastern Europe* (Washington D.C., Council for Research in Values and Philosophy 2005), p. 7.

[9] Tomka, Church, State and Society, p. 7.

church to go 'underground' where the state´s influence on the church would have been much more limited.[10]

Tomka concludes that two arguments motivated persecution of religious groups. In the first place, some sociological theories indicated that secularization would produce a society without a broad acceptance of religion; the Communists intended to accelerate the process of de-Christianization. Secondly, 'the political system adopted as obligatory the fight against habits and institutional arrangements which could have hindered the quick realization of the "historic necessity" of a religionless modern society'. [11] The consequences were devastating. 'The aggressive social policy criminalized the upper strata of the pre-Communist society and disarranged the middle class, while the collectivization of agriculture weakened rural society. The reorganization of the political system resulted in the elimination of the social institutions, including the political parties, movements, and the various security and professional organizations, which had played a role in the establishment and maintenance of previous public order and life. In a short time the churches remained the only institutions representing the traditions and the continuity with the previous system, which also meant that, willy-nilly, they became the single institution of opposition.'[12]

Paradoxically, although Communist governments were determined to eliminate churches, they also wanted to use them to help support the political purposes of the regime. Besides misusing the influence of religious leaders to manipulate society, the Communists took advantage of the influence of churches and of the international relationships they entered into, in order to further their own, foreign policy goals.

These partly contradictory intentions resulted in phases that varied between terror for churches and more tolerant church-state relationships.[13] This study is not intended to provide a detailed overview of these periods. The summary of the Communists' ways of threatening churches and religious people is limited to mentioning general paradigms that also became part of the development of the church-state relationship in Eastern and Central European countries. Kischkowski describes these phases in detail as they applied to the Soviet Union.[14] Later they became models for use by governments in the countries of the Eastern Bloc. Moscow`s 'experiments' with religions also created rules for

---

[10] For more information see: Martin G. Goerner, Die Kirche als Problem der SED: Strukturen kommunistischer Herrschaftsausübung gegenüber der evangelischen Kirche, 1945 bis 1958 (Berlin, Akademie, 1997, p. 23.

[11] Tomka, Church, State, and Society in Eastern Europe, p. 10.

[12] Miklós Tomka, 'Religiosity in Central and Eastern Europe. Facts and Interpretations', *Religion and Society in Central and Eastern Europe*, 3.1 (2010). <http://www.rascee.net/index.php/rascee/issue/view/3> [accessed 4 April 2012] (p. 2).

[13] Goerner, Die Kirche als Problem der SED, pp. 23-26.

[14] For more about the phases of church-state relationship and the politics of the Soviet union regarding religion, see Kischkowsky, *Die sowjetische Religionspolitik,* pp. 13–42.

others to adopt because the countries of the Eastern Bloc were under the influence of Moscow and the presence of the Red Army guaranteed unity in politics more or less throughout the region. The basic Communist paradigms for undermining the influence of churches in society can be observed in the various phases of church-state relationship in the former Soviet Union.

The period of the 'policy of weakening': 1917-27

The years from 1917 (the year of the Bolshevik Revolution) to 1927, form a period that Kischkowski calls the time of the 'policy of weakening'.[15] Thousands of priests were arrested and executed. Besides this, church property began to be expropriated, starting with overwhelming force. Religion became a private affair without any influence on social life, education, welfare work or societal activity. An aggressive anti-religious propaganda movement began, aimed at prejudicing the population against churches. The secret police registered churchgoers and exerted pressure on them.

Policy of destruction

Total terror started in 1927/28, imposed on all kinds of religious communities. This persecution lasted until 1939. Not even loyalty to the state could save church leaders or their churches from destruction. Demolition of church buildings, lawlessness that victimized the religious communities and divisions within the church characterized this period.

Policy of utilization

The religious policies enacted by the Communists entered a new phase at the beginning of WWII. 1939 brought about a radical change and released the churches from terror, but only so that the state could use them to help increase stability in the homeland. This policy continued, in the main, until 1958. The period reached its climax in November 1942, when Metropolit Sergius greeted Stalin as 'God's chosen leader of all military and cultural forces'.[16] The life of the churches in the region was still controlled by the government but churches received a certain measure of freedom to organize their affairs. As a consequence of this freedom, religious faith and commitment started to recover. The government responded with aggressive, atheistic propaganda and attacked the churches particularly vehemently in 1954 during the '100 days' anti-religious campaign. This event shows how the changes and tensions within the communist party influenced and could change the whole course of church politics, simply because of the personal interests of Communist leaders. This could also be observed in other countries as a prominent characteristic of totalitarian regimes.

---

[15] For a short overview of the various periods of the church-related politics of Moscow see: Goerner, *Die Kirche als Problem der SED,* p. 24.

[16] Goerner, Die Kirche als Problem der SED, p. 26.

The government still used the churches to help them promote Communist policies and goals. This state of limited tactical tolerance could also be observed in other Eastern Bloc countries and became quite common in the church-state relationship practised in Socialist countries. Since state archives have been opened to researchers in Hungary, it has become possible to form a clear picture of the 'ministry' of church leaders and how they supported the Communists. They were allowed to travel to international meetings but they had to report to the government about them and they also had to accomplish certain tasks the government gave them which were intended to further the government's international goals.[17]

Period of an aggressive atheistic propaganda

An article in *Pravda* in 1960 noted a clear sign of change in the course of religious politics on the part of the Soviet leaders. The church had to go underground and the state began to issue aggressive atheistic propaganda, followed by coercion and repression. Behind this situation was Khrushchev's political programme which was in operation until 1964, the year when Khrushchev's party colleagues removed him from power.[18] This brought release for Christians in the former Soviet Union.

Soviet exemplars for church-state relationships were often copied by one country's leaders from the models they observed in other countries of the Eastern Bloc. The leaders of these countries met in 1948 in Karlovy Vary, where they developed a common strategy to deploy against churches and religion in general.[19] The new approach resulted in dramatic changes in the religious attitudes of people and in the life of the Christian churches. Regarding Hungary, Eberts and Török identify three different ways in which the state related to the churches: (1) open terror including tormenting, terrorizing, imprisoning, deportation and even execution according to the Moscow paradigm, in other words employing all available means to stop church activities and gain the required behaviour from Christians; (2) carefully constructed methods of administration in order to destroy the influence of religious institutions in Hungarian society; (3) the conditional acceptance of churches that gave relatively more freedom for religious life, with the fundamental precondition of compromise by church leaders.[20] All these tactics can also be observed clearly

---

[17] The research in the recently opened state archives has found the reports and documents of church leaders including Adventists forwarded to the secret police.

[18] Goerner, Die Kirche als Problem der SED, p. 28.

[19] Interview with Dr Imre András, the director of the Hungarian Institute for Sociology of Religion, in Török, *Hungarian Church-State Relationships*, p. 77.

[20] Mirella Eberts, and Péter Török, 'The Catholic Church and Post-Communist Elections: Hungary and Poland Compared', in *Religion and Social Change in Post-Communist Europe*, ed. by Irena Borowik and Miklós Tomka (Kraków: Nomos, 2001), pp. 125–147.

during the various phases of church-state relationship that developed before the regime change.

Characteristics of 'the New Socialist Man'

From the very beginning it was clear that Communists were committed to eliminating religion and churches, along with their Judeo-Christian ethical norms.[21] The government aimed, not only at the forced rearrangement of the social, economic and political structures of society but, according to Anne-Marie Kool, 'individuals and societies were required to undergo re-education in order to conform to a certain ideological mould.'[22] Christian norms and traditions were hindering the collective value replacement attempted by Socialist governments in order to reach Socialist ideals, as the Hungarian sociologist László Medgyessy recalls: 'To ascertain future success, a new type of human being, the *homo Sovieticus* (in the Soviet Union) and the Socialist New Man (in Eastern Europe), had to be created.'[23]

The Socialist New Man was supposed to be the offspring of the new political system designed by Communists who wanted a new world, a new society and a new type of human being. However, while the government was focusing on destroying all elements of resistance, it failed to build a new society. As early as 1973, Gábor Czakó asserted that Hungarians had 'fallen between two stools' because the regime had started fighting against the churches in the early years of Communist rule and had focused on destroying all resistance, but attempted to introduce the international Socialist value system only later and failed to build a new society.[24] When Communism ended, it left behind a confused and sick society that can be described in a single adjective: anomic. In fact, only a relatively small percentage of people leaving the churches became Marxist; most of them were simply uprooted.[25]

The old way of life was destroyed but because the regime failed to create the ideal of the Socialist New Man, society descended into chaos. Tomka refers to two main characteristics of the *homo Sovieticus* who emerged as a consequence of the transformation process. Both of these characteristics have a strong connection to the social life of the country: extreme individualism and aggressive dependence.

Individualism

The Socialist Party carried out major changes without the agreement of the general populace, causing unnecessary and extensive damage. Growing social tensions and a feeling of insecurity may well be part of the modernization process

---

[21] Goerner, Die Kirche als Problem der SED, p. 23.
[22] Kool, 'Trends and Challenges', pp. 25–6.
[23] Medgyessy, 'Mission or proselytism?, p. 105.
[24] Gábor Czakó, *Indulatos jelentések* (Budapest: Magvető Könyvkiadó, 1973)
[25] See Miklós Tomka, 'A vallásosság változása – egy és több dimenzióban', *Kultúra és Közösség*, 5 (1985), 3–16, pp. 5–7.

but the steps taken by the government multiplied the adverse effects. According to the European Value Study and the International Social Survey Programme, the spread of individualism has been stronger in Hungary than in Western European countries.[26] Success, in economic terms, became the most sought-after goal and selfishness emerged as the leading principle but, without order and reason in the system, success was impossible. The high degree of uncertainty caused withdrawal, dependence and stress.[27]

Dependence

György Marosán describes what caused Hungarians' aggressive dependence. Individuals whose personalities were nurtured by dictatorship did not acquire the skills needed to assert personal interests. The ruling Communist system set the limits for behaviour and development and guided the nation within these limits towards the desired goal. The freedom of each individual was limited to acceptance of the given conditions.[28] The consequence was that *homo Sovieticus* was created as a dependent and vulnerable personality who expected the state to provide solutions for everything in life.[29]

According to Kopp and Skrabski, a significant proportion of Hungarians – forty six percent of men and fifty five percent of women – was characterized as having a so-called 'external-control attitude' at the time of the regime change of 1989: 'This attitude reflects fatalism, a belief that individuals are helplessly exposed to external factors; and it is beyond their ability to change their situation.'[30]

Historical development of the church-state relationship in Hungary

Communist discrimination against church-going people and persecution of them because of their beliefs changed the church-state association completely. According to Miklós Tomka, four main periods of church-state relationship can be observed in the period of totalitarian government.[31] These stages in the interconnection between the state and the churches started with extreme terror and antireligious oppression. It took forty years for the pressure to be slowly lifted and for a return to religious freedom to take place.

---

[26] Tomka, 'Vallás a rendszerváltás után', p. 19.

[27] Tomka, 'Vallási változások Kelet-Közép-Európában', p. 37.

[28] Marosán, 'A rendszerváltás "pszichológiája"', pp. 27–40.

[29] See more in: Tomka, 'Vallás a rendszerváltás után'.

[30] Török, Hungarian church-state relationships, p. 110.

[31] Miklós Tomka, 'A vallás mint változó rendszer (Religion as a System – and its Changes)', *Szociológiai Szemle*, 3-4 (1990), 155–84.

The time of confrontation: 1945-1956[32]

The new political power decided to transform the whole of Hungarian society and followed the Soviet example strictly. The government leaders created a single-party system with the support of the Soviet army and extinguished all other parties. After removing the political opposition from positions of influence, the Communists turned against churches. The system could not tolerate any different worldview or authority and autonomy of any kind among the public was inimical to those in power. That is why churches were considered to be potentially dangerous to the system.[33] The government decided to exercise its full authority over the leadership of churches.[34] Church institutions were nationalized, activities outside church programmes were forbidden and church leaders and other Christians who resisted the new regulations were arrested and sentenced to terms of imprisonment while such leaders as Bishop Ravasz, Bishop Ordass, Cardinal Mindszenty and others were put to death. The main goal was to force the churches to accept the situation as decreed by the Communist government and to arrange for state authorities and church leaders to work in compliance with the system. The Calvinist Church signed a contract with the state on 4 October 1948; the Lutheran Church did the same on 14 December 1948 and the Catholic Church followed suit on 30 August 1950. 'In these agreements the churches guaranteed their support for, and cooperation with, the new political leadership while the state, in its turn, guaranteed free religious practice and returned a few nationalized secondary schools and seminaries to ecclesiastical control.'[35]

The trials did not come to an end after this agreement. The year 1951 saw the beginning of the so-called 'priest-trials' that sent many priests and pastors of different denominations to prison. Another means of control over the churches was created in 1951: the State Office for Church Affairs. The SOCA was responsible for the secret police that was 'placed in every chancery, where they opened the bishops' mail, checked on their visitors, and were in possession of the diocesan seal.'[36]

Until 1949 the government's major purpose was to destroy the influence of the larger churches. During this time Adventists gained relative freedom. In 1944, along with other smaller denominations, Adventists had already formed the Alliance of Free Churches in order to obtain more effective representation of

---

[32] Tomka, 'A vallás, pp. 155-84. This study relies on the findings of Tomka concerning the main periods of church-state relationship. See also Rita Hegedűs, 'A vallásosság alakulása Magyarországon a kilencvenes évek kutatásainak tükrében' (PhD thesis, University of Economic Sciences and Public Administration, 2000) pp. 60-64.

[33] Hegedűs, 'A vallásosság alakulása Magyarországon', p. 60.

[34] Jenő Gergely, *A Katolikus Egyház Magyarországon, 1944-1971* (Budapest: Kossuth, 1985), p. 125.

[35] Török, Hungarian church-state relationships, p. 77.

[36] Imre András and Julias Morel, *Hungarian Catholicism: A Handbook* (Vienna: The Hungarain Inst. for Sociology in Religion, 1983), p. 22.

their interests through this cooperation. This also gave their pastors a chance to raise their voices against discrimination.[37] The state accepted the alliance as a partner but placed the churches under political control. They achieved a few more rights than others had but lost their independence. In 1949 the Hungarian press was nationalized and in 1950 the publishing house run by the Adventist Church was also taken into state control.[38] Also in 1950, an open declaration of war against the small churches appeared: 'We need to increase our efforts against the various sects. The leaders of Seventh-day Adventists, Jehovah's Witnesses, Baptists and other sects are, in most cases, in the service of American imperialism and these groups are nothing other than organs of imperialist propaganda.'[39]

The Adventist church left the Alliance of Free Churches, but continued to be treated like other small denominations. The intention of the government was:

- to limit the numbers of local congregations of these small church organizations;
- to allow only licensed pastors to preach;
- to prohibit the conduct of worship in homes;
- to control all printed materials and to prevent all support from Western countries.[40]

If no licensed pastor was present in a church, preaching was not allowed. A church member would be allowed to read aloud from a book but he had to remain sitting. If a pastor were preaching anywhere other than in a church building or doing outdoor evangelism, his licence would be withdrawn. The church lost about forty per cent of pastors and many small churches were also closed down.[41] The growing inner tensions and the increasing influence of the government in the church led to structural changes and challenges to spiritual life. Dissatisfaction on the part of church members resulted in a major crisis at the beginning of 1950s and pastor Zoltán Buday along with some 400 members left the mainstream Adventist Church in 1955-56.

The period of confrontation was not very successful for the government. Despite all its efforts to terrify Christians, the visible activities of the small churches continued to expand, even during the years from 1947 to 1953. Indeed, these denominations flourished during this period to an extent that they had not done prior to World War II.[42] However, the second period, just after the 'time of confrontation', brought much more satisfying results for Communists than the first period.

---

[37] For more see Rajki, A H. N. Adventista Egyház története, p. 48.

[38] Ibid., p. 48.

[39] József Révai, 'A klerikális reakció elleni harc feladatairól', *Magyar Nemzet*, Június 7. (1950), 3.

[40] Rajki, A H. N. Adventista Egyház története, p. 49.

[41] Ibid., pp. 49–51.

[42] Tomka, A magyar vallási helyzet öt dimenziója, p. 553.

The time of isolation: 1956 to 1966

Kadar's regime, characterized as 'goulash-Communism', started with a swift and cruel suppression of the revolution of 1956. Later the Communist Party sought to develop an apparently more peaceful relationship with the public. Open discrimination was softened without changing the original goal in regard to religion. The population was divided into religious and non-religious people. The churches were isolated from the rest of society and they had to reconsider their opportunities and their decisions in the context of the socialist state and its demands. 'A process of consolidation began, although it had a dual face. While the persecution of religion continued until 1964, the possibility of compromise began to emerge. Obviously, this rapprochement would mainly serve the interest of the church leaders, who, by now, realized, that Communism was likely to persist for an indefinite period of time. On the other hand, the Communists had come to the realization that religion would not die out soon either.'[43]

Many believers, not satisfied with the limited opportunities for experiencing spiritual life, started an underground movement in many churches. Besides the official churches, 'parallel churches', namely illegal small group gatherings sprang up in many denominations. These filled the need to maintain religious life, to provide education for youth and to cultivate fellowship among believers. Church members gathered secretly in homes, in forests and in various other places.[44] This time and this strategy of isolation were effective from the point of view of the Communist government. The official Adventist church became part of the system by making compromises and lost much of its former authority.

The Seventh-day Adventist Church became a state-recognized organization in 1957 at the price of having to join the Alliance of Free Churches and accept the direct influence of the regime upon church life. From 1958 onwards the regime not only put the church under pressure but also intervened in its inner life. The Alliance of Free Churches became the executive body of SOCA, exercising direct control over church affairs. This placed church leaders and pastors in a challenging position because usually the Alliance of Free Churches and local church members had exactly opposite expectations.[45]

The study by Rajki about the Adventist church's election of 1958 reveals how the Socialist regime manipulated processes within the church.[46] Communists used the institution of the church to weaken or even to destroy church-based faith

---

[43] See Török, *Hungarian church-state relationships*, pp. 80–90; István Lázár writes about the Kádár period that it was 'deeply contradictory and two- sided,' István Lázár and Albert Tezla, *Hungary: A Brief History* (Budapest: Corvina, 1989), p. 219.

[44] Rózsa Elemér gives an account of the 'illegal' way of maintaining faith and fellowship in the Lutheran church; Elemér Rózsa, 'Rövid bezsámoló az elmúlt negyven év illegális lelkigyakorlatairól', *Távlatok*, 11.3 (1993), 356–73.

[45] Rajki, A H. N. Adventista Egyház története, pp. 83-99. More about SOCA in: Rajki and Szigeti, *Szabadegyházak Története* Magyarországon, pp. 274-302.

[46] Rajki describes how it influenced life and work in the Adventis church in Hungary. Zoltán Rajki and Jenő Szigeti, *Szabadegyházak Története Magyarországon*, pp. 274-86.

in order to gain more freedom for building up the 'new social order'. After the revolution in 1956 the government made a series of attempts to take full control of churches, including those that were members of the Alliance of Free Churches. The SOCA analysed how free churches functioned, studying their history and the mentality and the way of life of their members. These steps laid the foundation for the later strategy of the secret police, a strategy that was put into operation against the twelve small Protestant churches united in the Alliance of Free Churches. Their members numbered 34,000-35,000 adults but their influence extended over about 100,000 people.[47] The government considered them to be dangerous because of their democratic structure and freedom of speech. From 1958 onwards the SOCA followed a carefully designed strategy detrimental to these small denominations.[48]

SOCA was responsible for matters directly affecting the churches, in terms of both fabric and personnel. It dealt with the administration of religious affairs, the implementation of agreements between the government and churches, and the administration of funds allocated for the support of church organizations. SOCA supervised church life strictly and expected church leaders to be accountable, not to the people of their own churches but to the political authorities. The local representatives of SOCA controlled all church activities and ensured compliance with government regulations. SOCA was an executive body, under state supervision, and always acted in harmony with the Party's internal instructions. It operated parallel to the state secret police. If the secret police could not provide enough evidence to the Ministry of Internal Affairs in order to sentence a particular person, SOCA acted against him or her at church level.[49]

The approval of SOCA was required before any pastoral position could be filled. SOCA also contacted many pastors and lay people and often played on the fear or opportunism of individuals or exploited their susceptibility to blackmail. Those collaborating with SOCA had to write reports about church programmes, targeted individuals and religious activities on a regular basis. Through these activities SOCA successfully exerted a destructive influence on the church.[50]

The officers of SOCA actively managed the preparation processes for the coming church election, achieving this through their agents who worked as pastors and leaders in the Adventist church. Conservative pastors, however, were intent on maintaining the biblical stance and democratic structure of the church. Some, like János Négyesi, Gyula Molnár and István Stoics were accused of manipulating preparations for the forthcoming elections. SOCA's goal was to

---

[47] Ibid., p. 268.
[48] Ibid.
[49] For more about SOCA see Edit Köpeczi Bócz, *Az Állami Egyházügyi Hivatal tevékenysége* (Budapest: Akadémiai Kiadó, 2004).
[50] András Emmerich, 'Basic Characteristics of Hungarian Church Politics', *Occasional Papers on Religion in Eastern Europe*, 4/1 (1984), Article 4.

force them to change their attitude. These pastors finally lost their licences and their right to be elected as future leaders of the church.[51]

At the union session of 1958 several officers were elected through the intervention of the state and remained in positions of leadership after 1962 because the next election was cancelled. The Duna and Tisza conferences ceased to exist and the leadership was centralized. Ödön Szabó became president but was too weak to make positive changes. Berzencey and Szakács were the acting leaders. Berzencey was an agent of the Hungarian State Security organization from 1957 to 1964 but he became isolated within the church. His financial unfaithfulness became more and more apparent and in 1971 he had to leave office.[52] Sándor Palotay had also been a 'secret police agent' until 1964/65 but he had a stronger connection with the State Office for Church Affairs. He had considerable power over free churches.

In 1957, during this period József Szakács was ordained as a pastor of the Adventist church. His faithful allegiance to the government during all his years in the ministry was revealed recently because it became possible to carry out research in the historical archives of the Hungarian State Security department. József Szakács, alias Pál Szaniszló,[53] started his work as an agent of the Hungarian State Security on 13 June 1956. His reports to the security agency reveal his dedication to the Communist regime very clearly and show how his work both undermined the life of the church and damaged its democratic structure. His influence within the Adventist church became significant only after 1965-6, by which time he had gained positions of leadership. Because of his loyalty to the state, he was able to develop a career in the Adventist church, to the extent that he became its president and made a huge impact on the life of the movement for decades.

The leadership crises affected the life of the church directly. Because of pressure from the state, the number of church employees fell from 86 to 33. Finances were controlled by the Alliance of Free Churches.[54] The departments of the church were also centralized and reduced in number at the end of the 1950s. An opposite trend, towards decentralization, began about ten years afterwards because of the schisms the Adventist church experienced in the '60s and '70s. This decentralization was also supported later by the political developments in Hungary.

In this context, one more person has to be mentioned: Sándor Palotay. In the 1950s he was simply a church member and lay evangelist but he established a

---

[51] Rajki, Az Egervári-mozgalom, pp. 4-7.

[52] Zoltán Rajki, 'Egy államilag manipulált kisegyházi választás. Az 1958. évi unióválasztás története a Hetednapi Adventisták Felekezete életében' (A tanulmány az OTKA K68299. számú pályázata és a Bolyai János Kutatási Ösztöndíj támogatásával készült. 2012).

[53] Zoltán Rajki has carried out an extensive research about Szakács' work for the Hungarian State Security department. See Rajki, Szigeti, *Szabadegyházak*, p. 5.

[54] Rajki, Szigeti, *Szabadegyházak*, p. 4.

strong connection with the secret police. His growing influence was felt in the church very quickly and about two years after 1958 he joined those who had become powerful instruments in the hands of the Communist regime, working to destroy the smaller Protestant congregations. Rajki's study reveals Palotay's unscrupulous ways of managing church life, his selfish motives and his destructive influence.[55]

The powerful way of the government also reached the local congregations and changed their lives completely. Only licensed pastors were allowed to preach in the local churches and the activities of church members were severely limited. The use of tape recorders was strictly forbidden. If a pastor provided sermons on a tape, he lost his licence immediately. If a local congregation decided to gather in a private home for worship purposes, SOCA transferred the ownership of the house to the state. Rajki describes in detail the steps used in the discrimination against the free churches.[56]

The growing influence of the regime on the church and the increasing inner tensions led to new disunion and the Négyesi group left the church in 1965-6.[57] The records in the historical archives of Hungarian State Security show clearly that at this time Szakács had already become deeply involved in collaboration with the Security Office and was therefore also influencing the election of new leaders.[58] With this election another new era began in the Adventist church. It was to include the greatest crisis Adventists had ever faced in Hungary.

The period of dialogue: 1966-1980
Political leaders in Hungary recognized the need for cooperation with the churches and their endorsement. In their turn, church leaders became more open to cooperation with the government. The state wanted to use the influence of churches to help them solve problems in society such as problems with youth refusing military service, underground groups and activities and certain kinds of religious activities not supported by the state. Religious leaders were often glad to receive more freedom and they were ready to rise to the government's expectations. This led to tensions within the church. The official church was often not only unable to ignite a renewal of interest in religion or to care for spiritual needs but often actually took action openly against renewal to the extent of blocking it. These tensions grew within the church and caused divisions in many denominations. There was, for example, the Bulányi problem in the Catholic Church, while the Evangelical Brethren split form the Methodists in 1974 and the Christian Advent Community (KERAK) separated from the Seventh-day Adventists in 1975, because of dissatisfaction with the political stance of the original, mainstream denominations. The relationship between religious institutions and religious culture was broken. This, of course, was

---

[55] Rajki, Szigeti, *Szabadegyházak*, p. 4.
[56] Ibid., p. 4.
[57] For the influence of this schism see Rajki, *A H. N. Adventista Egyház története*, pp. 100–8.
[58] Rajki, Szigeti, Szabadegyházak Története Magyarországon, p. 5.

among the goals of Communism. [59] Small groups and other underground Christian gatherings were the only alternatives for believers, if they were to obtain spiritual growth and renewal.

This divisive process developed into something extremely serious in the Adventist church. József Szakács became the president of the denomination in Hungary in 1971 and Sándor Palotay, the leader of the Alliance of Free Churches, collaborated with the regime and extended its influence at all levels of the denomination. This adherence towards the regime was slowly increased in tandem with political and ideological influence. As a consequence new theological debates took place, challenging Adventist identity in wider circles of the denomination and causing a new, more widespread crisis.

The relationship to other churches became a particularly serious issue. József Szakács participated in meetings organized by other denominations with the purpose of increasing ecumenical links among churches and made statements that appeared to many people to be provocative. As a consequence, the ecumenical question became the heart of the emerging new tensions and theological discussions in the denomination. This reveals a serious identity crisis in the Adventist church at the time.

In this process the church was perceived from being a faithful, mission-oriented, underground movement to becoming an instrument of the regime and cooperating in the fulfilment of its purposes. The more often some leaders of the Adventist Church made compromises, the more fervent the opposition became longing for genuine Christian values and lifestyle. A new kind of struggle arose in the church. Some felt that the status the Adventist Church received was no longer an advantage but merely a hindrance to a life of genuine Christian discipleship. Various influential pastors and lay people began to support the idea that it is better to remain a sect, suffering under the dictatorial authority of the state, than to be a recognized denomination.[60]

At the beginning of the 1970s new leaders emerged within the church and began to engage in a fight for positions and influence in the organization. Tensions grew rapidly and became noticeable, both within the church and in wider circles. Oszkár Egervári and Zsuzsanna Vankó started an opposition movement, acting cautiously at first and then extending their influence, first within congregations in the western part of Hungary and later throughout the whole union. A political struggle developed and resulted in a painful process of division and secession. This was followed by the withdrawal of between twenty and twenty-five per cent of members from the mainstream Adventist Church, to create a splinter group called after the name of one of the founders the Egervári group. All the efforts of the international body of the Seventh-day Adventist

---

[59] Tomka, 'Vallási változások Kelet-Közép-Európában', p. 29.
[60] Rajki, *A Hetednapi Adventista Egyház története*, pp. 131-91. Szakács was against these trends and also tried to establish a good relationship with other denominations. In addition, the state expected churches to live in peace and in harmony, under SOCA's guidance.

Church to restore unity were in vain. The two groups turned against each other and a very troublesome competition took place between them, overshadowing the mission and ministry of the Adventist Church for decades, during which many local congregations became weakened and many former faithful church members left the denomination.[61]

The Egervári group could not become an independent church organization because the SOCA refused its request. The group had to justify its existence, both to its members and also to the world church. Its identity was based on 'apostasy' of the official church. This division resulted in theological and intra-denominational arguments and in political battles between the denomination and the group. These unpleasant encounters involved many members and friends of the church and also the leaders of the world church.

Besides tension, the battles resulted in confusion in regard to theology among church members, as well as in broken relationships and painful and discreditable competition between the two church bodies.[62] The Adventist Church entered the new decade of 1980s with a weakened structure, attempting to cope with political struggles and inner tension and unable to recognize the new opportunities society was offering from 1978 onwards, opportunities that brought about another turning point in Hungarian society in regard to religious faith and practice.

The period of renewal of religious life in the context of the new regime change
The fourth phase, which began in 1980, has been a period of renewal of religious life, running later in tandem with regime change.

Criticism of the Communists and opposition towards them grew during the eighties. The system was shaking and freedom was growing. The dramatic history of Hungary in the twentieth century continued. This history is one of regime changes, political crises and loss of sovereignty.[63] In the first part of the century Hungarians longed to reform their country as a large independent nation within its ancient boundaries.[64] In the second half of the century they dreamed of freedom from oppression by the totalitarian regime that was controlled by Russian troops and politics. From the beginning of the twentieth century at least eight regime changes took place.[65]

An overview of the political changes shows clearly the dramatic history of Hungary in the twentieth century.

Republic. For centuries, Hungary had been straining under Habsburg occupation. In the wake of defeat in the First World War (1914-1918), the

---

[61] My observation. See for more: Rajki, Az Egervári-mozgalom.

[62] For more details about this split in the Adventist church and its consequences see: Rajki, Az Egervári-mozgalom.

[63] Ferenc Glatz and Kálmán Kulcsár, *Magyar Tudománytár* (Budapest: MTA Társadalomkutató Központ [u.a.], 2003), p. 304.

[64] For more see: R. J. Crampton, *Eastern Europe in the Twentieth Century*, 2nd edn (London: Routledge, 1997), pp. 78–94.

[65] Glatz and Kulcsár, *Magyar Tudománytár*, pp. 304-6.

Austro-Hungarian monarchy came to an end. In Hungary a short period of political confusion was followed by a bourgeois democratic revolution. On 29 October 1918 Hungary was declared a republic.

Hungarian Soviet Republic. Strikes, takeovers of estates and factories, demonstrations, and acts of violence intensified. Communism grew, gained power and the first Hungarian government lost power rapidly. On 21 March 1919 the Hungarian Soviet Republic was proclaimed. On the 1st of August, 133 days later, this heroic chapter in the history of the Hungarian working class was brought to a close with the entry of the White Rumanian army into Budapest.

The treaty of Trianon. In 1919 Romanian forces occupied Budapest. An anti-Communist government seized control and imposed 'white terror.' With the short Romanian occupation, and with the end of the white terror that replaced the red terror, a national assembly was convened, following elections. This formally restored the kingdom and elected Miklós Horthy as regent. In June 1920, at the Trianon, just outside Paris, the new regime signed the Treaty of Versailles,, the terms of which had been dictated by the victorious great powers. This move marked the de facto acknowledgement of the dissolution of historical Hungary.

German occupation. In 1944 German forces occupied the country and, after an unsuccessful attempt to pull out of the war, the extreme right-wing Arrow-Cross Party came to power in October 1944. Hungary had reached a low ebb in its history.

Russian occupation. In 1945 Russian troops liberated the country from the Germans and occupied Hungary. The nation was not able to regain sovereignty. Now, along with its neighbours, Hungary belonged to the Soviet sphere of influence. A Soviet-style Constitution was ratified and, the Hungarian People's Republic was proclaimed. Later a Stalinist political, economic and social system of government was imposed.

Revolution of 1956. On 23 October 1956 a popular uprising, which gradually turned into a revolution, broke out against the hated leadership and political party. This was a fight for freedom by the Hungarian people against Russian intervention. It was crushed by Soviet troops and the dictatorship was restored with Soviet support. Hundreds fell victim to reprisals.

Kadar's regime. János Kádár formed a new government, with the support of the Soviet Union, and after December 1956 steadily increased his control over Hungary.

Goulash Communism. János Kádár's Goulash Communism was relatively successful in the 1960es and early 1970s. Kádár introduced reforms and changed the totalitarian system to one of 'soft dictatorship'. This laid the foundation for the changes which came about in 1989.

All regime changes were accompanied by instability in politics, the economy and society at large. Most of the changes of government were followed by periods of reckoning, oppression, executions and aggression and left depressing impressions that were deep and long-lasting. Hungary was in a constant state of deprivation of democratic political procedures and consensual decision-making.[66]

The Hungarian regime change was influenced by many international factors and was part of an international transformation process that had enormous consequences. Until the 1980s the Soviet Union did not tolerate any deviation from the monolithic political system of state Socialism.[67] In the 1980s the Stalinist cold-war government was unable to compete with Western countries and fell behind in economic terms. Rising numbers of monetary, political and moral crises challenged the Soviets. In reaction, Mihail Gorbachev announced his reforms and expressed the intention of giving up superpower status on behalf of the Soviet Union. Under the pressure of this rising crisis, the Soviet Union changed its strategy.[68]

At this point in Hungary's history, the regime was giving more and more freedom to the struggling Adventist Church, permitting it to organize some basic activities that strengthened its members and repositioned the church itself within society. One of the most important steps taken by the church at this time was the initiation of an internal educational system for church members. The leaders started the training programme in order to overcome the devastating consequences of the schism and to educate new local church leaders in order to ensure smooth cooperation with the union. About 500 church members participated in the training programmes, at various locations.[69]

The SOCA gave the church a little freedom for evangelistic activities in the early 1980s.[70] The church started missionary activities among Romani people and alcoholics, a blood donation movement, initiated health courses aimed at helping people to give up alcohol and tobacco consumption and organized first-aid training but these activities were allowed only if the church did not use them as cover for 'religious propaganda'.

SOCA tried to demonstrate that there was religious freedom and declared that religious and non-religious people were working together to build up the socialist state. Renewal movements became more and more visible in the churches. Religious education became available to church members and others. Publishing

---

[66] For more see: Tomicah Tillemann, 'How to end an empire: The refugee crisis of 1989 and the collapse of the Eastern Bloc' (Ph.D dissertation, The Johns Hopkins University, 2009); Andrew Greeley, 'Religious Revivals in Eastern Europe', Society, 1 (2002), 76–77.

[67] Glatz and Kulcsár, *Magyar Tudománytár*, p. 308.

[68] James H. Billington, 'The Crisis of Communism and the Future of Freedom', *Ethics & International Affairs*, 5.1 (1991), 87–97. See more by Courtois: Courtois, and Kramer, *The black book of Communism*.

[69] 'Határozatok', *Lelkésztájékoztató*, 18 (1984), pp. 112-13.

[70] More about the changing face of SOCA towards Christian churches in: Konrád Szántó, *Az Egyházügyi Hivatal titkai* ([Budapest]: Mécses, 1990); Szilvia Köbel, 'Az Egyházügyi Hivatal működése az újjászervezéstől a megszűnésig 1959–1989' *Magyar Közigazgatás*, 10 (2001).; Edit Köpeczi-Bócz, *Az Állami Egyházügyi Hivatal tevékenysége* (Budapest, Akadémiai Kiadó, 2004).

houses started printing and distributing religious material. The number of openly religious people started growing at a steady pace from 1978 onwards. The SOCA was dissolved in 1989 and the agreements between the state and churches were terminated.[71] A new epoch began. The regime change brought freedom for religious groups. According to Tőkés, the roots of the regime change in 1989 go back to the sixties. The Kádár regime struggled with its inheritance of the revolution of 1956. Besides, its strategies left Hungary facing a severe economic crisis in the 1980s.[72]

However, the shadows of the totalitarian Communist regime were still current. SOCA ceased to exist in June 1989, without a legal successor, but the consequences of its activities persisted for decades after the regime change. These repercussions included distrust and suspicion towards church leaders because of their possible previous collaboration with SOCA, a high level of personal or family tragedy, and the aftermath of humiliation. The new government, under the leadership of Miklós Németh, decided that the next Hungarian administration would guarantee the separation of state and church. Using the 'Law on Freedom of Conscience and Religion', the new leaders accorded church-state relations a revised basis, providing freedom for churches in the new democratic society.

Socio-Economic Developments

An understanding of the position of Christian denominations in the community at the time of the regime change of 1989 requires examination of the context in which churches existed and of how socio-economic developments might have affected the religious developments in Hungary. The aim of this part of the present chapter is to study and evaluate publications related to the social life of the Hungarian people, their subjective sense of well-being and their satisfaction with life at the time of the regime change, in order to understand the expectations, motives and desires of these people in the period of time that is under scrutiny. This analysis may help to answer the question of why the population was becoming more trusting towards churches and why people flocked to Christian programmes.

General trends in Eastern Europe and Hungary

Trends in Eastern Europe
The revolutions of 1989 meant that Eastern European countries had installed a new system of government for the second time in just a half-century. The

---

[71] Hegedűs, A vallásosság alakulása Magyarországon, pp. 63–64.
[72] For more about Hungarian regime change see: Rudolf Tőkés, A kialkudott forradalom gazdasági reform, társadalmi átalakulás és politikai hatalomutódlás 1957-1990 (Budapest: Kossuth, 1998).

previous system had been established by force without the support of the vast majority of East Europeans and had lasted for about 40 years, creating a complex and challenging situation in every Eastern European country. The problem of 'overcoming the past' was, according to James F. Brown, more difficult in Eastern Europe than in post-Nazi Germany. Brown's argument is that the vast majority of Germans had supported the Nazis but the vast majority of East Europeans did not support their Communist rulers.[73]

A huge number of surveys and research studies produce a constantly growing number of publications about the transition period in Eastern European countries and there is a wide consensus of opinion that the process of change has not been easy. According to Minton Goldman: 'Communism had distorted everything it touched. When Communist Party rule collapsed, the whole structure of society, institutions, processes, and values collapsed along with it. People lost one way of doing things, but they have had difficulty finding an alternative. Popular behaviour and thought could not be transformed overnight.'[74]

Goldman sees the challenge of political and economic democratization in the vulnerability of post-Communist states, in the personal selfishness that is displayed and in primitive consumerism 'based on the principle that everything is now permitted'.[75] Miklós Lévai offers four partly different reasons as an explanation for the negative effects of the transformation[76] process on East European countries. 'The transformation started in societies living not in general wellbeing but in crisis. Changes took place in relatively homogeneous and closed societies that had forty years of socialist tradition behind them and the changes were intense and radical in character. Through the changes, these countries became open, subtle and pluralistic in their scale of values and norms. 'The past and its scale of values, symbols and institutions have all been nullified.' Social disharmony arose.'[77]

As early as 1991, James F. Brown submitted a checklist of the problems that he predicted Eastern European countries would face in the transition period. These problems exist in all post-Communist countries, forming both 'the legacy of communist rule and the work of its successors' (Brown) but also varying from country to country in both type and degree of tractability. Besides these difficulties, Brown lists the political, environmental and cultural challenges (including those relating to emigration) and the task of clearing away the 'pollution of the mind' (Václav Havel's expression), which comes with political,

---

[73] Brown, James F., *Hopes and shadows Eastern Europe after Communism* (Durham: Duke University Press, 1994), p. 3.

[74] Minton F. Goldman, Revolution and change in Central and Eastern Europe political, economic, and social challenges (Armonk, N.Y.: M.E. Sharpe, 1997), p. 51.

[75] Goldman, Revolution and change, p. 51.

[76] For more about the negative effect of the transformation see: H. G. Heiland and L. Shelley, Civilization, Modernization and the Development of Crime and Control: A paper prepared for the 50th Annual Meeting the American Society of Criminology (San Francisco, 1991).

[77] Lévai, 'Social Changes and Rising Crime Rates', pp. 45–46.

moral and intellectual deformation. According to Brown, it was caused by the contrast between Communist fiction and actual facts and it made an impact on both individuals and society as a whole and became an educational, moral and psychological problem.[78]

These malformations affected the whole process of building a new society, making it all the more challenging for it to develop into a Western-style democracy, take steps towards running a free-market economy or attain peace and unity for the people. Six years after the regime change, Minton Goldman concluded that the governments of Central and East European countries were still facing enormous difficulties: 'Although they have made great strides, they face horrendous problems in their search for political stability, material well-being, stability and tranquillity at home, and security abroad.'[79]

Goldman also lists the problems of post-Communist development. Like Brown he concludes that the main areas of challenge are establishing democratic government (a political challenge according to Brown), introducing a free-market economy, promoting social stability and diversifying foreign policy.

Researchers have defined several problem areas in the design of the transition process. According to Csite and Kovách, these 'horrendous problems' might be the consequence of focusing mainly on the question of how the transformation should take place and paying less attention to the assessment of the consequences. Politicians in post-Communist countries accepted that the route to modernization had only one option: privatization in tandem with a multi-party parliamentary system. Colin C. Williams aims to extend his critique of the powerful narrative of marketization by turning attention to Eastern and Central Europe and by asking questions about economic development in post-socialist societies. He describes diverse development paths and urges more openness to the evaluation of alternatives to capitalism.[80]

In the transition process politics had ascendancy over sociology. According to Csite and Kovách, the problem was increased because the country's leaders departed radically from the policy applied prior to the regime change, a policy of taking one small step at a time. A comparison of East European development with the growth of the economy of China showed that gradual reforms of the kind observed in the Chinese model result in more success than the East European 'privatization above all' strategy.[81]

Stark expressed his concerns in 1991 about the economic transition in East Central Europe, warning that it was not a 'problem to be solved by the rationalist

---

[78] See: Brown, *Hopes and shadows*, pp. 247–69.

[79] Goldman, Revolution and change in Central and Eastern Europe, p. 23.

[80] Colin C. Williams, 'Beyond Marketization: Rethinking Economic Development Trajectories in Central and Eastern Europe', *Journal of Contemporary European Studies*, 14.2 (2006), 241–254.

[81] Csite and Kovách, 'Posztszocialista Átalakulás', *pp.* 49–72. <http://www.szociologia.hu/dynamic/9502csite.htm> [accessed 4 April 2012] (p. 49).

design of economic institutions.'[82] His paper is highly sceptical in terms of its analysis and approach to the transition. He argues that the 'path dependence' of East European societies needs further study and understanding because it also strongly affects the economic transition process.

The negative consequences of this process mean, according to research studies on economics, that 'all the post-Socialist countries underwent a deep recession in the 1990s, and by the autumn of 1993 no recovery had begun in any of them except Poland.'[83] The results of the 'transformational recession' described by Kornai were falling national income, declining state redistribution, rising unemployment, inequality and poverty. 'All this has most likely contributed to growing unhappiness, according to the findings of the existing literature.'[84] Lelkes further concludes that seemingly an 'iron curtain' of unhappiness has replaced the political isolation of socialism. This is clearly visible in the survey evidence that 'suggests that the level of individual self-reported happiness in Central-Eastern Europe is much below that of Western Europe'.[85] Little is known about happiness or about subjective assessment of well-being during the era of Socialism. 'The official ideology claimed that every, or almost every, member of society was satisfied'.[86]

The problem areas noted above as listed by researchers show that the negative effects of the transformation process have been noticeable in all areas of European post-Communist society and that the countries were not well prepared for managing this crisis effectively. This resulted in growing unhappiness and diminishing social well-being in East European countries.

Trends in Hungary

Evans, Andorka, Rose and Haerper agree that among East European countries, and particularly in Hungary, a high proportion of the population was dissatisfied with the developments during the period of transition and felt that the standard of living was falling.[87] From data gathered by the Hungarian Household Panel survey, Szívós and Tóth conclude that Hungarians were dissatisfied with almost

---

[82] David Stark, 'Path Dependence and Privatization Strategies in East Central Europe', *East European Politics & Societies*, 6.1 (1991), 17–54 (p. 17).

[83] János Kornai, 'Transformational Recession: The Main Causes', *Journal of Comparative Economics*, 19 (1994), 39–63. <http://www.irisprojects.umd.edu/ppc_ideas/Revolutionizing_Aid/Resources/typology_pdf/transformational_recession.pdf> [accessed 12 July 2012] (p. 39).

[84] Lelkes, *Tasting freedom*, p. 4.

[85] Ibid, p. 1.

[86] Ibid.

[87] See: M. Evans, J. Kelley and T. Kollosi, 'Images of class: public perceptions in Hungary and Australia', *American Sociological Review*, 57 (1992), 461–482; Andorka, Richard Rose, William Mishler and Christian Haerpfer, *Democracy and its alternatives: Understanding post-communist societies* (Cambridge, UK: Polity Press in association with Blackwell Publishers, 1998); Richard Rose and Christian Haerpfer, *New democracies barometer III.: Studies in public policy* (Glasgow: Univeristy of Strathclyde, 1994).

all areas of life and that the tendency was for this discontentment to grow until 1997, when dissatisfaction reached its lowest point. According to the research data obtained by Szívós and Tóth, the biggest decline in satisfaction was measurable in views about future life prospects.[88] This pessimism had already begun to be felt by the beginning of the 1980s, before the regime change took place and Hungarians apparently had the most pessimistic expectations among East Europeans about their future standard of living. Sági suggested in 2000 that this pessimism had become even darker after the 1989 regime change.[89]

Only 17 per cent of adults were 'more or less satisfied' with their income and about a quarter were found to be happy with their standard of living. The cause Sági gives for the absence of satisfaction is that, instead of the hoped-for economic recovery, a severe economic crisis had occurred, surprising even the economists. The development was the opposite of what people had been expecting.[90]

Unemployment was an unknown issue during the decades of state socialism but it was changed after the regime change. Rapidly growing unemployment might have been one explanation for the pessimism among the people of Hungary. About 1.5 million jobs had been lost within a few years and unemployment had grown from 20,000 to 700,000 within three to four years after 1989. Sliding down to a lower social class had become a familiar experience and millions had had to give up their accustomed standard of living. Signs of poverty quickly became visible in the population. László Laki writes about the hunger, malnutrition and tuberculosis that appeared among the population again.[91] TÁRKI's (an independent Social Research Institute) analysis, based on the Household Panel Survey, shows that economic depression had forced a significant proportion of middle-class people to drift into a state of poverty.[92]

Péter Galasi and Gyula Nagy studied the changes in macroeconomic indicators in Hungary for the years 1989-1996, using data from the Hungarian Central Statistical Office. The seriousness of economic hardship among the Hungarian people is obvious from their chart, which shows how GDP fell by nearly a fifth between 1989 and 1993 and which also illustrates the decline in

---

[88] Péter Szívós and István György Tóth, 'Bevezetés', in *Stabilizálódó társadalomszerkezet: TÁRKI MONITOR JELENTÉSEK 2003*, ed. by Péter Szívós and István György Tóth (Budapest, 2004), pp. 5–9, p. 9.

[89] After Ukraine, Hungary came second in the table that recorded pessimism. Sági, 'Hogyan legyünk pesszimisták?' p. 41.

[90] Sági, 'Elégedettség, jövedelmi feszültség', p. 75.

[91] For further details see: László Laki, 'A magyar fejlődés sajátszerűségégnek néhány vonása', Szociológiai szemle, 3 (1997), 67–91.

[92] Tamás Kolosi and Péter Róbert, 'A magyar társadalom szerkezeti átalakulásának és mobilitásának főbb folyamatai a rendszerváltás óta idősoros illetve longitudinális nézőpontból', in *Stabilizálódó társadalomszerkezet: TÁRKI MONITOR JELENTÉSEK 2003*, ed. by Péter Szívós and István György Tóth (Budapest, 2004), pp. 10–22, p. 20.

employment and in real wages and how the number of those registered as unemployed increased from almost zero in 1989 to 14 per cent in 1993.[93]

'Although unemployment has fallen back somewhat during the slight recovery in output from 1994, employment continued to decline, as did real wages (in 1995-6).'[94] These serious tendencies created tensions among the populace, mainly associated with inequalities in income and living conditions.

Inequalities in living conditions
Surveys related to income inequalities have been carried out by the Central Statistical Office and information is also available from the Hungarian Household Panel survey.[95] The Household Monitor research by TÁRKI provides data that is useful for comparison and also supplies information about development of inequalities. Various publications reveal the historical and statistical development of income inequalities in Hungary, and provide comparisons of the Hungarian data with data from other East European countries.[96] They also show the reaction of the Hungarian population to growing inequalities and describe the expectations from Christian denominations which people had, hoping for solutions from the churches to the growing social problems, including the difficulties posed by new inequalities.

György István Tóth identifies three major periods in the development of income inequalities in Hungary between 1987 and 2000.

The first period covered (in approximate terms) the years between 1987 and 1992 and brought about the largest decline in the Hungarian economy since WW II. During this period inequality grew in all areas that were measured but the most significant change in household employment was caused by the polarization of the labour market.

In the second period, between 1992 and 1996, the economy was more or less characterized by stagnation, accompanied by relatively high inflation and unemployment. During this period inequalities continued and grew significantly.

---

[93] http://www.ksh.hu/statszemle_archive/2001/2001_04-05/2001_04-05_420.pdf; https://www.ksh.hu/docs/hun/xftp/idoszaki/mo/mo1989_2009.pdf

[94] Galasi, Péter, and Nagy, Gyula, 'Are children being left behind in the transition in Hungary?: The paper has been prepared for UNICEF International Child Development Centre.', *Budapest Working Papers on the Labour Market*, 1 (2000) <http://www.econ.core.hu/doc/bwp/bwp/bwp001.pdf> [accessed 4 April 2012], p. 2.

[95] For an analysis of theories about inequalities in Hungary and their causes see: Szívós and G. Tóth, *Feketén, fehéren*, p. 15.

[96] See data about the income inequalities and an overview of their further development in Hungary see: Szívós and G. Tóth, *Feketén, fehéren*, p. 15.

In the third period, from 1996 to 2000, the economy started to revive and unemployment and inflation fell. Those inequalities which were charted were only minimally different during this period.[97]

A comparison of Hungarian income inequalities with those in other East European countries shows that the 'strongest inequalities in living conditions can be observed for Hungary where the distribution is the most polarised. Every fourth respondent is above the country-specific average in both material and cultural respects, while almost every second respondent scores under the average.'[98] The analysis of consistency also provides a significant result: 'The "consistent uppers" are of a similar magnitude in Poland and Slovakia and are only somewhat smaller in the other three countries. The proportion of "consistent lowers" is about the same in Bulgaria and Hungary, only somewhat smaller in Poland and Slovakia and much smaller in [the] Czech Republic and Russia.'[99]

The ways in which these income changes affected Hungarian households are presented in TÁRKI's study. Matild Sági's study contains information about the income changes after the regime change and her data show clearly that the majority of Hungarian adults experienced decreasing salaries or wages. Overall, 61.4% suffered hardship because of income instabilities and losses and only 7.9% benefited from stable growth that could lead to feelings of satisfaction. The growing difference caused a gap between the highest income decile and the lowest, as presented by TÁRKI.

In TÁRKI's analysis of the data from the Hungarian Household Panel survey of the development of Hungarians households, 'Growth viewed from below', Kolosi, Róbert and Fábián present findings to the effect that in the 1990s, in the highest income decile, per capita income was 7 to 7.5 times higher than in the lowest income decile.[100] More details about the statistical development of income inequalities are presented in the study by TÁRKI.[101]

According to Szívós and Tóth, the growing inequality caused tensions in society and people expected the state to intervene in order to reduce these

---

[97] István György Tóth, 'Jövedelemelosztás', in *Stabilizálódó társadalomszerkezet: TÁRKI MONITOR JELENTÉSEK 2003*, ed. by Péter Szívós and István György Tóth (Budapest, 2004), pp. 30–38, p. 32.
[98] Péter Róbert, 'Social Determination of Living Conditions in Post-Communist Societies', *Czech sociological Review*, 5.2 (1997), 197–216 <http://sreview.soc.cas.cz/uploads/5012c60b1e99f0ed53fa02d36510e32313150031_431_19 7ROBER.pdf> [accessed 5 April 2012] (p. 202)
[99] Ibid.
[100] Róbert, 'Social Determination', p. 5
[101] Ibid., pp. 6–12

inequalities.[102] The vast majority of the population considered fundamental changes in the economic system to be necessary.[103]

In this challenging economic and social situation, the public also expected the churches to speak out and participate in the process of transition. According to the data supplied by the European Value Study, more than 55% of the population expected churches to make complaints about matters of unemployment.[104] This clearly demonstrates the attitude and the expectations of people in relation to the churches. The people felt that religious organizations ought to emerge from the isolation from society that had been forced on them by Communist government and become involved in the everyday problems and challenges faced by the general population.

Trends in poverty and employment issues
As a consequence of the above developments, unemployment and poverty became a major problem in Hungary. Csite and Kovách analysed the situation in six East European countries and concluded that the unemployment-to-employment ratio in Hungary in 1993 was one of the highest among those countries. Young adults living in rural areas were worst affected; many lost their jobs.[105] As a result of unemployment and of difficulties in the social system, poverty increased between 1987 and 1996.[106] One of the most radical sets of statistics on poverty comes from a World Bank publication of 1996 which says that, according to analysis based on reference to a defined poverty line, about 50% of the population lived in poverty at that time.[107]

Zoltán Fábián reviewed the main research studies on poverty in 1994. His work shows that Communists tried to hide the growing economic problems in the '80s.[108] TÁRKI's publication also provides data about the geographical distribution of poverty and supplies other important information about problems in Hungarian society related to hardship during the time of transition. Fábián refers to presentations interpreting the trends of inequalities at a conference in 1979: 'The most pressing needs in Hungary have, by and large, been covered by now. Hunger, mass squalor, precarious living conditions [and] general scarcity are problems of the past, and have hopefully been wiped out forever. The far from negligible hardships which still exist – inadequate living conditions and so

---

[102] Ibid., p. 9
[103] VALUES SURVEY DATABANK, Selected countries/samples: Hungary [1982], Hungary [1991], Hungary [1998], Hungary [1999]. European Value Study, http://www.jdsurvey.net/evs/EVSAnalizeQuestion.jsp.
[104] Values Survey Databank Hungary.
[105] Csite and Kovách, 'Posztszocialista Átalakulás', p. 55.
[106] Tóth, Jövedelemelosztás, p. 11.
[107] See: Förster and G. Tóth, *Szegénység és Egyenlőtlenségek,* TÁRKI, pp. 27–28; For more on the development of poverty see also: Tóth, Jövedelemelosztás, p. 12.
[108] Fábián, *Review of the main research on poverty* (Budapest, 1994) <http://www.tarki.hu/adatbank-h/panelcd/pub/wbp/povrev.html> [accessed 4 April 2012].

forth – are gradually being eased, and already they no longer affect the majority.'[109]

Nevertheless, poverty was quite obviously present in Hungary at that time.[110] A conference was organized in 1981 on 'Research into the Multiple Adverse Situation' in 1981 by the Hungarian Sociological Society. The event received a great deal of publicity, but the topic and the outcome were influenced by the ruling party. Fábián's conclusion is that 'poverty has been a central social problem in Hungary since the beginning of the economic crisis in 1978.'[111] Fábian also describes the challenge related to the research into poverty: 'Public debate started on social policy issues, even if the publicness was often limited and the roles of participants were determined by political factors. However, the political and economic reforms put this problem into foreground, and it turned to be an essential criterion in evaluating the process of democratic transition. Yet, there are relatively few social science research started after 1989/1990 due to the general bad financial situation of Hungary, in a country, where most of the research institutes are dependent exclusively on state support. Thus the challenging task remained for social sciences: to explore the social effects of a uniquely complex process of transition to a market economy based democratic political system.'[112]

Andorka, too, remarks: 'In the 1980s the number and proportion of those living on incomes below the subsistence level was estimated to be around one million, or, in other words, ten per cent [of the population]. It should be noted that even in those days there were different estimates of the number of poor.'[113]

The estimation of Tamás Kolosi about the proportion of those living below the Central Statistical Office subsistence level were supported also by others. According to his him the proportion was 22 per cent in 1992, 24 per cent in 1993 and 32 per cent in 1994.[114] Andorka's conclusion about the research of Kolosi shows what a significant problem poverty was in the 1990s in Hungary: 'He [Kolosi] made this estimate by adding the unreported income to the incomes recorded by the Household Panels which were revealed by the macro-statistical data collections… Whatever the opinion of social scientists may be about the subsistence level calculated by KSH, it is absolutely clear that poverty has increased very significantly, by at least three-fold.'[115]

---

[109] Fabian referred among others to the publication of Zsuzsa Ferge. Zsuzsa Ferge, *A Society in the Making: Hungarian Social and Societal Policy, 1945-1975.* (Middlesex: Penguin Books, 1979), p. 305.

[110] Fábián gives an overview of the research into poverty and describes the main steps taken to deal with it and the studies related to it. Fábián, *Review of the main research on poverty.*

[111] Fábián, Review of the main research on poverty.

[112] Ibid.

[113] Andorka and Spéder, 'Poverty in Hungary', p. 132.

[114] Ibid., p. 133.

[115] Andorka and Spéder, 'Poverty in Hungary', p. 133.

An extensive overview of surveys and research studies about poverty is to be found in the book by TÁRKI, edited by Förster and Tóth.[116]

Poverty tended to become especially critical for certain kinds of families. Large families and single-parent families were particularly vulnerable and were affected more than the rest of the population by the worsening situation. In three Visegrád countries, Czech Republic, Poland and Hungary, poverty levels for large families were twice those of the average for the general population and levels for single parents were two to five times as high. Nevertheless, poverty levels for single parents showed the most dramatic development: they doubled in the Czech Republic and in Hungary, and almost tripled in Poland.[117] Förster and Tóth also conclude that the intensity of the on hardship and the levels of poverty were higher for children than for the rest of the population. Others such as Galasi and Nagy agree that a very high percentage of Hungarian children experienced poverty. They conclude that 'at least once during 1992-96, 44 percent' of the children had to face undue neediness.[118] 'For many of them, however, poverty was transitory; one in five of all children experienced poverty only once and 13 per cent were poor for two or three years. About one tenth of all children were poor for four years or more.'[119]

Although the spread of poverty and its extent to which it spreads vary if different concepts of poverty are employed, all researchers agree that it was a major problem in Hungarian society during the time of transition. It made a negative impact on people's lives and on their outlook and made them open to new solutions, including searching for new ideologies and taking an interest in organizations that presented a common image of being 'social', even if they were religious organizations and churches.

Social life and social systems

Communists attempted to facilitate the complete centralization and bureaucratization of Hungary and systematically broke apart (Hankiss says 'atomized') the Hungarian way of life. Elemér Hankiss describes how traditional social networks – local, professional, cultural, religious and to some extent even family networks – were destroyed.[120] According to Hankiss' research, fragments of the social networks survived in a state of semi-dormancy and semi-legitimacy and a slow regeneration from these 'hibernating roots' began in the mid 1960s. He further remarks that this slow regeneration process within the social networks

---

[116] Förster and Tóth, Szegénység és Egyenlőtlenségek Magyarországon, pp. 27–28.

[117] See also the poverty indicators in: Michael F. Förster and István G. Tóth, 'Child Poverty and Family Transfers in the Czech Republic, Hungary and Poland', *Journal of European Social Policy*, 11 (2001), 324–41 <http://esp.sagepub.com/content/11/4/324.full.pdf> [accessed 4 April 2012] (p. 337).

[118] Galasi and Nagy, 'Are children being left behind?', p. 7.

[119] Ibid.

[120] Elemer Hankiss, *East European Alternatives* (Clarendon Press, 1990), Chapter 1.

went on after the mid-1960s 'despite the renewed efforts of the party and local oligarchies to thwart this process'. Hankiss also provides statistics for the changing number of clubs and social associations. His figures supply 'a good picture, not only of how social networks were destroyed in the late 1940s and 1950s, but also of how their slow regeneration began in the 1960s.'[121]

Living in a fragmented society forced Hungarians to pay a very high price for Communism in terms of their physical, mental and social wellbeing. Their workloads were increasing but their relative income was decreasing. Rising inflation and unemployment resulted in growing poverty. The segment of the population living below the poverty line grew from 10 per cent to 25 per cent between 1982 and 1992. In order to maintain their living standards, people had to find one or two more part-time jobs, in addition to their full-time positions. On top of their 40 hours of full-time work, they had to work at least 20 more hours per week to earn a subsistence wage.

Consequences for life expectancy
'In 1986 and 1987, on average, less than two thirds of the hours spent at work were spent at the main workplace. That means that after finishing work at the main workplace, people continued labouring somewhere else and spent again considerable time with work equalling to more than 50% of their main work time. One of the main consequences of this heavy workload was exhaustion. This, coupled with the unsatisfactory health care system and other factors [...] caused the life expectancy of Hungarian men to decline 1965 to 1994 when it started to increase again.'[122]

Consequences for social and family life
'Long working hours also caused a deterioration in Hungarian social relations... Communists destroyed the intermediary organizations that would normally have provided opportunities for socializing.' [123] Families were overloaded; modernization broke up wider family relationships and the emotional support system, even in networks of normally close family members and relatives.[124] This state of affairs naturally caused unhappiness within Hungarian families. They had the smallest younger generation and the greatest number of single-child families in the world. 'The short time that Hungarian parents could spend with their family, together with work related fatigue and stress, the unsupportive atmosphere of the home, and the inadequacy of the Communist educational

---

[121] Hankiss, East European Alternatives, p. 99.
[122] Török, Hungarian Church-State Relationships, p. 108.
[123] Ibid., p. 108.
[124] See in: Kopp, Mária and Árpád Skrabski, 'Magyar lelkiállapot – 1997', *Távlatok*, 2 (1997), 157–167.

system, created downward spiral in which the younger generations lost their orientation.'[125]

The consequence of these factors, in sociological terms, was devastating anomie. Kopp and Skrabski studied the results of three representative surveys carried out in 1988, 1994 and 1995 in order to analyse medical complaints and symptoms in relation to lifestyle characteristics and social, economic, sociological and psychological factors. One of their main conclusions is that between 1988 and 1995 an extraordinary decline took place in the perception of social support. The results show that people in Hungary felt left alone in 1995 to a much greater extent than they had in 1988. The characteristics and the extraordinary weakness of the social network are indicated in the results of the survey, which shows that in both 1988 and in 1995 people could not expect to receive or actually receive help in difficult life situations from those whose professions meant that they had a duty to help.[126] The most radical decline in social relationships is clearly recognizable in interactions made by professional people with colleagues and in exchanges between classmates made by students. The results of the survey indicate that the rate of possible help expected from colleagues declined by 60% from 1988 to 1995. The help expected from relatives, friends and parents was also significantly reduced. Both surveys asked questions in the same way about whose help people could count on in difficult life situations. The answers present subjective feelings, which also determine wellbeing.[127]

'According to the 1981 European Value Study, Hungarians were those among the surveyed European nations who wanted to spend the least time with their friends.'[128] Data from the Hungarian Household Panel survey carried out in 1993 and 1997 show that, in the four years between the one survey and the other, the average number of friends Hungarians claimed to have decreased by 36.61%. About 20% of the people answering the survey questions in 1993 said they did not have friends. This proportion rose in the next four years to almost 33%. The number of friends in 1993 was, on average, 7, and in 1997 it was 4.5. About 40% said they had from 1 to 4 friends. Fruzsian Albert and Beáta Dávid studied the various influences that affected the number of friends a person might have. Albert and Dávid recognized that women were in a more disadvantageous position regarding friendship. They also studied the following questions: 'What is the cause of the decline in the number of friends and why do people lose their

---

[125] Török, *Hungarian church-state relationships*, p. 187. Török relies strongly upon the results of Tomka's research. See in: Tomka, Miklós, 'Secularization or Anomy? Interpreting Religious Change in Communist Societies', *Social Compass*, 38.1 (1991), 93–102.
[126] See in: Mária Kopp, Árpád Skrabski, and Sándor Szedmák, 'A szociális kohézió jelentõsége a magyarországi morbiditás és mortalitás alakulásában', in *MTA Stratégiai Kutatások, Népegészség, orvos, társadalom*, ed. by Ferenc Glatz (Budapest: MTA Földrajtudományi Kutatóintézet, 1998), pp. 15–37, pp. 23-28.
[127] See: MTA Stratégiai Kutatások, p. 32.
[128] Török, Hungarian church-state relationships, p. 108.

friends?' They found out that the higher the level of education and the amount of income of a person had, the more friends he or she had.[129]

These statistics also indicate a declining tendency in emotional reinforcement and a growing lack of natural social support systems in the Hungarian social system. The hostile attitude, the lack of emotional comfort or help from others and the lack of security were seriously disruptive factors and affected health very negatively. Kopp is another researcher who concludes that a fundamental characteristic of the Hungarian state of mind is performance orientation,[130] indicating that the attitude that giving and receiving acceptance, value, worth and affirmation are primarily based on what people do or how they perform, rather than on who people are and on their self worth. The Communist way of building society affected people's lives, even after the regime change. Civic organizations could have taken steps to balance these tendencies but, as Éva Thun emphasizes, civic organizations were not able to accomplish this because their work was hindered and the government gave them neither encouragement nor adequate funding. 'In post-1989 Hungary, civic society and civic activism, as they are understood in Western democracies, hardly exist'.[131] She describes further challenges of civic organisations:

'Financial support for social and civic purposes is an unknown act of benevolence. Hungarian society prefers to support soccer teams and certain TV programmes. Those who possess the financial means to support civic organizations usually consider the provision of a social safety net for the masses to be the sole responsibility of the state. These people do not acknowledge any public responsibilities, and some of them hold the view that people should be able to prosper at the expense of others or by cheating the state. Most members of Hungary's economic elite regard those who choose to participate in civic work as either benevolent idealists or aggressive eccentrics. These people see civic activists as people who lack the courage or the talent to utilize Hungary's chaotic state of legislation for their own purposes in order to become rich. In such circumstances civic groups are tolerated only as long as they do not interfere with the activities of the rich and powerful.'[132]

Subjective well-being and satisfaction with life

The indicators of anomie in Hungarian society were the high suicide rate, alcoholism and erosion of mental health. The Hungarian suicide rate became the highest in the world in the 1960s. The suicide rate rose by 259% from 1954 to

---

[129] Endre Sík and István G. Tóth (eds), Magyar Háztartás Panel Műhelytanulmányok: Jelentés a Magyar Háztartás Panel 6. hullámának eredményeiről (Budapest: TÁRKI Társadalomkutatási Intézet Rt., 1998), p. 165.

[130] Kopp and Skrabski, *Magyar lelkiállapot – 1997*, pp. 160-163.

[131] Éva Thun, *Women in Hungary in Times of social and Cultural Transition* (1999) <http://epa.oszk.hu/00000/00010/00002/thun.htm> [accessed 29 November 2010].

[132] Thun, *Women in Hungary.*

1984 and reached a level 50% higher than the world's second highest rate, recorded in Sweden. Uzzoli's analysis indicates that the highest level of suicides was reached between 1988 and 1992 and that about 60% of suicides were caused by depression or symptoms related to it.[133] Studies of the causes of suicide reveal that this deviant behaviour is not usually the consequence of or a side effect of the development of depression but the outcome of a sense of failure, of falling behind the mainstream in society and of sensing the consequences of exclusion.[134] Moksony also indicated that he could prove his deprivation hypothesis, which showed that falling standards of living were associated with an increase the risk of suicide. All the available research suggests that suicide risk is especially high among young women aged 14-24: 5% of them have attempted it at least once.[135] Moksony's research presents a picture of the suicide problem in Budapest and compares it with rural areas.[136]

Kopp, Csoboth and Purebl analysed the data supplied by the representative surveys carried out in 1988, 1995 and 1998. The first two data collections related to the physical, mental and health wellbeing of Hungarians.[137] They appeared to prove a positive development in regard to the suicide rate after 1994.; fewer people committed suicide in the late 1990s than in the 1980s.[138]

The goal of the survey analysis undertaken by Kopp in 1998 was to carry out the same analysis among women in the age bracket of 14-24.[139] According to Kopp's research, the main health problem acknowledged by this group was depression. Their most serious health problem in 1988 was one of suffering from depression; eighteen per cent of the women had depressive symptoms. A quarter of these young women reported that sometimes during the year symptoms of depression reduced their ability to work and they experienced hopelessness and a loss of control. The frequency of symptoms of depression increased from 1988 onwards among young women although depression was decreasing among young men.[140]

Serious symptoms of depression in young women included self-accusation and tiredness. Forty-eight per cent of them were suffering because of self-accusation in 1988, 40% in 1995. Twenty-six per cent stated that they did not

---

[133] Uzzoli, 'A hazai egészségi állapot változásai 1990 után', p. 5.

[134] Ferenc Moksony, 'Társadalmi Mobilitás és Öngyilkosság', *Demográfia*, 48.1 (2005), 7–22
<http://www.demografia.hu/letoltes/kiadvanyok/Demografia/2005_1/Moksony%20Ferenc_t
an.pdf> [accessed 4 April 2012] (p. 17).

[135] Mária Kopp, Csilla Csoboth and Purebl György, 'Fiatal nők egészségi állapota', in
Szerepváltozások. Jelentés a nők és férfiak helyzetéről, ed. by Tiborné Pongrácz and István G.
Tóth (Budapest: TÁRKI Társadalomkutatási Intézet Rt., 1999), pp. 239–59 (p. 248).

[136] Moksony, 'A fejlődés ára, vagy az elmaradottság átka'.

[137] Kopp, Csoboth and Purebl, Fiatal nők egészségi állapota, pp. 239-59.

[138] See: Kopp and Skrabski, Magyar lelkiállapot, pp. 160-67.

[139] Kopp, Csoboth and Purebl, Fiatal nők egészségi állapota, pp. 240-253.

[140] Ibid., p. 241.

have any hope of a better future. Only 30% considered themselves as trustworthy. Tiredness was increasing most markedly; in 1988 it was estimated at 32.9%, in 1995 at 17.5% and in 1998 at 50%.[141]

The results of the surveys analysed by Kopp and Skrabski show that the most important background factor in relation to health deterioration was depression and its increase in frequency and severity. This does not indicate clinical depression (depressive illness) but a negative emotional state, of which the most important characteristic is powerlessness, feelings of loss of control, loss of interest in others, loss of ability to make decisions, self-accusation and a sense of hopelessness about the future. People in this state cannot make plans for future, consider the own situation to be hopeless and are unable to take active responsibility for changing the situation. This is a learned helplessness, which can have very serious physical consequences.[142]

Kopp and Skrabski observe that a significant proportion of Hungarians – 46 per cent of men and 55 per cent of women – have a so-called 'external-control attitude'. 'This attitude reflects fatalism, a belief that individuals are helplessly exposed to external factors; and it is beyond their ability to change their situation.'[143] People with this attitude feel that everything depends on their luck or fate and they hesitate to become active in using their opportunities in the changing environment. This attitude is an important background factor of anxiety.[144]

Alcoholism in Hungary is widespread. Alcohol consumption and its related problems multiplied under the Communist regime. 'While the yearly per capita consumption of alcohol in the mid 1930s was 5.5 litres (pure alcohol), it grew from the second half of the 1950s until 1980 when it peaked at 11.7 litres.'[145] The number of people who died from cirrhosis of the liver (the most frequently used indicator of alcohol-related problems) grew ten times from 1950 to 1991.

In summary, the characteristics of Hungarian society by the time of regime change were those of: 'a population struggling with increasing poverty, declining life expectancy, crumbling cultural institutions, a relatively low level of

---

[141] Kopp, Csoboth and Purebl, Fiatal nők egészségi állapota, p. 242.
[142] Kopp and Skrabski are relying in this regard on inputs from Endrőczi, Appels, Falger, Sklar and Anisman. Kopp and Skrabski, Magyar lelkiállapot, p. 160; See also: Elemér, Endrőczi, 'Stress és az immunrendszer', Psychiatria Hungarica, 1989.2 (4), 107–18; A., Appels, 'The year before myocardial infarction', in Biobehavioural bases of coronary heart disease, ed. by TM Dembroski, H Smidt and G Blumchen (Basel: Karger, 1983), p. 204; Falger, P, and A Appels, 'Psychological risk factors over the life course of myocardial infarction patients', Advances in Cardiology, 29 (19˙2), 132–39; Sklar, L, and H Anisman, 'Stress and coping factors in fluence tumour growth', Science, 205 (1979), 513–15.
[143] Török, *Hungarian church-state relationships*, p. 110.
[144] Kopp and Skrabski, 'Magyar lelkiállapot – 1997', p. 158.
[145] Török, Hungarian church-state relationships, p. 109.

education, a high rate of suicide and alcoholism, a growing rate of criminality, and an unsatisfactory level of mental health.'[146]

Security and crime

The crises people experienced during the transition period also became noticeable through analyses of the perceptions of security or insecurity on the part of the population and through studies of the development of crime rates. As Fritz Sack states, 'crime is one of the determining characteristics of social change'.[147] Social inequalities, the rising level of deprivation, the massive differences in property ownership and the lack of order in society led to an absence of ethical standards and also to a relatively high level of crime after the regime change.[148] The sudden rise in the number of crimes and the changes in the nature of crime were important common features of the social reshaping that took place after the Socialist system collapsed.[149]

Lévai explains the changes in the structure of crime and states that new phenomena can be observed:

> 'the increase of the role of violence in the field of crime which partly means the increase in the number of violent crimes and partly the increasing frequent appearance of brutality in the methods. [...] The latter feature leads to the forms of crime which had had no or few occurrences in the former "socialist" countries before. These are the economic crimes, drug-related crimes, organized crime and the connecting [associated] transnational crime, which can be regarded as the consequences of the transition to the market economy, of the privatization or the market economy itself.'[150]

Lévai comments on the growing number of recorded crimes, suggesting that by 1997 'Hungary can doubtlessly boast of having the highest ratio of crime among the countries concerned.'[151] The dramatic rise of officially recorded crimes can be seen in the statistics. The mean rate of registered crimes per 100,000 population grew from 1,843 in 1986 to 5,056 in 1997.[152]

According to Lévai, one of the main reasons for the growing crime rate was the dramatic rise in poverty in Hungary: 'The number of those whose income was less than the subsistence level officially published by the government had

---

[146] Ibid., p. 110.

[147] Fritz Sack, 'Társadalmi átalakulás és kriminalitás', in *Social Transformation and Crime: Hungarian-German Criminological Symposium: 20–25 August 1995 Budapest, 1995. augusztus 20 – 25*, ed. by Ferenc Irk (Budapest: Országos Kriminológiai és Kriminalisztikai Intézet, 1997), pp. 95–132.

[148] See: Lévai, 'Social Changes and Rising Crime Rates', pp. 47–48.

[149] Ibid., p. 37.

[150] Ibid., p. 40.

[151] Ibid., p. 43.

[152] Ibid., p. 38.

become as high as two, and two and a half million by 1994, and the ratio of unemployment had exceeded 10%. By the end of the 1980s, a large group of people had appeared on the periphery of society who were unable to adapt to the new economic system, meet the requirements of the labour market or improve their conditions on their own. Researches in Hungary have revealed that the different kinds of deviation accumulate and concentrate among them, furthermore the conditions of the increasing reproduction have also developed or as *Katalin Gönczöl* put it: 'Living conditions seem to reproduce crime in this case.'[153]

The emerging economic system not only challenged Hungarians to adopt it but also pushed them to the periphery of society if they were not able to cope with the new situation. When they found themselves in that position they had to find alternative ways to meet their needs because the system and the labour market disappointed them. The growing wealth of some people on the one hand and the growing poverty of many on the other hand created tensions in the population and increased the possibilities for committing crime. Korinek explains that, according to his findings, 'fear has mostly increased in the case of property crimes. We can conclude that this fear, which is specifically characteristic of Hungarian citizens, is embedded in the social reality of Hungarian society. In an impoverished society the relative value of assets is appreciated more than their real value.'[154]

Surveys are also available concerning the increase in fear of crime in post-Communist countries. Changes in people's personal feelings about security in Hungary and other countries relate to one of the main questions László Korinek's survey addresses. His work reveals that while in 1982 40% of the people participating in interviews said that they were not afraid at home, at night, in the area where they lived or anywhere else, people were later seen to be more and more afraid and 10 years later the ratio of unafraid to afraid was no more than one to four.[155]

The dramatic rise in crime rates, the downward spiral in feelings of security among the population and the worsening living conditions, which pushed a significant proportion of the community to the edge of poverty and social exclusion, also delivered an explanation for the rising interest of people in questions about the meaning of life, about where to find trustworthy ideologies and about institutions that were able to function supportively during times of struggle. Many people looked upon Christian churches as organizations that offered stability and possible solutions to questions about life and its struggles.

---

[153] Ibid., pp. 47–48.
[154] Korinek László, 'Békés egymás mellett félés, avagy félelem a bűnözéstől Közép-Kelet-Európában', in *Social Transformation and Crime: Hungarian-German Criminological Symposium: 20–25 August 1995 Budapest, 1995. augusztus 20 – 25*, ed. by Irk, pp. 145–50 (pp. 147–48).
[155] Korinek, pp. 147–48; See also Lévai, 'Social Changes and Rising Crime Rates', p. 43.

Religious Developments

Religious development before regime change

Religion before Communism

Christian churches held influential, even monopolistic positions in Hungarian society before Communist rule. A survey carried out in 1949 clearly indicates that 70.5% of the population belonged to the Catholic Church and 27.1% were members of Protestant churches.[156] Altogether, more than 97% of Hungarians were affiliated with a Christian church. Almost everybody was religious and weekly church attendance stood at 52% in 1947.[157] Less than three per cent of the population was non-religious. Almost 100% of Hungarian children received religious education in the schools, prior to 1948.

This was, according to Miklós Tomka, an age of triumphalism for churches. Besides their religious activities, the churches owned enormous tracts of land and ran respected educational and health institutions. The influence, the wealth and the institutions of the churches created a solid foundation for their political influence.[158]

The hegemony of the churches ended when a new political and ideological power emerged after WWII and focused on restructuring society. The Soviet system was the model for this new society and Communists followed it mechanically. Papp Zsolt says that Hungarian Socialist development was an exact copy of the Soviet modus operandi between 1949 and 1953. Its consequences were so devastating for society, the economy, for the lifestyle of the people and for the way people thought, that Hungary needed 30 years of struggle to try to recover.[159] The import of the Soviet system led to a fifteen-year period of confrontation between the churches and the political system, beginning in 1948.[160] This was the launch of a series of steps that changed the place of churches in society, reducing their influence dramatically.

The impact of Communism on religion before the regime change

The reorganization of society, transforming it into a Socialist state with abusive methods of governance and corrupt political means, resulted in a damaged scale of values and fragmented communities. This procedure not only affected social

---

[156] Pollack, 'Modifications in the Religious Field, p. 136.

[157] Tomka presents statistical data from A Magyar Távirati Iroda Magyar közvéleménykutató Szolgálat 5/1948 számú jelentése (Report of the Hungarian survey agency). Tomka, 'A vallás mint változó rendszer', pp. 155–84.

[158] Further information about the political influence of the churches is available in Andor Csizmadia: *A magyar állam és az egyházak jogi kapcsolatainak kialakulása és gyakorlata a Horthy korszakban*. Budapest. 1966. Akadémiai kiadó.

[159] Zsolt Papp, 40 Év – Avagy a Szocialista Magyar Út és Néhány Sajátossága. In: *Szociológiai Szemle*. 1992–3. p.103.

[160] Tomka, 'A vallás mint változó rendszer', p. 160.

values and health but also made a negative impact on religious developments[161] and on the position of religious people in the community at large.

Tomka describes three obvious factors that influenced the religious developments in the second half of the 20th century in Central Europe. 'In the first place, the demands for socio-economic progress supported the forced economic modernization policy of Communist states. Secondly, the less democratic legitimacy the political power had, the more it emphasized ideological legitimacy as derived from the supposed logic of history. The political power used Marxism as a universalist explanation of existence and as a system of moral and social order. Official Marxist ideology developed its own institutions, dignitaries, hierarchy, public creeds and rites. The holistic, fundamentalist and materialist interpretation of Marxism can be labelled a religion or at least a civil religion. At any rate, it collided, with any other faith. And thirdly, the totalitarian inclination of the Communist state required a grim fight against all kinds of cultural and social autonomy and, thus, against organized religion and religious institutions.'[162]

Because of discrimination, the religious were excluded from influential positions in society. Without compromise, it was almost impossible for Christians to become lawyers, teachers, journalists, scientists, doctors, leaders. Christians had to face discrimination, not only in the schools, but in their careers as well. Company promotion lists very seldom contained names of Christians, and their salaries were lower than those of others. Religious people slipped down to lower classes of society as a result of the discrimination. Tomka summarizes the impact of discrimination in his article. The dictatorial methods used by the Communist regime for creating the 'socialist world' ensured that religious people could not gain higher degrees and influential positions. Ideological filters were applied at all levels of society. The conclusion of Tomka's research is that this type of bias is a matter of history[163] and he lists its consequences, which still affect people, even today, in three areas of life.[164]

1. The discrimination put religious people at a disadvantage in economic, cultural and social respects. This was recognized as early as the seventies and recent studies show that nothing has changed as yet.[165] According to surveys, religious people are consumers on a much smaller scale than the average person. They tend to choose cheaper goods, and they have a low consumption potential. In general, religious people were in a disadvantageous position in Hungary, even

---

[161] Tomka, *Church, state*, p. 9.

[162] Ibid., p. 9.

[163] See in: Tomka, 'The Religious – Non-Religious Dichotomy', pp. 105–37.

[164] See in: Tomka, A magyar vallási helyzet öt dimenziója.

[165] György Fischer, 'A "köszszolgálati" médiumok és a vallásos közönség', *Vigília*, 3 (1997), 192–98.

in 2000, eleven years after Regime Change.[166] They are still considered to be in the lower classes of society. Non-religious people fill the leading economic, political and cultural positions in communities and through their dominance the non-religious worldview has become determinant.[167]

2. Discrimination caused a big difference to develop between the generations regarding their religious views. People born before 1941 had a similar religious life and worldview to people in Western Europe and they were more religious than the later generations.[168]

3. Tomka's study demonstrates that the first two consequences of Communist rule created a third disadvantage for churches. Because Christians tend to belong to the lower echelons of society, they also tend towards traditionalism. In order to protect themselves against the aggressive influence of the government, churches in Eastern and Central Europe guarded traditional rituals and other elements of religious practice and belief 'in a frozen, unchanged form, which often became obsolete over time'[169] Churches are under-represented among intellectuals. Religious people had fewer chances to take advantage of the existing opportunities in society to study, earn money or influence the development of the nation.[170] They were marginalized during Communist times.[171] This caused a detachment from society and has lowered the ability of church members to fall into line with society. The socialist government introduced 'numerous clauses' that allowed only people who accepted Marxist ideology to enter higher educational institutions. The result was that the percentage of believers (those following the teachings of the church) with university education fell to 1.4%.

The results of anti-religious propaganda became visible at all levels of the school system. Studies based on the data from ISSP 1991 show the trends among elementary school pupils. Weekly church attendance declined radically from about 80 per cent in 1946 to below 20 per cent in 1982 by those aged 11-12, as recalled by respondents in 1991. The number of those never attending church increased form about 5 per cent in 1946 to over 30 per cent in 1982.[172]

In 1948 almost all students attending secondary schools – 98 per cent of them – were religious. In 1988, under 1 per cent of secondary school students said they

---

[166] Fischer states that, according to surveys about consumerism, religious people are still at a disadvantage in society and have less purchasing power than others. Fischer, A vallásosság és a médiumok világa. (Budapest, 2000. Juni), pp. 1–12.

[167] Tomka, A magyar vallási helyzet öt dimenziója, pp. 554–57.

[168] Aufbruch/New Departures in 1997/98 provides evidence that Hungarian people born after 1941 are similar in their religious attitudes to Bulgarian, Czech and East-German people. Tomka, A magyar vallási helyzet öt dimenziója, pp. 554-57.

[169] Tomka, *Expanding religion*, pp. 16–17.

[170] Tomka, 'A vallásosság változása', pp. 8–10.

[171] Tomka, Church, state, and society in Eastern Europe, Chapter II.

[172] Paul Froese, 'Hungary for Religon: A Supply-Side Interpretation of the Hungarian Religious Revival', *Journal for the Scientific Study of Religion*, 40.2 (2002), 251–68.

were religious in the sense of following the teachings of the church. The schools turned religious education into an optional subject and discouraged pupils from joining classes on religion. If someone still decided to enrol, the employer of the parents would put the father or the mother in a disadvantageous position and under pressure from the requirements of the Communist party. The proportion of pupils taking religious classes fell from almost 100% before 1948 to 4-5% after 1948. Young people grew up without experiencing religious education.[173]

Christian students seldom enrolled in the study of the human sciences because of their worldview. This made it difficult for them to present Christian opinions and teachings publicly through the media and in public life. 'Religious people have, therefore, less connection with mass communication and fewer possibilities to move about than non-religious people.' Tomka further concludes: 'In summary: those who regard themselves as religious belong to social groups:

1. in which opportunity to take part in social life is reduced as a consequence of age;
2. which are in opposition to the main tendencies of social development (groups with low qualifications, agricultural workers, the economically inactive);
3. in which the possibilities for and space for personal and social development are relatively low (that is, in addition to the factors mentioned above, in the country);
4. in which financial and intellectual possibilities are relatively restricted. People of religious identification are thus mostly from the marginal parts of society and vice versa: a large proportion of those who take a relatively small part in social life – or more specifically, in public life – regard themselves as religious.'[174]

Another reason for the traditionalism of the churches is the geographical distribution of Christians. Many more religious people live in villages than in cities.[175] Only 5.6% of adults under the age of fifty, living in Hungarian towns, were practising Christians in 1988. Tomka concludes: 'The higher one looks in the social hierarchy of the countries of Eastern Central Europe, the fewer the number of Christians one finds. Belief tends to be limited to the lower levels of society.'[176]

The reorganization of society and the repositioning of Christians in public and economic life led to a significant loss of religious confidence in Hungary during the first decades of Communism. Kamaras states that at the end of the forties: 'Practically all Hungarians declared themselves as adhering to one religious denomination or another. [...] Twenty years later only half of the population

---

[173] Tomka, A magyar vallási helyzet öt dimenziója, Chapter II.
[174] Tomka, Church, state, and society in Eastern Europe, p. 48.
[175] See in: Tomka, A magyar vallási helyzet öt dimenziója.
[176] Tomka, Church, state, and society in Eastern Europe, p. 30.

declared themselves believers, and another ten years later only two-fifths did so. The loss of religious faith was faster and deeper in Hungary than in any [other] Western European countries during the same period.'[177]

Social survey data about religious beliefs are available from 1972. The question, 'Are you religious?' was answered by 46% of the people with 'yes' in 1972. Six years later, in 1978, only 36% of the people responded to the same question positively. Figures from 1978 reveal that religious trends had reached a turning point and that acknowledgement of religious belief had started growing again about that time. Surveys also reveal a slow rise in church attendance, beginning in 1980.[178]

Loss of religious adherence – a consequence of socialist modernisation or persecution and discrimination?

Hungarian sociologists explain the decline in religion during Communism in a different ways. Although sociologists differ significantly in their understanding of the causes and processes of secularization, 'There is substantial agreement over its definition as "the process in which religious thinking, practice and institutions lose their social significance" as a consequence of modernisation.'[179] Some, like Szántó and Tamás, question the impact of discrimination and conclude that socialist modernization was responsible for the dwindling numbers of churchgoers. Szántó acknowledges that churches sometimes experienced discrimination but questions its impact on religious developments. He sees the main reason for the decline of religious groups to be growing consumerism and similar aspects of the modernization processes.[180] Promoters of secularization theory claim that modernization eliminates religion and that the process of secularization is mainly responsible for the decline of religious commitment during the Communist period.[181]

It ought to be pointed out that Socialist modernization differed from the Western type of modernization. Far from expressing democratic principles, Socialist modernization was not a natural, democratic, cultural development but rather a forced reshaping of society by means of intense pressure from state authorities. The purpose was to achieve Socialist goals within a limited period of time. Pollack came to the conclusion in his research that: 'During the decades

---

[177] Kamarás, 'Tendencies of Religious Changes in Modern Hungary', p. 121.

[178] Andorka, 'A Magyarországi Evangelikus Egyház', p. 43.

[179] Herbert, 'Christianity, Democratisation and Secularisation', p. 278; See also: Detlef Pollack, 'Religiousness Inside and Outside the Church in Selected Post-Communist Countries of Central and Eastern Europe', Social Compass, 50.3 (2003), 321–34.

[180] János Szántó, *Vallásos családok társadalmi-gazdasági helyzete Magyarországon* (Budapest: TÁRKI Társadalomkutatási Intézet Rt., 1994), pp. I. m., Pál Tamási, 'Egyházi mozgásterek a társadalomban', in *Az egyház mozgástereiről a mai Magyarországon.*, ed. by Özséb Horányi (Budapest: Vigília, 1997), p. 49.

[181] See more in: Bögre, 'Társadalmi – politikai változások hatása, p. 32.

of Communist rule, many of the mainly agrarian countries went through processes of industrialisation, mobilisation, urbanisation and rationalisation, brought about forcibly by the state. This change in the distribution of work has weakened the capacity of families to hand down religion by about one third.'[182]

Socialist-style modernization also involved a clear plan for the suppression of religious practices in Hungary. Only those dissociating themselves from religious beliefs gained access to further education and, in turn, the higher-educated levels of society became, on average, less and less religious, as Pollack also states: 'On average, the more highly educated do not believe frequently in God as the less highly educated. This has been proven in Hungary [...]. Where migration from the countryside was especially drastic, the destruction of the traditional village milieu meant that the churches lost an important means of social demographic support.'[183]

These developments show that promoters of secularization neglect important processes in society, thus affecting religious developments significantly. Besides, Tomka concludes that the severe decrease in the practice of religion prior to the regime change was not simply the effect of modernization but also a consequence of the unresponsiveness of the churches. He sees, on the one hand that the conservatism of the church might be responsible, while on the other hand he acknowledges that the authoritarian system limited the autonomous activity of churches.[184]

In contrast to the secularization theory there is the belief that damage by the Communist dictatorship to the Hungarian people, and particularly to Hungarian churches, was mainly responsible for the loss of interest in religion. According to Zsuzsa Horváth, several factors contributed to this tendency. The period of terror, along with the Communist educational system and mass communication that included anti-religious propaganda, combined to cause loss of faith and/or loss of connection to religious denominations. Because the churches were compromised, their members also lost their trust in the churches.[185] Certainly the impact of the Communists on religion should not be neglected. Kool makes it clear how far-reaching the influence of the anti-religious activities of the government was and how these activities changed the life of the church: 'In the Communist era, people were under serious pressure to keep religion and faith within the private sphere. Churches were not allowed to be 'relevant', to speak to the context. Their message was made to appear outdated, "for decrepit old women wrapped in scarves." So Christians could not live for the present; the

---

[182] Pollack, 'Modifications', p.139.

[183] Ibid., p.139.

[184] Miklós Tomka, 'Vallás és társadalom Magyarországon: Gyakorlait teológiai és vallásszociológiai megközelítések' (Habilitation, Evangélikus Hittudományi Egyetem, 2001), p. 52.

[185] Zsuzsa Horváth, 'Az egyház kovásza: a bázisközösségi mozgalmak Magyarországon', in *Hitek és emberek*, ed. by Zsuzsa Horváth (Budapest: ELTE, 1995), pp. 243–82 (pp. 249–50).

relation between church and world was thus limited or was annulled. The ghetto mentality brought about a sort of Canaan language, especially within the free churches.'[186]

Some scholars acknowledge the devastating impact of the regime on church life and religious belief but hesitate to suggest that the regime was solely responsible for the decline.

One particular combination of these two theories leads to a third thesis. Separately, the secularization theory and the theory concerning discrimination cannot sufficiently account for the recent changes in religious belief and practice. For the correct interpretation both need to be considered. Zsuzsanna Bögre concludes that the data supplied in the international comparative surveys[187] prove that the impact of the persecution of religious people can be observed, along with the influence of secularization.[188] Kamarás and Tomka also support and substantiate the view that declining religious observance is the result of 'worldwide secularization combined with the atheism forced upon people by a Stalinist state'.[189] Tomka sees major differences between East-Central and Western European developments. The religious revival in East-Central Europe is a striking phenomenon that 'contradicts secularization theories and social trends in Western Europe. It surprised politicians and church dignitaries even in East-Central Europe. It should, however, never be mentioned separately from the fact of the relative weakness of the religious segment of society. In most East-European societies the committed and practising religious population is numerically a minority. In a few other countries it is weak because of the marginalized social position of believers.'[190]

Rita Hegedűs has also contributed significantly to the debate about religious developments. Her thesis and conclusions have been crucial for the conclusions made in this chapter. In her PhD research she analysed the available data on religious belief and practice in Hungary,[191] focusing mainly on the 1990s. Her study concentrates, not on the development of Christian churches per se, but on religious developments in general. Like Tomka and Kamarás, Hegedűs comes to

---

[186] Anne-Marie Kool, 'The Church in Hungary and Central and Eastern Europe: Trends and Challenges', *The Princeton Seminary Bulletin*, 28 (2007), 146–64, p. 152.

[187] See: EVS 1990, 1998, ISSP 1991, 1998, Aufbruch 1998, Ramp 1998. Bögre, 'Társadalmi – politikai változások hatása' p. 31.

[188] Bögre, 'Társadalmi – politikai változások hatása, p. 31.

[189] Kamarás, 'Tendencies of Religious Changes in Modern Hungary', p. 121;

[190] Tomka, Church, state, and society in Eastern Europe, p. 82.

[191] Hegedűs relied on the following sources of data in her research: European Value Study 1981 (Huingarian survey data) and 1990 (international survey data), International Social Survey Programme 1991 (Hungarian and international survey data), Hungarian Household Panel survey 1992, 1994 and 1997, Mobil TÁRKI 1992, Társadalmi Mobilitás Hungarian Central Statistical Office 1992, MKPK 1995 (about influence of the churches), Religious and moral pluralism 1997-1998, New Departures 1997-98, Monitor TÁRKI 1998, Europa TÁRKI 1998.

the conclusion that both the Communist type of modernization and also the discrimination meted out against church bodies by the Communist regime, combined to bring about the sharp decline in religious faith and practice.[192]

The conclusions drawn by Hegedűs about the development of religious life in Hungary can be divided into three groups. The end of 1940s and the 1950s witnessed the period of Socialist modernization. During this period churches also experienced heavy persecution. Even today, it can be observed that the younger generation of that time were the people who moved to cities or went to university and were also those who gave up religious interests and became secular. The higher the status gained by people in society, the less likely they were to be religious.

> The 1960s and 70s saw growing consumerism and individualism in Hungary. Hidden discrimination and growing visible hostility characterized the attitude towards churches. The generations growing up during this period became the most secular. Survey data present a change in the impact of Socialist modernization on this generation. It is clear that Socialist modernization no longer negatively affected the stratification of religious changes. In the 1980s Socialism was falling apart and society was characterized by economic crises and also by growing religious interest and presence. The younger generation of that time grew up mainly without religious socialization but the trend towards religion was very obvious. Notably, in direct contrast to the trends in the 1950s, religious attitudes were associated with higher status in society.[193]

The intensity of the growth of religious interest at the time of regime change is visible in the survey data. The turning point from religious decline to growing religious interest came in 1978. This was in contrast to West European religious tendencies and was a clear sign of a different type of modernization process in Communist and post-Communist countries.

While western counterparts of the population of Central and Eastern Europe experienced religious decline everywhere, the central and eastern European population went through a phase of significant religious growth. According to Tomka, 'it is without doubt that interest in religion became 'visible' and perhaps this interest even grew. Furthermore, from the mid eighties the prestige of the churches increased as well. This was the period of the visible disintegration of the party-state. This is the time when the population realized that the political and social system – conceived up to that point as more or less stable – was in a ruinous condition. This was contrasted by the people with the stability of the

---

192 Hegedűs, A vallásosság alakulása Magyarországon, p. 16. See also: Hegedűs, 'A vallásosság kérdése Magyarországon a nemzetközi és magyar kutatások eredményeinek tükrében'.
193 Hegedűs, A vallásosság alakulása Magyarországon, pp. 173–74.

churches which was believed eternal or at least which survived Communist persecution.'[194]

Table 1. Religiosity of Hungarians Between 1978 and 1993 (%)

Year	I am religious	I am not religious
1978	44,3	40,8
1980	51,5	38,3
1983	53,9	33,3
1984	59,4	29,1
1986	59,7	28,9
1988	58,1	35,3
1989	62,9	30,9
1990	67,7	27,3
1991	70	25,9
1993	70,9	25

Source: Tomka[195]

The growing religious interest that some called 'religious revival' surprised not only politicians and sociologists but also church leaders and members and it became a striking phenomenon. According to Tomka, this contradicts secularization theories and social trends in the Western part of Europe.[196]

Religion after the regime change

Before 1945, religion had been one of the main pillars of society and of the state, but during the Communist era its adherents were persecuted and it was relegated to the private sphere. According to Tomka,[197] since 1989 it has resumed its position as a public 'actor' whose precise role, however, has not yet been

---

[194] Tomka, Religiosity in Central and Eastern Europe, p. 6. He also stated: 'The increased value and role of religion and the churches must be seen by comparison with the other segments of social life and with the disintegrating institutions of the Communist state. The first optical illusion is that perhaps it was not so much that religion changed as that the standard that was used to evaluate religion was altered.'

[195] Tomka, 'The Changing Social Role of Religion', p. 18.

[196] It has to be stated too that, as Tomka concludes, the decline of interest in religion in recent decades might also have played an important role in these developments. Tomka's comment on the revival is apt: 'It should, however, never be mentioned separately from the fact of the relative weakness of the religious part of society. In most East-European societies the committed and practising religious population is numerically a minority. In a few other countries it is weak because of the marginalized social position of believers.' Tomka, *Church, state, and society in Eastern Europe,* p. 82.

[197] See also: Tomka, Religiosity in Central and Eastern Europe, p. 1.

determined. (See also Bremer, [198] Pollack, Borowik, Jagodzinski [199] and Spieker[200]).

It is clear that religious interest grew, even among the younger generation that was supposedly less religious, because of modernisation and the aggressive anti-religious propaganda of the Communist regime. The data analysis carried out by the International Social Survey Programme in 1998 shows the proportion of people aged 18-30 who had started to believe in God in recent years as compared with those who had lost their faith. The difference in certain Western and Central and Eastern European countries is clearly recognisable in the study of Tomka, presenting ISSP data analysis. While the proportion of people stating 'I do not believe in God though earlier I did' is significant larger (about 2-4 times) in the Western European countries as the proportion of people stating 'I believe in God though earlier I did not', Central and Eastern European countries (expect Slovenia) present clearly the opposite. The Proportion of those stating 'I believe in God though earlier I did not' is significantly larger (about 2-8 times) as those saying 'I do not believe in God though earlier I did'.[201]

In 1995 Kamarás, too, claimed that a religious renewal had begun and that: 'The interest of young people in religion is growing, as is the number of intellectuals who think of themselves as believers. There are thousands of small religious communities and self-supporting units striving to realise a religious way of life. There is an increasing interest in religious knowledge and in religious art. As a result of two opposing trends, the spread of atheism has stopped and, after the change in political system, a slight reversal can be anticipated.'[202]

'As a consequence of the renewal, religion could leave the isolated privacy and became a topic of public life and the process undoubtedly resulted in a higher public esteem of religion.'[203]

The research of World Value Studies in a number of Western and Central and Eastern European countries provides information about how people considered growth or decline in religious interest in the ten years preceding 1999. While in all Western countries people felt that less were religious in 1999 than 10 years ago, people of former Communist countries were quite sure that there had been a religious revival after the 1989 regime change. In Hungary over 60 per cent

---

[198] Thomas S. Bremer, *Religion and the conceptual boundary in Central and Eastern Europe: Encounters of faiths* (Basingstoke England, New York: Palgrave Macmillan, 2008), Studies in central and Eastern Europe.
[199] Detlef Pollack, Religiöser Wandel in den postkommunistischen Ländern Ost- und Mitteleuropas (Würzburg: Ergon-Verl, 1998), 6.
[200] Manfred Spieker, Katholische Kirche und Zivilgesellschaft in Osteuropa: Postkommunistische Transformationsprozesse in Polen, Tschechien, der Slowakei und Litauen (Paderborn: Schöningh, 2003), 22.
[201] See in: Tomka, Religiosity in Central and Eastern Europe, p. 8.
[202] Kamarás, 'Tendencies of Religious Changes in Modern Hungary', p. 121.
[203] Tomka, Religiosity in Central and Eastern Europe, p. 7.

chose the option 'More are religious today than 10 years ago' and only 18 per cent agreed with the option 'Less are religious today than 10 years ago'.[204]

Surveys at the time of regime change revealed that the churches already occupied a leading position among the most trusted and well-known organizations. Political changes had transformed society as well as the life and mission of Christian churches, and people had become more open towards religion. Society was accepting and supportive towards Christian churches after 1989. This resulted in many Hungarian churches and mission-oriented organizations in the western countries discovering rising opportunities for growth. Some denominations and congregations experienced renewal, others planted new churches, and multitudes of people joined evangelistic meetings and church activities. The Adventist Church was part of this renewal of faith.

The growing interest shown by people in religion at the time of regime change in Hungary is indicated in the survey data. World Values Survey shows that the new excitement about religion developed in tandem with declining atheism.[205]

The changing religious climate was accompanied by changes in religious activities. World Values Studies presents the alterations in the attitudes of people towards prayer and meditation in some European countries. World Value Survey also presented data about the change in percent of population who pray and meditate. It is clear that the proportion of people praying and meditating grew by 12% in Hungary between 1981 and 1990, a growth rate that is significant by comparison with the situation in some other European countries.[206]

Despite significant religious growth in Central and Eastern European countries and the increasing social prestige of the churches in the mid-eighties, the commitment to religious participation and church attendance remained only a minority feature of life, even among religious people. 'The groups that have, [...] very close ties to the church and that are "decidedly religious" are in most cases relatively small ones.'[207] Increasing ideological freedom was well understood by people and most of them designed their beliefs to suit themselves, exercising personal autonomy without depending on the institutional services of existing churches. Besides this, although the social role of the churches was growing, they were not able to tempt the majority of religious people to become regular churchgoers. Commitment to weekly church attendance and formalized church membership were affected very little by the religious revival experienced in Hungary. Pollack argues in his study of the modifications in the religious field of Central and Eastern Europe that denominational membership does not reflect a formalized church membership but merely a subjective feeling of belonging.[208] Monthly church attendance grew in the '80s and '90s but not as significantly as

---

[204] Ibid., p. 7.

[205] In: Froese, 'Hungary for Religon, p. 258.

[206] Ibid., p. 257.

[207] Tomka, Church, state, and society in Eastern Europe, p. 82.

[208] Pollack, 'Modifications in the Religious Field', pp. 140-158.

religious interest grew during the same period. After 1991, according to the data gathered by the International Social Survey, a decline in church attendance took place, although religious interest was still growing.[209]

Two thirds of religious people in Hungary think of themselves as religious, according to their own terms but only a third of them declare themselves to be believers in terms of the doctrines of their own church. A majority of the first group, according to Kamarás, 'do not practise their religion, lack a sense of identity with a congregation or parish, have minimal religious knowledge and some are anticlerical. The rest, a clear minority, lead more-than-average religious lives but feel their religion to be individual, cut to their personalities, and in some aspects they are critical of their church, particularly of its leaders.'[210]

Kamarás also concludes that the 'zone between religiousness and non-religiousness is broad. Some of those religious after their own fashion quickly drop out.'[211] Among university students, the number of those following the doctrines of a church is also very low. Two or tree times more consider themselves to be religious people, professing their own 'tailor-made' religion.

The different attitudes of people towards religion are difficult to slot into simple categories. Hegedűs attempts to do so, however. He relies on Tomka's publications[212] and says that three main types of ideological group exist in reference to religion:

1. Religious people declaring themselves to be believers in terms of the doctrines of their church
2. Non-religious people isolating themselves from religion and turning against religion
3. And people who are religious after their own fashion.[213]

The general religious developments in Hungarian society are mainly connected to the principal Christian denominations but besides them there are several smaller denominations, often called 'free churches' and also new Christian movements which play a minor but important role in the religious developments in the country. They initiated intensive missionary efforts at the end of the Communist era and tried to infiltrate society. While the main churches focused on the political repositioning of their denominations in society, the smaller denominations offered many different kinds of religious programmes.[214] The extent to which they were able to reach the people can also be seen from

---

[209] Froese, 'Hungary for Religon', p. 265.

[210] Kamarás, 'Tendencies of Religious Changes', p. 122.

[211] Ibid., p. 122.

[212] See Tomka's classification of religious people. In: Tomka, Miklós, *Magyar katolicizmus 1991* (Budapest: Országos Lelkipásztori Intézet Katolikus Társadalomtudományi Akadémia, 1991).

[213] Hegedűs, A vallásosság alakulása Magyarországon, p. 27.

[214] Presentations, seminars, meetings, concerts, health programmes….

their membership development. Szigeti and Török[215] interviewed the leaders of these denominations about the development and the size of the membership of their churches in 1990, 1994 and 1996/97. The question has to be asked as to how reliable these data can be considered. Török is aware of the problem that asking leading pastors about the number of their church members and the development of their denomination can result in subjective answers but because no other data collection has been done in this particular area, Török's and Szigeti's data remain the only figures to offer a picture of the membership growth of the above-mentioned denominations.[216]

The expansion in membership of the registered small churches, beyond 1,000 members, is indicated in the following table.

Table 2. The Expansion in Membership of the Registered Small Churches

Typical 'free churches'	Started in Hungary in the year	Török '90	Szigeti '94	Török '96/97
Baptists	1846	11,000	11,000	11,000
Pentecostal church	1920	3,900	4,980	6,000
Seventh-day Adventist Church	1890	4,125	4,530	4,717
Jehovah's Witnesses	1898	10,000	13,679	18,217
Church of the Nazarene	1839	2,500	3,000	2,200
Methodists	1898	1,700	1,000	1,967
Mormons	1888	100	250	3,000
Free Christian Church	1920	1,350	1,800	1,350
Early Christian Apostolic Church	1947	1,750	1,000	1,500
		36,425	41,239	49,951

Source: Török[217]

On average, these denominations experienced a 37.13% growth in the seven years covered by the study. This expansion seems to have been much larger than the equivalent change in the membership of Catholic, Calvinist and Lutheran churches but the relative impact of these denominations on society still remains very small; all of them together, including the new Christian denominations, represent less than 1% of the population of Hungary.

---

[215] See: Péter Török, 'A magyarországi bejegyzett kisegyházak tagságának alakulása 1990 és 1997 között', *Távlatok*, 48 (2000), pp. 290–300.
[216] Török, 'A magyarországi bejegyzett', pp 290-300.
[217] Török, 'A magyarországi bejegyzett', pp 290-300.

Christian communities around the world prayed for churches in the eastern block during the Communist period and fostered partnerships. The collapse of the Communist regimes was seen by many as an answer to their prayers and they recognized opportunities for Christian mission. During and after the years when there were changes, a massive invasion by missionaries took place. 'By far the majority arrived with no background knowledge in culture or language. Nevertheless they were convinced of the "need to bring Jesus" to Eastern Europe.'[218]

Peter Penner draws attention to the paradox that when the regime change opened up the way for free access to Christian mission by the churches, Western churches and organizations neglected the local churches they used to pray for. They had prayed that those congregations would survive persecution but after 1989 the Westerners often ignored those churches, failing to see them as valuable or interesting any longer.[219] According to Pachuau, many Western missionaries did not cooperate at all with the churches in Central and Eastern Europe in ways appropriate to the situation of the latter. Instead, says Kool, the Western denominations chose to carry out mission 'in ways that reflected their own cultural mores and missionary traditions'.[220] External difficulties were added to the internal ones in the life of those Eastern European churches. 'A massive influx of missionaries entered Central and Eastern European countries, including Hungary. These missionaries came mostly from the West but also from Korea and often there were virtually no attempts to engage in collaborative ministry with the local churches. Nor did the Korean missionaries endeavour to forge positive working relationships with Western missionaries.'[221] Participation in some worship services often simply meant financial and humanitarian benefits for the participants.[222]

The new religious freedom also gave birth to some new Christian denominations in Hungary. Török and Szigeti list seventeen of them. Their total membership in 1991, according to reports by the leaders, was 4,542 and in the following years these young groups achieved huge growth. In 1996/97 their membership reached 49,070, which is 10.8 times the number of members recorded in 1990.[223] Besides these churches, Török also lists fourteen recently established non-Christian religious groups. Their total membership grew from 8,878 in 1990 to 23,230 in 1996/97 but only two non-Christian groups

---

[218] Kool, 'Trends and Challenges', p. 25.

[219] Péter Penner, 'Critical Evaluation of Recent Developments in the CIS', in *Mission in the former USSR*, ed. by Walter Sawatsky, Peter Penner and and International Baptist Theological Seminary (Schwarzenfeld: Neufeld, 2005), pp. 120–63.

[220] Kool, 'Trends and Challenges', p. 25.

[221] Ibid., p. 29.

[222] Kool makes this statement mainly about Korean missions. Kool, 'Trends and Challenges', p. 29.

[223] Török, 'A magyarországi bejegyzett kisegyházak', 294-297.

contributed to this growth significantly: the Church of Scientology and the Krishna organization.

The study by Török also presents the development of five Orthodox churches. Their membership development shows a decline rather than growth. The total membership of these churches was 37,000 in 1990 but dropped to 34,800 by the year 1996/97. These numbers indicate that not all churches experienced revival after regime change. Jehovah Witnesses, Mormons, the charismatic 'Hit' church, along with a few other charismatic churches, the Krishna movement and the Scientology church grew significantly. The Orthodox churches and other churches with historical traditions were not able to use the opportunity for growth provided by the religious revival.

Figure 2. Fastest Growing Religious Groups in Hungary

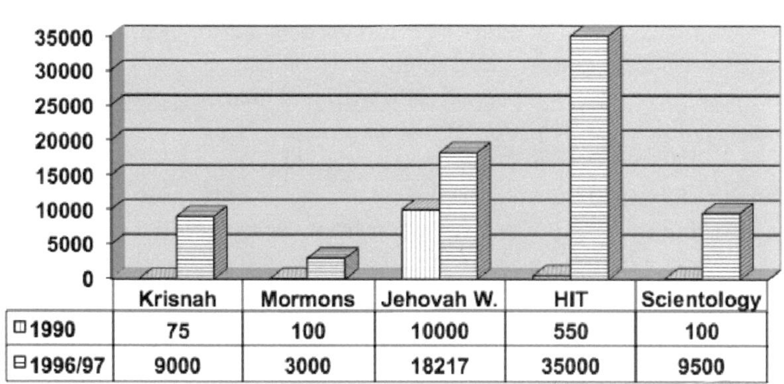

	Krisnah	Mormons	Jehovah W.	HIT	Scientology
1990	75	100	10000	550	100
1996/97	9000	3000	18217	35000	9500

Source: Török, Szigeti[224]

The above-mentioned growing denominations have some common characteristics that may have contributed to their expansion. All of them build strong relationships through personal care and fellowship, they try to be active in their communities and exercise influence through personal work, visiting in their neighbourhoods, using public media, music and social activities.[225] These

---

[224] Ibid., 294-297.

[225] Publications and researches provide information about the value system and the history of these fastest growing small enominations in Hungary. See more in: István Kamarás, *Krisnások Magyarországon* (Budapest: Iskolakultúra, 1998); Magdolna Banyán, 'Krisna Társadalma: Max Weber Hinduizmus Koncepciójának Társadalomtörténeti alkalmazása' (Történelemtudományok Doktori Iskola, 2011); *Tanok és szövetségek Tanok és szövetségek és az egyház története* (Belgium: Az Utolsó Napok Szentjeinek Jézus Krisztus Egyháza, 2002); Žofia Pažitná, '"Experiencing the Closeness of God": Mediated Religious Experience

activities, along with promises of peace, security, joy and hope, seemed to become relevant to a certain portion of society at the time of the regime change.

Possible reasons for growing religious interest at the time of the regime change and expectations within society

The population in Central and Eastern Europe, including Hungary, experienced significant religious growth at the time of the regime change. World Value Studies[226] and also the Aufbruch[227] research project produced results completely consonant with each other in this regard.[228] However, while the religious revival is widely accepted as fact, the explanations for it varies, as has been discussed. In short, the religious developments in former Socialist countries have been complex and have also been influenced by many other aspects of life. Possible reasons for growing religious interest may include the following situations.

Political changes
The Communist regime aimed to forbid and destroy all other parties, organizations, associations, federations and competing structures. 'Only the church was preserved as a parallel structure' and many expected the intensive and also political participation of the churches.[229] David Martin[230] and José Casanova[231] agree that it is always good for the church and for religion in general if church/religion and state/politics are not closely linked or seen to be intimately linked. Where the two are not separated from each other, the consequence is almost always a loss of authority and credibility. According to this theory, the intensive growth of the churches in the 1950s, despite Communist persecution, can be explained as a sign that people were putting their trust in the churches. In the 60s and 70s the state gained more and more influence in the life of the churches and compromised them. The fact that people were turning away from religion and churches may be interpreted as a possible consequence of this

---

and the Role of Authority in the Faith Church in Budapest' (Master Thesis, Central European University, 2008).

[226] World Values Survey Association, *Values Change the World: World Values Survey* (2011) <http://www.worldvaluessurvey.org/wvs/articles/folder_published/article_base_110/files/W VSbrochure6-2008_11.pdf> [accessed 27 June 2012].

[227] See descritpion of Aufbruch in: András Máté Tóth, and Csaba Máté Sarnyai, 'Egyházak a rendszerváltó Kelet-Közép-Európában: Egy nemzetközi vizsgálat tapasztalatai, különös tekintettel Magyarországra, Szlovákiára és Ukrajnára', in *Felekezetek, egyházpolitika, identitás*, ed. by Margit László Balogh (Budapest: Kossuth kiadó, 2008), pp. 355–59; See also: Margit Balogh: 'Egyház és egyházpolitika a Kádár-korszakban' *Eszmélet, 34* (1997), 69-79.

[228] Tomka, 'Religiosity in Central and Eastern Europe', p. 6.

[229] Tomka, Church, state, and society in Eastern Europe, p. 102.

[230] David Martin, *A general theory of secularization* (New York: Harper & Row, 1978).

[231] José Casanovas, *Public religions in the modern world* (Chicago: The University of Chicago Press, op. 1994).

influence.[232] Pressure from Communism led, to a certain extent, to the rise of autonomous groups and independent religious activities and the proliferation of these grass-roots communities[233] provided further support for the credibility of religion in general and for organized religion. This independent development was in complete contrast to the state's purposes but at the end of the 1970s it became stronger and also played a significant role in the revival of religious life.[234]

It is a paradox that, while Socialist modernisation weakened the position of religion in Central and Eastern Europe, 'the political arrangement strengthened it. Whereas the politics of the party-state persecuted religion, its social and cultural arrangement induced religion and the churches to become the institutions of opposition and [of] preserving traditions, thus creating a new, fertile soil for religion'.[235] The persecution was successful in the short term but in the long term religious opposition was strengthened because of it. In the 1980s it was already clear that religion had begun to revive in Hungary. The official propaganda had to change direction[236] and offer more tolerance towards religious developments. These political changes signalize the success of religion as the only possible opposition in a Communist state. Churches and these changes in behaviour in regard to religion broke the state monopoly and became forerunners of future developments. 'Religious communities can be interpreted as the first germs of local and civil society.'[237] Tomka also raises the question of 'whether the churches themselves understand and accept the responsibility which follows from their unique position'.[238] As opposition, they were not following a consciously designed process for revival and as a result of this their steps were very tentative.

Before 1989 the Communists pushed religions into the private sphere but 'since 1989, it [religion] has once again become a public actor whose precise role, however, has not yet been finalized'.[239] The political changes supported the revival of religion despite the opposing plans of the Communists.

Religious developments
The more political authority lost its credibility, the more previously hidden religious life gained new visibility.[240] For the correct interpretation of religious changes we also need to consider these developments. The seemingly intensive religious growth was not always in harmony with changes in how people

---

[232] See for more: Hegedűs, A vallásosság alakulása Magyarországon, p. 37.

[233] Tomka, Church, state, and society in Eastern Europe, p. 107.

[234] See for more: Hegedűs, A vallásosság alakulása Magyarországon, p. 37.

[235] Tomka, Religiosity in Central and Eastern Europe, p. 3.

[236] Tomka, Church, state, and society in Eastern Europe, p. 122.

[237] Ibid., p. 86.

[238] Ibid., p. 86.

[239] Tomka, 'Religiosity in Central and Eastern Europe', p. 1.

[240] Tomka, Church, state, and society in Eastern Europe, p. 82.

identified themselves or with their worldviews. It may also signalize that, due to the slowly changing political situation, behaviour had also changed during the decades of the '50s, '60s and '70s, many formerly religious people compromised by hiding their views on religion in order to avoid discrimination or persecution, or to gain access to studies or better job opportunities. They appeared to live as secular people, apparently adjusting to the Socialist way of life and accepting its values. People who rejected their religious background in those decades may also have supported religious revival after becoming aware of the political changes and the changing position of religion in society. Their consciences awoke and their religious feelings experienced a revival. Once again they openly confessed their religious views. Same facts indicate that the majority of interested did not belong to this category of people. The religious revival was supported by many young people who did not have any previous religious education.[241] They also expected something positive from the churches. Greely writes: 'The resurgence among the young of religious hope was linked to a rediscovery of a God who cares. When the burden of Socialist oppression was lifted, those born after 1970 found themselves more likely than their immediate predecessors, to believe in a God who is concerned about them personally. [...] Of its very nature this revival is invisible because it affects personal faith and hope.'[242]

The political changes and the growing interest people showed in religion provided a unique chance for the churches to present themselves and their message in society. Their religious activities could be presented more and more openly in public and they also used the opportunity to leave the hiding places that the Communists had forced them to withdraw into. National churches and also foreign missions gained unlimited access to the general public. The heritage of the past –holy books, historical traditions, religious teachings – flooded the country. Western churches and missions immediately released a vast amount of money and started countless projects in Central East European countries. Flocks of interested members of the public filled some churches to overflowing. Many people tried to compensate for their earlier lack of baptism, communion and confirmation. [243] All these developments added up to a very powerful concentration on religious issues throughout the country.

Developments in society
Hungarian society started changing its attitude towards religions and churches after the 1970s. The public acceptance of religions rose and the prestige of the churches increased too.[244] Religion could emerge from isolation and it now

---

[241] For more see the research of Bögre. She deals with questions related to the hypothesis that people became religious because they had belonged to a church prior to the political oppression. Bögre, Társadalmi – politikai változások hatása, p. 12.

[242] Andrew Greeley, 'Religious Revivals in Eastern Europe', *Society*, 1 (2002), 76–77.

[243] Tomka, 'Vallás a rendszerváltás után', pp. 24–25.

[244] Tomka, Church, state, and society in Eastern Europe, p. 12.

became a topic of public discourse. Tomka writes: 'Ecclesiastical dignitaries became celebrities'.[245] Public esteem for religion rose as a result of this process but it may be questioned how far it can be considered a genuine religious revival or to what extent the interest in religious issues was merely a demonstration of freedom that gave society a chance to deal with previously forbidden issues like religion. Tomka refers to an optical illusion generated by the media and, to a certain extent, by politics. 'The public visibility and the increase of religion's relative public significance aroused mass media interest. Religion in the media became a self-generating sensation.'[246] As already noted, despite the apparent growth of interest in religion, the number of churchgoers did not rise dramatically and it fell again several years after the regime change.

The massive growth in interest in religion may also have been the result of parallel developments in society and religion. Tomka highlights the fact that the autonomous reorganization of society and of religion happened at the same time. Just as society was able to recover after the dictatorship, religion was able to regain its vitality.[247] Because churches anticipated the reorganization and put new ideas into practice, rather than merely reflecting trends, traditional churches and faith groups could be seen as potentially supportive and as 'actual bearers of a kind of unifying, consolidating spiritual and institutional resource'.[248] Várhegyi comes to the conclusion, after analysing the position of the churches in 1995 that the public simply expected too much from the churches at the time of regime change. Apparently they expected 'morality and education, social service and charity, and even mediation in [regard to] the economy'.[249] In national, family and individual life an unprecedented moral vacuum emerged.[250] The new situation brought with it the greatest challenge to the churches. Tomka adds that in the 1980s the prestige of public institutions, governments and councils declined rapidly and that people were looking to two types of institution for solutions: the mass media and the churches. He states that 'more than three-quarters of the country's population pressed for the involvement of churches in social, cultural and societal issues'.[251]

Bogomilova describes certain differences among post-Communist countries with regard to expectations and hopes concerning the social and cultural role of the church.

> The greatest proportion of respondents in Romania (74.7%), Lithuania (74.4%), the Ukraine (63.1%), and Poland (62.7%) feel that the Church can contribute significantly to solving the moral, family, spiritual, and social problems of society.

---

[245] Tomka, Religiosity in Central and Eastern Europe, p. 7.
[246] Ibid., p. 7.
[247] Hegedűs, A vallásosság alakulása Magyarországon, p. 38.
[248] Bogomilova, Reflections on the contemporary religious "revival", pp. 5–6.
[249] Asztrid Várhegyi, 'Magyar egyház a fordulat után', *Egyházfórum*, 3 (1995), 91–94.
[250] Medgyessy, 'Mission or proselytism?, p. 105.
[251] Tomka, 'Az egyházak az ezredfordulón', pp. 78–82.

Among the most sceptical about the role of the Church in solving these problems are: the Eastern part of Germany (27.6%), Bulgaria (33.9%), the Czech Republic (36.4%) and Estonia (38.5%). In the middle range of the scale are Hungary (42.3%), Belarus (44.5%), Slovenia (46.8%), Latvia (52.8%), Russia (55.1%), Slovakia (59.7%) and Croatia (60%).[252]

The responses given by churches to these unrealistic expectations were not satisfying and caused later disappointments. However in 1995 many still expected the participation of the churches in social and public issues, of the kind Tomka identifies in the following list:

- Bringing peace and providing mediation in conflicts
- Promoting social cohesion and unity
- Creating community
- Educating on behalf of solidarity
- Demonstrating tolerance, with understanding, and giving moral guidance
- Presenting not teachings but practical love
- Helping with poverty reduction
- Caring for the homeless
- Treating addictions like alcoholism
- Caring for the elderly, sick and disabled.[253]

The high social expectations which people had in regard to the churches may also be accounted for by the churches' specific quality as large, organized bodies with country-wide networks and with specialized institutions and committed membership. They had preserved some autonomy during the previous forty years and had been able to offer alternatives to Socialism.[254] All other traditional social networks had been destroyed and society had become fragmented.[255] Civic activities hardly existed; the churches remained the only organizations giving evidence of strength and capability. The way, in which church members dealt with life's challenges also appeared to show personal autonomy, offering proof that 'people's utility does not depend on the social or political power of the institution they "belong to".'[256] Despite previous religious discrimination, religious commitment during the time of transition appeared to be a stable, positive correlate of life satisfaction.[257]

The growing needs of the populace and the vacuum in regard to trustworthy organizations, along with the positive image of the churches, turned people's attention to religion and resulted in high expectations. The revolution created a new chance of obtaining a higher quality of life, but it did not bring solutions to lawlessness and failed to create a perfect society overnight. Churches were seen

---

[252] Bogomilova, Reflections on the contemporary religious "revival", p. 6.

[253] Tomka, 'Az egyházak az ezredfordulón', pp. 78–82.

[254] See: Tomka, Church, state, and society in Eastern Europe, p. 85.

[255] Hankiss, East European Alternatives, p. 99.

[256] Lelkes, Tasting freedom, p. 24.

[257] For data about this correlation see: Lelkes, Tasting freedom, pp. 24-25.

as possible agents that could fulfil hopes and expectations of the kinds people held after the regime change.

Developments in the relationship between society and the churches

Several studies have shown how these expectations and hopes changed the relationship of the populace towards churches. According to Tomka, research had provided empirical data, as early as the late 1980s, on the growing trust people felt in churches and also indicated the somewhat unrealistic expectations. At the end of the '80s and during the '90s in many Eastern and Central European countries the churches enjoyed the highest prestige among all social and societal institutions.[258] According to an ISSP survey carried out in 1991, 77.3% of the population trusted churches and religious organizations (giving them middle-level, high-level and very high-level trust ratings). Only 22.7% of people stated that their confidence in the churches was low or very low. Bogomila compares these developments with Western European trends and comes to the conclusion that in most post-Communist countries higher trust was placed in the churches than was given to them in most Western European ones. 'The citizens of Austria, France, Great Britain, Sweden, Finland, Belgium, Spain [and] Denmark indicated smaller degrees of trust in their respective churches than in other public institutions, as evidenced by the European Values Study of 1999. According to the data provided by that survey, in most post-Communist countries (with the exception of Estonia, Bulgaria, Slovenia, the Czech Republic and the Eastern part of Germany), people placed greater trust in the church than in other institutions.'[259]

These trends opened dizzying perspectives for churches and made them one of the most important factors in the rebuilding of society. The clearest signs of this were that a multitude of previously non-religious people joined religious meetings, attended programmes and listened to religious leaders. With the visible disintegration of the party-state, the prestige of the churches increased. The ruinous condition of the political and social system was 'contrasted by the people with the stability of the churches which was believed eternal or at least which survived Communist persecution'.[260] Tomka also sees these changes as having a substitutionary function: 'People expected the church to fulfil those functions that had earlier been carried out by the state, local public authorities or secular social institutions.'[261]

---

[258] Tomka, Vallási változások Kelet-Közép-Európában, Chapter 3.
[259] Bogomilova, 'Reflections on the contemporary religious "revival"', p. 6.
[260] Tomka, Religiosity in Central and Eastern Europe, p. 6.
[261] Tomka, Religiosity in Central and Eastern Europe, p. 6.

Opinions about the decreasing interest and trust in the churches after the regime change

Studies reveal that, despite opportunities and growing interest towards religious matters at the beginning of the transition time, there was 'no religious renaissance' in Hungary. The appreciation of the church and the level of faith in society have not increased in the Hungarian society.[262] Church attendance most definitely fell in Hungary after 1991, although this does not appear to be true if one looks at figures for the development of interest in religion. Church attendance fell by almost 30% from 1991 to 1996, according to ISSP. Public self-assessment as being religious decreased by half that figure.[263] It is clear that the prestige of the churches was diminishing, although it was still higher than that of the average for public institutions.[264]

In addition, the development of the missionary programmes and of the membership of the Adventist church in Hungary shows falling interest in church issues only one or two years after the regime change.

Figure 3. SDA Church Membership Development from 1989 to 1999

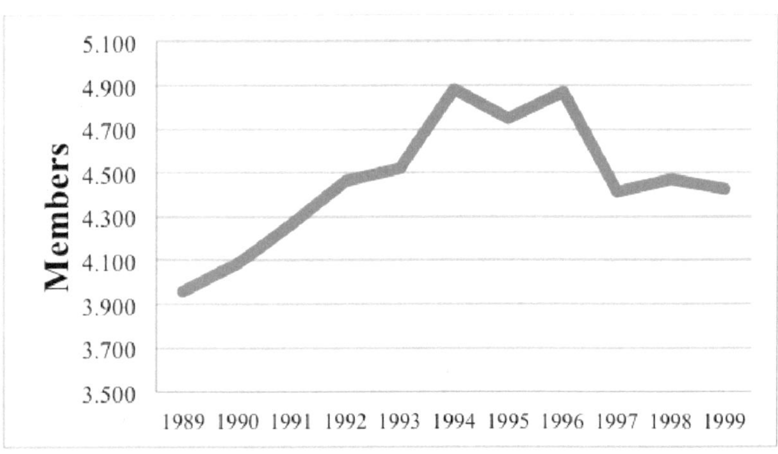

Source: Archive of Hungarian Union Conference

---

[262] For the conclusion drawn from GALLUP studies of religious developments in Hungary see: György Fischer, *A vallásosság és a médiumok világa (Religiosity and the world of media): (Nem elsősorban a közvélemény-kutató szemével)* (Budapest, 2000), pp. Slide 6.
[263] See in: Pollack, Modifications in the Religious Field.
[264] Tomka, Vallási változások Kelet-Közép-Európában, p. 27.

The reasons for the decreasing trust in churches can be examined in three areas.

Activities of chuches

In the first place, the life and activities of the church could not meet the sometimes unreasonably high expectations of the people. The aggressive nature of the Communist regime had affected the life of the churches and had forced them to protect themselves against changing forces. This resulted in frozen, old-fashioned forms of religious observance which did not seem to meet modern-day needs.[265] Church traditions and rituals had become obsolete over time and made the integration of new converts almost impossible. An analysis of Adventist Church statistics shows that the majority of baptized people and some newly established local congregations often left the church. This meant a major crisis for some districts.

The union president of the Adventist church in Hungary stated in his report in 1990: 'The majority of the members clung to the trend of maintaining legalistic traditions. As a result, the church found it hard to tolerate the youth. So the churches became old and weak. Because of that about 100-120 smaller or bigger church groups have died in the past 50 years.'[266]

The regime change also opened the door to new denominations, cults and new religious movements, and their appearance, along with the growing tensions among existing churches, encouraged competition.[267] The monopoly that had been held by some denominations, and their structural unity, was forcibly brought to an end. Some churches now focused more on the restoration of church hegemony[268] than upon the needs of their parishioners. The regime change also gave the churches new opportunities that kept them busy. They discovered the chance to reclaim their lost property, including schools and institutions.[269] Churches focusing on the restoration of their authority, social status and influence introduced anti-clerical voices and those of the disappointed. Churches were not prepared to face the responsibilities of the kind they had coped with in the past, or to bear the consequences of earlier actions. Under socialism, compromised leaders had brought discredit to the whole body of religious organizations.

Structure of religious population

Secondly, the structure of the religious population made it difficult, especially for Protestant denominations, to participate in rebuilding society. Church members had below-average social status and this resulted in church members

---

[265] Tomka, Expanding religion, pp. 16–17.

[266] Jenő Szigeti, Presidental report to the board of the Trans European Divison. St. Albans. 1990.

[267] Tomka, Church, state, and society in Eastern Europe, p. 13.

[268] Tomka, Expanding religion, p. 51.

[269] More opinions about it see: Várhegyi, 'Magyar egyház a fordulat után', pp. 91-92.

turning away from involvement in public life or in the mainstream social life of their country. Only a small proportion of religious people were to be found in socially advantaged groups and this hindered the churches from representing themselves properly to the non-religious segment of the population.[270] The age structure of the religious members of the population showed that the elderly were over-represented. In 1989, in the Adventist church in Hungary, 73.0% of all members were over the age of 50 and 74% of them were women. Only 7.15% of the members were men under the age of 40.

Figure 4. Age Structure of the Hungarian Adventist Church in 1989

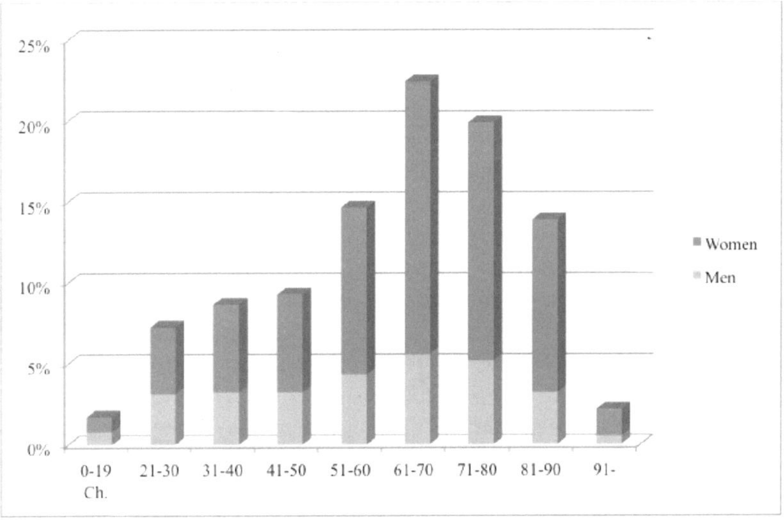

Source: Archive of the Hungarian Union Conference

This imbalance in terms of age within the Adventist church makes some major problems obvious. The majority of church members were women and were above 60 years of age. Yet, after the regime change, the majority of people coming to the programmes presented by the church were young people, as it is shown in the next graph.

---

[270] See: Tomka, Church, state, and society in Eastern Europe, p. 54.

Figure 5. Age structure of people joining the Adventist church in Hungary by baptism in the years 1989-93

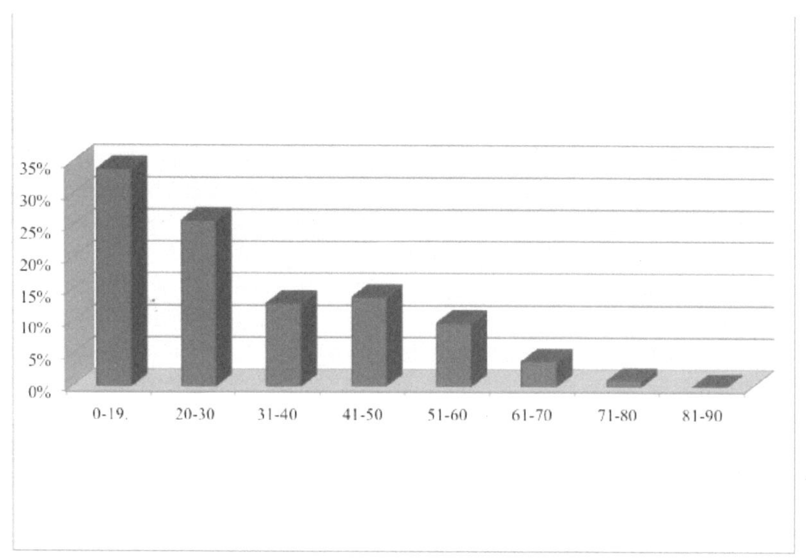

Source: Archive of the Hungarian Union Conference

The age structure of the church is exactly the opposite to the age structure of people joining the church after the1989 regime change. The difference instigated a generational conflict that resulted in many new church members leaving the church after only one or two years or even months of membership.

Missing religious values

In contrast to the situation in some other Eastern European[271] countries and to the USA, the appreciation of religious values did not grow significantly. Values are not rooted in the biological or physical functions of life. They are independent from the consensual principles and usually change slowly. The impact of Communism remained potent after 1989, regardless of the regime change. Schöpflin[272] and Kennedy[273] state that the legacy of the past, especially that of the political culture, intellectual traditions and ingrained mentalities, still

---

[271] For example in Russia. See: Andrew Greely, 'A Religious Revival in Russia', *Journal for the Scientific Study of Religion*, 33.3 (1994), 253–72.

[272] George Schöpflin, *Politics in Eastern Europe, 1945-1992* (Oxford, UK, Cambridge, Mass., USA: Blackwell, 1993).

[273] Michael D. Kennedy, *Envisioning Eastern Europe: Postcommunist cultural studies* (Ann Arbor: University of Michigan Press, 1994).

makes a very strong impact on later value systems. Fürtös and Szakolcai[274] began an empirical study in order to trace the changes in values during the period from 1977 to 1997. They used the method devised by Milton Rokeach,[275] designed specifically for the analysis of individual values. Their study was based on representative, empirical data[276] and showed that, for the Hungarian populace before the regime change, typical Socialist values were the most important: social image, work, peace, homeland security, equality and freedom. The regime change weakened these but they remained quite strong. Values which had previously been characteristic of the opposition became stronger: family, inner harmony and love. Values also connected to religion, such as 'forgiveness' and 'affection' also remained very weak after the regime change. The weakest value measured was, despite the religious revival, the only one with clear religious content: salvation. Regarding the appreciation of the value 'salvation', no change could be recognized between 1982 and 1989.[277] The data indicates that despite the increasing interest shown towards churches and the growing trust exhibited towards them, the interest in genuine religious values remained almost the same as before in Hungary.

These developments, along with the low percentage of churchgoers among 'religious' people, demonstrate that society had not adopted truly religious attitudes and values. The growing interest in religion had little impact on people's everyday lives and activities. Churches received the chance to present an alternative way of life and an opportunity to present Christian faith convincingly but the interest did not mean the implementation of Christian values or a real change in the lifestyle of the Hungarian population. The growing number of people attending Christian programmes and participating in church activities was a sign of openness and searching rather than a real revival of faith. However it is true that many people were on the road to rediscovering a God who cares.[278] The sad fact is that churches interpreted this unique opportunity wrongly and neglected to deal with deeper problems like hostile attitudes and distrust[279] among themselves and with other inherited consequences of the Socialist era. After one or two years of research, carried out in all eight Eastern European participating countries, it could be shown that 'confidence in church leaders has fallen sharply'.[280]

---

[274] László Fürtös and Szakolcai Árpád, 'Kontinuitás és Diszkontinuitás az Értékpreferenciákban (1977-1998)', *Szociológiai Szemle*, 3 (1999) <http://www.szociologia.hu/dynamic/9903fustos.htm> [accessed 4 April 2012]

[275] M. Rokeach, *The nature of human values* (Free Press, 1973).

[276] See for the detailed description of the samples and methods: Fürtös and Szakolcai, 'Kontinuitás és Diszkontinuitás'.

[277] Fürtös and Szakolcai, 'Kontinuitás és Diszkontinuitás'.

[278] Greeley, A Religious Revival in Russia, p. 77.

[279] See in: Kopp and Skrabski, Magyar lelkiállapot – 1997.

[280] In: Greeley, A Religious Revival in Russia, p. 77.

'In every country, they report, the principle concerns of the churches were to reassert their political power, their religious monopoly, and their moral control of the population. Small wonder that they lost the confidence of their people. One would think that the religious leadership in Eastern Europe would have to be brain dead not to notice the possibilities for evangelization among those under thirty years old. However, since one hears nothing about this revival of faith in a God who cares, one suspects that they are not aware of it. Like religious leaders in the West, they do not need sociology to tell them about the needs and the problems of their people. Nor the opportunities.'[281]

---

[281] Ibid., p. 77.

3. The Development of Missionary Thinking behind the Activities of the Seventh-Day Adventist Church

The Background of Changing
Missionary Activities of Adventists in Hungary

Communism not only changed Hungarian society radically but also changed the life and activities of the Adventist church, including its missionary thinking and praxis. During the years from 1920–45 and from 1948-52 the Adventist church experienced very difficult periods of persecution, illegality and discrimination but, despite all these difficulties, emerged as a maturing organization with clear missionary zeal and activities that were able to mobilize a significant proportion of church members. Hundreds of lay people without theological education were involved in evangelistic activities and, despite its often illegal status, the denomination in Hungary grew steadily, sometimes even doubling its membership within one to two years.[1] During those years the young church showed maturity and a sense of independence in designing the life and mission of the church.

The international headquarters of the organization supported local activities but the work was done mainly by local congregations and church members, without relying heavily on international projects, strategies and support. Adventists had good community relationships and seemed to be aware of the needs of people around them. The ministry carried out by the denomination within society was strongly related to the recognized needs. The mission of the church appeared to be concentrated not so much on a truth-oriented proclamation as on holistic service to the people of the country.

Even during WW II the church leaders were able to organize supportive programmes, offering all the church members a chance to participate. Adventist mission activities were organized in 1944 in three major areas:

1. Evangelism, including conducting meetings, visiting people in their homes, correspondence group and prayer groups
2. Distribution of literature such as tracts, journals and books

---

[1] In 1920 Adventists had 611 church members in Hungary. This number grew steadily, reaching 3,608 in 1945 and 6,810 by 1952. See: Szigeti, *Fejezetek a H. N. Adventista Egyház magyarországi történetéből.*; Rajki, *A H. N. Adventista Egyház története,* pp. 16-7.

3. Welfare work, including feeding the poor, weekly ministry for people in need, visits to families, mediation regarding job opportunities for unemployed people, and more.

The mobilization of membership was successful, as is apparent from the statistics. About 220 lay evangelists and 140 voluntary preachers were working in Hungary in 1947. The lay evangelists gave 10,332 bible studies to 21,210 people usually in small groups and conducted 17,344 visits in 1947. Between 1945 and 1949 Adventists established fifteen new local congregations annually, on average, reaching mainly young people.[2] The welfare ministry of the church made a significant contribution to meeting the needs of the public after WWII.

A comparison of Adventist ministry before and after Communism reveals major differences. During the forty years of Communism the young, dynamic denomination lost a significant portion of its momentum, autonomy and ability to mobilize its members. Instead of recognizing people's current needs and relating to the community through relevant ministries and personal service by church members, Adventist mission mainly relied on proclamation- oriented concepts of mission and on Western plans and projects.

The headquarters of the world church, called the General Conference, and its European representative, the Trans European Division, created worldwide strategies for the whole church regarding mission. 'Harvest 90' was a plan for the years 1985-1990 and 'Global Strategy' was created to direct the mission activities of the worldwide denomination in the period from 1990 to 1995. These plans were aimed at fostering traditional Adventist values and mission activities, unifying church undertakings internationally. The local activities in Hungary were merely determined by international programmes and trends in mission, largely dependent on Western instructions.

Behind the mission activities a certain kind of underlying missionary thinking and mission theology can be observed. In this chapter I am going to analyse the developments and changes that have taken place in Adventist missionary thinking in order to understand the roots and the underlying traditional concepts of mission that appeared during the period 1985–1995. Some of the form and content of Adventist mission often seems to be unique. To understand it a study is needed about how Adventists viewed their role as a church within the community. The answer to this question reveals the basis of the denomination's mission theology. The goal is to understand missionary thinking and its consequences for the mission activities carried out by the denomination in Hungary in the period of time under scrutiny.

---

[2] For statistics on, and further development of, mission activities, see: Rajki, Zoltán, *A H. N. Adventista Egyház története 1945 és 1989 között Magyarországon* (Budapest: Advent, 2003), p. 32.

The Need for Critical Reflexion and
Evaluation of Applied Mission Theology

The nature of mission theology

Mission theology is a relatively new discipline. Gerald Anderson's definition, which has influenced other scholars in this field, including Adventists[3] is that 'in this 'post-Constantinian' age of church history, mission is no longer understood as outreach beyond Christendom, but rather as 'the common witness of the whole church, bringing the whole gospel to the whole world'.[4]

The definition clearly indicates that mission theology refers to beliefs about the content and direction of Christian mission.[5] Goals, motives and methods provided through mission theology should not lead to an excessive emphasis on activities because mission theology is not a one-way street. The complexity of mission theology is shown in an article by Charles van Engen and Arthur F. Glaser. In their attempt to define mission theology they describe eight characteristics: mission theology is multidisciplinary, integrative, biblical, theological, praxeological, definitional, analytical and seeks to be truthful.[6] It is a process that is influenced not only by theory but also by practice. Orlando Costa emphasizes the relationship between reflection and action: 'Missiology is fundamentally a praxeological phenomenon. It is a critical reflection that takes place in the praxis of mission [… It occurs] in the concrete missionary situation, as part of the church's missionary obedience to and participation in God's mission, and is itself actualized in that situation […] Its object is always the world, […] men and women in their multiple life situations […] In reference to this witnessing action saturated and led by the sovereign, redemptive action of the Holy Spirit, […] the concept of missionary praxis is used. Missiology arises as part of a witnessing engagement to the gospel in the multiple situations of life.'[7]

While this 'witnessing engagement' is taking place in order to serve 'God's purpuses in the world',[8] the church also needs to test theory and praxis by maintaining an on-going critical reflection of mission theology. This is because

---

[3] See: Borge Schantz. See: Schantz, *The Development,* p. 191.

[4] Stephen Neill, Gerald H. Anderson and John Goodwin, *Concise Dictionary of the Christian World Mission* (Nashville: Abingdon Press, 1971), p. 594.

[5] See: Frances S. Adeney, 'Why Biography? Contributions of Narrative Studies to Mission Theology and Mission Theory', in *Mission Studies: Journal of the International Association for Mission Studies* (Leiden: Brill, 2009), 26 (p. 155).

[6] *Global Dictionary of Theology: A Resource for the Worldwide Church, ed. by* W.A Dyrness and others (Downers Grove: Intervarsity Press, 2008), p. 550.

[7] Orlando E. Costas, Theology of the Crossroads in Contemporary Latin America: Missiology in Mainline Protestantism, 1969-1974 (Amsterdam: Rodopi, 1976), p. 8.

[8] Stephen Bevans, The Mission has a church: Perspectives of a Roman Catholic Theologian, *in:* Kirsteen Kim and Andrew Anderson, *Edinburgh 2010: Mission Today and Tomorrow* (OCMS, 2011), pp. 201-08.

its primary task is 'to validate, correct and establish on better foundations the entire practice of mission'.

'Theology of mission acts, then, as a means of validating, correcting and establishing on better foundations the motives and actions of those wanting to be part of the answer to the prayer, "Your kingdom come, your will be done on earth as in heaven". In brief, it has the task of keeping under review and validating best practice in all areas of missionary obedience. It tests theory and practice against the apostolic Gospel and history read eschatologically.'[9]

Theology of mission is simultaneously 'missiological action-in-reflection and theological reflection-in-action'.[10] The aim of biblical and theological reflection is to achieve a trustworthy perception of the mission of the church that 'seeks to interface with the appropriate missional action, and creates a new set of values and priorities that reflect as clearly as possible the ways in which the church may participate in God's mission in specific contexts at particular times'.[11] People are always at the heart of mission: 'Theology of mission is at its best when it is intimately involved in the heart, head and hand (being, knowing and doing) of the church's mission in the world. Theology of mission is a personal, corporate, committed, profoundly transformational search for always new and more profound understanding of the ways in which the people of God may participate more faithfully in God's mission in a lost and broken world so loved by God.'[12]

That is why missionaries must also become theologians; it is the very nature of their task and mission needs theological reflection.[13] The increasing range of the dominant questions asked at the World Missionary Conferences is a good example of this search for a new understanding of certain aspects of mission.[14]

---

[9] J. A. Kirk, *What is Mission?: Theological explorations* (Minneapolis, MN: Fortress Press, 2000), p. 21.

[10] Dyrness, Global Dictionary of Theology, p. 550.

[11] Ibid., p. 561.

[12] Ibid., p. 561.

[13] Paul G. Hiebert, Tite T., *Missional Theology*. (2005). <http://www.globalmissiology.org/cms/images/stories/hiebert/Heibert_Tienou_Missional_T heology.pdf> [accessed 28 February 2012] (p. 6).

[14] Gerald Anderson tried to summarize the main content of the conferences in the form of one dominant question for each. At the World Mission Conference in Edinburgh in 1910 the dominant question was, 'How missions?'; in Jerusalem in 1928 it was 'Wherefore missions?'; in Tambaram, India, in 1938 it was 'Whence missions?'; in Whitby, Ontario, in 1947 it was 'Whither missions?'; in Willingen, Germany, in 1952, the question that dominated was 'Why missions?' and so on. See Gerald H. Anderson, *Theology of the Christian Mission* (Nashville,: Abingdon Press, 1961).

The need for critical reflection and re-examination of the theological underpinnings of mission

The Christian faith is intrinsically mission-oriented and in this respect it is similar to many other religions and also to Marxism.[15] Karl Marx himself stated that 'Philosophers have only interpreted the world differently; the point is, however, to change it.'[16] His words indicate his conviction that it must be possible to change the world if philosophy is oriented towards the possibility of action, rather than simply towards interpretation of theory. Because both Christianity and Marxism aim to influence the world, the conflict between them was inevitable during Communist times. Adherents of each belief system tried to change not only society but each other too. In this interaction the Christian missionary enterprise needed a clear and adequate ideological foundation. Indeed, Christians have experienced the same inner challenges, not only in post-Communist countries, during socialism and at times of regime change, but throughout history.

Christian missionary thinking has never remained constant but has gone through major changes. In recent centuries Christians – both Protestants and Catholics – have discovered and have come to give more and more emphasis to the missionary task of the church. The roots of Protestant missionary development go back to the beginning of the nineteenth century when Protestants in Europe and in North America became more and more involved in mission after experiencing the influence of William Carey's famous preaching.[17] 'By 1817 the missionary cause had become the great passion of the American churches.'[18]

The development of missionary thinking needed time but it became more and more widely understood and accepted that the mission of the church involves accepting God's command to 'go forth' and believing that the church should participate in the divine mission.[19] The world mission conference of major Protestant denominations and missionary societies held in Edinburgh in 1910 'was one of the great landmarks in the history of the Church. [...] In Edinburgh a decisive attempt was made for a global gathering in order to facilitate cooperation across denominational barriers'.[20] The importance of the role that mission plays in the life of the Christian denominations is also clear from the fact that this event is considered to have been the 'symbolic beginning' of the modern

---

[15] Bosch, *Transforming Mission*, pp. 7–8.

[16] Karl Marx's last thesis on Feuerbach, thesis XI in *Marx/Engels Selected Works*, 1. (Moscow: Progress Publishers, 1969), p. 13-14.

[17] For more about the development of Protestant mission see Bosch, *Transforming Mission*, pp. 239-511.

[18] Bosch, *Transforming Mission*, p. 279.

[19] Ibid., pp. 389–93.

[20] Daryl M. Balia and Kirsteen Kim, *Edinburgh 2010 Volume II: Witnessing to Christ Today* (Oxford: Regnum Books International, 2010), pp. 199–200.

Protestant Christian ecumenical movement. The conference focused on certain events because they appeared in its context as most relevant and urgent, but it neglected other important questions. 'In Edinburgh, a major concern was the absence of missionary enthusiasm in the churches of the West; the theological question of the relationship between church and mission was hardly touched.'[21] A sentence from the closing statement of the world mission conference forty-two years later in Willingen supplies a picture of the development of missionary thinking among Protestants. The whole church was addressed and mission was seen as a 'self-revelation' of God: 'There is no participation in Christ without participation in His mission to the world.' The 'Missio Dei' is God's self-revelation, which declares that he loves the world, and the mission of the church refers to particular forms of participation in the Missio Dei.[22]

Catholics also experienced a growing desire to 'bring the light of Christ to all men'.[23] The twenty-first Ecumenical Council of the Catholic Church, the Second Vatican Council, led the process of the missionary development of the church, marked by missionary encyclicals in the twentieth century,[24] to the rediscovery of a missionary ecclesiology of the local church. At Vatican II 'the real breakthrough in respect to mission occurred not in the missionary decree but in Lumen Gentium (LG) right at the outset [...] (the church present itself) as a servant community. LG ecclesiology is missionary through and through'[25] and it starts with the statement that 'Christ is the Light of nations'.[26]

At the beginning of the missionary movement optimism dominated and some Protestants in particular believed that it was just a matter of time before the whole world would be Christianized.[27] This enthusiasm disappeared in the following

---

[21] Bosch, *Transforming Mission*, p. 369.

[22] For more about the role of the church in mission, see: Johannes C. Hoekendijk and Erich-Walter Pollmann, *Kirche und Volk in der deutschen Missionswissenschaft,* Theologische Bücherei (München: Chr. Kaiser, 1967), p. 346.

[23] The growing urgency of the missionary task of the Catholic Church is rooted in 'the present-day conditions of the world' as stated in the 'Dogmatic Constitution on the Church', *Lumen Gentium*, p. 1.

[24] See especially *Maximum Illud* (1919), *Rerum Ecclisiae* (1926), *Evangelii Praecones* (1951), and *Fidei Donum* (1957).

[25] Bosch, Transforming Mission, p. 371.

[26] This appears in Chapter I, 'The Mystery of the Church'. For more on this see Nigel Johnson and Paddy Moloney, *The light of the Nations: Lumen Gentium the Dogmatic Constitution on the Church of the 2nd Vatican Council* (Harare: Catholic Students Chaplaincy, 1996 – 2002).

[27] In 1900 Lars Dahle, the General Secretary of the Norwegian Missionary Society, calculated the growth rate of Christianity in the entire world and developed a mathematical formula to predict by which year the entire human race would accept the Christian faith. His conclusion was that it would happen in 1990. Others such as Johannes Gustav Warneck presented evidence of the superior power of Christianity by comparison with other religions. See Johannes G. Warneck, *The living Christ and dying heathenism: The experiences of a missionary in animistic heathendom,* The Living forces of the Gospel series (Grand Rapids, MI: Baker, 1954).

decades, not only as a consequence of the world wars which led many to disappointment in the Christian faith but also through crises affecting church life and missions.

In his comprehensive work about paradigm changes in Christian mission, David Bosch concludes that the manifestation of the crisis in the Christian church, in relation to theology, and to mission, can be described as having six factors. Among these factors is the worldwide process of secularization, the dechristianization of the West that used to be the heart of the entire modern missionary enterprise,[28] and also the influence of Western theology and Western ecclesial ways and practices as undisputed norms for others.[29] The shift of Christianity's numerical centre of gravity to the global South also raises questions about what its implications are for mission.[30]

Like the ecumenical movement and the Catholic Church, the Seventh-day Adventist Church displayed growing missionary zeal. In 1874 the Adventist church began sending its evangelists and other workers around the globe and became a missionary movement, resulting in considerable growth for the denomination. A well-organized international organization with almost twenty million members worldwide grew out of these missionary activities. It can be stated with confidence that the Seventh-day Adventist Church is a mission-oriented denomination and that outreach towards non-Adventists has a high priority. However, in recent decades Adventist missionary thinking has also gone through a process of change and pragmatic goals have often determined the agenda of the denomination in terms of mission, while deeper questions about mission theology and the biblical foundations of mission have seldom been asked. An analysis of the mission plans and activities of Adventists at the time of regime change in Hungary support the conclusions of Gordon Doss that Adventists were so preoccupied with the practical opportunities for expanding the mission of the church that 'they tended to overlook the theological underpinnings of mission'. In his comprehensive study of structural models for mission, Doss calls for 'harmonizing mission theology, structure, strategy and methodology in the Adventist church.'[31]

The sudden rise of religious interest in Eastern Europe and the expanding opportunities for mission strengthened the prevailing attitude within the Seventh-day Adventist Church that missiological agendas needed to be dominated primarily by the strategy and practice of mission. Charles van

---

[28] David Barrett calculated that, in Europe and North America, an average of 53,000 people leave Christian churches permanently every week. *World Christian Encyclopaedia: A Comparative Survey of Chruches and Religions in the Modern World A.D. 1900-2000*, ed. by David B. Barrett (Oxford: Oxford University Press, 1982), p. 7.

[29] Bosch, Transforming Mission, pp. 3–4.

[30] See: Philip Jenkins, *The Next Christendom: The Coming of Global Christianity* (Oxford: Oxford University Press, 2002).

[31] Gordon R. Doss, 'Structural Models for World Mission in the Twenty-first Century: An Adventist Perspective', *Andrews University Seminary Studies*, 43/2 (2005), 301–13 (p. 305).

Engen's observation (leading to his statement in 1996) gives the impression that this situation represented a general trend among Christian denominations, especially in the second part of the twentieth century: 'For the past thirty years mission theology has taken a backseat to mission practice... missiology concerned itself with a host of activist issues and agendas like [...] evangelism, church growth [...]. Unfortunately, in the midst of such busy global activism, the deeper questions of mission theology were too seldom asked.'[32]

Scholars within the church have been similarly critical of the mission praxis of the denomination. Adventist lecturer in mission studies, Gorden R. Doss, draws a parallel with other Christian denominations and considers the harmonization of theology of mission and the praxis of mission to be an urgent need. 'Like most Christian groups, twentieth-century Adventists were so preoccupied with the practical realities of doing missions in the midst of two world wars, a global depression, a cold war, a shift from colonialism to political independence, and many other historical factors, that they tended to overlook the theological underpinnings of mission. However, the experience of the twentieth century and the fresh challenges of the twenty-first century have forced upon many denominations and groups the realization that they must work harder in bringing their theology, structure, strategy, and methodology for world mission into closer harmony. The global reach and cultural diversity of our own denominations make this harmonization an urgent need. [...] The range of Adventist cultural, economic and educational diversity is vast, yet mission demands a high degree of unity.'[33]

Adventist scholars have called again and again for more reflection on the mission of the church. Besides Doss, other distinguished academics within the denomination such as Gottfried Oosterwal and Borge Schantz have raised their voices and argued for the urgency of the matter. As long ago as 1983, Schantz listed five problem areas that he believed called for reflection on self-identity and mission. He noted that, by its efforts in terms of missionary work, the Seventh-day Adventist Church had experienced remarkable expansion and growth throughout the world but that 'at present the SDA movement is facing certain problems arising from its distinctives which call for renewed reflection on its self-identity. These problems have raised a series of basic missiological questions'.[34]

The five problem areas, according to Schantz, are:

1. *The Problem of Size*. For many year the Seventh-day Adventist Church has been a worldwide denomination with a strong emphasis on unity. Schantz addresses some of the difficulties that have arisen because of these factors: 'Can it be that the many problems facing the SDA church today arise from its desire

---

[32] Charles E. v. Engen, *Mission on the way: Issues in mission theology* (Grand Rapids, MI: Baker Books, 1996), p. 17.

[33] Doss, 'Structural Models for World Mission', p. 305.

[34] Schantz, *The Development*, p. iv.

to achieve world-wide uniformity despite the great cultural diversity of its members?'[35]

2. *The Problem of Organizational Structure.* In cultural terms, Adventists' desire for world- wide uniformity has created an anthropological challenge. Schantz asks, 'Can it be that the SDA commitment to methodological uniformity tends to deculturalize its members and disorient them from their own peoples?'[36]

3. *The Problem of Exporting Western Models.* 'Can it be that the SDA pattern of exporting its Western institutional models is hindering its growth as [a] world-wide spiritual movement?'[37] This question is especially important for the present study of the missionary activities in the former Communist countries in Central Eastern Europe. After the regime change multitudes of western evangelists came with their concepts of mission to European countries and conducted their meetings in exactly the same way as they did in their home countries. In some places, as this research has discovered, local congregations, conferences and even unions simply copied Western models of evangelism. In the archive of the Adventist church in Prague for example documents show that the church received well designed proposals from Western evangelists for projects, with budgets which they were to follow exactly.

4. *The Problem of Growing Self-understanding.* The distinctive beliefs held by Adventists are increasingly being preached worldwide to all peoples. 'Can it be that the SDA [church's] failure to culturally contextualize its distinctives has produced a movement reflecting some of the major weaknesses of Western colonialism?'[38] Schantz states that Adventism served at the beginning as a renewal movement within Protestantism. The distinctiveness of the church played an important role. After Adventists began penetrating the non-Christian world, apart from preaching the basic evangelical message, missionaries often failed to seek to contextualize certain unique [or specific] Adventist doctrines. This could be also observed in the missionary activities of the church in Eastern Europe.

5. *The Problem of Ecclesiastical Exclusivism* – 'Can it be that the SDA tendency to live in isolation from other segments of the world-wide Christian movement has impoverished her thought and understanding of the missiological task? The SDA Church has from the outset, due to its unique mix of belief and practice, and probably also as a result of the treatment it has received from other Christians, taken a fairly anti-ecumenical stance.'[39]

---

[35] Schantz states that in many cultures local patterns of leadership roles and organization have been ignored and the church tends to be regarded as a foreign presence. Schantz, *The Development,* p. iv..

[36] Ibid., p. iv.

[37] Ibid., p. iv.

[38] Ibid., p iv.

[39] Ibid., p iv.

Since 1983, the year in which Schantz published his research about Adventist mission, the changes taking place in society have added some new, problematic aspects to these questions and the Seventh-day Adventist Church is now facing a growing crisis, both in Western countries and in Central Eastern Europe. Political, economic and social changes and the increasing percentage of immigrants in European society and also in Adventist churches have become huge challenges for the denomination, as have dying churches. The Adventist church in Hungary alone has lost more than 150 local congregations in the past sixty years. The stagnation of the church, according to statistics in many countries, is being prevented only because immigrants from the third world or from developing countries join the church. The history of Adventist mission experiences, including its failures, in the former communist countries examined in this research, also highlights the need to reflect on and evaluate Adventist mission theology, theory and praxis.

Mission theology was not a separate discipline before the 1960s when the publications and work of Gerald Anderson initiated changes.[40] However, even before the 1960s, reflection about theological issues concerning mission became more and more important for quite a number of prominent theologians. Karl Barth, Gustav Warneck, Martin Kaehler, Hendrick Kraemer, Max Warren, Josef Schmidlin, Walter Freytag, Harold Lindsell and others reflected on theological issues of mission without considering it as a separate discipline of theology. For example 'Barth's major discussion of the church's mission occurs in his fourth volume, The Doctrine of Reconciliation. Here he focuses on the definitive work that God accomplished in the cross and resurrection of Jesus Christ. The event of reconciliation – and its prerequisite, God's free covenant of union with man – becomes the "horizon" framework or starting point of missions.'[41]

This reflection is needed because, as is shown by the changing and varying meaning and character of the fundamental term 'mission',[42] the presuppositions underlying the mission enterprise and the differences in its interpretation have been evolving, not only throughout history but also in recent times, placing missiology in a state of confusion. Pachuau describes the cause and the consequences of this confusion: 'Differences in the understanding of mission and the contrariety between the different renditions of the field of study have placed missiology in a state of confusion, thereby preventing it from occupying its proper place in theological academia. The confusion is the result of drastic changes of mission understanding and the resultant multiple faces of mission.'

---

[40] The collection of essays edited by Gerald Anderson has been considered by many ecumenical theologians to be the pioneering text in this discipline. Anderson, *Theology of Christian Mission.*

[41] Waldron Scott, *Karl Barth's theology of Mission* (Downers Grove IL: InterVarsity Press, 1978), p. 10.

[42] 'Until [the] sixteenth century the term was used exclusively with reference to the doctrine of the Trinity [...] the sending of the Son by the Father.' Bosch, *Transforming Mission*, p. 1.

This underlines the necessity of dealing with the 'problem of identifying the nature and characteristics of missiology.'[43]

David Bosch claims that mission is always in a state of crisis: 'This is because mission functions at the nexus of history, culture, and faith.'[44] The world is complex and varied and each new generation of Christians is challenged by newly arising questions and issues not previously faced or adequately addressed.[45] The diversity of Christian denominations increases this challenge because the differences among faith groups require each of them to develop distinct mission theology in order to describe how they understand God's purpose for them, to design steps to meet that expectation and to discover answers to arising questions. In his comprehensive work on the history and theology of mission Bosch concludes: 'At no time in the past two millennia was there only one single 'theology of Mission'. This was true even for the church in its pristine state. However, different theologies of mission do not necessarily exclude each other; they form a multi-coloured mosaic of complementary and mutually enriching as well as mutually challenging frames of reference.'[46]

The unique structure and self-understanding of the multi cultural and multinational Seventh-day Adventist Church and its mission require thoughtful reflection, with careful and unbiased consideration of the basic foundation of Adventist missional enterprise. The central administration of the worldwide denomination has to understand, to cooperate with and serve people with an overwhelming richness of ethnic, cultural, religious, social and political diversity found in the countries, nations, tribes and people groups the church is actively working in. These people continue to raise new questions and challenges that often need to be dealt with promptly and thoroughly. Because the Adventist Church has a hierarchical structure and it manages its worldwide network through a central administrative system reflections on mission theology are even more important and challenging.

Adventist churches in Western countries have had a strong influence on churches in the third world and in developing countries, including Eastern Central Europe. The growing mission challenges in the West may have contributed to the rising interest in the promising mission fields in the East. The results of a comparative survey of churches and religions in 1982 were supposed to be warning signs for the Adventist church as well as for others. As early as 1982, Christian churches in Western countries were losing ground and influence

---

[43] Lalsangkima Pachuau, *Missiology in a Pluralistic World: The Place of Mission Study in Theological Education* (2000) <http://www.religion-online.org/showarticle.asp?title=1177> [accessed 5 March 2012].

[44] See: Doss, 'Structural Models for World Mission', p. 301.

[45] Kirk, *What is Mission?*, p. 21.

[46] Bosch, *Transforming Mission*, p. 8.

in society. It was calculated that in Europe and North America an average of 53,000 people left Christian churches permanently every week.[47]

Adventists in Western countries experience falling membership, a decline in influence in society, the problem of changing and dying churches, the challenge of spending all their energy on maintenance, and vanishing missionary enthusiasm in the churches of the West.

The crisis of mission is also the crisis of the church itself. Kraemer states that it is not a temporary condition but 'strictly speaking, one ought to say that the Church is always in a state of crisis and that its greatest shortcoming is that it is only occasionally aware of it'.[48] He goes one step further and says that the church 'has always needed apparent failure and suffering in order to become fully alive to its real nature and mission'.[49] Even if at present, at some locations, the suffering is minimal because the church has already been established and seems to be functioning well, this should not be interpreted as a sign of success.[50] It is only a matter of time before there will be a wider crisis of mission and also a general crisis in the church because, as David Bosch states, 'An inadequate foundation of mission and ambiguous missionary motives and aims are bound to lead to an unsatisfactory missionary practice.'[51] Past experiences are teaching Christian churches an important lesson about the need to be humble and willing to constantly re-evaluate the theological underpinning of their missionary activities.

The Development of Missionary Thinking of the Adventist Church and Paradigms Influencing Later Missionary Praxis

Roots of the message and mission of the Seventh-day Adventist Church

In order to understand the development of Adventist mission theology and the changes affecting it, it is necessary to trace the movement from its origins in the United States of America, where the church grew out of nineteenth century apocalyptic fever.[52] The heartbeat of Seventh-day Adventist identity originated in the Millerite expectation of Christ's imminent return. The theological and

---

[47] For more information see David B. Barrett, *World Christian Encyclopaedia: A Comparative Survey of Churches and Religions in the Modern World A.D. 1900–2000* (Oxford: Oxford University Press, 1982), p. 7.

[48] Hendrik Kraemer, *The Christian message in a Non-Christian World* (S.l: [s.n.], 1947), p. 24.

[49] Kraemer, *The Christian Message*, p. 26.

[50] Bosch states, 'And for many centuries the church has suffered very little and has been led to believe that it is a success.' Bosch, *Transforming Mission*, p. 2.

[51] Ibid., p. 5.

[52] John Skrzypaszek, 'Conversion and identity in the context of the Seventh-day Adventist faith tradition', *Melanesian Journal of Theology*, 28.1 (2010), 61.

missiological aspects of this historical heritage linked to the Millerite movement are keys to an understanding of the formation of Adventist theology of mission and providing a short overview of these factors is the main purpose of this chapter.

A Protestant context with few official bonds to existing churches
At the beginning of the nineteenth century American Christianity was predominantly Protestant.[53] Damsteegt refers to the *Yearbook of American Churches that* 'only a small section of the population was officially associated with a church at the time of Independence even though the colonies had experienced the Great Awakening in the 18th century'.[54] Damsteegt presents figures which show that in 1800 the percentage of the population holding membership in the churches was estimated to be 6.9%; in 1840 the percentage was, 14.5%; by 1850, it had reached 15.5%; in 1900 it stood at 35.7 %. The majority of the people were religious without belonging officially to a church. By the time the Millerite movement reached its zenith in the 1840s, only about fifteen per cent of the American population held membership in Christian churches.[55]

Philosophical trends in society, eschatological trends among Christians
Church and state were officially separated with the adoption of the Constitution. Religious pluralism contributed to the formulation of the principle of religious freedom in the constitution and in turn, as Damsteegt[56] states, the Constitution, as well as increasing immigration, stimulated the further development of religious plurality.[57]

David Bosch discusses the way in which the Enlightenment shaped missionary thinking and also addresses the different features of Enlightenment. The development of Adventist thinking and mission also reflects these characteristics. 'The fact of the matter is that each of these (nine missionary) motifs, as they shaped missionary thinking since the middle of the eighteenth century, betrayed the features of the Enlightenment [...]: the undisputed primacy of reason, the separation between subject and object, the substitution of the cause-effect scheme for belief in purpose, the infatuation with progress, the unsolved tension between "fact" and "value", the confidence that every problem

---

[53] Damsteegt, Foundations, p. 3; Cf. Kenneth S. Latourette, *Christianity in a Revolutionary Age: A History of Christianity in the Nineteenth and Twentieth Centuries* (New York: Harper, 1958-62), III., p. 4.

[54] Damsteegt, *Foundations of Seventh-day Adventist*, p. 3.

[55] Ibid., p. 3.

[56] Ibid., p. 4.

[57] Kenneth Scott Latourette notes that the result was that, by 1914, 'nearly every kind of Christianity found anywhere else in the world was present'. Latourette, *Christianity in a Revolutionary Age*, p. 10.

and puzzle could be solved, and the idea of the emancipated, autonomous individual.'[58]

Also deism had an impact on the development of Protestantism. Miller himself also held deistic views for a time. 'Born into a Christian home, Miller abandoned his religious convictions for deism in the first years of the nineteenth century.'[59] While undertaking military service during the War of 1812, he experienced a great personal crisis which made him think about life issues and revise his world view. He described his struggles in the following words: 'The heavens were as brass over my head, and the earth as iron under my feet. Eternity! What was it? And death – why was it? The more I reasoned, the further I was from demonstration. The more I thought, the more scattered were my conclusions. I tried to stop thinking, but my thoughts would not be controlled. I was truly wretched, but did not understand the cause. I murmured and complained, but knew not of whom. I knew that there was a wrong, but knew not how or where to find the right.'[60]

The unprecedented geographical expansion of the nation as well as of its churches also played an important role in laying the foundations of the Millerite movement and in encouraging its expansion. Movements among Christians, such as the Great Awakening and the later Second Great Awakening exercised a profound influence on theological development and mission and led to fervent eschatological anticipation. The Presbyterian Jonathan Edwards became the leading figure of the Great Awakening. He understood the need to lay down an appealing theological basis and also to present a motivating personal example and commitment. In his teaching, eschatology became a central issue and it 'was postmillennial [...] there was a sparkle of excitement in his eschatology, in that he believed that the Awakening really heralded the beginning of the latter days'.[61] 'These expectations were linked to the proclamation of a gospel of repentance and faith, not of inducing people to do good works. [...] Those touched by the Awakening were characterized by a burning seriousness with regard to the ultimate issues of life.'[62]

At the beginning of the nineteenth century eschatology became a central issue for proclamation by theologians and evangelists. Chaney writes, in reference to this period of time, that 'not a single sermon or missionary report can be discovered that does not stress eschatological considerations'.[63] Premillennialist views had been held by some influential religious leaders in earlier times. For

---

[58] Bosch, *Transforming Mission*, p. 342.

[59] George R. Knight, *Anticipating the advent: A brief history of Seventh-day Adventists* (Boise Idaho: Pacific Press Pub. Association, 1993), Anchors, p. 7.

[60] Everett N. Dick, *Founders of the Message* (Takoma Park, Washington DC: Review and Herald Publishing Association, 1938), pp. 20–21.

[61] See: Bosch, *Transforming Mission*, pp. 277-78.

[62] Bosch, *Transforming Mission*, p. 278.

[63] Charles L. Chaney, *The Birth of Missions in America* (South Pasadena, CA: William Carey Library, 1976), p. 269.

instance, John Wesley appears to have been inclined towards premillennialism in the early part of his career. He considered the new earth state to indicate the millennium and expressed this in a 1748 edition of their hymnal called Hymns for Our Lord's Resurrection. Hymn 22 contains the following lines:

> Then the whole earth again shall rest,
> And see its paradise restored.
> O wouldst Thou bring the final scene,
> Accomplish the redeeming plan,
> Thy great millennial reign begin.[64]

However, by the early nineteenth century, 'the dominant theological position in virtually all protestant denominations was explicitly postmillennialist'.[65] The events of the time seemed to support the theological position that the kingdom of God, the possible millennium had come near and would be revealed gradually. Developments in western countries, and especially the dramatic technical advances in North America, as well as the worldwide impact of the American missionary societies, were suggesting that America was going to play a central role in the millennium. Damsteegt mentions a sermon by Benjamin Trumbull, delivered at North Haven on 11 December 1783, that provides a good example of Protestant attitudes and Protestant views on how the newly formed republic was to lead the world to millennial glory. The American 'wisdom, liberty and happiness, knowledge and religion would be diffused throughout the earth' and 'mankind would be prepared for the universal reign of the Son of God in the glories of the latter day'.[66] It was also generally accepted that the final event would be the visible and literal Parousia of Christ.[67] The Parousia became the major event focused on by William Miller and also, later, by Sabbatarian Adventists, with the difference that in their premillennialist view the visible coming of Christ was an immense soon-coming event which could be expected to take place in the immediate future and needed urgent preparation.

After the Great Awakening Methodist, Baptist and Presbyterian churches experienced marked growth.[68] Notably, 'Miller was among those who returned to a belief in the Bible during the Awakening.'[69] The movement played an important role in the history of the Millerites and was later to influence Adventists too.

---

[64] See more: LeRoy E. Froom, *The Prophetic Faith of Our Fathers: The Historical Development of Prophetic Interpretation*, 4 vols. (Washington, DC: Review and Herald, 1948-53), II (1950), p. 694.

[65] Bosch, *Transforming Mission*, p. 282.

[66] Damsteegt, *Foundations of Seventh-day Adventist*, p. 6.

[67] Bosch, *Transforming Mission*, p. 283.

[68] Bosch concludes that 'the dramatic rise after 1776 is to be attributed almost solely to the Second Great Awakening', Bosch, *Transforming Mission*, p. 279.

[69] Knight, *Anticipating the Advent*, p. 7.

Discovering the worldwide aspects of mission, a voluntary movement
Besides church renewal, the worldwide aspect of mission received more and more attention. One reason was that the conviction grew among Protestants that their call was to reach out and take the gospel to all parts of the world. The urge to convert the heathen around the world started with a British Baptist, William Carey, considered by many to have been the father of modern Protestant missions. In 1786, according to anecdote, Carey stood up at a pastors' meeting and asked his fellow ministers whether or not they accepted that it was every Christian's obligation to help share the Gospel with the rest of the world's population. About a decade later he published his revolutionary booklet, *An Enquiry into the Obligations of Christians to use Means for the Conversion of the Heathens*, and – along with others – founded the Baptist Missionary Society, the first of a number of Protestant missionary organizations.[70] In addition, the stories of the explorations carried out by men such as James Cook were widely read and opened up new horizons for worldwide travel, for missionaries as well as for scientists and adventurers. Protestants discovered enticing opportunities and 'by 1817 the missionary cause had become the great passion of the American churches, resulting in a number of missionary societies'.[71] The way Millerites thought about mission was deeply influenced by the activities of these societies.

The spirit of voluntarism
The impact of the great awakenings waned and after a while they lost impetus. Awakenings and revivals were becoming routine, each contributing to the fashion for such excitement. People longed for new activities and ideas to interest them and were not satisfied with waiting for official organizations to make something happen. 'Those touched by the awakening were no longer willing to sit back and wait for the official churches to take the initiative. Rather, individual Christians, frequently belonging to different churches, banded together for the sake of world mission [...] Church renewal and mission were simply in the air.'[72]

The spirit of voluntarism also included respect for such support in the Adventist movement during later decades. The Millerite Adventists and also the Sabbatarian Adventists worked outside church organizations and depended on the voluntary support of enthusiastic lay people.

Anti-Catholic attitude
Another important matter to consider, in the context of the development of the Millerite movement and the formation, later, of the Adventist church, is the increasing percentage of Catholics in the population. The accelerating speed of Catholic immigration can be traced in statistics which show that in the period

---

[70] See: F. Deaville Walker, *William Carey, Missionary Pioneer and Statesman* (Chicago: Moody Press, n.d., repr. 1925), p. 54.
[71] Bosch, *Transforming Mission*, p. 279. Carey's famous slogan aptly characterizes the enthusiasm of Protestants: 'Expect great things from God, attempt great things for God!'
[72] Bosch, *Transforming Mission*, p. 280.

from 1790 to 1840 the population of the United States rose by four point five times but the number of Catholics within that population grew by nearly nineteen times.[73] What is more, the foundation of several Roman Catholic missionary societies in Europe, to promote evangelistic work in America, created anxiety and tension among many American Protestants. By 1850 Catholics had become the largest single church organization in the USA.[74] Their progress in terms of Americanization was very slow. 'It was felt that the near monopoly of the Protestant churches was threatened by a church known for its authoritarian government and persecuting policies. [...] There was a resurgence of the anti-Catholic bias exhibited by the colonial fathers, who in turn had received their ideas from Reformation literature – especially in sixteenth- and seventeenth-century England. A flood of anti-Catholic publications supported this "no-popery" crusade.'[75] No wonder that the Catholic Church, with its hierarchical structure, received special attention from Adventists in their Bible study and teaching.

Growing social needs and growing individualism concerning religious issues
The Second Great Awakening was losing its impact by the fourth decade of the nineteenth century and a new revival began,[76] but it was challenged by major social and financial issues which also influenced eschatological views. [77] 'Revivalism had increased the individualism of the people. Much seemed to depend upon the personal decision of the individual. Non-conformity was both acceptable and desirable, and the quest for truth became paramount.'[78] All this in combination created a fruitful atmosphere for the development of new ideas, religious movements and churches, especially in the so-called 'Burned-over District' of the state of New York.[79] Damsteegt also describes the development of extremists, including ultraist parties, and also the rise of perfectionism. He mentions central and western New York State as one of the areas most conducive to the rise of new religious movements. The area was called 'the Burned-over District' because it was swept over so often by the fires of revivalism.

---

[73] H. S. Smith, *American Christianity: An Historical Interpretation with Representative Documents*, 2 vols (New York: Scribner, 1963), II, p. 6.

[74] Sydney E. Ahlstrom, *A Religious History of the American People* (New Haven: Yale University Press, 1972), p. 513.

[75] Damsteegt, *Foundations of Seventh-day Adventist*, p. 6.

[76] This was the time when another revival started, under the leadership of Charles G. Finney (1792-1875). Bosch, *Transforming Mission*, p. 282.

[77] See Reuben E. E. Harkness, 'Social origins of the Millerite movement' (unpublished doctoral thesis, University of Chicago, 1927).

[78] Damsteegt, *Foundations of Seventh-day Adventist*, p. 12.

[79] For more see: Whitney R. Cross, *The Burned-over District: The social and intellectual history of enthusiastic religion in western New York, 1800-1850* (Ithaca, NY: Cornell University Press, 1950); Glenn C. Altschuler and Jan M. Saltzgaber, *Revivalism, social conscience, and community in the Burned-over District: The trial of Rhoda Bement* (Ithaca, NY: Cornell University Press, 1983).

Mormonism began in this region, as did Adventism and Spiritualism, all developing there within two decades.[80]

Growing emphasis on the imminent Parousia and the Day of Judgement
Among evangelical Christians in the early part of the nineteenth century the emphasis on Bible study increased and led many to new concepts in eschatology. According to the comprehensive study of Damsteegt historical events together with new discoveries in the Bible stimulated the key people. 'First, the emphasis on eschatology, which was stimulated by the events of the French Revolution, took place in Europe; later it arose in America. Many participating in these studies became convinced that Christ's return and the Day of Judgment were imminent and would inaugurate the millennium– a view designated as premillennialism. Consequently, these individuals strongly opposed the current postmillennial views. The principal exponent of premillennialism in America during this period was William Miller (1782-1849).'[81]

Miller studied intensively, devoting himself to the Bible alone. His method of study was to allow the Bible to explain itself. His system of interpreting scripture by comparing the text with history later became typical for Adventists too: 'I then devoted myself to prayer and to the reading of the word. I determined to lay aside all my presuppositions, to thoroughly compare Scripture with Scripture, and to pursue its study in a regular and methodical manner [...]. I found that by a comparison of Scripture with history, all the prophecies, as far as they have been fulfilled, had been fulfilled literally; [...] I was thus satisfied that the Bible is a system of revealed truths, so clearly and simply given, that the "wayfaring man, though a fool, need not err therein".'[82]

The prophecies not yet fulfilled, especially those that focused on the second coming of Jesus Christ, forced Miller to make difficult decisions. Miller reached that conclusion through a study of the prophecies of the book of Daniel, especially Daniel 8:14. 'Unto two thousand and three hundred days; then shall the sanctuary be cleansed.' Operating on the commonly accepted interpretation of Numbers 14.34 and Ezekiel 4:5, 6, that a day in prophecy equals a year, Miller calculated that the 2,300-day prophecy would conclude in 1843. And, interpreting the sanctuary of Daniel 8:14 as the earth and its cleansing as the last-

---

[80] Damsteegt, *Foundations of Seventh-day Adventist*, p. 12.

[81] Damsteegt, *Foundations of Seventh-day Adventist*, p. 13. Sylvester Bliss and James White published details of Miller's life and ministry and his memoirs: James White and Sylvester Bliss, *Sketches of the Christian life and public labours of William Miller* (Battle Creek, MI: Press of the Seventh-day Adventist Publishing Association, 1875; repr.New York: AMS Press, 1972). Some doctoral dissertations have also been written concerning his ministry. See: Tommy L. Faris, 'A Common Sense Life', unpublished doctoral thesis, Columbia University, 2007.

[82] Miller, *Apology and Defence*, p. 6.

day cleansing of the earth by fire, Miller reasoned that Christ would return to the earth at the end of the 2,300 days – about 1843.[83]

'His common sense logic told Miller that if prophecies had literally come true in the past, then if they had not yet come true, they would in the future.' [84] '[He came to the shocking,] solemn conclusion, that in about twenty-five years from that time all the affairs of our present state would be wound up; that all its pride and power, pomp and vanity, wickedness and oppression, would come to an end; and that, in the place of the kingdoms of this world, the peaceful and long-desired kingdom of the Messiah would be established under the whole heaven; that, in about twenty-five years, the glory of the Lord would be revealed.'[85]

Because of this findings Miller spent another five years (1818-23) re-examining his Bible. At the end of his second Bible study period he became even more certain about his conclusion but people did not seem to be interested in his message. For another nine years (1823-33) Miller continued his study, with increasing conviction that it was his duty to present his findings to others.[86]

After further study, Miller became quite convinced of the truth of what he had discovered. In 1831, after more than fifteen years of Bible study, Miller began to preach about the imminent coming of Jesus Christ. His eschatological message and the way he presented his lectures – by appealing to the accepted authority of Scripture and giving high priority to reason in his study of the Bible – was in accordance with the spirit of the age and familiar to the people. The message was widely accepted. In his comprehensive work about Miller's life David Rowe concludes: 'To all appearances he was just like them, and he reaped the benefit of democratic culture that valued commonness. […] Patterned on the schedule of a protracted meeting, his course of lectures on the second coming of Christ gathered people for as many days as they requested, as often as three times a day, lasting into evening candle time. He […] would present a tightly framed argument that progressed from one lecture to the next, setting forth his expectation of Jesus' imminent return and the reasons he believed in it.'[87]

Schwarz and Greenlaf add that Miller had a strong missionary zeal. In order to reach people he organized his sermons cautiously but he was not merely aiming for agreement that his calculations were reasonable: '[He was not interested in] simply securing intellectual assent to his mathematical calculations; his greatest desire was to see men and women, especially agnostics and infidels, accept Jesus Christ as Saviour and look forward with joy to His

---

[83] See Knight, George R., *Millennial fever and the end of the world: A study of millerite adventism* (Boise, Idaho: Pacific Press, 1993), p. 8.

[84] Tommy L. Faris, *A Common Sense Life* (Columbia: Columbia University, 2007, p. 37).

[85] Sylvester Bliss, *Memoirs of William Miller: With appendices containing three other contemporary biographical sketches* (Berrien Springs MI: Andrews University Press, 2005), p. 76.

[86] See: Darmsteegt, *Foundation of Seventh-day Adventist*, pp 13-20.

[87] David L. Rowe, *God's strange work: William Miller and the end of the World* (Grand Rapids MI: Eerdmans, 2008), p. 105.

soon return. Miller's sermons were known for their careful organization and heavy reliance on numerous Bible texts.'[88]

Miller studied the Bible by comparing verses with each other and giving priority to the cognitive process for understanding God's will, without paying much attention to the teachings of existing denominations. The urgency of the discovered message led to aggressive proclamation that remained a characteristic of the Sabbatarian Adventist movement which emerged after Miller's own period of evangelistic fervour. Later a similar style also characterized the Seventh-day Adventist Church. Miller, this self-made, common-sense theologian, set out fourteen rules for the interpretation of the Bible, influencing, for decades to come, not only the hermeneutics of the later movements but also their development and the changes which took place in their mission theology.

I. Every word must have its proper bearing on the subject presented in the Bible.

II. All Scripture is necessary, and may be understood by a diligent application and study.

III. Nothing revealed in Scriptures can or will be hid from those who ask in faith, not wavering.

IV. To understand doctrine, bring all the Scriptures together on the subject you wish to know; then let every word have its proper influence; and if you can form your theory without a contradiction, you cannot be in error.

V. Scripture must be its own expositor, since it is a rule of itself. If I depend on a teacher to expound to me, and he should guess at its meaning, or desire to have it so on account of his sectarian creed, or to be thought wise, then his guessing, desire, creed or wisdom, is my rule, and not the Bible.

VI. God has revealed things to come, by visions, in figures and parables; and in this way the same things are often time revealed again and again, by different visions, or in different figures and parables. If you wish to understand them, you must combine them all in one.

VII. Visions are always mentioned as such.

VIII. Figures always have a figurative meaning, and are used much in prophecy to represent future things, times and events – such as mountains, meaning governments, beasts, meaning kingdoms, waters, meaning people, day, meaning year, etc..

IX. Parables are used as comparisons to illustrate subjects, and must be explained in the same way as figures, by the subject and Bible.

X. Figures sometimes have two or more different significations, as day is used in a figurative sense to represent three different periods of time, namely, first, indefinite; second, definite, a day for a year; and third, a day for a thousand years.

---

[88] Richard W. Schwarz and Floyd Greenleaf, *Light Bearers: a History of the Seventh-day Adventist Church* (Nampa, ID: Pacific Press, 2000), p. 32.

The right construction will harmonize with the Bible, and make good sense; other constructions will not.

XI. If a word makes good sense as it stands, and does no violence to the simple laws of nature, it is to be understood literally; if not, figuratively.

XII. To learn the meaning of a figure, trace the word through your Bible, and when you find it explained, substitute the explanation for the word used; and, if it makes good sense, you need not look further; if not, look again.

XIII. To know whether we have the true historical event for the fulfilment of a prophecy: If you find every word of the prophecy (after the figures are understood) is literally fulfilled, then you may know that your history is the true event; but if one word lacks a fulfilment, then you must look for another event, or wait its future development; for God takes care that history and prophecy shall agree, so that the true believing children of God may never be ashamed.

XIV. The most important rule of all is, that you must have faith. It must be a faith that requires a sacrifice, and, if tried, would give up the dearest object on earth, the world.'[89]

By the year 1840 the message about the second coming of Christ had become widely accepted and the Millerite movement expanded. 'From 1840 onward the Millerite movement was no longer a one-man project but was led by a large and increasing group of men of various denominations. His teachings gained prominence in major cities when Joshua Vaughan Himes (1805-95), a minister of the Christian Connection, and pastor of the Chardon Street Chapel in Boston, began taking an interest in Miller's message.'[90]

The focal point of their concept for mission was Matthew 24.14, the text prophesying that 'this gospel of the kingdom shall be preached in all the world for a witness unto all nations' and that then the end would come. Millerites believed that it was their duty to preach the gospel and according to their understanding that meant proclaiming the imminent second coming of Christ. As the movement grew, Miller's followers used all the available time and means at their disposal to spread their message around the world. Their attitude towards mission can be summed up in the following words of Joshua Himes: 'From my first knowledge of the doctrine of Christ's Second Coming being at the door, I have felt it to be my duty to make proclamation of it to the greatest possible extent. If it was true (which as already stated above, I believed) then the church

---

[89] Miller's rules for interpretation of the Bible (a shortened version without Bible texts): Bliss, *Memoirs of William Miller*, pp. 70–71.

[90] Rex Riches, *The Establishment of the British Mission of the Seventh-day Adventist Church, 1863-1887* (Seventh-day Adventist – BUC Historical Archive, 1995). <http://www.adventisthistory.org.uk/documents/rexriches/index.php> [accessed 5 January 2011].

and the world ought to know it. The time being short, what was done, was to be done quickly.'[91]

Their mission activities can be organized into three major groups:

1. Preaching in existing churches
'This was the way Miller started his public ministry in 1831.William Miller and his followers did not have the intention of separating from the various churches in which they held membership, but rather they wanted 'to warn all Christians everywhere that the Advent was near. Indeed, in the beginning, Millerites proclaimed their message in the existing churches only when invited.'[92] The followers remained loyal to their established churches and denominational beliefs but, as the excitement increased, more and more tensions arose between Millerites and their home churches and they were increasingly rejected by the various established denominations. They developed a loose organization among themselves without wanting to establish a new denomination.

2. Publishing ministry
Miller's views were first printed in 1832 as a series of letters to a Baptist paper, The Vermont Telegraph. He continued with a sixty-four page pamphlet and was prepared to answer inquires. In 1836 a more comprehensive version of his ideas, expressed in sixteen lectures, was published in book form.[93] Joshua V. Himes became involved in the Millerite's movement in 1839. Impressed by Miller's prophetic explanations, he decided to assist Miller by using his talent for organization to help spread the message across America and also internationally. The historian Nathan Hatch has referred to Himes's work as 'an unprecedented media blitz'. Himes stated that 'Our first object was to start a newspaper, which should be exclusively devoted to the exposition of the Word of God, relating to the Second Advent, and the events connected with it. This, by the blessing of God, has been sustained and widely disseminated.'[94] Beyond periodicals, Himes also guided the publication of a vast array of pamphlets, tracts, and books.

> Most of the works written by Miller, Litch, Fitch, Cox and others have been sent to all the Missionary stations that we know of on the globe. They have been sent also to many parts of Europe, Asia, and Africa, as also to the Islands of the Ocean. In this country they have been scattered profusely. [95]

---

[91] Joshua Himes, 'Camp-Meeting Notice', in *The Signs of the Times and Expositor of Prophecy* (Silver Spring, 1841-1844), p. 148.

[92] Schantz, *Foundation of Seventh-day Adventist*, p. 203.

[93] Schwarz and Greenleaf, *Light bearers*, pp. 32–33.

[94] Himes, 'Camp Meeting Notice', p. 148.

[95] Schwarz and Greenleaf, *Light bearers*, pp. 32–33. Publishing was also one of the central missionary activities later, for the Seventh-day Adventist Church.

3. Organizing conferences and camp meetings.
'Millerites began holding camp meetings in the summer of 1842 and conducted more than 130 of such conventions before the autumn of 1844. For more information see Himes, 3, p. 148. According to estimations, the combined attendance at these meetings was in excess of one and half million people. The Millerite tent with a seating capacity of approximately 4,000 'was apparently the largest of its kind in the United states up to that time.'[96]

Rex Riches summarizes the development of the Millerite movement:

> Millerism became a mass movement distributed across the Northeast and Midwest of the United States from Maine to Michigan and beyond... By the summer of 1843 they were working in the trans-Appalachian West, in the states of Kentucky, Missouri, Illinois, Indiana, Wisconsin, and Iowa. In the South, speaking invitations came from such cities as Charleston, Savannah and Mobile. Millerite literature was sent to Robert Winter, an Adventist preaching in the streets of London, England, with thousands there looking for the advent. Their publications also reached other parts of the world.[97]

The Millerite motives for mission
As members of an active interconfessional movement, the Millerites had really only one specific message for the world: 'The End is near.' Their motives for mission were of an apocalyptic-eschatological nature, coming as they did from the belief that they were living in the 'time of the end'. The interpretation of Daniel 12.7 led to the conclusion that the 'time of the end' came in 1798. 'The "time of the end" is not a single point of time, but a period, extending from 1798 to the end itself.'[98] 'The Millerite concept of 'the time of the end' was determined by use of a historicist hermeneutic which interpreted a number of transpiring historical events during the 18th and 19th centuries as fulfilment of Bible prophecy.'[99]

Millerite theological interpretations of three historical events were basic to their understanding of this end time.

1. the captivity of the pope in 1798. Like many other Protestants of that time who employed historicist hermeneutic, the Millerites identified the Roman Catholic Church with Babylon, especially during the early years of their movement. The fall of Babylon as presented in Revelation 14.8 was seen by Litch as the fall of Rome, caused by the French. Prophecies about the Catholic Church became crucial in the interpretation of Bible prophecies during the Millerite movement.[100]

---

[96] Knight, *Millenial fever*, p. 11.
[97] Riches, *The Establishment of the British Mission*, Ch. 1.
[98] Himes, p. 59.
[99] Damsteegt, *Foundations of the Seventh-day Adventist*, p. 20.
[100] For more about this see Damsteegt, *Foundations of the Seventh-day Adventist*, pp. 20–46.

2. the cosmic phenomena of sudden darkening of the sun and of the full moon. This happened over a section of the eastern part of the North American continent on 19 May 1780. It was seen as a fulfilment of Matthew 24.29, Revelation 6.12 and Joel 2.31. Many interpreted this event in America as a sign of the Second Advent and it was referred to in literature as the 'Dark Day'. Similarly, the falling of the stars on 15 November 1833, when the most spectacular meteor shower in living memory occurred over the Western Hemisphere, was also understood as a fulfilment of Bible prophecy.[101]

3. the fall of the Turkish (or Ottoman) empire.[102] This historical event was another important sign for the Millerites, especially because Litch had discovered the prospect of the event through his studies of Bible prophecies and had already published the results of these studies in 1838, predicting that the Ottoman Empire would fall in 1840. Litch's excitement in 1840 can be understood; it certainly gave even more urgency to the evangelistic activities of the Millerites:

'I am entirely satisfied that on the 11th of August, 1840, the Ottoman power according to previous calculation, DEPARTED TO RETURN NO MORE. I can now say with the utmost confidence, "The second woe is past and behold the third woe cometh quickly." "Blessed is he that watcheth and keepeth his garments, lest he walk naked and they see his shame.".'[103] They also felt that other 'historical events supported their interpretations of Bible prophecy and the prediction of Litch about the fall of the Ottoman Empire convinced many prominent infidels to renounced their infidelity and accept the Christian religion. Loughborough reported that Litch received letters from over one thousand prominent infidels (some of them had been leaders in infidel clubs) who, on the fulfilment of the predicted fall of the Ottoman independence, renounced their infidelity, and accepted the Christian religion, and declared their faith in the word of God'.[104]

The results of their prophetic calculations can be seen in their attitude towards mission: 'According to their prophetic charts and timetables, the end-time prophecies of Daniel and Revelation had been fulfilled in their day. No time prophecy went beyond 1844. Therefore, Jesus was just at the door of human history and was about to return. As there was little time left before the end of the world, all energies were used in an extensive warning campaign of preaching and publishing. There was no need for anything else whether it be church organization, institutions of one sort and another, or even agreement on fundamental beliefs.'[105]

---

[101] Damsteegt, *Foundations of the Seventh-day Adventist*, pp. 20–46.
[102] John N. Loughborough, *Last Day Tokens* (Pacific Press, 1904), pp. 151–52.
[103] Himes, p. 162
[104] Loughborough, *Last Day Tokens*, pp. 151–52.
[105] Schantz, *The Development*, p. 267.

The doctrine of an imminent Second Advent motivated many to search the Scripture in order to find the exact date of the second coming of Christ. Some 'Non-timeists' like Henry D. Ward published their views against definite time setting:

> I think you wrong in urging the matter of the date; but I honor your zeal, your fidelity, your learning, your industry.[106]

Although a number of 'non-timeists' were opposed to trying to identify precise dates for the Parousia, the time element received increasing emphasis as the year 1843 approached.[107] Eventually the Millerites set specific dates for the Coming of Christ, first for 1843 and later for 22 October 1844. They felt that other signs of the times also supported the likelihood that the Millerite position was true. Faris believes that the harmony of many different observed events and theological aspects led them to this conclusion:

> The proliferation of missionary and Bible societies, the spread of the gospel in spite of human interference, and the ongoing revivals of religion, all indicated Christ's presence at the door, knocking to be allowed entry into the church, into the world, and into the lives of individuals. It was clear to Miller that all of this was evidence of Christ's near return.[108]

Setting the date became a turning point in the further development of the movement. During this time some Millerites developed the 'shut door' theory. Miller believed that the door of mercy (as it is called) was shut. He wrote: 'I know we cannot satisfy the sceptic nor the world that we are right, neither do I believe we are called on by God to do it. They are now in the snare prepared by themselves, and so that day [will] come upon them unawares.'[109]

The shut door theory[110] came from Miller's explanation of the Parable of the Ten Virgins found in Matthew 25.1-13, a passage that would come to provide one of the most important stories told in the Millerite Adventist movement.

> The kingdom of heaven in the parable meant the age of the gospel dispensation, which had begun with the preaching of John the Baptist and would continue to the Second Advent. The ten virgins as a group represented "mankind in general," with the wise virgins standing for Christian believers and the foolish virgins for unbelievers. The lamps the virgins carried referred to the Bible and the oil in them

---

[106] Letter, H. D. Ward to Miller, 29 October 1841. Miller was hesitant about setting the exact date but he published his opinion that Jesus Christ was going to return about the year 1843: Miller, William, *Evidence from Scripture and History of the Second Coming of Christ about the Year 1843: Exhibited in a course of lectures* (Boston: Joshua V. Himes, 1842).
[107] Miller, *Apology and Defence*, p. 13.
[108] Faris, *A Common Sense Life*, p. 135.
[109] Ibid., p. 288.
[110] Joshua Himes, 'The ten Virgins', *Signs of the Times* (1844), p. 77.

to faith. The vessels the wise virgins used to carry their oil were "the persons or mind that believes or disbelieves in the word of God." The bridegroom whose arrival the virgins were awaiting represented Christ. The door that shut against the unprepared foolish virgins signified the ending of the gospel age. Marriage in the parable referred to the second coming of Christ. The midnight cry, which would become a watchword of the Millerite movement as well as the title of one of the major Millerite newspapers, was the group of people who discerned the time of the second coming and devoted themselves to warning the world of it. Finally, the trimming of the lamps meant that the light of the word of God would become stronger and clearer. Miller took it as an indication of the work of translating the Bible into various languages, distributing Bibles where they were in short supply, and sending out missionaries who could teach it.[111]

Under this pressure, and facing the intolerance of various churches, some extreme views about other churches emerged among Millerites as a consequence of shut-door theory. William Miller tried to warn against extreme views, setting out his original purpose and example in ministry in *Signs of the Times* on 31 January 1844. He also advised against separation: 'I have not advised any one to separate from the churches to which they may have belonged, unless their brethren cast them out, or deny them religious privileges. I have taught you no precept of man; nor the creed of any sect. I have never designed to make a new sect, or to give you a nick name; this the enemies to Christ's second advent have done; and we must patiently bear it until he comes; and then he will take away our reproach. I have wronged no man; neither have I sought for your honours or gold. I have preached about 4,500 lectures in about twelve years, to at least 500,000 different people. I have broken my constitution and lost my health; and for what? That if possible I might be the means of saving some.'[112]

Among others a well-known Millerite preacher called Charles Fitch started expounding his ideas powerfully in Ohio in 1843 on the subject of Revelation 18: 'Babylon the great has fallen. [...] Come out of her my people!' (Rev. 18:14)[113] Millerites, like most other Protestants, had usually identified the papacy with the Babylon of this text but 'Fitch went far beyond this by labelling the entire Christian world as Babylon because of its opposition to the doctrine that the time of Christ's return was at hand'.[114] The Millerites had to struggle with growing tension because of such extreme views, which later almost crippled the missionary activities of Adventists.

After the first disappointment in 1843 and after the close of 1844, the year which brought the Great Disappointment to Millerites, the group faced an

---

[111] Faris, *A Common Sense Life*, pp. 143–44.

[112] William Miller, 'Address to Second Advent Believers', *Signs of the Times*, VI.144 (1844), p. 196.

[113] Revelation 18.1.4. KJV 1900.

[114] He appealed to all true Christians to come out into the light of the 'Advent near' or risk perishing. Quoted in: Schwarz and Greenleaf, *Light bearers*, p. 45.

unexpected challenge. They spent the weeks before the last date that had been set in intensive preparations for the coming of the Saviour, and naturally they had no plans beyond that crucial date and no other orientation in life. Employees had given up their jobs, businessmen had closed their shops, farmers had left their crops in the fields; practically no provision had been made for the coming of the next winter. Christ had not returned, as they had expected. Instead, confusion and despair had become the universal experience of the Millerites. Besides the disappointment experience, the development of their theological views contributed to this attitude. They believed that the date 1844 was right but the interpretation of the event was wrong. According to new insight, after the disappointment, what had been prophesied was not that Christ would come to this world as they expected but that (on 22 October 1844) he would enter the most holy place in the heavenly sanctuary as High Priest and begin his work of investigative judgement. This view was based on a Bible text, Daniel 8.14. The coming of Christ is to be expected soon, after the completion of the judgement, these early Adventists believed, and Advent believers should live in expectation of that soon coming. Their missionary zeal slowed down and their vision of world mission was gone. A commonly held view was that the door of mercy had been shut and that it was therefore pointless to carry a burden for lost sinners.[115] They combined the investigative judgement with the 'shut door' referred to in Matthew 25.10 and with the marriage feast described in Revelation 22.11,12, in which the following words appear: 'Let the evildoer still do evil, and the filthy still be filthy, and the righteous still do right, and the holy still be holy. Behold I am coming soon.' They interpreted this to mean 'that a short time before Christ's return man's eternal destiny would be forever sealed. This "sealing" took place in 1844 on October 22 and on that day the door of mercy was shut (Rev 3:7, 8). There would be no need after this to seek to convert anyone. In other words, it was pointless to seek a burden for lost sinners. Only those who had gone through the heart-breaking experience in connection with the "Disappointment" would be saved. Their concern inevitably turned inward; their main task was to comfort and encourage one another.'[116]

This view was not accepted by all. Joshua Himes published several articles against it and in addition 'Miller joined his colleague in attempting to quell, or at least to discredit, the radicals. He was surprised, however, that an earlier remark, which appeared in the 12 February 1845 issue of the Advent Herald, had caused some people to believe he had decided the door of mercy was shut. He was by no means certain it was shut, but his study of the subject had led him to conclude there would come a time, before Christ's return, when sinners would find the door shut against them.'[117] Miller also wrote, 'I say with our present light it would be impossible for any man to prove that the door is shut; ... I think at

---

[115] Schantz, *The Development*, pp. 213–14.
[116] Ibid., pp. 213–14..
[117] See in: Faris, *A Common Sense Life*, pp. 281–82.

present the evidence is strong against the idea…'[118] But, as is shown in the next chapter, the shut door theory influenced the mission theology of Sabbatarian Adventists for years and was maintained by many, even into the 1870s.

An evaluation of the Millerite mission
Evaluation of the Millerites' mission activities shows clearly that their self-understanding definitely determined both their methods and the content of their outreach. From the heavy emphasis they placed on presenting eschatological urgency it is obvious that the Millerite Advent movement 'defined itself with reference to the future', as Malcolm Bull and Keith Lockhart conclude.[119]

William Miller was a child of his age; he came from deism, experienced great 'awakenings' and was influenced by the Enlightenment in his emphasis on reasoning and on the importance of a personal understanding of the Bible. He was also a man of his time in that he spoke the contemporary language of the people, referring in his preaching and prophetic interpretations to events and challenging signs that intrigued other people and which they found interesting enough to ask questions about. In his presentations about the soon-coming 'end of time' he emphasized points of argument that were independent of other authorities and usually relied only on Bible texts in order to convince his hearers. He presented his topics with a sense of urgency because this was simply the nature of things in his eschatology. Using the Protestant principle of 'Sola Scriptura', Miller also challenged existing views and was able to draw the attention of multitudes to the case he was representing. Millerites used strong cognitive methods for the proclamation of their teachings. These included preaching, lecturing and publishing their theological views and missionary thinking.

Establishing fellowship as the goal of the missionary endeavour was not something stated by the Millerites. They did not actually intend to form a new denomination, with local congregations. The 'cause' united them and brought them together but the focus was an eschatological one. 'Table fellowship' as Jürgen Becker describes it, had been an essential aspect of the ministry of Jesus.[120] The Millerites do not appear to have emphasized this feature of Jesus' approach to communication but through their intensive Bible study programmes, conferences and meetings Millerite Adventists practised table fellowship and developed community bonds.

Need-oriented service and healing was not a real issue for Millerites. Community service did not appear to them to be relevant because of the urgency

---

[118] Ibid., pp. 281–82.

[119] Malcolm Bull and Keith Lockhart, *Seeking a Sanctuary: Seventh-day Adventism and the American Dream*, 2nd edn (Bloomington: Indiana University Press, 2007), p. 39.

[120] One distinctive way in which Jesus communicated the gospel was through table fellowship, which demonstrated that God welcomes sinners into his kingdom. For more detail, see: Jürgen Becker, *Jesus von Nazaret* (Berlin, New York: W. de Gruyter, 1996), pp. 176–233.

of their expectations. Their later theological development also inhibited connection to wider society and made social service almost impossible.

The way in which the Millerite movement developed can be regarded as a warning to later Adventists. Seeing only the urgency of the message, the Millerites failed to develop a well-defined biblical mission theology and as a consequence of this they were both thwarted and confused in their mission activities. Their history also shows that it is not enough to be in tune with contemporary thought and clearly understood by people – relating to current issues and trends and speaking the language of the people in lectures. Nor is it sufficient to challenge other views and to present an attractive alternative way of living the Christian life. This is because, if the foundations of biblical views and mission theology are flawed, disappointment will result again and again. The same lesson had to be learned by Sabbatarian Adventists.

Development and changes in Adventist missionary thinking in the early phase of the church's history

Although, during the twentieth century, Seventh-day Adventists supported one of the most ambitious mission outreach programmes in the history of Christianity, the Adventist movement started with a mission theology that was quite the opposite in terms of attitude.

Because of its specific historical development, Adventism was not really part of the process that formed Protestant missionary thinking. In the early years of their history Adventists went their own way and took a unique approach in developing their mission theology. It later became a priority for Adventist leaders to observe, participate in and learn from World Missionary Conferences. For instance, Arthur Daniells, the president of the General Conference, did this.

Some basic similarities with the development of Protestant missionary thinking can be seen, especially in the role of ecclesiology in the development of mission theology. As David Bosch notes in the twelfth chapter of his book, ecclesiology was a leading element and driving force in the shifts in missionary thinking and led to Mission Dei. Ecclesiology, along with eschatology, was also a crucial element in the formation of Adventist mission theology from the early days onwards.

At the outset the church accepted the concept of world mission developed by Millerites in the early 1840s. This was strongly determined by their interpretation of Matthew 24.14. [121] Miller and his followers saw the universality of the proclamation of the gospel in the first part of the nineteenth century as unparalleled in history. 'There was no doubt in the mind of Miller that this prediction had been accomplished as one of the signs of the time of the end.'[122]

---

[121] 'And this gospel of the kingdom shall be preached in all the world for a witness unto all nations; and then shall the end come.' KJV.

[122] Damsteegt, *Foundations*, p. 50.

As evidence for his views, he stated: 'The Bible [has been] translated into more than 200 different languages; missionaries sent among all the nations known to us on the globe, and reformation succeeding reformation in every town, nook or corner in this land. The gospel has now spread over the four quarters of the globe. It began in Asia. In the apostles' day, that quarter was full of light. From thence it went into Africa; and, for a number of centuries, Africa stretched out her hands, unto God. Europe, too, has had a long visitation of gospel blessings; and now America, the last quarter of the globe, is reaping a harvest of souls for the last day. The gospel, like the sun, arose in the east, and will set in the west.'[123]

He believed that the sign given in Matthew 24.14 had been fulfilled and this conviction also supported his prophetic calculations that Jesus would return in about 1843 or 1844. Damsteegt also states that although 'the Millerites did not think the Advent message had to be preached to every individual, their concept of world mission was that they thought it necessary to send their publications to every reachable Christian community on earth so that the news of the message would reach those unaware of the imminence of Christ's coming. Therefore, the Millerites did everything to increase their publications, giving them a circulation as wide as possible.'[124]

Later he also established the exact date for Christ's second advent as October 22, 1844. 'Miller likened his message to the "midnight cry" in the parable of the ten virgins (Matt. 25).

From Miller's point of view, the Bible societies had fulfilled the parable's picture of virgins trimming their lamps. According to his interpretation, the 'trimming' of lamps symbolized the translation of the Bible into all kinds of languages and the activity of making it available to people of all nations. 'This closed door signified to Miller the closing up of the mediatorial kingdom, and finishing the gospel period when the time of grace and mercy for the world was expected to end sometime before Christ's return, a view he supported with Revelation 10:5-7.'[125]

Because Christ did not return on the predicted date, Miller interpreted the 'shut door' to mean that 22 October 1844 marked the close of human probation. In December of the same year, according to George Knight, Miller wrote: 'We have done our work in warning sinners, and in trying to awake a formal church. God, in his providence has shut the door; we can only stir one another up to be patient; and be diligent to make our calling and election sure.'[126]

This was the main starting point of 'Sabbatarian Adventism' which came to be known to other post-Millerite Adventists, in derogative terms, as the church of 'the seventh day shut door people'. Various views have been proposed about

---

[123] Miller, William, 'A Lecture on the Signs of the Present Times', *Signs of the Times*, 20 March 1840, p. 4.
[124] Damsteegt, *Foundations*, p. 53.
[125] Ibid., p. 43.
[126] Knight, *Historical sketches*, p. vii.

the development of Adventist understanding in relation to mission. In keeping with Oosterwal, Schantz writes that his 'study promotes the existence of three distinctive periods in SDA mission history, namely, The American Experience 1830-1869, The Christendom Experience 1860- 1890, and The World Experience 1890 to the Advent. Each era was a preparation for what followed. At the same time there were also overlappings, as well as developments in each period that, in turn, became foundational to more distant future developments.'[127]

Some other concepts describe five distinctive periods. The first phase in the development of Sabbatarian Adventist[128] mission theology started with this theological inheritance from Millerites.

Phase I: The Shut Door Mission Era (1844-1852)[129]

During the 'shut door' period of Sabbatarian missiology it was believed that Revelation 22.11-12 had been fulfilled and that the 'sealing took place in 1844 on October 22 and on that day the door of mercy was shut'.[130] Arthur White states, 'It has been declared of Seventh-day Adventists that in their early history they held firmly to the position that on October 22, 1844, probation closed for the world generally and there was beyond that point no more mercy for sinners.'[131]

They believed that the gospel had already been preached throughout the whole world but that 'the churches of their day had rejected the special message of Christ's soon return and the preparation it required on man's part. For that reason they confined their particular mission to those converted Christians who already believed in the soon coming of Christ and who had gone through the experience of the Great Disappointment.'[132] Ellen White, one of the founders of the church and among its leaders at that time, stated later, 'For a time after the disappointment in 1844 I did hold in common with the advent body that the door of mercy was then forever closed to the world.'[133]

Schantz argues that 'shut door' theory was not accepted by all Sabbatarian Adventists: 'However, evidence exists which shows that between 1844 and 1851 some proselytizing was going on despite the considerable slowing down of mission activities.'[134] Evangelistic reports in the *Review*[135] mention this activity

---

[127] Schantz, *The Development*, p. 237.

[128] The Sabbatarian Adventists organized and formed the Seventh-day Adventist Church in 1863.

[129] See Knight, *Historical Sketches*, p. VI.

[130] Schantz, *The Development*, p. 214.

[131] Arthur White, *Ellen G. White and the Shut Door Question: A Review of The Experience of Early Seventh-day Adventist Believers in its Historical Context* (1982) <http://www.whiteestate.org/issues/shut-alw.html> [accessed 5 January 2011], p. 1.

[132] Oosterwal, *Mission Possible*, p. 24.

[133] White. *Selected Messages*, p. 63.

[134] Schantz, *The Development*, p. 216.

[135] August, 1850:14, 15; April 7; 1851:64; June 24, 1852:28, 29.

and the first issue of *The Present Truth* (1849) also indicates that some 'Adventist believers went beyond the shut-door, otherwise there would have been no point in printing it'.[136] Ellen White had already indicated, in 1848, that the Adventist message should become 'streams of light that went clear round the world'[137] and she urged her husband to start a publishing ministry. Her statements went beyond 'shut-door' theology and indicated that 'the present absence of mission among non-Adventists was of a temporary nature'. On the other hand, some facts support the belief that the shut-door view was held so firmly that one of the future organizers of what was later to become the Seventh-day Adventist Church 'nearly refused the message' because the person presenting it to him had doubts about the possibility of his salvation.[138] This was because 'he was not in the 44 move'.[139] These contradictions reinforce the feelings Waggoner expressed in 1861. Looking back at the development of the movement up to the early 1850s, he said, 'Our views of the work before us were then mostly vague and indefinite.'[140]

The movement needed time for the development of a consensus regarding basic doctrines among a core group of leaders and believers. The process of establishing a doctrinal foundation brought people together, including future leaders. A series of conferences allowed the process to take these people beyond the establishment of a doctrinal base towards the formation of a membership base. Without them Adventists would not have had a message to preach and would have been without a compelling sense of purpose. At the end of the 1840s a new theological framework for mission had been developed in the form of 'the third angel's message', which was understood as a sealing communication.[141]

Conversion of individuals to Sabbatarian Adventism made a reinterpretation of the shut door missionary doctrine unavoidable. People who had not made a public profession of religion prior to 1845 joined the Adventists and caused James White to make a statement to the effect that 'the door was shut to those who heard the everlasting gospel' message and rejected it, but the door of conversion was still open for three classes:

---

[136] Schantz, *The Development*, p. 216.

[137] Based on a vision received regarding the proclamation of the 'sealing message', she indicated several times that the message would have an impact on other churches in the future.

[138] Ellen White became involved and encouraged this individual 'to hope in God and to give his heart fully to Jesus, which he did then and there [...] Waggoner identified himself as being this non-Adventist and added that none of the leaders had any doubts about his chances of salvation.' Waggoner's experience is a good example of the confusion about the 'door of mercy' as they called it. Damsteegt, *Foundations*, p. 152.

[139] Knight, *Historical Sketches*, p. vii.

[140] Ellet Joseph Waggoner in his Conference address of 1861. In: Knight, *Historical Sketches*, p. viii.

[141] Darmsteegt describes in detail the influence of this message on the development of the church in: Darmsteegt, *Foundations*, pp 153.

1. 'Erring' post-Millerites who had not as yet sided with the Sabbatarians,
2. Children approaching the age of accountability, and
3. 'Hidden souls' who had not bowed to Baal and would be converted in the future.[142]

This was the beginning of a slow move towards the second phase in the development of Adventist mission theology. White still held that the primary task of the church was to work for the salvation of ex-Millerites but because of the increasing accession of converts to Adventism, especially from the third category noted above, he was forced to adopt a reinterpretation of the 'shut door'. From February 1852 onwards he began to teach the 'open door' theory of mission: 'This open door we teach, and invite those who have an ear to hear, to come to it and find salvation through Jesus Christ.'[143]

Phase II: A Partially Opened Door (1852-1874)

Millerite apocalyptic eschatology had, in essence, only one specific message – that the end was near and that the post-millennial perspectives of other churches were not biblical. This message resulted in the shut-door theology which caused the 'no mission' position. This had to be radically revised after 1844. A basic formation of distinctive Adventist beliefs had taken place by 1852. These tenets of faith were published and explained in the *Review* under the title 'Leading Doctrines Taught by the Review'. Five principal topics appeared between 15 August and 19 December 1854, regularly followed by further theological explanations:

- 'The Bible, and the Bible alone, the rule of faith and duty.
- The Law of God, as taught in the Old and New Testaments, unchangeable.
- The Personal Advent of Christ and the Resurrection of the Just, before the Millennium.
- The Earth restored to its Eden perfection and glory, the final Inheritance of the Saints.
- Immortality alone through Christ, to be given to the Saints at the Resurrection.'[144]

Researching the Review and Herald of the time, Schantz added to this 'official' list two important eschatological proclamations[145] articles were focusing on: 'The theological significance of the three angels' messages of

---

[142] Knight, *Historical Sketches*, p. viii.

[143] White, James, 'Call at the Harbinger Office', *Review and Herald*, 17 February 1852, p. 95.

[144] James White published a series of articles of an unidentified author about leading doctrines in the musthead of the Review and Herald from Aug. 15 to Dec. 19, 1854. 'Leading doctrines', *The Review and Herald* VI.01- VI.18. (1854) (p. 1).

[145] 'These last two points are found in several Review articles' (19 August 1851:12; 2 September 1851:20; 27 May 1852:13; 10 June 1852:28; 12 May 1853:204; 7 July 1853:25; 29 November 1853:164; 6 December 1853:172; 21 March 1854:69). Quoted in Schantz, *The Development*, pp. 268–69.

Revelation 14:6-12 as a part of the gospel of Jesus Christ, and their relationship to the historical Advent movement. The work of Jesus Christ on man's behalf in the heavenly sanctuary as Mediator, Advocate, Judge and Priest with special emphasis on the investigative or pre-Advent Judgment.'[146]

These leading doctrines present a clear shift from the Millerites' apocalyptic eschatology towards eschatology relevant to present life.[147] However, they do not provide a foundation for salvation through Jesus Christ. Schantz concludes in his comprehensive study that sermon titles, articles in the *Review* and tracts all reveal the content of their message clearly: 'When Adventist ministers started their evangelistic campaigns in the USA in the late 1850s and 1860s, both in New England and on the frontiers, the message they preached was the Sabbath, Judgement, and the pre-Millennial Advent of Jesus Christ.'[148] The omission of the doctrine of salvation through Christ led to a crisis that culminated in 1888. However, in the pre-1888 period, Adventists focused mostly on distinctive beliefs with a legalistic attitude and their mission activities were still strongly influenced by earlier shut-door theology.

The absence of the doctrine of salvation among the 'Leading Doctrines' did not mean that Adventists rejected it. They simply believed that other missionary societies should fulfil the task of bringing people, including non-Christians, to Christ. The *Review and Herald* observed the work of Bible societies carefully and also reported on it regularly but Adventists still partly upheld the 'shut door' and felt that their duty was to bring to the people the 'last warning'. 'SDAs felt they should concentrate on God's few elect in other churches and call them out to follow their distinctive message.'[149] James White was one of those working towards widening the missiological horizon but although he was one of the most influential leaders and was supported in his efforts to change the 'shut door' theology by Ellen White and other leaders, the door was not opened very far. Some aspects of Adventist mission theology remained the same until the 1870s.

Theological views and factors still upholding the 'shut door' position
Five main factors of significance can be observed relating to this period in the historical development of Adventism, when the 'shut door' position was sustained within the developing denomination.

The conviction that the worldwide dimension of proclamation had been fulfilled and there was nothing more to do
Adventists accepted the Millerite interpretation of Matthew 24.14 and believed that others had accomplished the task of mission prior to 1844. Leading Adventist ministers were still preaching, as late as 1872, that the taking of the

---

[146] Schantz, *The Development*, pp. 268–69.
[147] Ibid., pp. 268–69.
[148] Ibid, p. 269.
[149] See: *Review*, 16 July 1872:36; 15 December 1874:197. Quoted in Schantz, *The Development*, pp. 252–53.

gospel to the entire world (referred to in Matthew 24.14) had been essentially fulfilled.[150] The Bible societies had proclaimed (and were still proclaiming) the gospel and Adventists believed that Miller's movement made the last warning message available to everybody. In *The Signs of the Times* in 1842 Joshua Himes wrote an account of his personal motivation; this testimony is a good example of the missionary attitude adopted by Millerites: 'From my first knowledge of the doctrine of Christ's Second Coming being at the door, I have felt it to be my duty to make proclamation of it to the greatest possible extent. If it was true (which as already stated above, I believed), then the church and the world ought to know it. The time being short, what was done, was to be done quickly.'[151]

Himes stated that most of the published works of Miller, Litch, Fitch and others were sent 'to all the Missionary stations that we know of on the globe'.[152] This enthusiasm on the part of the Millerites led to three different kinds of activities described by Himes and they account for the expansion of the Millerite movement: 'Our first object was to start a newspaper, which should be exclusively devoted to the exposition of the Word of God, relating to the Second Advent, and the events connected with it. This, by the blessing of God, has been sustained and widely disseminated.' [153] Another mode of spreading these views was by publishing Mr. Miller's works on Prophecies. 'These have produced an immense influence. Besides these, the works of Brethren Litch, Fitch, Cox, and others, have been published, with various Tracts, all of which have been very widely scattered. Most of these works have, been sent to all the Missionary stations that we know of on the globe. They have been sent also to many parts of Europe, Asia, and Africa, as also to the Islands of the Ocean. In this country they have been scattered profusely.'[154]

Also public lectures were considered as another important way of publishing their views to the world. 'Arrangements were early, made to visit the principal towns and cities in the Union, and give full courses of lectures on the subject.'[155]

Viewing America as a 'providential place in history' where every nation, tribe, language and people are present
On the one hand the intensive activities carried out by Millerites supported the conviction that the worldwide dimension of proclamation had been fulfilled and there was nothing more to do in terms of evangelism. On the other hand it was also believed that the whole world was represented in America by its immigrant population and there was no need anywhere to fulfil other Bible texts like

---

[150] Dudley M. Canright, 'Present Condition of the World', *Review and Herald* (16 April 1872), pp. 137-138.

[151] Joshua Himes, 'Camp-Meeting Notice', in *The Signs of the Times and Expositor of Prophecy*, 3, ed. by Ellen G. White Estate (Silver Spring, 1841-1844) p. 148.

[152] Joshua Himes, August 10, 1842 – Camp-Meeting Notice, p. 148.

[153] Ibid., p. 148.

[154] Ibid., p. 148.

[155] Ibid., p. 148.

Revelation 14 that played an important role in the Millerite understanding of judgement and salvation. Damsteegt describes how Adventists discovered the apocalyptic-eschatological aspects of this message and how it became central point in their proclamation.[156] Revelation 14.6 says: 'Then I saw another angel flying in mid-air, and he had the eternal gospel to proclaim to those who live on the earth—to every nation, tribe, language and people.'[157]

The international character of this text raised the first questions and doubts concerning the 'shut door' position. In 1859 a reader of the *Review and Herald* was troubled by the text, wondering what it means by 'to every nation, tribe, language and people', and asked the editor if he understood to whom the Third Angel's message had been given. Uriah Smith's answer presents an argument that was used over and over again. It supports the view that worldwide mission was not necessary anymore 'since our land is composed of people from almost every nation'.[158] According to many Adventists of that time, the 'proclamation of Seventh-day Adventist beliefs to all nations, tribes, and languages was being fulfilled right in the United States, where the representatives of the whole world lived'.[159] According to their interpretation of the text, it was not necessary to preach the gospel to every individual. They viewed America as a 'providential place in history'[160] because 'in what other land could the proclamation of the truth reach at once so many "peoples, nations and tongues?" (See Rev. 10. 11.) People from every civilized part of the globe are here to be found, as a settled and abiding portion of our population.'[161] As a consequence of this, the proclamation, as witness to all nations, could be fulfilled in the United States of America.[162]

The negative attitude of people towards Adventists after the Disappointment
Some of the believers continued to hold on to the extreme 'shut-door view' as a result of their personal experiences with others after 1844.[163] In some areas such as Vermont, New Hampshire, Maine and Canada in 1850 the view was supported by the fact that it was 'next to impossible to obtain access to unbelievers' because the Disappointment 'had confused the minds of many, and they would not listen to any explanation of the matter'.[164] These experiences, along with their

---

[156] Chapter V deals with the basic structure of the theology of mission, 1850-74, in which Revelation 14 plays an important role. Damsteegt, *Foundations*, Ch. 5.

[157] Revelation 14.6. The Holy Bible, New International Version (electronic ed.) (Grand Rapids MI: Zondervan, 1996).

[158] In: Oosterwal, *Mission Possible*, p. 25.

[159] Ibid., p. 25.

[160] These are words used by Smith to describe the unique position of the States in God's plan, according to his understanding.

[161] Damsteegt, *Foundations*, p. 285.

[162] See for more: Damsteegt, *Foundations*, p. 284.

[163] Ibid., pp. 270-274.

[164] Ellen G. White's words from 1851 described the challenges Adventists were facing after the Disappointment. In: Damsteegt, *Foundations*, p. 272.

theological heritage, made Adventists into reluctant missionaries who tended to withdraw from society and focus on issues within the denomination instead of turning towards others, especially non-Christians.[165]

Lack of a unified theological concept of church life and mission
At the beginning of this second phase in its development the church did not have educational institutes and as a result it also lacked educated workers, trained for ministry. Training would also have been difficult because Adventists did not have a unified theological concept of church life and mission. Besides this, their basic theological views and interpretations were not in harmony. Some were still writing and preaching about the 'shut door' as applied to all those who had rejected or ignored messages about the second coming of Christ before 1845, while others were translating publications into new languages in order to send them to relatives, friends and other people.

Inadequate church structures
As a result of inadequate structures for foreign mission in the first part of this phase, early Adventist leaders were reluctant to support proposals for mission outside North America. They also tried to avoid making mistakes that would involve financial loss. They were eager, at this stage, to protect the stability of the church's life and structure. On the other hand, according to some scholars, Adventist leaders came from a rural background, as distinct from the cities, and were nationalistic or provincial in outlook, with a very limited understanding of global mission. Schantz presents a differing opinions related to Czechowski's ministry. Regarded by some as the first, though unofficial Adventist missionary in Europe, Czechowski 'is described as being a man of foresight and a cosmopolitan in contrast to the SDA leaders who were rural, nationalistic, and parochial, with a narrow understanding of global mission. The line between the opinions of Czechowski can roughly be drawn with American SDA scholars defending the stand of the leaders of the Church in the 1860s, while European SDA scholars largely defend Czechowski.'[166]

The entire structure of the church was organized in such a way as to support no more than the expansion of the Adventist movement in America. This made leaders reluctant to make decisions about new projects or to underpin unusual initiatives. The best example of such an initiative is the story of the first Adventist to venture beyond the borders of North America to work as a missionary in Europe. Michael Belina Czechowski, an ex-Roman Catholic Polish priest, was converted in 1857 to Sabbatarian Adventism in the USA. A year later he was more than anxious to go to his home continent: 'How I would

---

[165] Some gave up the extreme 'shut-door' theory and 'had a theoretical understanding that their mission was to warn the whole world' but Haskell complains about them, which also shows the general attitude of Adventists concerning worldwide mission. See Damsteegt, *Foundations*, p. 291.

[166] Schantz, *The Development*, p. 259.

love to visit my own native country across the big waters, and tell them all about Jesus' coming, and the glorious restitution, and how they must keep the Commandments of God and the Faith of Jesus.'[167]

However, because he was new in the faith and seemed to have some personal instability, he was unable to gain the trust of the church leaders. Sabbatarian Adventists did not send him to Europe as a missionary. Czechowski went in frustration to the Advent Christian denomination and received sponsorship for his mission. Arriving in Europe, he promoted his Sabbatarian Adventist views through public evangelism, publishing a paper and circulating tracts. As a result of his work he planted the seeds of the Seventh-day Adventist Church in Switzerland, Italy, Hungary, Romania and other parts of Europe.[168] His life – ministry, suffering and tragic death[169] –viewed in the words of the first official missionary, Andrews, helps to provide some understanding of the on-going processes and struggles of the young movement. He remarked of Czechowski in 1870 that he saw the 'hand of God' in his ministry but that that was too late for Czechowski. In January 1870 Andrews wrote in the *Review and Herald* about the 'cause in Switzerland' and stated that 'in consequence of our fears to trust money with Bro. Czechowski, and our lack of care to patiently counsel him as to its proper use, God used our most decided opponents to carry forward the work'. These opponents were the Adventist Christian denomination keeping Sunday as the Sabbath, as well as another group stemming from the Millerite movement.

Adventist leaders were still hesitating about what to do about calls for missionaries coming from Europe. Another pastor, B. F. Snook, was later considered for missionary service in Europe. The *Review and Herald* included a comment in 1863 that 'the General Conference Executive Committee may send him [as] a missionary to Europe before the close of 1863',[170] but he was not sent, neither to Europe nor elsewhere. This gives a short insight into the struggles Adventists experienced in relation to world-wide mission and how difficult it was for leaders to take certain necessary steps towards opening the 'shut door' wider.

Supporting factors for widening missiological horizons
The 'shut door' view was challenged and the young denomination was forced to widen its missiological horizons for several reasons. These can be divided into three groups: the personal influence of leaders with changing theological views, organizational factors and unexpected influence from outside the church.

---

[167] In: Knight, "Historical Introduction", p. X ii.
[168] For the most complete description of Czechowski's life and work see Rajmund Ł. Dąbrowski and Bert B. Beach, *Michal Belina Czechowski, 1818-1876: Rezultaty sympozjum naukowego o jego życiu i działalności, które odbyło się w Warszawie, 17-23 maja 1976 roku, z okazji setnej rocznicy jego śmierci*, 1st edn (Warzawa: Wydawn. "Znaki czasu", 1979).
[169] He lost his support and actually starved, lonely and friendless, in Vienna in 1876.
[170] 'God's Free-men', *The Review and Herald* (1863), p. 8.

Personal influence of leaders with changing theological views
Although Sabbatarian Adventists had very little interest in overseas missionary work, a few of them were not satisfied with the 'no responsibility'[171] position in reference to such a mission. Several leaders and pastors started writing and teaching about the need to change their mission theology. A sense of progress can be observed when one looks at this transition time. From the position that the 'door of mercy' was shut for others, including other Christians, some argued for extending mission to other churches. Joseph Bates and James White, both of them prominent leaders at that time, urged: 'A missionary spirit should be cherished by those who profess the Message. Not to send the gospel to the heathen; but to extend the solemn warning throughout the realms of corrupted Christianity. 'Blow ye the trumpet in Zion, and sound an alarm in my holy mountain.' Joel ii,1. 'Cry aloud and spare not; lift up thy voice like a trumpet, and show my people their transgressions, and the house of Jacob their sins.' Isa.lviii,1[...] We say a missionary spirit is wanted to raise the cry more extensively in new fields, and sound the alarm throughout Christendom. There is yet, no doubt, much work to be done in each State where the Message has been given; but not in those towns where the alarm has been given, and the few who had ears to hear and hearts to obey have been gathered out.'[172]

Because of this focus on other Christians, Adventists were later accused of 'sheep stealing' but it was the beginning of a new understanding of mission for the church. Both Joseph Bates and James White were pioneers in the development of Adventist mission theology and very soon they did take further steps towards opening the 'door of mercy' even wider.

In 1849 James White signalled a shift in the focus of ministry. Instead of advocating that the church withdraw into a corner and focus on the development of its own holiness, excluded from the world, he set a new tone with a remarkable sentence. Like a military captain, he ordered, 'Let the message fly', proving and strengthening his position as a leader. He also had experience of past struggles and was able to bring the Advent movement's period of hesitation to an end. 'The scattering time since 1844, has truly been 'a dark and cloudy day.' The weary and torn flock have been grieved, driven, and scattered upon the mountains; but the gathering time has come, and the sheep are beginning to hear the cheering voice of the true Shepherd, in the commandments of God, and the testimony of Jesus, as they are being more fully proclaimed. The message will go, the sheep will be gathered into the present truth, and the breach restored. All the powers of earth and hell combined, cannot stop the work of God. Then let the message fly, for time is short.'[173]

---

[171] The phrase is George Knight's.
[172] James White, 'The Third Angel's Message', *Review and Herald*, 8.18 (1856), 141.
[173] James White, 'Repairing the Breach in the Law of God', *The Present Truth*, September 1849 (pp. 25–29), p. 28.

The theological framework which Adventists inherited mainly from the Millerite movement and which continued to influence them was inadequate for developing any theology for world-wide mission. This had to be addressed and the thinking changed. The process required new understanding of God's mercy and also new eschatological interpretation. In 1853 James White discussed 'shut door' theology in the pages of the *Review and Herald*, challenging its biblical basis and its connection to the mercy of God. He stated clearly that all those Bible texts used in support of the 'shut door' theory are unconnected with the 'door of mercy', a phrase which is not even present anywhere in the Bible. If this is true, it also has consequences for the time of the 'Second Advent', meaning after 1844: 'The phrase 'door of mercy' is much used; yet it is not found in the above texts, or elsewhere in the scriptures. It has been handed down to the Advent people by those who have not closely studied the Bible, and it is to be regretted that they should so freely use it. The impression has been made upon most minds, that this so called 'door of mercy' would be closed when Christ is revealed from heaven. But the Lord's mercy, strictly, will never close. 'His mercy endureth for ever.' In all past time, the mercy of the Lord has ceased to men, and to nations, when they have rejected all the means of salvation which the all-wise Creator could, according to his plan of saving men, set before them. The Lord can do no more than this at the period of his Second Advent.'[174]

In the same issue of the *Review and Herald* White began applying his new views concerning mercy and turned towards readers who did not reject the Adventist message, assuring them that they still 'stand on the same ground for salvation, as though such a movement had never taken place. Those, therefore, who are now looking for the Lord, and are obeying the present truth, may now rejoice.'[175] Concerning the shut door theory, White showed the 'absurdity of applying it to the Second Advent'. Indeed, with this statement he openly contradicted the theory. James White gave another explanation of the 'shut door' in the same article of the *Review and Herald*: 'We can see no other application of the shut door, that will harmonize with other parts of the parable (of the ten virgins in Matthew 25), and with other scriptures, than to our High Priest entering upon the antitype of the ancient tenth day of the seventh month atonement, at the end of the 2300 days, in the Autumn of 1844. His work, performing the antitype of the daily ministration, then must cease in the Holy place of the True Tabernacle, in order for him to enter the Most Holy place to cleanse the Sanctuary. And as his work closed in the Holy, it commenced in the Most Holy. We think the following, addressed to the Philadelphia church, applies to this subject.'[176]

---

[174] White, James, 'The Shut Door', *The Advent Review and Sabbath Herald*, 3 (1853), p. 188.

[175] White, 'The Shut Door', p. 189.

[176] Ibid., p. 189.

He also wrote with considerable animation:' Yet we rejoice to publish to those that have an ear to hear, that there is an Open Door [...] Reader, come along with us to this open door, and see what we will show you. [...] God help you to see this open door, and by faith, view the ark, and see the law of God in all its strength and glory.'[177]

With this statement he opened the 'shut door' much wider for all who had not yet 'rejected all the means of salvation'. This move meant taking significant steps towards a theology of worldwide mission. As his main message he presented the law of God. In 1863, a month or two before the General Conference session, James White went even further and challenged every member of the church to adjust his or her way of life in accordance with the significance of the message: 'Ours is a world-wide message. Its very nature, and its destined growing influence, will bring us into notice, to fill important and critical positions before the world. It is a grand mistake to suppose that the message we teach is to test the world and thus ripen the harvest of the earth, while those who bear it are shut up in a corner, so excluded from the world, or so singular in their general deportment, as to have no influence in the world.'[178]

James White was one of the first to employ the expression 'world-wide' in connection with Adventist mission. Another leading Adventist minister, B. F. Snook, wrote in 1863 concerning the world-wide dimension of the work of apostles: 'The same great commission that authorized them to go out into all the world is yet in force, and Christ yet says to his people, "Go ye into all the world, and preach the gospel to every creature. For lo, I am with you always, even unto the end of the world." Go, and I will go with you, is the sentiment of the Lord. But the Lord does not ordinarily call and send men independently of the church. He will lead out by his Spirit in his church, and the church will follow in the direction in which his Spirit moves.'[179]

Snook made one of the first attempts to create an Adventist mission theology when he published an article in the *Review and Herald* in 1863 with the title 'The Great Missionary Society'. His earnest call has a clear message: 'Arise, shine, for thy light is come; and the glory of the Lord is risen upon thee.' Isa.lx, 1. The subject of missionary operations is one that should begin to receive the candid considerations of the people of God. What are the duties of God's people in this direction? What are their agencies?'[180]

Snook answers these questions in three major statements which present a clear new voice promoting a systematic mission theology:

I. The church is a missionary society: 'In order to present a few thoughts on this subject, we will first consider the church as a missionary society. [...] He commits to it the holy light of his divine word, with which he would have all

---

[177] Ibid., p. 189.
[178] White, James, 'The light of the World', *Review and Herald* 21 (1863), p. 165.
[179] Snook, B.F, 'The Great Missionary Society', *Review and Herald*, 6 (1863), p. 46.
[180] Shook, 'The Great Missionary Society', p. 46.

enlightened.' He then said, "Ye are the light of the world, a city that is set on a hill cannot be hid. [...] He has therefore made it their duty to present the light to their fellow men.[...] The only source through which the world can receive light is through the church of Christ, to which he has entrusted the light.'[181]

II. The church has to send missionaries to all nations and proclaim the gospel in the whole world: 'The church, as a missionary society, sends out her chosen ministers to proclaim the words of life. The Lord selected from his church certain disciples who he called apostles, and licensed them as missionaries to go out into the world's wide field to preach the gospel. He said, 'Go ye therefore, teach all nations'. [...] The same great commission that authorized them to go out into all the world is yet in force.'[182]

III. The church supports its missionaries: 'The church as a missionary society sustains her missionaries in the field of labor, and co-works with them for the salvation of souls.'[183]

He also suggested very clearly how it should happen: 'This is done:

By those means which satisfy the temporal demands of the missionaries. While the brethren and sisters cannot go out and preach, by being industrious and economical they can act well their part by contributing to the sustenance of those whom they send out. Each one does something in this way. All should desire to be doing what they can in this way. The means placed in the missionary fund will go to sustain your poor brethren who labor in the missionary work. Who among this people is there that does not desire to have a donation in the treasury? Not one, we hope. Let all strive to do something for it. And especially let me say to my brethren and sisters in Iowa, that when God calls for help, he means you, and does not intend that you shall be deprived of that special love for giving to his cause. The Lord loves a cheerful giver. We are running no tent this season, and we must do a good part for the Association, and missionary cause.'[184]

Eschatological urgency as one of the main motives for mission still played an important role in the missionary thinking of Adventists. This is clear in Snook's conclusion: 'Time is short and our mission is great [...] O, that every one may feel a share of the burden of this work; and may it move on, and on, till by the power of God it shall close in the salvation of all his honest children.'[185]

Ellen White also argued in favour of worldwide mission and, as early as 1848, wrote about 'streams of light that went clear around the world'.[186] Along with others, she tried to counteract the 'shut door' view and urged the church to

---

[181] Ibid., p. 46.

[182] Ibid., p. 46.

[183] Ibid., p. 46.

[184] Ibid., p. 46.

[185] Ibid., p. 46.

[186] Based on a vision received regarding the proclamation of the 'sealing message', she indicated several times that the message would also have an impact on other churches in the future.

undertake international work. In 1871 she wrote: 'Our publications should be printed in other languages, that foreign nations may be reached. [...] When the churches see young men possessing zeal to qualify themselves to extend their labors to cities, villages, and towns that have never been aroused to the truth, and missionaries volunteering to go to other nations to carry the truth to them, the churches will be encouraged and strengthened far more than to themselves receive the labors of inexperienced young men.'[187]

Ellen White urged young people to learn new languages so that God could use them as missionaries among other nations and by these statements she showed the way clearly for further development of Adventist mission theology.

> Young men who feel stirred by the appeals that have been made for help in this great work of advancing the cause of God [...] Young men should be qualifying themselves by becoming familiar with other languages, that God may use them as mediums to communicate His saving truth to those of other nations. These young men may obtain knowledge of other languages even while engaged in labouring for sinners.[188]

The Danish pioneer missionary J. G. Matteson [189] introduced another important theological argument for launching into mission. He argued that, despite limited resources in personnel and funds, the early church went to every place possible.[190] He raised the question of whether, if Adventists really believed in the soon second coming of Jesus Christ and that the time was short, how much more they should seek to do the same as the early Christians and use all available means for spreading the truth.[191]

Organizational factors influencing the change of mission theology
A look at the organization and numerical size of the church makes it possible, on the one hand, to appreciate the significance of the statements about the worldwide extent of Adventist mission and, on the other hand, it helps to explain why the leadership of the church was reluctant before 1874 to take further steps towards international evangelism. When the church was organized in 1863, it had a membership of about 3,500, 'not many of whom had much in the way of financial resources'.[192] By 1875, 8,000 members (the official number) were attempting to manage two publishing houses, a medical institution and a college, to supply a growing demand for workers, and to fund rapidly expanding work in

---

[187] Ellen G. White, *Life sketches of Ellen G. White* (CA: Pacific Press Publishing Association, 1915), pp. 204–205.

[188] Published first on 10 December 1871. White, *Life Sketches of Ellen G*, p. 204.

[189] A Danish convert in the USA went back to Denmark, Norway and Sweden in 1877 in order to preach the Adventist message there.

[190] Matteson quoted 1 Thessalonians 1.3, 8.

[191] *Review and Herald*, 5 December 1871 – p. 197 in: Schantz, *The Development*, p. 251.

[192] Damsteegt, *Foundations*, p. 285.

North America.[193] These facts show the visionary leadership of the Whites, Bates and others who promoted the worldwide extension of Adventist mission, even before the organizational structures had been stabilized or before supporting institutions had been established for the international dimension of the work. The precondition of this development was the abandonment of the 'shut door' inheritance of Millerites and the inception of a visionary structure that was able to form the foundation for future growth.

The formation of the Foreign Mission Society in 1869 was also a clear step towards overseas evangelistic efforts. The constitution of the society stated clearly that its task was to deal with growing activity involving mission, as the official missionary society of the Adventist church: 'This society shall be known as the Mission Society of the Seventh-day Adventists. The object of this society shall be to send the truth of the third angel's message to foreign lands, and to distant parts of our own country, by means of missionaries; papers, books, tracts, etc.' [194] Along with the Tract and Mission Society and the Publishing Department, Adventist mission showed rapid progress in the following years.[195]

Influences from outside the church

As early as 1858 James White had the following remarks to make about printing literature in foreign languages for European immigrants: 'In the ranks of Sabbath-keepers are those who speak German, French, Norwegian, Swedish, Dutch, etc. These, as it would be natural to suppose, feel a deep interest for those of their tongue. They desire to see publications on the present truth printed in their native languages, to circulate in America and in Europe.'[196]

On behalf of the Publishing Committee he reported on plans and steps to be taken for printing Adventist materials in German, French, Norwegian and Swedish, while admitting the difficulties and financial challenges involved.[197] He suggested covering the costs of printing in other languages by asking for donations – a clear step towards involving more and more people in international missionary work. By 1861 'mission work was carried on among the French, Polish, Italian, Swedish, Danish, Norwegian and German immigrants in the U.S.A. For years these immigrant converts had already been calling for publications in their native languages and pamphlets had been published in

---

[193] Damsteegt, *Foundations*, p. 285.

[194] Schantz, *The Development*, p. 254.

[195] Schantz, *The Development*, p. 252.

[196] James White, 'Publications in other Languages', *Review and Herald*, XI.25 (1858), p. 200.

[197] 'We have printed in French 1500 copies of a work of 36 pages on the Sabbath, and have a work on the Second Advent in the press the same size. Of this we print 2000 copies. The entire cost of both will be $175.00, or $5.00 per hundred. Of this sum, $100,64 has been received. Due, $74,36. We suggest that it would be best to meet the entire cost of publications in other languages by donations. Most of them must be circulated gratuitously. The avails of those which may be sold, the translators, preachers, or colporteurs, will need to help them in their work.' White, 'Publications in other Languages', p. 200.

French, German, and Dutch.'[198] In 1869 James White acknowledged the international pressure they experienced: 'We have almost daily applications to send publications to other lands. Means are wanted. Other lands are reaching out their hands to us for help.'[199]

European immigrants also played an important role in changing and extending mission theology. They not only talked about the international aspects of mission but also became actively involved in foreign mission work. They became converted to Sabbatarian Adventism in the United States and started translating their literature into other languages in the mid 1850s in order to send these materials to their relatives and friends in their home countries. Thus the third angel's message was being preached silently in Europe, and by the early 1860s overseas converts were beginning to make themselves known to Adventists in America.[200] Since the early 1860s American Adventists had known that converts in Ireland, England, and later in Africa, had accepted the Adventist message through the literature they had received. These converts called first for publications and later also asked for missionaries. This meant that Adventists' hesitations about world mission were challenged, regardless of their views on this matter.

Czechowski raised Sabbath-keeping companies in Europe. This led the General Conference to revise its attitude towards Czechowski and the work in Europe. In 1872 the General Conference acknowledged officially that God's hand had helped to plant the truth in Europe in the work of Czechowski.[201] He worked successfully in Switzerland, Hungary and Romania. As a result, James Erzberger, a Swiss convert, was invited to the General Conference in 1869 and became the first ordained European minister in the Adventist church.

A gradual expansion of the Adventist view of the missionary task was unavoidable. The Seventh-day Adventist Church arrived at a new phase in the development of mission-related thinking. Despite how reluctant the leaders were, facts, and increasing international pressure from abroad for more literature in different languages and for Adventist missionaries, led to a decision and in 1874 J. N. Andrews, the first official Adventist missionary was sent to Europe. In addition, the first missionary periodical to be published by the church – *The True Missionary* – was established by James White in 1874.

---

[198] Damsteegt, *Foundations*, pp. 286–87.
[199] James White, *Review and Herald* (23 November 1869), p. 197.
[200] Knight, "Historical Introduction", p. xi.
[201] General Conference of SDA, *The Review and Herald* (2 January 1872), p. 20.

Developing Adventist Interest in Worldwide Mission

Phase III: Mission as proclamation of the distinctive message to Christians,
1874 -1889

In this third phase the missionary task of evangelizing non-Christians was still regarded as having been fulfilled by other missionary societies; Adventists felt that they had the duty of bringing the distinctively Adventist doctrines to previously converted Christians. The first overseas missionary, J.N. Andrews, revealed in his first letter home from Europe how he understood the task of Adventist mission: 'I firmly believe that God has much people in Europe who are ready to obey his holy law, and to reverence his Sabbath, and to wait for his Son from Heaven. I came here to give my life to the proclamation of these sacred truths concerning the near advent of Christ and the observance of God's commandments.'[202]

Andrews was not concerned about bringing the gospel of salvation to the "heathen" but about reaching those interested in distinctive Adventist doctrines. Christian Europe seemed to be the right location for this kind of mission. 'Mission to non Christians was approved of and praised.'[203] However: 'It was regarded as the task that other evangelical missionary societies could take care of. When they [evangelicals] had brought people to Christ, the SDAs were committed to bringing them the last warning.'[204]

Knight comes to the conclusion that, despite openness and support related to mission to non-Christians, 'responsibility to the heathen would remain outside the scope of Adventist missiology until the 1890s'.[205]

The theological foundation of the Adventist mission explains this attitude. Adventists understood their ministry as a fulfilment of the commission of the three angels of Revelation 14. According to their interpretation of this text, Adventists felt that they had been instructed to call people out of Babylon, which for them meant corrupted Christianity.

As a consequence, Andrews and Erzberger started their work in Europe among Sabbath-keeping Christians in Switzerland and extended their ministry to Sabbath-keeping Christians in Germany. The next stage in the growth of Adventist mission was also confined to Protestant populations – in England, Australia, New Zealand and South Africa.

---

[202] J. N. Andrews, 'Our Arrival in Switzerland', *Review and Herald* (1874), p. 166.
[203] This is the conclusion drawn by Schantz about the period from 1874 to 1890. See Schantz, *The Development,* pp 252-53.
[204] Schantz, *The Development,* pp 252-53..
[205] Knight, "Historical Introduction", p. xvi.

Factors hindering the further development of Adventist world mission

Adventists challenged – more and more focus on apologetics
Because Adventists focused on proclamation of the Sabbath, Judgement and the pre-Millennial Advent of Jesus Christ, Christians of other denominations challenged them regularly about their distinctive beliefs. This forced Adventist ministers to spend even more time studying and reasoning about these doctrines, neglecting other areas of the Bible message, such as righteousness by faith. Although they accepted the doctrine of salvation through Christ, they believed that this was widely accepted by Protestants and that there was no need to explain it again. This led to one-sided legalistic and doctrinal preaching concentrating on apocalyptic prophecies and created a crisis, not only in Adventist mission but also in the Adventist church itself.

Eschatological urgency
Adventist pioneers called their message 'present truth' or 'the last warning' and felt that it was their duty to deliver the message as quickly as possible and then go on to enlighten other people, in other places. The missionaries spent only limited periods of time on ministry in any one area. This urgency also determined the target groups they could reach with the message – mainly Christians with a prior interest in deeper Bible knowledge.

Differences in understanding of basic teachings among pioneers
Adventist pioneers came from different denominational backgrounds and accepted differing theological concepts. Schantz sees the main differences to be those 'concerning the Trinity, the deity of Christ, the personality of the Holy Spirit, and the atonement'.[206] A conflict in the process of acceptance of their theological framework was inevitable. These differences appeared mainly when the church addressed the doctrines just listed, as happened at the 1888 General Conference of Seventh-day Adventists in Minneapolis.

Organizational problems in the expanding church
The church's organizational framework was formed in 1863 and at the end of the eighteen eighties it was clear that the young church had quickly outgrown the highly centralized structure. The burden of leadership rested upon the shoulders of too few people. The General Conference Executive Committee consisted of only five members until 1886.[207] Their work was characterized by extensive travelling, slow communication with each other and with the overseas workers, lack of familiarity with the situation existing in other countries and very slow progress of the work. Several studies of the development of the Seventh-day Adventist organization have been published. They provide further information about the structural development of the denomination –

---

[206] Schantz, *The Development*, p. 272.
[207] The number of the General Conference Executive Committee members was increased to seven in 1886 and to thirteen in 1897.

development which played an important role in the growth of missions and also in changes in missionary thinking.[208]

Supporting factors widening the horizon of Adventist mission

Extending the power base of the church to new continents
The decades prior to 1890 provided Adventists with time for building a power base, first in North America and later also in Europe, Australia and New Zealand. The General Conference sponsored more and more mission activities in those countries.

Organizational developments
The European mission demonstrated its growing maturation by undertaking major steps in organizational development. The first general meeting of workers from the various Seventh-day Adventist missions in Europe was held in 1882 'for consultation concerning the general wants of the cause'. This session became known as the European Council of Seventh-day Adventists.[209] As an outcome of the council, the range of languages in which periodicals were published was extended beyond French to include German, Italian and Romanian.

The organizational developments also included discussion of the need for European educational institutions. This discussion began at the 1884 session of the European Council and ended as far as I am aware with the 1899 acquisition of the Klappermühle – now Friedensau Adventist University.

Doctrinal developments and structural changes made at the General Conference in Minneapolis
Several major steps were taken at the 1888 session of the General Conference in Minneapolis, Minnesota. One major issue at the meeting was the reorganization of the structure of the denomination. 'Immediately, an attempt was made under the leadership of W. C. White to decentralize the jurisdiction of the General Conference.'[210] The process of reorganization took years and was painful for many. The organizational reform started at the conference in Minneapolis led to a major crisis in the life of the denomination. It highlighted organizational difficulties and at the same time it also revealed doctrinal problems and showed

---

[208] Andrew G. Mustard, *James White and the Seventh-day Adventist Organization: Historical Development, 1844-1881* (Berrien Springs, MI: Andrews University Press, 1988); Barry David Oliver, 'Principles for reorganization of the Seventh-day Adventist administrative structure, 1888-1903: Implications for an international church' (doctoral dissertation, Andrews University, 1989); Richard W. Schwarz, and Floyd Greenleaf, *Light Bearers: A History of the Seventh-day Adventist Church* (Nampa, ID: Pacific Press Publishing Association, 2000), chaps. 6, 10, 17 and 23.

[209] Knight, "Historical Introduction", p. xvii.

[210] Oliver, Barry David, 'Principles for reorganization of the Seventh-day Adventist administrative structure, 1888-1903: Implications for an international church' (doctoral dissertation, Andrews University, 1989), p. 69.

the urgency of the need to carry out major changes in the organization and content of the mission of the Seventh-day Adventist Church. At the General Conference session a major correction in theological emphasis was made.[211] A. T. Jones and E. J. Waggoner emphasized at the session that distinctive Seventh-day Adventist doctrines are not of real value if the central principle of the gospel – righteousness by faith – is ignored.[212] Adventists turned their focus more and more on Christ-centred teachings related to soteriology, including righteousness by faith. This growing emphasis on the ministry of Christ resulted in major changes in the theological development of the denomination.

The Seventh-day Adventist Foreign Mission Board

In 1886, according to Ernest R. Sandeen, the Student Volunteer Movement for Foreign Missions[213] stimulated 'the greatest demonstration of missionary interest ever known in the United States'.[214] European countries also experienced a growing interest in mission involvement. In turn, these developments had a strong influence on Adventist mission theology. 'The dynamic thrust of Protestant, and particularly Anglo-American, missions in the 1890s was of crucial importance to Adventism, especially since the denomination was dominated by Americans and was heavily influenced by developments in the Anglo-American sphere. Thus, just as the foreign mission movement was picking up speed, Seventh-day Adventism began to take a larger interest in its own missiological role in the world.'[215]

At exactly this time, in 1886, when Moody challenged young people and one result was the establishment of the Student Volunteer Movement, Adventists published their first book on foreign missions: *Historical Sketches of the Foreign Missions of the Seventh-day Adventists.*

In 1889, in order to take up the challenge and survey the opportunities offered by foreign missions, S. N. Haskell and Percy T. Magan were sent by the denomination on a two-year journey around the world. Their reports about Africa, India and other places captured the attention of Adventist young people and motivated them to take an active interest in mission. In November of the same year the General Conference session created the Seventh-day Adventist Foreign Missionary Board 'for the management of the foreign mission work'.[216]

---

[211] See more: Höschele, Stefan, *From the end of the world to the ends of the earth: The development of Seventh-day Adventist missiology* (Zomba, Malawi: Kachere Series, 2004), p. 24.

[212] Schwarz, *Light bearers*, pp. 183-97.

[213] The movement grew out of an 1886 appeal by Dwight L. Moody for college students. First hundreds and later thousands of students joined the movement and yielded their lives to mission service.

[214] R. E. Sandeen, *The Roots of Fundamentalism: British and American Millenarianism 1800-1930* (Grand Rapids, MI: Baker Book House, 1978), p. 183.

[215] Knight, "Historical Introduction", p. xix.

[216] 'General Conference Proceedings: Seventeenth Meeting', *General Conference Bulletin* (1889), pp. 141–42.

and also the periodical *Home Missionary* which 'was a periodical aimed at promoting the various aspects of missionary work'.[217] The rapid worldwide growth of the Adventist movement made this step really urgent. 'By the end of the 1890s Adventism had been established on every continent and on many of the islands of the sea.'[218]

Growing emphasis on health message and education
Adventists established numerous health institutions after 1863. These flourished and became known as 'the right arm of the message' with growing influence. In the first two decades after 1874 several colleges, academies and industrial schools emerged, both in the USA and abroad. The Seventh-day Adventist Educational Society was formed in 1874 and promoted Christian education. These two new types of outreach – the use of the health message and education – gave the young denomination alternative ways of advancing the church's relationship to society beyond its distinctive message. More and more publications appeared with a focus on health topics rather than being limited to Adventism's special or unique dogmas. Adventists presented a basic, healthful diet. Over 100 years ago they warned of the harmful effects of tobacco while doctors were still prescribing smoking for health. They urged moderation in using high-fat foods, especially meat, encouraged a diet of fresh fruit, vegetables and grains, and recommended plenty of exercise and fresh air.

A vibrant eschatological vision
Adventists now felt a sense of eschatological urgency. According to Barry David Oliver, this played a principal motivating role in the growth of the church's missionary movement. 'Not only were increasing numbers of Seventh-day Adventist missionaries leaving the shores of America to go to the 'regions beyond', but they were doing so with a sense of optimism and urgency. Their concept of the mission of the church and that urgency with which the missionary task was to be executed arose from a vibrant eschatological vision. The evangelization of the world was considered attainable. It was anticipated that the return of Christ would occur within the life-span of those who had experienced 'great disappointment' in 1844.'[219]

Phase IV: The Gospel to all Nations 1890-1956

In this fourth phase of evangelistic outreach, Adventists aimed to reach Catholics and as well as the 'heathen'. This mission included medical, educational and publishing work almost everywhere. Barry David Oliver analyses in his research the growth rates of the denomination throughout its history and comes to the conclusion, in his comprehensive study of the history of the reorganization of the Seventh-day Adventist Church between 1888 and 1903, that those fifteen

---

[217] Knight, "Historical Introduction", p. xix.
[218] Ibid., p. xix.
[219] Oliver, *Principles for Reorganization*, p. 360.

years encompassed a time of unprecedented growth in the life of the denomination. 'Not only was the denomination experiencing outstanding numerical growth, but it was also expanding institutionally, organizationally, and geographically. At no other time in its history has there been a period of fifteen years when the denomination has witnessed multi- lateral growth to the same extent that it did in that period.'[220]

The study of the historical development of Adventism reveals what caused this outstanding progress. The structure of the denomination was created in 1863 but mission was not its driving force at that stage, although the question of mission did play an important role. The spectacular growth of the denomination reached a climax at the end of the 1880s. The growth had at least four dimensions:

1. It was numerical; new members were attracted to the church, particularly in the mission fields.
2. It was geographical; the church commenced working in at least one new overseas country each year, and in most years, in three or four new countries.
3. It was organizational; three new auxiliary organizations were established, and those that had existed at the beginning of the period were themselves spawning auxiliary organizations and becoming more complex.
4. It was institutional; no period in the history of the Seventh-day Adventist Church has ever seen a more spectacular rate of institutional expansion than the 1890s.[221]

However, since the existing organization was not able to meet the needs of the growing movement, administrative crises arose repeatedly, especially during the 1890s. 'Change was necessary in order to accommodate the growing church– to prevent over-centralization and to promote the delegation of responsibility and decision making prerogative–and in order to facilitate greater growth. More than anything else, the reorganization of denominational structures in 1901-1903 was to be necessary because the church was encountering great success in its missionary endeavours.'[222]

According to Oliver's study,

> [the] administrative structures and methods were not equipped to cope with either the task it had set itself or the growth that resulted. Lack of role clarity between the various organizations, continuing centralization of decision making prerogative, financial shortage, dispute over the purpose and control of institutions, the question of the authority of the General Conference, and competition for scarce resources between the church in North America and the management of the expanding missionary enterprise of the church arose as a consequence of the unprecedented

---

[220] Oliver, *Principles for Reorganization*, p. 359.
[221] Ibid., p. 129.
[222] Ibid., p. 66.

success that the church had encountered as it responded to its commitment to preach the gospel to the world.[223]

For fifteen years Adventists struggled with indecision about which way they should go in regard to further developments. Bruce Bauer offers a comprehensive study[224] of the choice between congregational and mission structure as two possible options for reorganization at that time. The decision in regard to this caused one of the most serious crises and on-going struggles experienced by Adventists and also made an enormous and lasting impact on the mission activities of the denomination.[225] A bipolar approach to church structure characterized Adventist ecclesiological thinking in those years and led to a division 'between those, on the one hand, who chose to emphasize a congregational form of organization with diversity as its greatest value, and those, on the other hand, who chose to emphasize a hierarchical form of organization with unity as its greatest value. [...] the polemical attitudes of denominational leaders prevented any attempt to bring both of those viewpoints together.'[226]

The eventual structure of the Seventh-day Adventist Church developed during the period 1901-1930. The present five-tier level of organization 'resulted in both, delegation to the lower levels and centralization, especially in the area of policy making, to the higher levels. It was therefore, the duty and responsibility of the General Conference to set policies, decide procedures and guide in the larger problems.'[227]

The struggle for reorganization and the process involved in attaining it reached a climax at the General Conference session of 1901. The regular business agenda was suspended and a Representative Committee was appointed to study the matter of reorganization. The recommendations brought by the committee urged strongly that there should be decentralization.

The four most significant recommendations of the Representative Committee to the General Conference in 1901 were the following:

1. The organization of union conferences and union missions around the world to replace the local conferences as the constituent parts of the General Conference.

2. The enlargement of the General Conference Executive Committee to 25 members, including the presidents of the union conferences. As the number of unions grew, so the size of the Executive Committee would increase.

---

[223] Ibid., p. 360.

[224] Bruce L. Bauer, 'Congregational and Mission Structures and How the Seventh-day Adventist Church Related to them' (doctoral dissertation, Andrews University, 1982.

[225] Ibid., pp. 13-44.

[226] Oliver, *Principles for reorganization*, p. 270.

[227] Bauer, 'Congregational and Mission Structures', p. 189.

3. The auxiliary organizations to be placed under the administrative control of the General Conference through the formation of departments.
4. The office of General Conference president to be replaced by a chairman. The 25-member executive committee would appoint a chairman from among its number who would serve as the chief administrative officer of the church.[228]

The guiding principles for the reorganization were not systematically illuminated but Oliver reconstructed them in his comprehensive study and came to the conclusion that five major topics directed the process:

1. the need to hold unity and diversity in balance;
2. representation;
3. legitimization of authority;
4. simplicity; and
5. adaptability.[229]

Arthur G. Daniells was elected as chairman with remarkably limited power, not president, of the General Conference, but a few weeks later he started acting as president without requesting new authorization.[230] This strong personality became one of the key elements in the further missionary development of the denomination. 'Daniells made the GCC into a virtual Mission Board during the early years of his administration.'[231] 'Daniells was a mission strategist. He put into practice the "spring- board plan" of investing into fields that could soon be self-supporting and send missionaries, too. Under his leadership during 20 years, missionaries [were] sent out and new territories were entered. Many European Adventists were sent into their nations' colonies and started missions there as early as the first decade of the 20th century, e.g. in Kenya, Tanzania, and Algeria. Others "adopted" countries, such as the Scandinavian Seventh-day Adventists who chose Ethiopia as their mission field. Australians reached out into the Pacific, and from South Africa, Zimbabwe and Zambia were reached.'[232]

In this fourth phase, Adventist mission can be characterized as holistic in its approach. The growing world-wide denomination gave priority to building hospitals and educational institutions, translating the Bible into local languages and preaching not only distinctive Adventist teachings but also the whole gospel. This emphasis can be readily seen from the words of William Spicer, former missionary in India and co-worker with Arthur Daniells, as Secretary of the General Conference. Spicer writes clearly about the Gospel message as the

---

[228] Andrew G. Mustard, 'The Church and Society', 1–18 <https://adventistbiblicalresearch.org/sites/default/files/pdf/AMustard-SDA%20polity.pdf> [accessed 12 June 2014], p. 13.
[229] Oliver, *Principles for reorganization*, p. 361
[230] Apparently he began using the title 'president' within a few weeks of the 1901 session. In 1903 the General Conference gave him the right to act officially as president. See: Andrew G. Mustard, *Seventh-day Adventist Polity: Its Historical Development*, p. 14
[231] Bauer, 'Congregational and Mission Structures', p. 189.
[232] Höschele, *From the End of the World*, p. 23.

primary content of Adventist mission: 'The cause of world wide missions is not something in addition to the regular work of the church. The work of God is one work the wide world over. The Gospel message can never have accomplished its purpose until it has reached all lands.'[233]

The General Conference paid particular attention to the European field. Ludwig Richard Conradi was sent to Europe in 1886 and travelled widely throughout Germany, Switzerland, Russia, Turkey, Romania and Hungary. In 1889 he established the headquarters of the German Seventh-day Adventist Church in Hamburg and in 1901 he became the first chairman of the General European Conference. Later he was elected president of the European Division and vice-president of the General Conference.

Conradi's interpretation of his role, and his approach to mission and to methods of conducting that mission differed significantly from the American Adventist models. From the beginning, other, established denominations observed Adventist mission activities in Europe with stubborn resistance. The population also looked at them with deep distrust, since these Adventists were regarded as the representatives of a North American 'sect' alien to European culture.[234] According to Adventist historian Daniel Heinz, one of the reasons for Conradi's outstanding missionary accomplishments, despite the challenging European context, was his decision not to follow American approach in undertaking mission. He dismissed the ethnocentric view of American Adventists that success in missionary work in Europe requires the implementation of the American model.[235] For example, he rejected revival camp meetings because these were unusual for European churchgoers and instead he trained Adventist pastors to become 'neutral' public lecturers, able to introduce the Adventist message by pointing to the common historical and theological heritage of the various Christian denominations.[236]

Conradi's main focus was on serving people's needs and addressing issues relevant to society in Europe. His approach was proved successful in the European field and under the leadership of Conradi Adventists experienced a radical and international growth. This was true not only throughout the continent; they also reached out to other areas far beyond Europe.

---

[233] Spicer, William A., *Our Story of Missions* (CA: Pacific Press Publishing Association, 1921), p. 11.

[234] See in: Heinz, Daniel, 'L. R. Conradis missionarischer Durchbruch: Ein Modell für die Zukunft?', in *Die Adventisten und Hamburg: Von der Ortsgemeinde zur internationalen Bewegung*, Baldur Ed. Pfeiffer, Lothar E. Träder, George R. Knight (Hrsg.), ed. by Baldur E. Pfeiffer, Lothar E. Träder and George R. Knight (Frankfurt am Main: Lang, 1992), 4: Archives of international Adventist History, p. 148.

[235] 'Our European Missions', *Review and Herald*, 7 (1877), 181.

[236] See: Daniel Heinz, 'Exklusivität und Kontextualisierung: Geschichte und Selbstverständnis der Siebenten – Tags – Adventisten in Deutschland', in *Spes Christiana: A Journal of Theology*, 12, ed. by Stefan Höschele (Lüneburg: Saatkorn-Verlag GmbH, 2001), 12, pp. 121–39 (p. 128).

Also Conradi's relationship to other denominations differed from the original American Adventist model. Many non-Adventist missionaries and theologians like Professor Richter in Berlin and Bodelschwingh expressed words of appreciation about his approach towards extending Adventist mission, because Conradi targeted rather unentered mission fields in order to avoid emerging competition among different Christian missionary societies.[237] Heinz concludes in his comprehensive study about the life and mission of Conradi that because of his non confrontative approach and of his genuine interest on the needs of the local society, language [238] and geography, Conradi gained not only wide acceptance for his missionary work but especially in Africa he received also governmental support for his ministry.[239] Conradi also participated at the first world mission conference in Edinburg although Adventists were not participating in the ecumenical movement. He was interested on building relationships with other influential denominational leaders outside of Adventism.

Conradi's way of designing mission has received strong support also within the denomination. Not only in Africa but also in Europe he was able to motivate and integrate laity into the missionary work. European Adventists were mature enough to design their mission activities within Europe but also in the mission field without heavily relying upon instructions and leadership coming from America.

The formation of the Hungarian Union Conference

Also in Hungary Adventists presented clear signs of growing organisational maturity. The Hungarian Union of Seventh-day Adventist was formed in 1925 with 43 local congregations and 1063 church members. Szigeti's comprehensive study about the development of the denomination in Hungary before 1945 outlines how the formation of the union also contributed to the consolidation of local leadership. Talented young pastors joined the leadership that initiated trainings for church members, equipped pastors for mission with useful materials and trainings, supported the further development of charity work, laid special emphasis on health ministry and advanced also many other existing areas of Adventist mission.[240] The mission of Hungarian Adventists after WW II was still a lay driven movement giving a chance for participation to hundreds of lay evangelists and Bible workers.[241]

---

[237] See: Heinz, Daniel, L. R. Conradi: *A Hetednapi Adventista Egyház misszionáriusa, evangélistája és szervezője Európában* (Budapest: Élet és Egészség Könyvk., 2004), p. 62.

[238] Conradi encouraged missionaries to learn local languages. Some of his missionaries like Kotz were pioneers in linguistics and their publications about tribal languages generated interest also outside of the denomination.

[239] Heinz, L. R. Conradi: *A Hetednapi Adventista Egyház misszionáriusa*, p. 63.

[240] Szigeti, Fejezetek a H. N. *Adventista Egyház magyarországi történetéből*, pp. 186-193.

[241] See reports in Idők Jelei, 1948 July.

*Phase V: Decline in cross-cultural mission –
growth in national churches: 1956 onwards*

In this study the year 1956 has been chosen as a landmark for phase V because of the steps taken by the General Conference that signalled significant changes in Adventist mission.

Since the beginning of the 20th century Adventism has experienced rapid growth. The worldwide membership reached 756,712 in 1950, indicating baptized members of the church. The later years of the century brought even more remarkable results and the denomination had grown to over 14,000,000 by the year 2005. Membership figures were approaching 20,000,000 a year or so later. An increasing portion of this growth now takes place outside North America, demonstrating that Adventism is a worldwide movement.

This new period of mission is a kind of managerial one. Missionaries mainly work in administration. The Annual Council of 1956 recommended a new type of training for missionaries because of the challenges in the mission fields. This indicated the struggle that the denomination was having with issues concerned with mission that had been brought about by changing times, processes in mission and intercultural relationships. Political changes after WW II also contributed significantly to reshaping the structure of Adventist mission.

The development of Adventist foreign mission started with slow, painstaking growth encouraged by expatriate presence. By the second half of the 20th century strong national institutions had been established by the church around the world 'where cross-cultural interaction becomes the norm in the leadership and life of the national church'.[242] Most mission fields became Conferences. These had some independent economic strength and participated at all levels in the administration of the world church. As part of the internationalization process, indigenous leaders replaced foreign missionaries in nearly every area, reducing the level of administrative control from the United States and other sending countries. Although, in its earlier phases, Adventist mission had been quite haphazard, lacking a conscious plan to evangelize the world systematically, a more proactive outreach had later been developed, with the definite goal of 'preaching the three angels' messages to every nation, and kindred, and tongue, and people'.[243] This process resulted in a reduction in the number of missionaries sent overseas; the responsibility for outreach in countries outside the USA was handed over to locals. Oosterwal describes this new phase of Adventist mission, which began in the 1950s and 60s, as a managerial one 'in which missionaries

---

[242] G. Ralph Thompson, 'The Role of the New Missionary: From Pioneer and Parent to Partner and Participant', in *Adventist missions facing the 21st century: A reader*, ed. by Baldur Pfeiffer (Frankfurt am Main, New York: P. Lang, 1990), Vol. 3: Archives of International Adventist History, p. 65.

[243] Knight, "Historical Introduction", p. XXIV.

went out to supervise the national ministers, lead in departmental work, administer and direct institutions'.[244]

These developments towards confining mission administration to General Conference based personal resulted in isolating the mission fields from home fields. Several Adventist scholars pointed out the dangers and negative consequences of the change, not only for mission fields but also for home fields. Bauer concluded, 'Present administrative structure and practice has effectively eliminated the possibility of cross-cultural missionary endeavours for most of the countries in our world.'

> Unless a local conference or mission makes a specific request for a specific type of missionary there is no other way for Adventist Church members to officially become involved in reaching the unreached groups who may live within the geographic boundaries of a national church. Even when the national church is weak and has few members it is still totally responsible for all the unreached peoples within its territory.[245]

In his analysis of the home field-mission field relationship, Pekka Pohjola concluded that recent developments had led to a broken relationship between home churches and mission, to disorientation, to a loss of funds and missionary enthusiasm and to a decline in the number of missionaries.[246] A new type of relationship had been created.

The leaders of the administration were aware of this loss of missionary enthusiasm[247] and developed programmes for revitalizing the spirit of worldwide Adventist outreach. Such initiatives by the General Conference took place during the period of time before and after the 1989 regime change in Hungary, when the programmes called 'Harvest 90' and 'Global Strategy' were examined and assessed. Both major strategies will be discussed in this study later.

Conclusion

The present study of the development of missionary thinking in the history of Seventh-day Adventism shows that the denomination was not one made up of a missionary people by conscious design. In its first phases Adventist mission

---

[244] See Gottfried Oosterwal, 'Training for Missions Tomorrow', in *Adventist missions facing the 21st century: A reader*, ed. by Baldur Pfeiffer (Frankfurt am Main, New York: P. Lang, 1990), Vol. 3: Archives of International Adventist history, pp. 78–91.

[245] Bauer, *Congregational and Mission Structures*, p. 195.

[246] See more in: Pohjola, Pekka, 'Home Field – Mission Field: Isolation of Symbiotic Relationship?', in *Adventist missions facing the 21st century: A reader*, ed. by Baldur Pfeiffer (Frankfurt am Main, New York: P. Lang, 1990), Vol. 3: Archives of international Adventist history, pp. 92–106.

[247] In his study Pohjola describes the falling number of missionaries, the loss of financing and also the challenges still affecting Adventist mission.

endeavour was quite haphazard. Knight rightly concludes that 'Adventism had been pushed from one missiological stage to the next by converts who called for missionaries'.[248] In the first decades of Adventist mission no plans or clear theological framework for mission were created at headquarters. The personal influence of leaders, influential pastors and administrators played a crucial role in developing and shaping mission, without having much direct connection to the worldwide mission of other denominations. On the other hand, despite all these struggles, the denomination was growing constantly. From a small group of Adventists at the beginning of its existence, it has now become a church of almost 20 million members, worldwide, with a presence in about 200 countries.

At the time of regime change in Eastern Europe in 1989, the worldwide administration of the denomination and its local representatives played crucial roles in designing mission, setting the programme and content for missionary activities and coordinating the use of funds and budgets. The question arises as to how it was that Adventists wanted to reach post-Communist society with a traditional message and methods that focused mainly on apologetics and eschatology. This method was successful in the past but it must be asked whether it remains suitable for the special situation of the population of Eastern Europe.

---

[248] See: Knight, "Historical Introduction", p. XXVI.

4. Adventist Missionary Thinking in Hungary at the Time of Regime Change in the Light of Publications and Training Programmes

Introduction

The Seventh-day Adventist Church was not prepared for the growing interest in church programmes shown by people in Hungary, starting in the 1980s. The historical and political developments of the previous decades had caused many changes, not only in society but also in daily life, in demographics and in different areas of church ministry. The denomination was no longer the same as it had been before the time of Communism. Up to the beginning of the 1950s Adventists had a strong vision for mission and could also implement it. Educated and experienced Bible workers and lay pastors carried out most of the missionary activity, establishing new congregations. Thirty years later the denomination looked quite different.

Adventists in Hungary had lost almost fifty per cent of their members and had struggled with schisms during the previous three decades before 1989, losing mainly young, educated members. By the time of regime change the denomination had lost more local congregations (over 150) that had been established in the past than the number that still existed in 1989 (about 120). Those who remained in the church had maintained a religious lifestyle mainly oriented towards keeping traditions alive and surviving in spite of difficulties. The elderly, especially women, were over-represented in the age structure of the denomination and the church members were not trained or experienced in doing mission.

The new, expanding opportunity for mission in the second half of the 1980s caused a burst of enthusiasm in the church, especially among the leaders. They hoped to regain some lost strength for the denomination and 'mission' was considered as the solution to many problems. At the international board meeting of the Trans European Division in England the union president stated: 'First of all we would like to express our conviction that all the problems of the life of the Hungarian Union Conference will be solved if missionary work is given priority in our efforts.' A report about the growth in the Hungarian Union Conference followed this introductory statement. 'We are glad to report that the stagnation or declining tendency turned this year. Even so, the number of members of our denomination has grown.'[1]

This statement well expresses the hopes and the longing of Hungarian Adventists for successful mission endeavour. Mission seemed to become 'the solution' for everything and the words of the union president about the struggling church signalled the beginning of a new era: 'Like other socialist countries, Hungary is experiencing a time of far-reaching change, and this influences the work as well. That is why we need new efforts and why we must search for new ways to conduct our work in the field of mission. We have to strengthen the influence of the Church. In recent months new paths have opened up before us, so we can take part in public health and social programmes....'[2]

Characteristics of Adventist Teachings about Mission in Hungary

Major sources of influence on Adventist missionary thinking in Hungary

New challenges required support and training and the struggling Hungarian part of the denomination turned towards the Western part to receive assistance. Leaders at the General Conference of the Adventist Church in the United States also recognized the changes in Eastern European countries. This is clear from the words of Ralph Thompson, Secretary of the General Conference, when he spoke at the meeting of worldwide delegates in Indianapolis in 1990: 'Major changes have taken place in Eastern Europe and we have to find a new approach to the needs of these times.'[3]

Scholars, lecturers, pastors and administrators came to Hungary in order to teach, train, care for the youth and conduct public meetings. They were welcomed with joy and high expectations. Some had an outstanding impact on the Hungarian church, even before the regime change in 1989. They included Mark Finley, Gottfried Oosterwal, James Huzzey and Borge Schantz. Kenneth Wood must be mentioned too, although he did not have a directly significant impact on East Central Europe. His study, *The role of the Seventh-day Adventist Church in the great controversy in the end time,*[4] published by the Biblical Research Committee of the General Conference of the SDA church and issued on behalf of the North American Bible Conference in 1974, was widely used in

---

[1] Executive committee of the Hungarian Union Conference, 1989, HUC Archive Pécel, p. 1.

[2] Jenő Szigeti, Report on the work of the Hungarian Union Conference December 1987-April (1988), p. 1.

[3] My own translation from the Hungarian text published in: 'Misszió', *Adventhírnök, 6* (1990), pp. 6–7.

[4] Kenneth H. Wood, 'The role of the Seventh-day Adventist Church in the great controversy in the end time', in *North American Bible Conference 1974*, ed. by the General Conference of Seventh-day Adventists Biblical Research Committee (Silver Spring, MD: Biblical Research Committee, 1974), p. 17.

the training of church administrators and leaders, including personnel in all divisions and union leaders worldwide, including Hungarians. The impact of the study on missionary thinking was much larger than the distribution of the study itself. An analysis of these authors' influence, activities and publications in Hungary shows that there were similarities among them but also significant differences.

Those publications dealing with mission can be systematically organized according to the positions their writers held in the denomination. Three different kinds of influence can be observed to have shaped the variable understanding of mission in the Hungarian Adventist church:

Firstly, Adventist scholars and researchers who came from Western countries influenced Hungarian understanding of mission through their publications, lectures and training programmes. They came to Hungary either because the General Conference or the Trans European Division sent them or the Hungarian Union Conference invited them for educational purposes.

Secondly, pastors and administrators working for or on behalf of the General Conference or the Trans- European Division visited Hungary and/or published material about mission in Hungary.

Thirdly, Hungarian pastors and administrators wrote papers or articles on Hungarian Adventist mission and reflected on what they had learned during training sessions, mostly led by foreigners.[5] The following sections indicate the major differences among these writers, and their way of reflecting on mission, its goals and methods.

How did the teaching of Adventist scholars and
lecturers influence missionary thinking?

Visiting scholars and Adventist writers usually focused on a purely academic type of teaching about the nature, the foundation, the relevance and the methods of mission. Their publications and thoughts, including those of Schantz, Oosterwal, Booth and also Wood, were often received with great interest in Hungary. Usually they not only presented a biblical mission theology but also reflected critically on the mission praxis of the denomination and evaluated past experiences. Their conclusions urged changes and new ways of meeting needs in contemporary society.

Schantz's comprehensive study of Adventist mission, comprising over 950 pages, reveals not only his mission theology but also the views of his critics about the mission praxis of the denomination. These findings were the result of his research tracing the development of Adventist missionary thinking. Schantz's book has never been translated into Hungarian but he visited Hungary and trained pastors for mission. His name and also the content of his lectures are still remembered and quoted, even decades later, among Hungarian Adventist

---

[5] This part will be discussed later and also their publications and articles will be analysed.

pastors. He places strong emphasis on the right and holistic approach, starting with critical reflection challenging pastors and administrators who face biblical fundamentals. 'Questions mission must ask' are well defined and appropriate to the Adventist situation. Schantz actually returns to the questions posed by Bavinck but the selection and the way in which he extends them shows the relevance Schantz attributes to these questions.[6]

'What are the motives for mission? What position do they occupy within the total framework of the Scriptures, its commands and its promises?'[7] Mission, for Schantz, is not automatically equal to evangelism. He addresses the need for 'clearance of the relationship between mission and the work of evangelism'. Evangelism is actually a component of mission and less comprehensive than mission.[8] He also challenges the traditional Adventist mission praxis: Is it to be restricted exclusively to the preaching of the Word, or does it also include medical, educational, and agricultural assistance?[9]

Schantz indicates that mission is the total task of the church in witness and that, besides evangelism, it includes social action.[10] He argues for reflection on past failures, relevance to the culture in which the mission is practised and a holistic approach. He presented his mission theology to Hungarian pastors during his visit in Hungary and also in trainings organized in Friedensau also for participating Hungarian pastors.

Oosterwal's book, *Mission Possible,* and his presentations represented, during the period of time under examination, the most extensive and comprehensive lectures about mission theology available to Hungarian Adventists. Several of his other publications had already been printed before the regime change but *Mission Possible* is the most significant among them.[11] There are three reasons for its importance:

First, although it was published in America and addressed to readers living in a mainly American context, it had been widely translated and circulated in Eastern European countries, including Hungary, by 1982. Oosterwal's personal visits to Europe helped to give him a good understanding of the cultural milieu. While there he received the support of the local leadership of the church also in Hungary and had excellent opportunities to promote his insights and to exert a unique and strong personal influence on mission. He became one of the leading Adventist missiologists of his time, influencing missionary thinking in Europe for decades.

---

[6] J.H Bavinck and D.H Freeman, *An Introduction to the Science of Missions:* (Phillipsburg: Presbyterian & Reformed Publishing Company, 1992).

[7] Schantz, *The Development*, p. 5.

[8] Ibid., p. 191.

[9] Ibid., pp. 5–6.

[10] Ibid., p. 191.

[11] Oosterwal, *Mission Possible.*

Secondly, *Mission Possible* not only studies the major steps taken in the course of Adventist mission history but also focuses on the development of the community or population targeted by that mission. Oosterwal presents clear, carefully planned steps towards developing a contemporary missionary ministry, going beyond the traditional understanding of Adventist mission. He challenges readers and listeners to leave behind the apologetical eschatological approach and to turn towards their intended cultural context in order to understand, to present love and to serve its people. He urges the church to develop a fresh, contemporary approach to mission, a strategy proving that Adventists can serve meaningfully and offer a relevant ministry in the community.

Thirdly, Oosterwal looks into the future and outlines a prognosis for future Adventist mission. He challenges church administrators and leaders to act with more openness and to change church structures to supply better support for mission. He stresses the importance for the church of making wise use of such opportunities as may offer themselves in the future and of avoiding traps that may be lying ahead. His purpose was understood well in Hungary and through its impact Hungarians even changed the original English title of his book, *Mission Possible; its* Hungarian edition (1982) means 'Mission in a changed world'.[12] The importance of this book for Hungarian missionary thinking is clearly discernible from the fact that the book was reprinted and widely circulated in the church decades later, in 2006.[13]

In addition to reading Oosterwal's book, a group of pastors travelled to Friedensau in Germany in order to take his training course for mission. As a lecturer with international experience, he addressed the issue as relevant, not only for North Americans but also for international readers and listeners. The efforts he made to solve the terminological confusion about mission, missionary and evangelism challenged the existing traditions of the denomination. Three features stand out clearly in the Adventist interpretation and use of the term 'missionary': 'First, a missionary crosses national or cultural-geographical boundaries. Second, he goes out in the service of the church. That is, he carries church credentials and is financially supported by it. Third, he can be called to do any type of work: office secretary, minister, school superintendent, physician, or builder.'[14]

Oosterwal then continues to ask: 'Is it not striking that none of these criteria by which we define a missionary apply to Jesus Christ, our great model of mission?'[15] The word 'mission' is used in the Adventist terminology similarly to the term 'missionary' to mean 'first of all, any type of church work done outside of one's own country'. In addition, a unit of church organization within the

---

[12] The Hungarian translation of his book was based on the German text.

[13] Gottfried Oosterwal, *Misszió egy megváltozott világban* (Budapest: Boldog Élet Alapítvány, 2006).

[14] Oosterwal, *Mission Possible,* p. 86.

[15] Ibid., p. 86.

Adventist Church is called 'mission', describing a form and function similar 'to that of a conference, the basic difference being that missions cannot elect their own officers'. 'Adventists also use the term "mission" for mission stations, for the organization that pays the workers' salaries, or an evangelistic campaign-Mission.'[16]

Oosterwal also addresses the problem of presenting dominant Western culture in other areas when he adds to this complex matter the problem of 'the identification of mission and the missionary with Western imperialism and paternalism'.[17] He concludes with an imperative: to look at that 'good old term "mission" anew' and urges the younger generation to accept the challenge to 'discover for itself the true Biblical meaning of being a missionary and follow it. It may differ from what Christians have believed to be "true mission" in the past, but since when are Seventh-day Adventists bound by their own or other Christians' traditions?'[18] The urgent need to rediscover the 'true Biblical concept of mission' is given more prominence than before: 'The need to rediscover the true Biblical concept of mission is even more pressing because the traditional one is faltering under the present circumstances. It fails to inspire us and to arouse us to action. It fails to come up with answers to questions posed by the radically changed situation in which we live today. And worst of all, it leaves the work for which Christ established His church largely undone, and the church without a valid sense of purpose.'[19]

If the present generation does not want to lose opportunities for mission, currently held concepts of mission have to go through a process of revision.

> This is most imperative, since much of the church's missionary structure and organization reflects a concept of the world and of mission that is no longer capable of solving the problems and issues of the new missionary situation. Thus, many opportunities and challenges of mission go unanswered.[20]

Oosterwal's radical message was well understood when it was first presented in various Central European countries. I have carried out several interviews in Hungary a in the Czech Republic twenty years later with pastors who were working at the time of the regime change in both countries. During the interviews those pastors answered the question, 'Who impacted the missionary thinking strongly in your country at the time of the regime change?' Usually Oosterwal's name was mentioned as one of the first three among the most influential people, in reference to missionary thinking whom these ministers had encountered (in person, or through their reading). Very often people put him in first place.

---

[16] Ibid., p. 84.

[17] He cites white supremacy and oppression in the countries of Africa and Asia.

[18] Oosterwal, *Mission Possible,* p. 86.

[19] Ibid., p. 86.

[20] Ibid., p. 51.

His definition of mission shows a strong intention to rely on the example of Christ. He makes it clear that no initiative by an organization, missionary or any other person can adequately define mission; true mission originates in God.[21] 'The one and only source where we can find the true meaning of mission in its authentic setting is the Bible, the same Book that testifies of Christ, 'the greatest missionary the world has ever known'. Only in Him can we understand what 'missionary' really means.'[22]

Oosterwal calls on Adventists to understand and bear the consequences of the knowledge that 'Christian mission is the imitation and the continuation of Christ's work on earth'. [23] The church as a 'living image of God' has to recognize that its mission is 'to participate in God's own mission' and reflect 'His fullness and sufficiency through unselfish love, service, and a holy way of life'.[24]

The question concerning the practical steps the church is supposed to take did not remain unanswered. Oosterwal presented exactly the same three methods for the communication of the gospel as Becker did in his comprehensive study of the life of Jesus.[25] The church has the responsibility to make the gospel known in 'all the world through proclamation, service, and fellowship […] and to urge the people for whom Christ died to accept this gospel and to avail themselves of its benefits.'[26]

These steps would lead to 'reconciliation, the restoration of the union between God and man'[27] and to the restoration of His kingdom.[28] People going through this process of reconciliation and restoration become not only members of the church, participating in the programmes and supporting church activities, but active 'missionaries' who cooperate with their Master. Mission is, therefore, not the task of a few professionals but of everyone in the church: 'Mission is the heartbeat of the church. If it stops, the church ceases to be. […] And every believer by baptism not only publicly declares himself a follower of Jesus Christ but also pledges himself to work with Him for the salvation of men. Mission, then, is the hallmark of a Christian, his test of faith.'[29]

Oosterwal's is a voice urging radical changes, urging service and fellowship that supplements the proclamation of the Gospel and urging the involvement in missional endeavour of all institutions and church members. Along with Schantz, he clearly challenges Adventist missionary thinking and has succeeded in bringing about new impulses for change.

---

[21] Ibid., p. 87, cf. p. 13.

[22] Ibid., p. 85.

[23] Ibid., p. 51.

[24] Ibid., p. 69.

[25] Jürgen Becker, *Jesus of Nazareth* (New York: W. de Gruyter, 1998).

[26] Oosterwal, *Mission Possible*, p. 72.

[27] Ibid., p. 90.

[28] Ibid., p. 70.

[29] Ibid., p. 15.

Publications by two other scholars, Kenneth Wood and Carlton Booth, have had a less direct impact on Hungarian missionary thinking due to their lack of direct connection to Hungary. Their approach to mission also differs from the methods advocated by the authors of the two previous publications, men who come from a European background. Just two years after Oosterwal's book appeared, another study was published by Wood. At first the target readership of this book was seen as the North American Division but as time went on many more administrators working in leadership positions, including some who later came to Hungary, were influenced by the book, through the training programmes organized by the General Conference. Wood's publication on the mission of Adventists, presented in 1974 at the North American Bible Conference, signalled from the title that he focuses mainly on the eschatological perspective of Adventist mission: 'The role of the Seventh-day Adventist Church in the great controversy in the end time'. His approach presents some similar characteristics to the Millerites' and early Adventists' view of mission: 'Part of the general mission assigned to this church is to preach the gospel to the entire world. This assignment is rooted in Christ's command, rooted in Matthew 28:18-20, and is restated in Revelation 14:6. This assignment is so intimately connected with God's purposes for this world that Jesus pointed to its fulfilment as being one sign of the nearness of the end of all things. Said Christ in Matthew 24:14: "This gospel of the kingdom shall be preached in all the world for a witness unto all nations; and then shall the end come".'[30]

Wood studies the unique and distinctive aspects of the SDA church that play an important role in its mission and concludes that it has a general aspect and a specific component.

He views the general mission of Adventists as being similar to the roles of ancient Israel and of the apostolic church: 'revealing God, showing results of obedience, witnessing verbally to world and inviting them to decision and vindicating God's character and wisdom'.[31]

The most important part of mission seems, from Wood's point of view, to be the specific mission of Adventists – the responsibility that makes them unique among Christians. This mission consists of the distinctive teachings of Adventists, such as the messages of the judgement, of the imminent second advent of Christ and the law of God. Within the activities of this specific mission of the SDA church Wood lists:

1. Preaching gospel in the context of the judgement-hour message that is God's final message;
2. Preaching the imminent advent of Christ;
3. Reaching the entire world with the message;
4. Defending God's law and demanding a choice between the Sabbath of the fourth commandment and man's counterfeit Sabbath;

---

[30] Wood, 'The Role of Seventh-day Adventist Church', p. 17.
[31] Ibid., p. 17.

5. Setting forth the full meaning of righteousness by faith;
6. Preparing people for translation, people who reflect the image of Jesus fully and receive the divine seal;
7. Proclaiming the fall of Babylon and urging people to come out of that evil realm.[32]

Unlike Oosterwal and Schantz, Wood gives relatively little attention to present realities in society or to lessons the church can learn from recent developments, failures and successes. Instead, his understanding of mission is dominated by the urgency of proclaiming distinctive truths. Wood concentrates almost exclusively on the eschatological elements influencing missionary motives and on providing 'present truth' as the content of missionary work.

Wood's influence has been felt most strongly in the administration of the Church in North America. The plans and activities of the General Conference, described later in this study, reflect his views much more than those of Oosterwal or Schantz. The leadership has seemed to be much more open to the traditional voices representing the Adventist eschatological apologetic approach than to questions and surveys resulting from past experiences and failures in Adventist mission.

Another person who published an article entitled 'Evangelism in the church' was Carlton Booth. His thoughts were translated and published in Hungary as early as 1986. He supported proclamation-oriented mission and defined the goal of God for the church as 'bringing the message of Christ to all people'.[33] Booth's essay encourages very high expectations on the part of the church in terms of evangelism as proclamation and also describes how the denomination can fulfil these expectations. For him, 'the church [is] the centre for evangelism' and everybody should consider evangelism to be his personal duty. The special contribution of Booth's article to the development of Adventist missionary thinking was that, besides presenting evangelism as an overwhelming task and burden, he also described practical steps to be taken by missionaries and listed a number of activities Adventists could undertake in order to accomplish the missionary task: public evangelism, friendship evangelism, personal witnessing, small-group evangelism, Sabbath school as evangelism, 'visitation' evangelism, evangelistic camps and retreats, youth evangelism, literature and media evangelism.[34] By setting out these concrete methods, Booth created the foundation of the later missional theory that was adopted by Adventists in Hungary.

---

[32] See: Wood, 'The role of Seventh-day Adventist Church', pp. 1–4.
[33] Carlton Booth, 'Evangélizáció az Egyházban', *Lelkésztájékoztató* (1986), 392–400.
[34] Booth, 'Evangélizáció az Egyházban', p. 392-400.

*How had teachings of foreign administrators and pastors influenced
missionary thinking?*

The Hungarian Union Conference together with division leaders took a major
decision in the period from 1985 to 1986 by leaving the mainly German-speaking
territory, the Euro-Africa Division of the Seventh-day Adventist Church,[35] and
by joining the Trans-European Division, which has its headquarters in England.
Hungarians acquired new international partners to cooperate with and another
common language: English. The international predominance of Western
countries determining the missionary thinking and activities of Hungarian
Adventists grew far beyond their influence on Hungarian leaders and scholars.[36]
The majority of the publications –especially articles in church magazines –
contributing to the understanding of mission were clearly by foreigners and often
Hungarian writers simply reflected or reported what they had heard from
Western colleagues. The majority of Hungarian mission-related contributions in
church publications in Hungary were about baptisms, projects, experiences and
plans and not about mission theology or theory.

Pastors and administrators who come from Western countries have mostly
chosen a pragmatic way of talking about mission. The Trans-European Division
launched the worldwide church programme 'Harvest 90' and also Hungary
adapted it in 1986. This global programme created a framework for mission and
strongly influenced the meaning, the content and also the methods of mission
promoted by Hungarian leaders and presented to the church. The Union
Secretary, László Hangyás, conveyed Mark Finley's[37] message to Hungarian
Adventists, emphasizing that harvesting has to be given first priority, put into
first place: 'We don't have time; people are waiting. The only thing that has
value for the kingdom of God is winning people for Christ.'[38]

Finley's job description as ministerial secretary responsible for mission in the
division's territory also indicates how the division understood mission and which
activities were expected to fulfil the plan for outreach: 'During this
quinquennium, the Ministerial Secretary will be active in evangelistic crusades,
sponsor three major Festivals of Evangelism and co-ordinate a major
evangelistic strategy in harmony with North American Division evangelists. We
envision each Adventist minister using His God-given gifts within the context of

---

[35] With its headquarters in Bern.

[36] These were Germany, England, The USA and also, later, other European countries and
Australia.

[37] Finley and Schantz came to Hungary and conducted training programmes in mission for
pastors. See the report of the president about past mission-related developments in the
Adventist church in Hungary: Jenő Szigeti, 'Az 'Aratás '90 a Magyar Unióban',
Lelkésztájékoztató (1990), 136–38, pp. 136–37.

[38] László Hangyás and Mark A. Finley, 'Aratás '90: Jelszó vagy bibliai motiváció?',
Lelkésztájékoztató (1986), 169–74.

his culture to win souls for Jesus Christ. We envision each church within the Division as a dynamic, pulsating evangelistic centre.'[39]

Pastors working in position of leadership gave more emphasis to the Biblical and the practical 'How to?' side of mission in order to make public meetings as successful as possible. Public presentations of the Adventist message as truth-oriented lectures became the major paradigm for mission promoted by the administration.

Some exceptions to this approach can be found. For example, Huzzey, an English pastor promoted a more need-oriented strategy in his lectures in Hungary in 1986, four years before the regime change. On the 24 January he preached at a youth meeting in Budapest and addressed issues related to the needs of Hungarians. His sermon, 'Being free in Christ' and also a summary of his recent training of young pastors were published in the church magazine in Hungary and were among the first articles to point to a new era of freedom for mission. His approach to mission was not proclamation oriented but holistic, focusing more on improving the quality of church life. He promoted consideration of the present situation in society and presentation of the gospel not only through words but also through actions demonstrating love and care. Huzzey defined the foundation of the ministry as fellowship with God and put pressure on people to develop that fellowship with God and with others. Starting with the words in Luke 4.18-2, he explained: 'The good news of Jesus is not the proclamation of theories but practical ministry to people. This is also our task. […]. The gospel brings about the solution to people's physical and spiritual needs.'[40]

Like Booth, Huzzey describes practical steps that church members can take in order to carry out 'mission' but these steps are different and more holistic. They include maintaining friendship, supporting the old and sick, telling our personal experiences to others, setting a good example, helping people struggling with problems related to tobacco, alcohol and drugs, and distribution of literature.[41]

During the training of young pastors on 26 and 27 January 1986 Huzzey also addressed internal problems faced by the church. He argued that 'mission' should start within the church. Young people leave the church because 'the church is a boring place, the church is concerned about her own future and is forgetting the youth'.[42] Accordingly, the missionary task also has to be taken seriously within the church. He went on to suggest practical steps, which church members and leaders could take. These included expressing love towards the

---

[39] Trans-European Division Ministerial Department, 'A vision of the Future 1990-1995: A report of the ministerial department presented to TED spring meetings, 22 April 1990', A22-A26, pp. A24.

[40] The presentations by James Huzzey were summarized by his translator, Hangyás and published in the church's magazine *Adventhírnök*': László Hangyás, 'James Huzzey testvér látogatása', *Lelkésztájékoztató* (1986), 18–21, pp. 18–21.

[41] Hangyás, 'James Huzzey testvér látogatása', pp. 18-21.

[42] Ibid., pp. 18-21.

young among them and visiting young people in their homes and recognizing their crisis situations. He felt that pastors might usefully learn how to understand and even speak the kind of 'youthspeak' young people adopted. Pastors should also try to establish good relationships with children, and should encourage young people to develop a positive vision of the future....[43]

Although Huzzey's advice was very much appreciated, his voice did not become the overall trend-setter for the praxis of Hungarian Adventist mission. The study of strategic plans and publications reveals that the promotion of the truth-oriented proclamation as the main approach became the leading one. Articles and publications by several other administrators, pastors and church entities were translated and printed in Hungary after 1985. The majority of them concentrated on a strategy for mission that resembled Wood's system, which highlighted the proclamation-centered missional method with its emphasis on eschatology.

Neal Wilson, General Conference President, stated firmly: 'Global Strategy requires from us that we give a chance to everybody, regardless of his position in society, to hear the eternal gospel.'[44] His successor, Robert Folkenberg said: 'Our church exists in order to fulfil a call: the proclamation of the gospel.'[45]

Jan Paulsen, president of the Trans-European Division, wrote: 'We have to proclaim the gospel because this is the only way in which we can accomplish our mission and the end can come. (Matthew 24.14).'[46]

Mark Finley, leader of the ministerial department of the Trans-European Division, addressed the 'Harvest 90' programme with following words: 'In a society which is becoming increasingly secular, dominated by materialism, affluence and pleasure, [...] the church has received a mandate from the Lord of harvest. He affirms, 'I sent you to reap.' [...] The church would be unfaithful to her Lord if we did not participate in winning people. [...] We have to put Harvesting into first place. [...] We don't have much time because people are waiting. [...] The only thing that has value for the kingdom of God is winning people for Christ. 'Harvest 90' presents us with the most important opportunity. It calls on all church members to focus on lost souls with all our energy.'[47]

Charles Taylor, who was working for the Global Mission office of the General Conference, declared: 'Global mission is not only a motto. This is the way in

---

[43] Ibid., pp. 18-21.

[44] Neal Wilson, 'Globális Missziói Stratégia' *Adventhírnök*, 6-8 (1990), 8.

[45] Robert S. Folkenberg, 'Meghatározni a gyülekezet misszióját', *Adventhírnök*, 4 (1994), 2 (p. 2),

[46] Jan Paulsen, 'Tegyünk valami rendkívülit Krisztusért 1990-ben', *Adventhírnök*, 1 (1990), 4–5 (p. 4).

[47] 'Reaping' means for Finley the proclamation of the gospel and urging people to make decisions for God and baptism. Mark A. Finley, 'Aratás 90', *Lelkésztájlékoztató*, 2 (1986), 169-174.

which Seventh-day Adventists fulfil their missionary mandate: the proclamation of the gospel to every people and tribe and language and nation.'[48]

Other administrators spoke in a similar way at the major international gathering of the denomination called the General Conference. [49] Official statements issued by church departments disseminated the same views: 'We envision each Adventist minister using His God-given gifts within the context of his culture to win souls for Jesus Christ. We envision each church within the Division as a dynamic, pulsating evangelistic centre.'[50]

Church administrators have had a much stronger influence on developing mission praxis in Hungary than other voices have had. The results clearly demonstrate their impact. The research which formed the basis of this present study did not produce much evidence of theological reflection behind the 'missional effort' of Harvest 90. Questions of cultural anthropology, conscious planning for the process of inculturation of the gospel and a focus on the actual needs expressed by the struggling Hungarian population were not really included in the mainly administration-led implementation of Harvest 90.

How did the views of Hungarian writers influence missionary thinking?

Hungarian writers seem to have been both influenced by foreign approaches and to have taken positions that depended on the local context. In 1984 a formal decision by the executive committee of the Hungarian Union Conference marked the beginning of a new era in the life of the church in Hungary: 'In line with our previous decisions, we still believe that our call is to proclaim the three angels' message (Revelation 14.6-12). [...] We are convinced that this message contains the gospel and this gospel must be preached to all humans so that people may discover the solutions of Jesus that guide us in all kinds of life situations. We commit ourselves to the view that all our churches should proclaim the full gospel based on the message of the three angels.'[51]

This decision on the part of the leadership demonstrates clearly that Hungarian Adventist leaders were at this point following a truth-and-proclamation-centred approach to mission, with a strong eschatological emphasis. Although it was also announced at the meeting that the message

---

[48] R. C. Taylor, 'Globális missziói eredmények', *Adventhírnök*, 2 (1995), 2 (p. 2).

[49] Presentation at the Uttrecht General Conference in 1995 Frank Ottati, 'Hadd kongajanak a szabadság harangjai', *Adventhírnök*, 4 (1995), 18–20 (pp. 18–20), G. Ralph Thompson, 'Nem mesterkélt mesék', *Adventhírnök*, 4 (1995), 10–12 (pp. 10–12), Joel N Musvosvi, 'Egyek az Ő szavában', *Adventhírnök*, 4 (1995), 14 (p. 14).

[50] Trans-European Division Ministerial Department, 'A vision of the Future 1990-1995: A report of the ministerial department presented to TED spring meetings' April 22-23. 1990. HUC Archive. p. 24. Also the methods were proposed in the same paragraph: evangelistic crusades, major festivals of evangelism, a major evangelistic strategy in harmony with North American Division evangelists.

[51] Executive committee of the Hungarian Union Conference, *Lelkésztájékoztató*, 18 (1984), p. 108.

should be proclaimed in an up-to-date way, to meet the expectations of modern people, this actually involved not much more than updating the technical methods, materials and devices used by pastors. In 1986 Szigeti called for renewal of the ministry within the organization and for training of church members, a call that was to be repeated within the framework of Harvest '90.[52]

When Szilvási, the Secretary of the union, reported in 1986 on how many baptismal candidates the worldwide church had planned for each division and for Hungary specifically, he also proposed appropriate programmes. All of them reflected the truth-and-proclamation-centred approach. The step suggested in the article were: to motivate and train church members for mission, to conduct seminars, especially Revelation seminars, to train evangelists and to provide supporting materials like slides, pictures and videos for pastors.[53] The first reports already showed a positive welcome for this approach, as the president of the Duna Conference stated: 'We have received Harvest' 90 with joy and made it our life purpose. We conduct evangelistic meetings in many churches in our conference.'[54]

Later reports show how ambitiously Adventists had been planning their public campaigns, even before the regime change. The leadership planned a big 'harvesting' campaign for the autumn of 1988 with the clear goal of increasing membership and baptizing new people.[55] With these growing ambitions uncertainty increased. Questions that leaders started asking revealed their almost unattainable expectations in regard to public evangelism: 'Have we presented the fragrance of the knowledge of Christ everywhere? Have we made every possible effort? Have we learned to live and to serve and to work in such a fellowship that the fragrance of Christ, His character, can become known more and more widely?'[56]

What Hungarian leaders wrote in 1990 is clear evidence of enthusiasm for public evangelism but it also reveals a degree of disappointment in the methods and shows that these leaders were searching for new ways forward: 'The main point about mission is how we should *do* mission. We always have to do it as

---

[52] Jenő Szigeti, 'A szolgálat Bázisa', *Lelkésztájékoztató*, 1986, pp. 341–44.

[53] József Szilvási, 'Aratás '90', *Lelkésztájékoztató*, 1986, pp. 353–54.

[54] László Erdélyi, 'Események tükrében [A report on the ministry of the executive committee]', *Lelkésztájékoztató* (1986), 355–58 (pp. 355–56).

[55] Hungarian Union Conference of the Seventh-day Adventist Church, *Harvest '90*, 31 March 1988, Seventh-day Adventist – HUC Historical Archive, 1, p. 1, Youth training program for mission: Peter Zarka, 'Ifjusagi nap Nemesvámoson', *Adventhírnök*, 3 (1988), 157 (p. 157), Reports about 'success' in public evangelism: András Szilvasi, 'Keresztség Békéscsabán', Adventhírnök, 3 (1988), 155; Árpád Szöllösi, 'Lelkészcsaládok közös üdülése', *Adventhírnök*, 4 (1988), 210; Szöllösi Árpád, 'Debrecen', *Adventhírnök*, 4 (1988), 212.

[56] Sándor Ócsai, 'Tiszavidéki Egyházterület Elnöki Beszámolója az 1987-1990 konferenciai időszak munkájáról', *Adventhírnök*, 9-12 (1990), 3–6 (p. 3).

Jesus did it.'[57] 'We have to get to know the people we have been sent to. These people don't need explanations; they need real help.'[58]

A statement issued by the union president in 1991 at the international meeting of denominational leaders at the division headquarters in England indicates that Hungarian Adventists seemed to be overwhelmed by the expectations and possibilities related to missionary work in the community: 'Never has the world's need for teaching and healing been greater than it is today. The world is full of those who need to be ministered unto–the weak, the helpless, the ignorant, the degraded.'[59]

Two years later, as president of the church in Hungary, Szigeti announced that Hungarian Adventists had failed to achieve their goals and that there was a need for change in the interpretation and accomplishment of mission. By that time Hungarians had experienced enough mission activity led from abroad to draw their own conclusions about it and a kind of disillusion could be recognized. This led to challenges to the way in which mission was understood and fulfilled: 'Our mission has arrived at a crossroads. The traditionalism of our churches does not tolerate the different lifestyles of people searching for Christ. […] Our witnessing is often just a matter of words. Social service is strange for many. I consider it to be a major challenge that Adventist homes are not open to our friends. We need a new view of mission, free from the chains of our traditions.'[60]

This statement indicates that the influence of Oosterwal, Schantz and Huzzey was still being felt among Hungarian Adventists as an alternative to the 'truth-and-proclamation'-oriented approach to mission. Despite the challenges and the growing tensions in some churches, the official programme of the church and the concept of mission still remained the same: the proclamation of the gospel to all people.

> The ministerial department obeys the comission of the Master: teach the eternal gospel to all people. The task of the ministerial department is to train and lead our lay members as well as pastors and administrators to cooperate in the ministry and in the proclamation of the end-time gospel.[61]

---

[57] id. Árpád Szőllősi, 'Az evangélizálás', *Adventhírnök*, 2 (1990), 2 (p. 2). Szőllősi rasied the issue theoretically but did not present practical solutions.

[58] Jenő Szigeti, 'Ne félj, hanem szólj, ne hallgass!', *Adventhírnök*, 1 (1990), 2.

[59] Szigeti relied on the words of Ellen White in this sentence: Szigeti, Jenő, 'Jelentés a Transeurópai Divízió évvégi üléséről', *Adventhírnök*, 6 (1991), 3–4. See: Ellen G White, *Counsels to Parents, Teachers, and Students Regarding Christian Education* (Mountain View, CA: Pacific Press Publishing Association, 1913), p. 467.

[60] Jenő Szigeti, 'Beszámoló ülés: Hálát adok érettetek Istennek', *Adventhírnök,* 3 (1993), p.3.

[61] The official statement by the Duna Conference repeated the previous statements. See: Duna Conference, 'A Dunamelléki Egyházterület Választokonferenciájának határozatai', *Adventhírnök*, 2 (1993), 9; József Szilvási, 'Irányelvek az osztályok munkájáról', *Adventhírnök*, 6 (1993), 7–9; See also József Szilvási, 'Számvetés – toronyépítés előtt',

The influence of the administration had significantly more impact on the development of missionary thinking than had the publications and training programmes of the lecturers. Their input was not strong enough to assist the Adventist church, at different levels, to recognize the importance of reflection on and analysis of the social context and to develop methods that would implement a holistic approach to mission. Mission was understood as proclamation of the 'truth' and this led to the truth-and-proclamation oriented approach.

What was considered to be the main message Adventists should proclaim in Hungary?

Oosterwal obviously wanted to prevent Adventists from ignoring past shifts in emphasis in the Seventh-day Adventist missionary message. He took definite steps in order to encourage the church to note carefully how previous decades of Adventist mission and closer contact with other Christian missions in the mission fields through established interconnection had led to a different concept of the church and its mission. He illustrated the shift by comparing how Andrews, the first Adventist missionary, summarized the essence of the three angels' message in 1874 as the content of mission – 'preach the Sabbath, warn of the coming judgment, and teach obedience to the commandments' – with how Eckenroth defined the message in 1952 for the denominational Bible Conference held that year: 'Conversion, the cross, and the love of Christ are the center of the three angels' messages'. Oosterwal did not hide his opinion about this shift; it is clear that it was important to him to emphasize it in strong terms: 'Apparently Seventh-day Adventist doctrines have now found their proper relationship to Christ, the center of all doctrine. Adventists have begun to rediscover that "the present truth presents Christ, not only humiliated and crucified, but risen and glorified. It holds up Christ as our example while upon earth, our advocate above and our approaching king in the world to come. It points to Christ as the only means of escape from eternal death, and to his second coming as the blessed hope of the people of God in all ages.'[62]

Oosterwal wrote and taught in strong terms that mission as proclamation is 'Christ centred saving good news' and 'involves salvation first for every person' and that Adventists should see the people of the world first and foremost as 'the object of God's love and God's own mission.' Consequently the burden of our message should be 'the mission and life of Jesus Christ'.[63]

The same approach is also found in reports by Finley. He describes the practical consequence of the church's cooperation with God and says this serves

---

Adventhírnök, 2 (1994), 3–5; Zoltán Mayor, 'Jól gondoljátok hát meg e naptól fogva az elmúltakat is…', *Adventhírnök*, 2 (1994), 8 (p. 8); H. N. Adventista Egyház, 'Állásfoglalás a H. N. Adventista Egyház megbízatársáról', *Adventhírnök*, 4 (1994), 2 (p. 2).

[62] See: Oosterwal, *Mission Possible*, pp. 32-4.

[63] Ibid., pp. 32-4.

to 'meet a variety of needs in the community'.[64] The official programme of the worldwide Adventist church from 1990-95, called 'Global Strategy', also emphasized that following Christ's example leads to a holistic approach in mission. Therefore the SDA church wants to meet the 'physical, mental, social, and spiritual needs' of men and women.[65] The wording is very similar to descriptions of Huzzey's approach to teaching Hungarian pastors back in 1986.[66]

Although advocacy of this approach can be found in several articles and publications, it was not the one determining the main content of Adventist proclamation; the majority of the publications and training courses focused on the unique content of the Adventist message. Seventh-day Adventists had come to believe that there is a message relevant to a particular time in a very special and historical situation. Each generation, it was felt, has a definite message to proclaim and a special responsibility to fulfil in the world. Adventists call this special message for a particular time the 'present truth'.[67] The present truth for the Seventh-day Adventist Church was mainly related to the eschatological urgency of the second coming of Jesus Christ and this was the main foundation and also the driving force of Adventist mission during the period of time under examination. The Biblical Research Institute of the SDA church expressed this through Wood's words: 'But unlike God's individual or corporate emissaries in the past, whose gospel message was of a general nature, the Seventh-day Adventist Church has been assigned the special mission of preaching the everlasting gospel in the context of the three-angels' message of Revelation 14. In the spectrum of both secular and sacred history, this is God's final message to the world. Carrying this message to every human being is the raison d'être of the church This message is not just another message among many good messages, it is the only message that meets man's needs on every level of experience. It is the only message that is absolutely relevant to the human predicament in the contemporary scene.'[68]

Both programmes of the General Conference of the SDA church setting the direction for mission in Hungary from 1985 to 1995 were influenced by this message. 'Harvest '90' 1985-90 and 'Global Strategy' 1990-95 focused mainly on the end-time message because of its perceived urgency: 'There is temporal time set to harvesting. It's the same with God's harvest. There is an immediacy about harvest. The priority needs to be set on reaping. All efforts need to be

---

[64] Mark Finley Harvest 90 – Administrative slogan or Compelling Biblical Motivation, HUC Archive (1985), Finley, p. 5.

[65] General Conference of SDA, Global Strategy of the Seventh-day Adventist Church, 1989, HUC Archive, 1–51 (14–36).

[66] See the comments by Huzzey in: László Hangyás, 'James Huzzey testvér látogatása', *Lelkésztájékoztató* (1986), 18–21.

[67] Oosterwal, *Mission Possible*, pp. 16–17.

[68] Wood, 'The role of the Seventh-day Adventist Church', p. 17.

concentrated on this task. Jesus' return will set an end to the reaping. People will be lost for eternity.'[69]

This message and the strong sense of responsibility that was felt created, in their turn, a powerful feeling of urgency and placed all levels of the church under pressure. Apparently many were convinced that they were living shortly before the end of the world and this seemed to be the last chance for them to warn the world and to save the lost. Revelation chapter 14 – presenting the 'three angels' message'[70] – was considered to be the foundation of the last warning message because it announces that the 'hour of the judgement' has come and that the history of the earth will soon end. The Hungarian Union Conference leaders took a stand and demonstrated their conviction about it with a firm vote: 'As in shown in our previous decisions, we still believe that our call is to proclaim the three angels' gospel (Revelation 14.6-12). [...] We are convinced that this message contains the gospel and that this gospel must be preached to all humans....'[71]

Adventists understood that their major task was to urge people to 'fear God' and accept the last warning message.[72] They believed that, according to Matthew 24.14, the proclamation of this last warning throughout the whole world will prepare and make possible 'that the end comes' through the second coming of Jesus Christ.[73] The administration sent out regular encouragement to motivate the church to participate in proclaiming this exhortation. The presidential message from the General Conference, published in 1987, set the tone for Adventist mission in the whole world, including Hungary: 'There must be no stumbling, delays, or retreats. There must be continuous and unrelenting advance. Events taking place in our world tell us that the Lord is holding back the winds so that the harvest and sealing can be completed. Jesus is coming soon and this compels us to press on with added vigour and soul-saving action.'[74]

---

[69] Mark Finley, Harvest 90 – Administrative slogan or Compelling Biblical Motivation, 1985, HUC Archive, p. 7.

[70] Revelation chapter 14 was the main biblical foundation of these programmes. See: the words of the General Conference president, Neal Wilson, in 'Globális Missziói Stratégia', *Adventhírnök*, 6-8 (1990), 8; the decision of the Hungarian Union Conference: Executive committee of the Hungarian Union Conference, 'Határozatok', *Lelkésztájékoztató*, 18 (1984); the decision of the Duna Conference: Duna Conference, 'A Dunamelléki Egyházterület Választokonferenciájának határozatai', *Adventhírnök*, 2 (1993), 9.

[71] Executive committee of the Hungarian Union Conference, 'Határozatok', Lelkésztájékoztató, 18 (1984), 108; see also later decisions: H. N. Adventista Egyház, 'Állásfoglalás a H. N. Adventista Egyház megbízatársáról', *Adventhírnök*, 4 (1994), 2; and an article by Taylor in the Hungarian church magazine: R.C. Taylor., 'Globális missziói eredmények', *Adventhírnök*, 2 (1995), 2.

[72] József Szilvási, 'Számvetés – toronyépítés előtt', *Adventhírnök*, 2 (1994), 3–5 (3).

[73] Jan Paulsen, 'Tegyünk valami rendkívülit Krisztusért 1990-ben', *Adventhírnök*, 1 (1990), 4–5 Paulsen, p. 4.

[74] Neal C Wilson, 'Special Message: President, General Conference', in *Half-Way Point of Harvest 90*, ed. by Carlos E. Aeschlimann (Washington D.C., 1987), Ministerial Association Bulletin Harvest 90, p. 2.

As part of the Global Strategy programme, the Global Mission programme was established within the church with the same purpose: to proclaim Christ and his Three Angels' Messages to every nation, kindred, tongue and people.[75] The Hungarian Union Conference joined this initiative by the General Conference and decided to set aside ten per cent of its tithe income to support the campaign. Adventists increased their efforts of proclaiming the 'present truth' because their interpretation of the development of world history seemed to support their eschatological views: 'Seventh-day Adventists are familiar with the signs of Jesus' coming. Every newspaper illustrates Matthew 24 and points to the nearness of His return.'[76]

A message by Robert Folkenberg, the next General Conference President, was also published in Hungary in 1994. He urged the church to ask questions: 'Why are we here? How could we reach people more effectively with the three angels' message?'[77]

The Secretary of the Hungarian Union also reminded the church: 'Our task is to educate people to fear God and glorify him through the everlasting gospel because the hour of his judgement has come, according to Revelation 14.7.'[78]

In addition to his statement and to the declaration by the leadership of the Hungarian Union in 1994 that the church has received a call to carry out 'the proclamation of the everlasting gospel to all people, based on Revelation 14.6-12', the leaders voted that a holistic approach to people's needs and the ministry of healing were also to be part of their strategy.[79]

At the end of the 1980s Hungarian pastors received prewritten sermons for use in their public evangelistic meetings. The most widely copied and circulated sermons were written by Finley. Many pastors were given copies of these sermons and preached them in different locations. Analysis of the content of the 22 sermons in the series reveals the following categories:

1. Topics addressing personal needs such as loneliness or hope of survival in difficult times: 3 sermons, 13%
2. Topics focusing on Christ, salvation and forgiveness: 3 sermons, 13%
3. Topics dealing with the origin of sin and focusing on the past: 2 sermons, 9%
4. Topics focusing on the law of God and the Sabbath: 4 Sermons, 18%

---

[75] Global Mission Objectives, 1990, HUC Archive Pécel, p.1.
[76] Michael Ryan, 'Into all the world: the meaning of Global Mission: The Seventh-day Adventist Church has launched the most ambitious plan in the history of missions. An introduction', *Ministry Magazine*, 11 (1992), 5- 7 (p. 6).
[77] Robert S. Folkenberg, 'Meghatározni a gyülekezet misszióját', *Adventhírnök*, 4 (1994), 2.
[78] József Szilvási, 'Számvetés – toronyépítés előtt', *Adventhírnök*, 2 (1994), 3–5.
[79] H. N. Adventista Egyház, 'Állásfoglalás a H. N. Adventista Egyház megbízatársáról', *Adventhírnök*, 4 (1994), 2.

5. Sermons with a strong emphasis on eschatology, explaining prophecy, the second coming of Christ, the Judgement and eternal life: 10 sermons, 45%.[80]

Many pastors gave archaeological presentations, illustrated by pictures of the Holy Land, in order to attract more people to the meetings.[81] Pastors also often used the 'Choose life' series of evangelistic material. These ready-made sermons encouraged them to conduct meetings by themselves, but without struggling to create the content for their meetings. The heavy dependency on help in conducting mission that Hungarian pastors displayed may have been the consequence of the previous decades. They relied a great deal on external support and it took a further decade before the growing demand for native sermons and content created by Hungarians was realized.[82] Because of the prewritten materials, the presentations seemed schematic and dissatisfying. The administration addressed this issue in 1994, when they complained in strong terms that evangelistic presentations had become routine and lifeless: 'We have to prepare new series capable of meeting the needs in Hungary. We have to lead the people's attention to repentance, acceptance of Christ and conversion.'[83]

In the same year the union leaders cast votes concerning the goal of mission and also arrived at a position about its content. They stated that the SDA church proclaims the everlasting gospel and aims to lead people to Jesus Christ as their personal Saviour. The leaders also declared that education plays an important role in mission, as well as direct evangelism. The focus was strongly directed towards supporting people in their needs, a holistic approach in ministry, healing the sick and caring for poor people. The leaders urged that these ministries must be given a prominent place in the mission of the church.[84]

A growing understanding of the needs of society can be observed in the publications of the church in Hungary and in the decisions made by its leadership. These answered an increasing desire for a shift from a truth-oriented approach to mission to a need-oriented approach. The church had experienced Hungarian reality and those who were at its head in the country urged that its mission should expand beyond proclamation-oriented evangelism, loaded heavily with eschatology. These voices were growing stronger in the early 1990s, but not strong enough to change the methods and content of evangelism. Due to a lack of different paradigms, Hungarian Adventists continued to rely

---

[80] The Hungarian translation of the printed sermons manuscripts,

[81] 'Tony Campbell előadás sorozat Zalaegerszegben', *Adventhírnök* (1991), 8; József Panek, 'Malcom Potts előadás sorozat' *Adventhírnök* (1991), 9; Árpád Szőllősi, 'Evangélizációs sorozat Nyíregyházán 1990. Február 3-17-ig', *Adventhírnök*, 3-5 (1990), 3.

[82] Interviews with pastors coming from abroad also mention the topics they usually addressed. See, for example,: József Panek, p. 9; p. 8; Szilvási (1991), p. 8.

[83] Szilvási refers in particular to the programme 'Choose life', József Szilvási, 'Számvetés – toronyépítés előtt', *Adventhírnök*, 2 (1994), 3–5.

[84] H. N. Adventista Egyház, 'Állásfoglalás a H. N. Adventista Egyház megbízatársáról', *Adventhírnök*, 4 (1994), 2.

heavily on influence from the West and on the official directions given by the worldwide church.

The General Conference repeatedly issued guidelines for conducting evangelism in 1994. The President emphasized three criteria for planning evangelism and for determining its content. Evangelism has to:

Be based on the teachings of the Bible,
Be gospel oriented and
Present our special message, the 'present truth'.[85]

What content is needed in order to reveal the 'present truth'? The same document listed key elements in detail: the mission commission of the church, the hour of the Judgement, worshipping the creator God, the law of God, the Sabbath, the 'great controversy', Christ's second coming and the gift of prophecy. The simplest approach seemed to be for Hungarian Adventists to deal with these topics biblically, by offering Revelations seminars. As union president, Szigeti stated that Hungarian Adventists had not yet discovered the real potential of offering Revelation seminars. 'The ministry of the foreign evangelists should encourage us to become active and start the ministry by ourselves.'[86]

What were seen as key elements of effective proclamation?

The suggested methods, principles and plans for Adventist mission in Hungary are the focus of this part of the chapter. What was taught among Adventists about the actions required to bring the message to the people?

Oosterwal's approach to mission also indicates his anthropological thinking.[87] He calles persistently for reassessment and for an upgrade of methods and ways of presenting Christ to the world so that Adventists can fulfil their mission as the denomination understands it. His book on mission was originally addressed to the American Adventist church and he stressed the importance of being culturally sensitive and relevant right at the beginning. He considered the changing environment, size, age, structure and culture of the church and listed six strong arguments aimed at forcing Adventists to reflect and readjust their way of doing mission in light of current challenges in every specific community or cultural context:

Mission involves personal commitment and 'it is accomplished only through individual men and women in whom Christ lives and works. [...] The Christian

---

[85] József Szilvási, 'Számvetés – toronyépítés előtt', *Adventhírnök*, 2 (1994), 3–5, p. 3.
[86] Szigeti (1989), p. 5. See also the decision of the Hungarian Union Conference to print 10,000 copies of Revelation seminar lessons in 1989: H. N. Adventist Egyház Unióbizottsága, *Jegyzőkönyv*, Protocol of the meeting (1989), p. 9. See also: József Szilvási, 'Aratás '90', *Lelkésztájékoztató* (1986), 353–54; David Currie, *Models of Christian Witness*, 1993 – TED Winter Meetings, HUC Archive Pécel, pp. 1–5.
[87] Dr Oosterwal holds advanced degrees in religious studies and also in anthropology.

who receives the legacy of mission and thinks that it will work of its own accord is mistaken.' Oosterwal emphasizes that the way to a relevant ministry lies in the personal commitment of each member, using the God-given abilities and talents for ministry.

Each generation of believers faces a different world. Today's generation faces challenges never seen before. Confusion arises 'about what to do first and how to spend the limited funds'. But since the object of our mission is the world we are living in, 'each generation must come to grips with that different world in which it lives. This may be the greatest challenge of mission today.'

God has a particular message to proclaim for each generation. Adventists call this message 'present truth'. 'The challenge of mission today is to find God's very special truth for our time and our world and then to accept it ourselves and proclaim it to others.'

The position of the Christian churches has changed throughout the world but Christian churches themselves have also experienced major changes. A new revival is needed in order to meet this new situation and its challenges.

The Seventh-day Adventist Church changes too with each generation. From a largely Western church, 'it suddenly has become a largely non-white and non-Western church with some 80 percent of its membership living outside North America.'

Many parts of the world have witnessed a 'sudden receptivity to the gospel, preparing thousands and thousands of people for membership.'[88]

Oosterwal's evaluation of past experiences of Adventist mission led him to the firm conclusion that new forms of mission must be developed, that new methods and new strategies are necessary and that the church should not just continue to practise the traditional way of doing mission: 'The danger of merely perpetuating certain established institutions and tested programs looms very large in our generation of continuous and rapid change. The challenge of mission today, then, is for the church to develop new forms and methods of mission that will stimulate and help implement its missionary role.'[89]

Oosterwal's interest in mission motivated him to draw lessons from past experiences in order to find the key elements of effective mission. This led him to carry out an analysis of the factors that usually make Adventist churches grow rapidly. He identified seven of these factors as most important. According to him, not all of them need to be present in every area all the time but 'there is usually a combination of these factors at work to cause the church to grow, and grow rapidly'.[90] These factors are:

1. A crisis situation that has been created through major changes in society

---

88 Oosterwal, *Mission Possible*, pp. 18-21.
89 Ibid., pp. 18-21.
90 Gottfried Oosterwal, "Servants for Christ the Adventist Church facing the '80s", ed. Robert E. Firth (Berrien Springs, MI: Andrews University Press, 1980) pp. 7–8.

2. A mobilized laity made up of people who understand their role in ministry

3. A message that is relevant and in harmony with the crisis situation

4. Holistic ministry recognizing the needs of people comprehensively. The message is integrated within a holistic process.

5. Local churches recognized as the basis of evangelism

6. Pastoral leadership that is able to motivate, coordinate and support church laity

7. Faith and commitment to the service of people and to mission activities.[91]

Oosterwal's enthusiasm for fulfilling the goals of Adventist mission is clearly observable in regard to the opportunities offered by the new technical resources of his day. He sees the combination of growing potential, resourcefulness, power and opportunity in his Christian generation as a unique opportunity to meet the challenges of an end-time urgency of a kind never seen before.[92]

An analysis of the recommendations for mission indicates that Adventists in the 1990s' wanted to be modern and open to new ways of doing mission in modern times. Certain principles and steps were strongly emphasized.

Diversity in ministry

One major principle to be given prominence in several publications from the period under consideration was diversity. Oosterwal warned against traditionalism and urged that certain programmes of a kind that had once stimulated the mission of the church should be relinquished because they were no longer effective to use. Besides this he called for relevance in each particular context because certain programmes and institutions, 'which in one area of the world greatly contribute to the success of mission do not perform that role in other areas. Promoting such institutions there would mean not only wasted money, effort and time but also disobedience to our great calling.'[93] He urged acknowledgement of diversity, as that is what makes Adventist mission culturally relevant and colourful. The Harvest '90 programme emphasized that the church 'needs unity but not uniformity. Different approaches and opinions are accepted'.[94] Finley was one of the main leaders of the 'Harvest '90' campaign and also requested diversity but the difference between Finley's approach and Oosterwal's is remarkable. While Oosterwal focused on context and called for relevance, to promote effectiveness in each particular context, Finley instead concentrated on the church and called for diversity in order to involve every kind of human being in the 'greatest' endeavour in mission: 'Diversity is needed to bring in this great harvest. Everyone has different talents and gifts from God. He/she shall use it for finishing God's plan in Harvest 90. All church members shall find out what gifts God gave them and in what area they can be most

---

[91] Oosterwal, "Servants for Christ", pp. 7-8.

[92] Oosterwal, *Mission Possible*, p. 21.

[93] Ibid., pp. 19–20.

[94] Mark Finley, *Harvest 90 – Administrative slogan or Compelling Biblical Motivation*, 1985, HUC Archive p. 4.

effective in helping to reach the lost. This is also the way Jesus worked. For him people were more important than the method.'[95]

Whereas Oosterwal talked about the different needs of society, Finley saw one main need: people 'outside of the church' were lost. According to him diversity was needed in order to design the message colourfully, appealing to more and more members of the public. The possibility of developing new methods and ways in which to conduct ministry had been made clear. However, analysis of the suggestions made by Finley and other church leaders concerning practical methods of conducting mission reveals contradictions among these statements and, possibly because of the strong feeling of urgency about accomplishing the vision, little attention was spent on developing new methods of evangelism in praxis. Instead the tendency was to maintain the continuation and further development of a limited number of existing methods, with few updates of a more technical nature. The use of tape recorders, slides and projectors brought changes to the technical aspects of the presentations and made them more attractive to many people.

All church members should be involved in ministry
Oosterwal strongly recommended the development of a lay mission programme. He had had two primary reasons, one theological and one practical. The theological reason was based on Ephesians Chapter 4. According to Oosterwal's interpretation of this Bible passage, the main responsibility of key leaders was: 'to nourish, equip, help, and sustain the community of believers in carrying out its mission. In other words, God has called the ministers and leaders to assist His people in carrying out the mission of the church, not vice versa, as is often the case.'[96]

The practical task, as Oosterwal saw it, was to develop and coordinate the many varying gifts held by those active in the church and to prepare them for use. In his writing about the subject, Oosterwal makes a clear distinction between the duties of ministers and those of laity in order to avoid confusion.

'Pastors have no right to ask others to do what God has entrusted in particular to them. And never can the minister perform the work that God has entrusted to the laity. Rather, he should recognize the specific role of the laity as God's representatives in the world and lay plans for training and coordination according to that role. But the discovery, training, and coordination of the manifold gifts are not merely the work of the minister. The whole church should be involved.'[97]

It is very clear from these statements that the emphasis of any good mission plan must, according to Oosterwal, be on the mobilization of the whole church, using all kinds of different talents and gifts in order to accomplish its task. These

---

[95] Finley, *Harvest 90*, pp. 5–7.
[96] Oosterwal, *Mission Possible*, p. 64.
[97] Ibid., p. 64, p. 118.

steps would have required the complete reorganization of the life and structure of the denomination.

Building interpersonal relationships and maintaining a long-term process of evangelism

Building interpersonal relationships as the basis of public evangelism was strongly emphasized by leaders.[98] The instruction was to maintain friendships unselfishly, to display empathy, to care about people and to invite friends to the 'harvesting events'. Finley presented a lecture on evangelism in Miskolc in 1987 describing. He based his approach on Psalm 126.5-6, stating that evangelism requires three steps: going to people unselfishly with love, crying with and praying for others because they matter to us, and harvesting through evangelistic meetings.[99] This strategy was also built into the 'Harvest 90' programme and putting it into practice was considered the preparation phase: 'Every harvest is preceded by a period of sowing. A harvest does not occur automatically at the end of the growing season. There is a process or cycle that must be followed to ensure an abundant crop. [...] Harvest 90 speaks of a process of sowing and reaping. It calls for church members to develop a network of interpersonal relationships among friends, neighbours, and working associates. It challenges Seventh-day Adventist Churches throughout the world to become caring centres of love and redemption for their community.'[100]

Finley also called this 'Friendship evangelism'.[101] The focus was still on public meetings but church members were requested to contact, to care for and to maintain the friendship of new people.

Need- oriented ministry

From 1990 onwards a slight shift can be recognized in the missionary approach used in Hungary. This change brought evangelistic methods more into harmony with Oosterwal's need-oriented approach to the community. An increasing emphasis on the health ministry can be observed in the church magazine and also in the plans of the denomination.[102] As early as in 1988 Szigeti reported to the division that 'in recent months new ways were opened up before us so we can take part in the health and social programmes of the community.'[103] He

---

[98] Jenő Szigeti, 'A Lélek esője már hullik', *Adventhírnök*, 3-5 (1990), 1.

[99] Mark Finley, 'Hogyan lehetünk eredményes evangélisták?', *Lelkésztájékoztató* (1988), 67–72; Booth, pp. 392–400; David Currie (1993), pp. 1–5.

[100] Finley, *Harvest 90*, p. 2.

[101] Booth, *Evangélizáció az egyházban*, pp 392–400.

[102] In the period of time examined here 45 articles were printed in the church magazine about health-related topics such as health seminars, health mission, cancer, diet and health camps. See the statement by the health department of the church: Szigeti, Jenő, Report of the Hungarian Union Conference for the TED winter meetings – 1990 (1990); Jenő Szigeti, 'Az 'Aratás '90' a Magyar Unióban', Lelkésztájékoztató (1990), 136–38;

[103] Jenő Szigeti, Report on the work of the Hungarian Union Conference December 1987 – April 1988 (1988).

mentioned smoking cessation programmes, weight-control courses, and connection with and support of anti-drug and anti-alcohol organizations. The importance of healing was also discussed.[104]

Small-group evangelism
Members were encouraged to invite friends into their homes and to discover the opportunity of studying the Bible together at home with their friends.[105] Szőllősi also presented advice about how such Bible-study groups could be led by church members in their homes. The suggested approach was not a holistic one, involving nurturing growing fellowship and training members for the implementation of the need-oriented approach. The main focus of the small groups was on Bible study and it emphasized a cognitive learning process. Beyond a few examples, further data cannot be found about the possible expansion of small-group ministry among Hungarian Adventists. The missing data concerning further activities in small groups may indicate that the mobilization of Adventist church members was one that failed, in terms of autonomous mission activities in small groups.

Considering regular church programmes as evangelistic opportunities
Various church activities were also promoted as opportunities for mission. The Bible study period each Sabbath morning, referred to as 'Sabbath school', was considered the right place for leading conversation in small groups with friends.[106] Sermons and other teaching activities during the regular worship services were also presented as possible opportunities for evangelism.[107] In addition, youth programmes and events conducted by the church received priority among the various missionary activities of the church.[108]

Book and media evangelism
Adventists placed heavy emphasis on literature evangelism.[109] Leaders placed particular emphasis on its promotion. The door-to-door visitation was considered as the true method of bringing Adventist literature to non-Adventists.

---

[104] H. N. Adventista Egyház, 'Állásfoglalás a H. N. Adventista Egyház megbízatársáról', *Adventhírnök*, 4 (1994), 2; Jenő Szigeti, 'Jelentés a Magyar Unió 1992. évi tervkészítő üléséről: Vajon elérjük-e az el nem értet?', *Adventhírnök*, 6 (1992), 5–6.

[105] Booth, 'Evangélizáció az egyházban', pp. 392–400; Árpád Szőllősi, 'Országos lelkészértekezlet Boglárlellén', *Lelkésztájékoztató*, 4 (1988), 208.

[106] Booth, 'Evangélizáció az egyházban', pp 392–400.

[107] 'Állásfoglalás a H. N. Adventista Egyház megbízatársáról', *Adventhírnök*, 4 (1994), 2.

[108] Booth, 'Evangélizáció az egyházban', pp. 392–400; David Currie, Models of Christian Witness, 1993 – TED Winter Meetings, pp. 1–5.

[109] See for example: Executive committee of the Hungarian Union Conference, Report on the Work of the Hungarian Union (1989); Sándor Ócsai, 'Tiszavidéki Egyházterület Elnöki Beszámolója az 1987-1990 konferenciai időszak munkájáról', *Adventhírnök*, 9-12 (1990), 3–6; Javaslat a könyvevangelista munka megszervezésére, HUC Archive, 13; Jenő Szigeti, Report of the Hungarian Union Conference (1989), p. 2; 'Vakok is olvashatják a Jézushoz

Also a growing interest in television and radio programmes as possible channels of proclamation is recognizable in relation to the years under analysis.[110]

Public evangelism

The most widely promoted method of conducting mission was public evangelism.[111] The call of the President was clear: 'Prestigious presentations are needed.'[112] Some other activities were required in order to make public meetings more effective. Public evangelism is aimed at leading people to making decisions. For this purpose several training courses were organized for pastors and publications were printed about how to help people to make decisions for Jesus Christ and for baptism.[113]

An analysis of the job description of pastors in the SDA church in Hungary shows that the expectations of the leaders regarding pastoral ministry were mainly based on the traditional role of the pastors in the local congregations, without real consideration of the key elements of effective ministry seen in the publications and teaching programmes and the goals set for church activities. Job description of pastors was in 1988: responsible for worship services, offering Bible studies as preparation for baptism, supporting the departmental work in the church, administration, visitation of members – once a quarter,education regularly.[114] Oosterwal's suggestions and recommendations were obviously not taken into account in the pastors' job description.

Adventists' Views about Integration and Fellowship as Part of Their Mission

Observations

The message of Jesus was fundamentally oriented towards the coming kingdom of God and thereby strongly eschatological, but throughout his life, and in the way he related to people, he also clearly and continuously emphasized the importance of fellowship. Becker considers fellowship to have been Jesus'

---

vezető utat', *Adventhírnök* (1993), 12 (p. 12); Duna Conference, 'A Dunamelléki Egyházterület Választokonferenciájának határozatai', *Adventhírnök*, 2 (1993), p. 8.

[110] Jenő Szigeti, 'A Lélek esője már hullik', *Adventhírnök*, 3-5 (1990), p. 1.

[111] See: Jenő Szigeti, 'Hogyan lehet misszió munkára serkenteni a gyülekezetet?', *Lelkésztájékoztató*, 2 (1988), 122–28; Booth, Evangélizáció az egyházban, pp. 392–400, H. N. Adventista Egyház, 'Állásfoglalás a H. N. Adventista Egyház megbízatársáról', Adventhírnök, 4 (1994), 2.

[112] Jenő Szigeti, 'A Lélek esője már hullik', *Adventhírnök*, 3-5 (1990), p. 1.

[113] László Hangyás, 'Az evangélista felelőssége a döntsére hívásban', *Lelkésztájékoztató* (1986), 328–30.

[114] See in: Hetednapi Adventista Egyház, Job description of pastors, 6 May 1988, Seventh-day Adventist – HUC Historical Archive, HNAE 4314, 2.

second major method for communicating the gospel. Jesus established fellowship with people, regardless of their social status or interest in his teachings and gave them the opportunity to be admitted into the kingdom of God through table-fellowship with the Master.[115]

Becker emphasizes that, in His eschatological message, Jesus not only presented God's intervention at the end of time in order to alleviate human needs but also offered the 'continuous providential care of the creator that enables his creature to live'.[116] When Jesus sat in the company of all kinds of people, listening to their needs, healing the sick and offering genuine fellowship, regardless of the social status of those people, 'He made their concerns God's concerns. He introduced into their drab lives the excitement of the coming Kingdom of God.'[117] The fellowship with Jesus, and His participation in the table-fellowship demonstrated in the present what they hoped for in the future.

Evidence in Adventist teachings of emphasis on maintaining fellowship as a significant method for the communication of the gospel

A search covering international and national Adventist publications in the period of ten years under examination has shown that there were voices calling for more attention to be given to fellowship and to more holistic ministry. Nancy Vyhmesiter published an article on this subject in *Ministry* magazine (read worldwide by Adventist pastors), urging that mission must include proclamation, service and fellowship. 'Mission must meet the needs of human beings: whole mission to whole persons.'[118] It is also notable that the president of the Trans-European Division, Jan Paulsen, stated in an article that was translated into Hungarian: 'We are bound together.' He urged that more attention should be given to fellowship and unity.[119]

Oosterwal challenged the church in similar terms, arguing; '[The] Christian church cannot find its goals merely in the rescuing of individual souls and the planting of churches. Surely, God's mission is always to seek and to save what is lost (Luke 19:10), but the kingdom of God is not identical with the sum of converts. It embraces much more than individual acts of salvation.'[120]

He called for true signs of God's mission activity. The world is heavily overburdened by conflicts and the church has a special task in God's mission because Christ has enlisted the church in His mission of reconciliation.[121]

---

[115] Becker, *Jesus of Nazareth*, p. 157.

[116] Ibid., p. 156.

[117] Ibid., pp. 168–69.

[118] Nancy Vyhmeister, 'Why world mission?: What is the mission of the Seveth-day Adventist Church? Must the mission be worldwide? And if so, why?', *Ministry Magazine*, 8 (1990), 8–10 (p. 8).

[119] Jan Paulsen, 'Egymashoz vagyunk kötve', *Adventhírnök*, 1 (1991), 4–5.

[120] Oosterwal, *Mission Possible*, p. 71.

[121] Oosterwal, *Mission Possible*, p. 77.

Oosterwal called it 'the very essence of mission and the true task of the missionary'.[122] He recalled Paul's example as a model for the ministry of the church and stated that 'Christ has restored man's relationships with God and with his fellows. Christ has called His church to serve as living evidence of the ensuing peace, that new relationship of peace and reconciliation, of wholeness, well-being, and righteousness.'[123] The church can present the evidences and benefits of this new reality and make it available to all, not only through proclamation and service but also through fellowship.[124]

Huzzey also emphasized, in his1986 training courses for mission, that witnessing involves maintaining friendship and being present in people's lives whenever they feel challenged by life's difficulties such as sickness, age problems or addictions. He based his teaching on the first letter of John, arguing strongly for fellowship with God and others as the exemplary Christian life. Adventist homes should be open to their friends, helping their young people to establish good relationships and offering support for the future.[125]

The history of the Adventist church in Hungary shows that young people in particular, put fellowship into practice more and more often. Young pastors started a fellowship called FILEK or 'young pastor's fellowship' and aimed at maintaining not only companionship and brotherhood but also unity in the ministry.[126] In 1995, another initiative was started for a similar purpose but it was open to all young people. The GYICSŐ scheme was organized for the youth of the church and was aimed at reducing the focus on programmes for the youth and on improving the relationship of young people with the church through regular gatherings.[127]

Maintaining this fellowship may have been a significant step to take in post-Communist society, since it was intended to meet current needs and aspirations of people interested in Christian activities and the Christian message. However, the traditional structure of the church and its mainly 'truth-oriented' approach kept the denomination too busy and very little attention could be spared for these innovative kinds of activities at the local church level.

The analysis of publications clearly shows that Adventists rarely directed their main focus beyond proclamation and towards fellowship and integration. Public evangelism occupied local congregations intensely and the expense involved was a huge challenge to the budgets of all the church bodies. The focus on public evangelistic meetings required the investment of all available resources and kept active church members fully occupied. This brought enthusiasm and a

---

[122] Ibid., p. 90.

[123] Ibid., p. 71.

[124] Ibid., p. 72.

[125] László Hangyás, 'James Huzzey testvér látogatása', *Lelkésztájékoztató* (1986), 18–21.

[126] László Restás, 'Mit varhatunk a FILEKtol?', *Adventhírnök* (1993), 6 (p. 6).

[127] Zoltán Szilvási, 'Kapcsolat vagy programközpontú ifjúság?', *Adventhírnök*, 1 (1995), 30 (p. 30).

feeling of revival to the congregations for a certain period of time. Interviews with church members show that old tensions were often laid aside and willingness to cooperate and to participate in more action-oriented integration grew. The intense combined efforts at various levels of Adventist church organization were usually motivated by common numerical goals formulated by administrators, without focusing on the development and maintenance of real fellowship of the kind Jesus encouraged.

Adventists later paid a high price for this rather one-sided proclamation oriented approach. When the public meetings were over and the newly baptized members were supposed to be integrated into the local congregations, the church had to face major and sometimes overwhelming challenges. Not only did the old, unsolved tensions and hidden problems appear again but also new and unexpected issues had to be faced. Adventist congregations had an elderly age structure with long and firmly established traditions in regard to church life and Christian behaviour. The newly baptized members, usually converted because of public meetings which had not offered them a long enough social learning process to allow them any depth of familiarity with the Adventist way of life, were much younger, on average, than the established members and often found it difficult to tolerate the traditions of the church. This led to tensions and disappointments and to people leaving Adventist congregations with strong feelings of dissatisfaction.

A research project carried out in 1999-2000 among those leaving the Adventist church in Hungary in the '80s and '90s delivered evidence about the situation.[128] Along with students attending the Hungarian Adventist Theological Seminary I tried to contact former church members. Their number was constantly growing, according to the available statistics. The actual number of those leaving the church was much higher but because their names remained on the church books for years, the statistics do not give a true picture of the fluctuation in membership. [129] Our attempt to contact the hundreds of ex-members was in vain because of the broken relationship between local congregations and those former church members.[130] We received back only 28 answers out of the hundreds of questionnaires we had sent out. The small number of replies made it impossible to form a representative picture of the reasons why people had left the Adventist church but gave a small insight into the problems. It appears that 78 per cent of those who filled in the questionnaires were female, with an average age of over 55. The majority of them had joined the church

---

[128] A quantitative analysis with some semi structured questions at the end.

[129] The statistical office of the General Conference provides an annual overview of the membership figures. See: http://www.adventiststatistics.org/view_Summary.asp? FieldInstID=2014096.

[130] Our personal visits to several former church members showed that they often felt hurt by some people in the church and experienced personal conflicts which caused their exit from the denomination.

because of its teaching and had become active church members. In their answers, the number one reason they gave for leaving the church was the tension between doctrine and lifestyle; expectations had been too high and the standards presented in the teaching had turned out to be very different from the actual situation among the members. There had been too many disappointments and social tensions.[131]

It was only rarely possible to find evidence that Adventist local churches practised this communication method of the gospel – the practice described by Becker as Table-Fellowship.

Adventists' Views about Healing and Ministry
According to the Needs Expressed by the Local People

Observations

Becker considers the miracles of Jesus to have been a vital aspect of His ministry. 'To no miracle worker in all of Antiquity were as many miracles attributed as there were to Jesus. All four gospels, including their sources, without exception bear witness to Jesus as a powerful miracle worker.'[132] His miracles were an expression of the closeness of the eschatological dominion of the kingdom of God. They happened not as the result of a miraculous elixir or something similar but as the consequence of the presence of the kingdom of God. Because Jesus presented a holistic concept of humanity, his actions also demonstrated the closeness of His kingdom in all areas of human life. Along with-proclamation of the gospel as the good news for human beings and with his participation in table-fellowship with hungry people, Jesus made it clear that his kingdom is at hand and that believing this makes a difference in the lives of those suffering because of sickness and death. These sad conditions do not have a place in his dominion and the reality of his kingdom does not tolerate their existence. 'To overcome them was a fundamental goal for Jesus as healer'[133] and he did it by performing miracles and signs. These healings provided a foretaste the closeness of the kingdom and also made His eschatological message relevant to the present. People could experience the knowledge that God's care is comprehensive and includes all areas of life.

---

[131] For more details see: Róbert Bicskei, 'Felmérés a HNA Egyházból kimaradt, illetve kizárt személyek okairól és körülményeiről' (seminary paper, Adventista Teológiai Főiskola, Pécel, 2000).

[132] Becker, *Jesus von Nazareth*, p. 221.

[133] Ibid., p. 221.

*Evidence in Adventist teaching of the emphasis on healing as a purpose of
Adventist mission to people in physical, social or spiritual need*

This research study has indicated that undeniably crucial needs among the population may have played an important role in the rising interest of people in religious matters in Hungarian society at the time of the regime change.

Certain approaches were present in Adventist publications and emphasized the relevance of healing ministry and need-oriented service, but this area may have been-the most neglected aspect of Hungarian Adventist mission. Although James Huzzey did not spend much time in Hungary, he recognized the need and preached that the 'gospel brings solution to the physical and spiritual needs of people.'[134] As early as 1988, Szigeti presented to the international leadership board the growing opportunity offered by social programmes and health services. Hungarians were indicating the potential in this area and expected support. Szigeti stated, 'We can take part in the health and social programmes of society' because, like other socialist countries, Hungary has 'experienced a far reaching change and it influences the work as well'.[135] In 1990 he called for more efforts related to social and health issues. 'There is a need for more social participation and better health education work.'[136] Szigeti also added. 'We need the insight to understand those people we have been sent to. They need our help, not our preaching.'[137]

As union president in Hungary, he was confronted with the growing needs among the populace and urged that 'the methods of mission should not be set by the church but by the human conditions of those we are ministering to'.[138]

The executive committee of the Trans-European division voted in 1993 that healing is one of the three methods by which the church seeks to achieve its mission: 'Affirming the biblical emphasis of the well-being of the whole person, we make the preservation of health and healing of the sick a priority and through our ministry to the poor and oppressed [we] co-operate with the Creator in His compassionate work of restoration.'[139]

The church has chosen to establish institutions for social and health ministry. A branch of the Adventist Development and Relief Agency (ADRA) was set up in Hungary and started national and international ministries for people in need.[140]

---

[134] László Hangyás, 'James Huzzey testvér látogatása', *Lelkésztájékoztató* (1986), 18–21.

[135] Jenő Szigeti, 'A félamatőrök országa: Elnöki beszámoló', *Adventhírnök*, 6 (1993), 6–7.

[136] Jenő Szigeti, 'A Lélek esője már hullik', *Adventhírnök*, 3-5 (1990), 1.

[137] Ibid., p. 2.

[138] Jenő Szigeti, Report on the work of the Hungarian Union Conference December 1987 – April 1988 (1988), p. 1.; Szigeti writes similarly also in: Jenő Szigeti, 'Hogyan lehet misszió munkára serkenteni a gyülekezetet?', *Lelkésztájékoztató*, 2 (1988), 122–28.

[139] Trans-European Division Executive Comittee, *Mission Statement of the Seventh-day Adventist Church*, Global Mission (1993), p. 1.

[140] Edit H. Erdélyiné, 'Az ADRA Hungary tevékenysége', *Adventhírnök*, 2 (1994), 11 (p. 11).

The Health Department of the church was organized and within several years it was able to demonstrate significant achievements in health-related issues.[141]

The union leadership declared in 1994 that the Hungarian Union Conference accepts the biblical emphasis on ministering to people holistically. This means working for prevention of diseases, supporting the sick in their healing processes, and ministering to the poor and oppressed.[142]

The institutions started their work but the local churches were mainly involved in public evangelism and failed to pay significant attention to the felt needs of people or to healing ministry. On the other hand, this research has shown that the main requirements in the community were related to lack of orientation, social integration, financial challenges, low self-esteem and other issues linked to mental health.

Conclusion

The present study has revealed that at the time of regime change various factors were influencing the Hungarian Adventist way of thinking. These factors not only suggested different priorities to be urgent but they often also contradicted each other. Before 1990 the official programme distributed by the General Conference of the SDA Church and the administrators working for the implementation of 'Harvest 90' and 'Global Strategy' dominated the church's evangelistic work in Hungary and played a key role in the publications and direction of Hungarian Adventist mission. The traditional 'truth-and-proclamation'-oriented approach, focusing to a large extent on the doctrines and duties of Adventists, overshadowed the more anthropological alignment of mission, which also concentrated strongly on the relevance of Adventist mission in the context of the changed circumstances in Hungary. Because the process of 'revision'[143] indicated by Oosterwal, Schantz and partly also by Huzzey had to give way to widespread proclamation, the needs related to Adventist mission which these men pointed out remained mainly without response:

1. the need to rediscover the true biblical concept of mission
2. to find out what inspires and motivates Adventists to take action
3. to discover relevant answers to questions posed by the radically changed situation in which Adventist live
4. to develop (through a revision process) new concepts for Adventist mission that may help local churches to become the true bases for evangelism
5. to describe the role of local pastors in this process.

---

[141] See the list of activities in: László Szigeti, 'Egészségnevelés, mértékletesség', *Adventhírnök*, 2 (1994), 9.

[142] H. N. Adventista Egyház, 'Állásfoglalás a H. N. Adventista Egyház megbízatársáról', *Adventhírnök*, 4 (1994), 2.

[143] Oosterwal, *Mission Possible*, p. 51.

However, because Hungarian Adventists failed to achieve goals set by their leaders, more and more voices were raised. People both required and suggested a new orientation for mission. The whole concept of doing mission was questioned and the desire to go back to the model of Jesus was expressed.[144] Some of the more courageous leaders announced openly that Hungarian Adventists should turn back towards the understanding of mission presented by Oosterwal and Schantz and some like-minded men. The union president, Szigeti, stated this unequivocally in 1990 '…people don't need explanations; they need real help…'.[145]

---

[144] Szőllősi raised the issue theoretically but did not present practical solutions in Árpád Szőllősi, 'Az evangélizálás', *Adventhírnök*, 2 (1990), 2 (p. 2).

[145] Jenő Szigeti, 'Ne félj, hanem szólj, ne hallgass!', *Adventhírnök*, 1 (1990), 2.

5. Adventist Mission Activities in the Years of Regime Change in Hungary, 1985-1995

Introduction

This chapter is focused on a description and analysis of the mission plans and activities of the Adventist church in Hungary from 1985 to 1995, the years just before and just after the regime change. The aim of this part of the study is to provide an understanding of the strategic plans and activities that characterized the life and work of the Seventh-day Adventist Church in Hungary in the period of time under examination, within the given regime-change context.

Fundamental Changes before 1984 Influencing Later Developments in the Mission Activities of the Hungarian Union

The study of the development of the historical situation has presented the various consequences religious people faced due to the lack of religious freedom in Hungary prior to the regime change. Because of the on-going political changes, freedom was constantly growing during the 1980s. Like other religious bodies, the Seventh-day Adventist Church was given more and more independence in the planning and designing of its life and mission.

The slowly changing aspect of the church-state relationship in the years at the end of the seventies and the beginning of the eighties also introduced modifications into the inner development of the denomination. Adventist leaders in Hungary increasingly gained the courage to discuss mission-related issues openly and to admit and address the failures of the past decades.[1] Back on 21 December 1975 the union leadership, along with the delegates of the union session declared: 'We regret that we have not used our opportunities adequately in the past. We have not found the appropriate form or locations for our ministry. We have not understood the paths and opportunities that God has opened up to us.'[2]

These changes in context and in attitude became fundamental to the process of restructuring the denomination's life and ministry. In the analysis of the

---

[1] In: *Boldog Élet*, 1 (1976), 5-6.
[2] Final report of HUC leaders at the session. 21 December 1975, HUC Archive, Pécel.

original documents it was not possible to discover an overall strategic plan for the transformation process that affected different departments and areas of church life, sometimes contrarily. The way in which the leadership initiated changes can often be regarded as a spontaneous reaction to felt needs within the denomination[3] and as the result of interaction with others serving in western countries. The transformations can be observed in four major areas of church life: the ministry and life of pastors and their families, the conscious development of community and fellowship within the denomination, the changed attitude towards and concepts of evangelism and the establishment of the health department of the Adventist church in Hungary.

The life and ministry of pastors and their families

A study of the reports about pastoral meetings and training programmes leads to the conclusion that, in the years before the end of Communism, the Communist authorities exerted less and less influence on the agenda for evangelistic meetings and for training sessions for pastors. At pastoral meetings, too, Adventists received increasing opportunities to address issues according to their own priorities and needs. Analysis of the reports of the conferences from 1981 to 1984 shows that education and training of pastors immediately became one of the most urgent and crucial issues conference leaders wanted to deal with.[4] A team of pastors formed a working group in order to provide background and direction for the further development of pastors. The denomination also turned attention to the retired pastors and spouses of pastors, providing fellowship, support and community for them. Conferences organized meetings for them and offered opportunities to discuss their concerns and relate to each other, talk about relevant issues and receive information from leaders. After careful consideration of the historical development of the denomination, this step appears all the more important. It was a way of establishing fellowship among pastors in order to create a healthy atmosphere among workers and among pastors' families.

Steps for developing community and fellowship within the denomination

Community development programmes within the denomination focused on different age groups and became essential features of the life of church members. Adventists started regular youth programmes. The introduction of youth camps was an especially significant step. Communists strictly forbade youth programmes but Adventists referred to the illegal youth camps of the Egervári group and argued that in order to avoid Adventist young people joining those

---

[3] The schisms within the denomination in the 60s and 70s played an especially important role and motivated leaders and delegates to take steps towards providing solutions to felt needs within the denomination in order to solve critical issues and avoid further tensions.

[4] This shift in the content of pastoral training is noticeable in the official reports in the Hungarian 'Ministry magazine' for pastors. See in *Lelkésztájékoztató*, 1 (1981) 11.; 2 (1981) 23.; 6 (1983) 18-19.; 2 (1984), 18-20.

camps, the church must organize some for its own youth.[5] From sixty to a hundred young people gathered for a week at a time in the camps for sport, Bible talks and prayer. The number of youth-related items recorded in the minutes of various committees indicates the major interest in youth that was taken by denominational leaders. [6] Besides the camp meetings, special church programmes were started in local churches for children and young people.[7] The youth were not the only people who received special attention; other age groups in the church were also catered to. Various programmes were organized for them regularly: mothers' day, a special day for elderly people, children's day and other such events. Extraordinary occasions for all age groups included the church music festivals at which several choirs joined together and offered their music programme at larger meetings. The music programmes became highlights from 1981 onwards and during the next two decades they remained among the most important gatherings.[8] Besides the major programmes the church also began a welfare department and a ministry for the sick, set up in 1978.[9] The social activities reached a high point when the denomination joined the international Red Cross in 1983 to participate in an interdenominational and international project to give assistance in Angola and Mozambique.[10]

Changes in the attitude and concepts of evangelism

The understanding and praxis of evangelism also underwent some major changes. As early as 21 December 1975 the delegates and leaders attending the union session voted in favour of the following resolution. Later published, it read: 'We are open to proclaim the Adventist message here and now to the people, the good news about the second coming of Christ.'[11] This voice proclaiming eschatological urgency set the mood for later years but development was slow and needed some major changes, especially in the education of new workers. Analysis of the protocols of the conference executive committees leads to the conclusion that the church suffered lack of coordination and integration of mission activities. The structure was not capable of giving enough support to

---

[5] See: Zoltán Rajki, A. H. N. Adventista Egyház története 1945 és 1989 között Magyarországon (Budapest: Advent, 2003), p. 158.

[6] See for example in the Tisza Conference: Pécel, Archive of HUC, 24 February 1981; 4 August 1981; 9 November 1983; in the South Conference: 25 January 1981; 15 June 1981; 28 January 1982.; *Lelkésztájékoztató* 1 (1981), 5.; 3 (1983), 13.; 4 (1983), 3.; 2 (1984), 20.

[7] These were weekend programmes for youth. One example was the Bible club in Érd. See: Rajki, *A.H. N.* Adventista Egyház, p. 159.

[8] See the presidential reports of the South and Tisza Conferences. Pécel, Archive of HUC, 1984.

[9] See the annual report of the Welfare Department of the Hungarian Union Conference. In: Pécel, Archive of HUC, 1978.

[10] Rajki, A H. N. Adventista Egyház, p. 158.

[11] The union session summarized the decisions in eight paragraphs and communicated them to the whole church in Hungary: *Boldog Élet*, 1 (1976), 5-6.

organizing the cooperation of local congregations in terms of lay pastors and evangelists. The conference leaders considered allocating lay evangelists and Bible workers to local churches in order to provide better continuity for their evangelism and counselling and to increase the involvement of congregations in the ministry.[12] This step shows that evangelism was mainly understood as a short-term and cognitive project; there was very little emphasis given to on-going personal relationships, nurture and care.

Two rapidly growing mission-oriented media ministries conducted by the denomination supported the mission activities. One of these was the publishing work – constantly producing not only hymnals and training manuals but also pamphlets for use in mission outreach.[13] The literature committee, organized in 1980, was in charge of this work. The other media ministry involved the Advent Studio, which was founded in 1982 and produced tapes of lectures, sermons and evangelistic presentations.[14] These developments, along with the planned changes in the organization of evangelistic programmes,[15] show that Hungarian Adventists still continued to conduct evangelism in the traditional style that dated back to 1947.

Conferences changed the focus from short-term evangelistic series, conducted mainly at weekends, to long-term evangelistic programmes involving church members and guests in a more extensive series of meetings presenting Adventist beliefs.

The direction in mission and evangelism had been set after WW II by the South-European Division, with emphasis on a merely cognitive way of carrying out evangelism. It followed the directives issued by the division and gave greatest weight to public lectures in order to achieve the highest possible results in 'soul winning'.[16]

Growing intensity of the activities of the health department

Through the activities of the health department Adventists could present their message more intensively not only in the church but also in the community. Besides participating in blood donation programmes and writing articles for

---

[12] Minutes of the executive committee of the Tisza Conference. September 1984. Minutes of the executive committee of the Central Conference. September 1984. Pécel, Archive of HUC.

[13] Reports about the work of the Literature Committee see in: *Lelkésztájékoztató*, 6 (1981), 7.; 2 (1983), 12.; 2 (1984), 24-25.; Pécel, Archive of HUC of SDA, Intézőbizottsági jegyzőkönyv [Protocol of the executive committee], Oct. 3. 1983.

[14] *Lelkésztájékoztató*, 2 (1984), 30.

[15] For more details, see the following protocols of the South-Hungarian Conference and Tisza Conference: Pécel, Archive of HUC of SDA, June 15, 1981.; January 28. 1982.; January 20. 1983.; March 17, 1982.; April 13, 1983.; *Lelkésztájékoztató*, 4 (1983), 55-56.

[16] See the official letter from the South-European Division to the churches. Budapest, Archive of Jenő Szigeti, 31 December 1947.

church magazines, Adventist health workers also conducted seminars and gave public lectures.[17]

Consideration of these historical developments in the denomination at the beginning of the 80s, the last decade of Communism, shows that these processes led inevitably to a critical period in the life of the recovering Adventist church. The growing interest of the denomination in mission activities and the desire to be more and more relevant in relation to the public challenged the underdeveloped structure, overloaded the inadequately trained membership and raised new issues Adventists were not yet prepared for.

The Expanding Mission under Growing Influence
from the West after 1984

The years from 1984 to 1986 established the agenda for the next decade for Adventists in Hungary. Several major factors can be recognized as change-supporting agents during this period of time.

Firstly, the decisions made at the union session in 1984 signalled the start of a new era.[18] Delegates representing all the local Adventist congregations in the entire country gathered in 1984 for a quinquennial meeting in order to conduct union business. Besides the election of new leaders one of the main topics at the conference was the mission of the Adventist church. Although the mission at the beginning of the 1980s had not achieved very much success,[19] those present at the session seemed to be aware of the changing political context and of growing freedom as a new opportunity for mission and they took serious steps towards consciously advancing the mission of the church. The session resolution presented and clearly emphasized the proclamation-oriented approach to mission. It stated that all people have to hear the message: 'Therefore, we commit ourselves [...] that all the local congregations should preach the whole gospel to the whole world.'[20]

The call to 'maintain a healthy missionary spirit' resulted in two practical duties to be undertaken and the session communicated them to the church leaders in clear terms. These duties also reveal the areas of mission-related needs of the denomination at that time. Delegates felt that too few people were involved in mission activities and that the number of lay missionaries had to be increased radically. The first part of the resolution declared that leaders ought to start

---

[17] Report of the Health Department, Pécel, Archive of HUC of SDA, 1984.;
Lelkésztájékoztató, 3 (1983), 12.

[18] See the decisions of the Executive committee of the Hungarian Union Conference in:
'Határozatok', *Lelkésztájékoztató*, 18 (1984).

[19] The number of visitors attending public lectures averaged 8-20. Rajki came to this conclusion by examining the reports of both conferences between 1981 and 1984. See: Rajki, A H. N. Adventista Egyház, p. 159.

[20] Report about the session, *Lelkésztájékoztató* (1984), 108.

searching for talented people: 'We call upon the executive committees of the conferences to invite into the ministry of the proclamation of the gospel spiritually and intellectually suitable men and women who are ready to work as a team.'[21]

The second section of the resolution revealed the dissatisfaction of the delegates with the level of missionary education. The session urged leaders: 'to develop plans for the training and further education of church members carrying out ministry in local churches. We want to put particular emphasis on holding regular courses for lay evangelists, teaching them the rules of modern witnessing.'[22]

These steps and the actions that followed pointed to a new era in Adventist missionary undertakings in Hungary. The process actually started years prior to the session with some courageous steps that were taken in the Adventist church.[23]

Secondly, as part of the worldwide church, the Hungarian Union planned its mission-based initiatives mainly under the international direction of the denomination's leaders. The General Conference began two major worldwide programmes determining the activities of the Seventh-day Adventist Church from 1985 to 1995. These had a specific focus on 'soul winning'. The programmes were designed, led and supported by the General Conference of the denomination and putting these campaigns into action involved all four levels of the church's organization – the central office of the General Conference, the local divisions of the General Conference, the unions and the conferences. The plans were created according to the principles voted by the delegates at the fifty-fourth General Conference session in 1985, to the effect that the role and function of Denominational Organizations Commission was to preserve the unity of Church and its message. The resolution of the session states: 'In contrast to most other churches, the Seventh-day Adventist Church is a world church. Its structure permits both a centralized structure (an authoritative and effective world headquarters with division offices) and a decentralized sharing of administrative and promotional responsibilities with many individuals and organizations on four constituency levels in all parts of the world.'[24]

Unity was considered to be a biblical mandate, as found in John 17.21 and 'basic to the nature of the Seventh-day Adventist Church'. The session also decided on steps by which such unity could be maintained. Three items agreed on by the delegates are especially important in relation to the mission activities of the denomination in the following decade:

---

[21] My own translation. 'Határozatok', *Lelkésztájékoztató*, 18 (1984), p. 112.

[22] 'Határozatok', p. 112.

[23] The denomination had put growing emphasis on the publishing activities and youth ministry, even prior to 1984.

[24] See: 'Session actions: Role and Function of Denominational Organizations – Commission report', *Adventist Review*, 7 (1985), 9, p. 9.

First, strong evangelistic proclamation of the Advent message in its time-of–the-end setting.[25] Second, development and strengthening of a universal ethos that will characterize Adventists as a unique, world-wide, evangelistic, moral, healthy, happy, caring family.[26] Third, strong, effective leadership with the ability to achieve the mission of the church.[27]

The massive eschatological emphasis, the accent on the universality and unity of the church and on the goal of establishing a strong leadership able to carry out the mission of the church led to the introduction of the most extensive worldwide programmes for mission in the Adventist church. The General Conference drew up and accepted a worldwide strategic plan for the next quinquennium, starting in 1985. Because the leaders focused merely on the quantitative growth through a continually growing number of baptisms, Neal C. Wilson called the campaign 'Harvest 90'. The second major programme was 'Global strategy' which started in 1990 and was designed to continue for the next five years.

Thirdly, in 1986 the General Conference restructured the European field and in this process Hungary was shifted from the Swiss-based Euro-Africa Division (EUD) to the Trans- European Division (TED) based in London, England. This change in the leadership was probably part of the process related to the desire to recover from past schisms the denomination had experienced in the 1960s and 1970s and to make a new start. The leadership of the EUD had been involved as mediator in the conflict-overloaded process of reconciliation, especially with the Egervári group which left the Adventist church in 1975. The leadership of the TED seemed to be neutral in terms of ongoing Adventist church politics in Hungary and also made the resources of the huge English-speaking segment of the denomination available for Hungarians to use. TED leaders stepped in immediately and exercised a growing influence on Hungarian Adventism.

A number of other national factors also played an important role in the further development of the denomination. In January 1985 all the Adventist youth leaders in Hungary gathered in order to draw up a plan for future regional and countrywide youth meetings, weeks of prayer and camp meetings. They also decided to join the initiative of the United Nations to consider 1985 as International Year of Youth, by putting strong emphasis on participation, development and peace. From 1985 on, the official publications of the Hungarian Adventist church have reported on a regular basis about local and national Adventist youth programmes, presenting the growing interest of the denomination in keeping, motivating and training youth in the church and for the ministry.

---

[25] Report I.A.3, p. 9.
[26] Ibid., p. 9.
[27] Ibid., p. 9.

'Harvest 90', an International Adventist Plan for Evangelism and Its Implementation in Hungary from 1985 to 1990

The motivation and the vision behind 'Harvest 90'

Harvest 90 did not only involve implementing of the principles voted in 1985. It was also the manifestation of the mission theology adhered to by the leaders of the denomination at that time. The selection of biblical motifs highlights these leaders' understanding of the mission of the church, the gospel commission and the practical steps necessary for the fulfilment of the mission. The steps were taken in the hope of leading millions of church members on every continent towards a successful harvest of souls.

Three major biblical motifs stand out in relation to the 'Harvest 90' programme. Their interpretation set the tone for the whole programme and also determined the message that would be a key feature of the denomination's missionary activities. All three motifs carry a strong eschatological urgency, indicating in no uncertain terms the expectations of the leadership towards the worldwide church.

The harvest motif

The Harvest 90 plan was named after a particular motif in the Bible that became the leading metaphor for the worldwide Adventist church during the following five years. The selection of this image reveals how leaders understood the historical setting of the denomination and the task that they must undertake. Keeping in mind the words of Jesus in John 4. 34, as he urged his disciples to discover that the harvest was ripe and their duty was to gather it in, Adventists felt that the time they were living in and the missionary task they had been given are well described in this message of Jesus. These words of Jesus are connected to his experience with the Samaritan woman at Jacob's well. Her sudden conversion and enthusiasm convinced her whole village that Jesus does not only have life-changing power but that He is also the expected Messiah and Saviour. As a consequence of her witness, the whole village came to believe in Jesus. When the surprised disciples saw this happening, the commission of Jesus was made clear to them and they understood that they would see many more occasions similar to the conversion of the Samaritan village because people are waiting for the gospel and ready to be 'harvested' for the kingdom of God.

According to the Adventist interpretation of world events and in view of the openness of many people towards their proclamation and to church programmes, the time that was starting in 1985 was the right time for the 'harvest' and a unique opportunity for mission had arrived. The General Conference' president stated: 'Events taking place in our world tell us that the Lord is holding the winds so that the harvest and sealing can be completed. Jesus is coming soon and this compels us to press on with added vigor and soul-saving action.'[28]

Many events taking place in the world were seen as eschatological fulfilment of the prophecies in the book of Revelation, signalling the very end of the world: 'The harvest concept speaks of finality, of end events, of final things. So, you have the whole concept of harvest tied in with the second coming of Christ and Adventist eschatology.'[29]

Mittleider expresses the consequences of the eschatological urgency and the required steps even more concretely: 'We live in the final years of earth's history. The challenge is to reach every person with the gospel to complete God's work. We need to dedicate ourselves more [passionately] to this cause.'[30]

The running-the-race motif
The selection of the second biblical motif underlines the leaders' expectations in regard to pastors and church members. The conviction appears to have been that there was no time to waste and that 'the maximum effort is needed to bring home the victory'.[31] The race motif was taken from Paul in I Corinthians 9.24. There was a sense that the church was running to reach the finishing line and this historical reference set uniquely high expectations in front of the church. This metaphor certainly communicated to the church members the need to intensify their efforts and to carry out their commission with endurance right up to the finishing line – the second coming of Jesus Christ. This also indicated that 'Harvest 90' was supposed to end with the return of Christ. The motif put the whole church under very heavy pressure because it suggested that individuals not participating fully in 'Harvest 90' risked failure.

The apostolic church motif
The choice of the last motif was intended to convince church members about the achievability of the high expectations and to promise success because the model of the apostolic church was considered to have been a successful one. The apostolic church motif served as an encouragement and as an example for all. If the church followed the original pattern, Harvest 90 could not fail: 'We will succeed in our world strategy for evangelism only as we realize that for us, as for the apostolic church, it is Pentecost or failure! Only the power of the Holy Spirit will enable us to plan wisely and to execute effectively. Only a Latter Rain outpouring will provide power to herald God's last day message to a secular,

---

[28] Neal C. Wilson, 'Special Message: President, General Conference', in *Half-Way Point of Harvest 90*, ed. by Carlos E. Aeschlimann (Washington, DC, 1987), Ministerial Association Bulletin Harvest 90, p. 2.

[29] Ray Dabrowski, *Harvest 90 – Interview with Mark Finley*, Mark Finley (1985), p. 2.

[30] Kenneth Mittleider and Carlos Aeschlimann, *Harvest 90 Affirmation* (Nairobi, Kenya, 1988), p. 1.

[31] Carlos E. Aeschlimann, *Harvest 90 Victory Special Edition*, Ministerial Association Bulletin Harvest 90 Number 11 (Washington, DC, 1988), p. 5.

materialistic, heathen, or indifferent Christian world. There is no succeeding in our world strategy of evangelism without a repetition of Pentecost.'[32]

According to Aeschlimann, the success of the work of the church depends on the work of the Holy Spirit and His special ministry at the 'end of the times' but it also places heavy responsibility on the shoulders of church leaders and members. If they want to finish the 'Lord's work', they need to live, work and believe like the members of the apostolic church. The example of the apostolic church is the model everyone must follow. 'Harvest 90 strategy for world gospel conquest must include the same experience that came to the apostolic church.'[33]

Vision and numerical growth

Harvest 90 was created with the intention that it would involve all levels of the international body of the church in one action, presenting and experiencing unity and effectiveness. This goal required a motivating vision that could be understood by different cultures, groups and people. The vision was designed for each of these groups according to their abilities and possible contributions. The unifying elements of the vision were the urgency of eschatological reality, the possibility of something great that united effort can accomplish and the impact of these factors on the life and development of the Adventist church.

The GC president put strong emphasis on eschatological urgency in 1987 and interpreted the events of the world as signs that the second coming of the Lord was imminent. The major events and political changes taking place in Central East Europe supported this feeling and church members in this part of the world tended to agree with the president. Wilson stated: 'There must be no stumbling, delays, or retreats. There must be continuous and unrelenting advance. Events taking place in our world tell us that the Lord is holding the winds so that the harvest and sealing can be completed. Jesus is coming soon and this compels us to press on with added vigor and soul-saving action.'[34]

The programme was understood as 'a milestone toward a finished work'.[35] Behind this expression was the conviction that Jesus is coming soon and that the major task of the church is to prepare church members first to meet Jesus and then to prepare those who listen to the witness of the church members. The vision and eagerness of the leaders are obvious in the statement, 'May our motto be: Everyone a conqueror in the name of Jesus and by the power of the Holy Spirit.'[36]

---

[32] Aeschlimann, WorldWide Evangelistic Campaign, p. 6.

[33] Ibid., p. 6.

[34] Neal C.Wilson, 'Special Message: President, General Conference', in *Half-Way Point of Harvest 90*, ed. by Carlos E. Aeschlimann (Washington DC, 1987), Ministerial Association Bulletin Harvest 90, p.2.

[35] General Conference, A Bold Plan to Culminate Harvest 90: An Interview with Carlos Aeschlimann, Coordinator of Harvest 90 (1988), pp. 7–8.

[36] A Bold Plan to Culminate Harvest 90, pp. 7-8.

The action taken at Annual Council to implement 'Harvest 90' also included quantitative goals and concrete numbers. 'This gigantic global program of total and permanent evangelism would use all the forces of the church in order to obtain the greatest harvest of souls in the history of the Adventist Church.'[37]

The plan was to double the number of accessions[38] and to extend Adventist mission to all towns, houses and people: 'Town by town until the last town. House by house until the last house. Person by person until the last person.'[39]

For many ministers, 'Harvest 90' became more than just a series of tasks to be dealt with at work. Strong emotions are apparent in many of the statements associated with the campaign. The way in which administrators and pastors talked about it expressed their enthusiasm and firm belief in the goals and themes of 'Harvest 90'. This is especially obvious in statements by leaders from countries and areas of the world where the culture encourages the use of quite emotional language: 'It is harvest time. The work is to be finished in a blaze of glory and power that will astonish the world. God's ministers and people will become a flame of fire for him.'[40]

The Harvest 90 vision for pastors
The programme included visions for different levels of the church and its workers. The vision of ministry for pastors was set accordingly. The pastor was 'to be a dynamic leader of evangelism in his district or church.'[41] The General Conference leadership's vision for pastors was expressed by Aeschlimann: 'Each pastor is the leader and example in evangelization, constantly promoting the winning of souls and involving the largest number possible of lay persons.'[42] A wise pastor sees 'his congregation as a school of people waiting to be inspired, trained, and organized for service – an evangelistic team waiting for direction'.[43] The sharp focus on achievements in the words of the coordinator of Harvest 90 reflects the mindset leaders maintained at that time. While they focused on 'victory', they had little time or opportunity to pay attention to the diverse needs, different cultural settings and local contexts people live in around the world. For the accomplishment of Harvest 90 they felt that they simply needed everyone. 'We are eager for all to reach the Harvest 90 victory. We encourage you to outline daring plans so your local field can have an extraordinary victory.

---

[37] Ibid., p. 3.

[38] Ray Dabrowski, *Harvest 90 – Interview with Mark Finley*, 1985, HUC Archive, p. 1.

[39] Carlos E Aeschlimann, *The Inter-America Division reached One Million Church Members June 1987*, Ministerial Association Bulletin Harvest 90 Number 7 (Washington DC, 1987), p. 5.

[40] 'A Bold Plan to Culminate Harvest 90', pp. 7–8.

[41] Ibid., p. 5.

[42] Carlos E., Aeschlimann, 'Harvest 90's First Anniversary', Ministerial Association Bulletin Harvest 90 Number 3 (Washington, DC, 1986), p. 8.

[43] Carlos E. Aeschlimann, Inter-America and its passion for Evangelism: Public Evangelism, Ministerial Association Bulletin Harvest 90 Number 10 (Washington DC, 1988), p. 5.

Challenge everyone to launch a total evangelistic offensive. With Christ, the victory is sure!'[44]

The Harvest 90 vision for local congregations

Wilson's vision, as part of Harvest 90, was for the local churches to see that 'every local field and every church of the world field will implement a permanent program of evangelism and harvest'.[45] The perception was that the involvement in Harvest 90 would change the life of the church completely and make it to be 'a center of evangelism and the winning of souls, through a continuous program of evangelism with the participation of all its members.'[46] All available forces had the responsibility to support Harvest 90[47] and this should lead to the fulfilment of the 'dream', as Aeschlimann described it, of 'every local field in the world reaching its harvest 90 baptismal goal by the power of the holy spirit.'[48]

Harvest 90 vision for church members

The Harvest 90 statement was created in order to inform, motivate and challenge all church members and to show them ways of active participation in the programme. Two major aspects of the vision for laity, as presented in the statement, are important to note. First, personal qualification was a precondition for participation and success. This qualifying factor was seen as fulfilment of the expectation that men and women should be in 'right relation with God – themselves prepared to meet Jesus. The messenger must be what he desires his hearers to become.'[49] The three main biblical motifs of Harvest 90 indicated what 'right relation with God' and being 'prepared to meet Jesus' meant. All of them demanded that church members should accept eschatological urgency, focusing on the second coming of Jesus Christ, and, in accordingly, maintaining a lifestyle that led to the second precondition of success, total participation by every church member. The goal was the 'total involvement of the church membership in evangelization and in pastoral and administrative activities.'[50]

The numerical goals of the Adventist church for Harvest 90

The study of the General Conference plans for mission reveals that numerical goals played a very important role in all areas of Harvest 90 project. At the beginning leaders had to prove the legitimacy of numeric goals because some of those involved in the evangelistic campaign were against setting such goals. The communication department of the General Conference published an interview with Mark Finley, one of the main leaders of Harvest 90, which contains his statement on the legitimacy of numerical goal-setting. His answer makes it

---

[44] Ibid., p. 5.
[45] 'A Bold Plan to Culminate Harvest 90', p. 4.
[46] Aeschlimann, 'Inter-America and its passion', p. 8.
[47] 'A Bold Plan to Culminate Harvest 90', p. 3.
[48] Aeschlimann, 'Inter-America and its passion', p. 24.
[49] Ibid., p. 5.
[50] Aeschlimann, 'Harvest 90's First Anniversary', p. 9.

obvious that the General Conference works with clear and measurable expectations: 'Numbers merely represent people if they are rightly understood. Some people look at numbers and almost have a defeatist attitude. [...] Numbers of baptisms are merely indicators of people redeemed for Christ, and if God is hungry for a harvest, if God desires that all men and women [should] be saved and come to a knowledge of the truth, it would seem to me that God wants large numbers of people ready. [...] I think that numerical goals are significant statements of faith of what we believe God can accomplish, and is going to accomplish.'[51]

Statements by other leaders indicate that these numerical goals were set very high in all areas of church life and represented a challenge to the whole church body.

Further statements by Finley show the unachievably high expectations held by leaders in terms of numerical planning. In an American context the words might sound different but for Europeans they create very high pressure: 'All genuine, worthwhile goals are born in the secret place of prayer. All valuable goals are measurable. All worthwhile goals are realistic and achievable. All worthwhile goals must be owned or shared by the body whose goals they are. To achieve worthwhile goals one must be willing to sacrifice.'[52]

Neal C. Wilson, the president of the General Conference, focused on the possible results too, but his statement also reveals his concern about the essence of Christian life, the personal relationship with Christ: 'Now that we are at the midway point of this gigantic outreach program, I challenge you to continue on with courage and even more enthusiasm. From here on, Harvest 90 should be more productive in terms of our personal relationship with Christ and each other. We should reap the benefits of seed sowing and planning, and there should be accelerated redemptive action. The results should be greater!'[53]

In their publications and speeches leaders presented overwhelming optimism and the conviction that the time had come to reach such idealistic goals. This study has not found any clear explanation as to why leaders considered the years 1985-1990 to be ideal for such a plan. What is clear is that, in their efforts to realize their plans, they used emotionally overloaded language to convince people and to build upon the trust church members placed in their leaders. 'The possibilities are excellent; however, time is short. Therefore, it is necessary to involve the entire church in order to produce a great evangelistic explosion. Now

---

[51] Dabrowski, 'Harvest 90', p 4.

[52] Mark Finley, 'Goals: Man-made or God inspired?', in Finley, Mark, 'Goals: Man-made or God inspired?: Sharing ideas and methods', in *Harvest 90's First Anniversary*, ed. by Carlos E. Aeschlimann (Washington D.C.: GC, 1986), Ministerial Association Bulletin Harvest 90, p. 10.

[53] Neal C Wilson, 'Special Message', p. 2.

is the time to accelerate our efforts to the maximum. [...] Now is the time to launch a total evangelistic offensive.'[54]

The expressions used to describe expectations give the impression that leaders try to achieve the highest possible results by emphasizing eschatological urgency, just as in the days of Miller at the beginning of the Advent movement:

'Make definite plans to have the best year in baptisms in the history of the church.'[55] '[Maintain] the goal of achieving an unprecedented harvest of souls [...]'[56] 'Launch a gigantic campaign of recruitment and training of workers and laity for the final stage of Harvest 90. Prepare hundreds of thousands of interested persons ready to be harvested during the last part of Harvest 90.'[57] 'A time to lift our vision, a time for greater exploits for God, a time for an unprecedented evangelistic emphasis throughout our division. A time under God's blessing to double our results.'[58] 'To gain the final victory, it is necessary to accelerate evangelistic activities to the maximum. Soul winning must be a priority for administrators, departmental leaders, pastors, and churches. The baptismal results should drastically increase.'[59]

The words 'gaining the final victory' indicate an eschatological urgency without explanation the real meaning in any detail. Some people might receive the impression that with the end of the quinquennium in 1990 the end of the world might also be expected. Besides this, the fulfilment of the eschatological expectation seemed to depend on the efforts and achievements of church workers, who were expected to work at maximum capacity. How long this kind of impetus could last was not clear but nobody can work at 'full steam' forever. The language used in drawing up plan probably increased pressure on church members significantly.

Harvest 90 set numerical goals for local fields, churches, pastors, laity, families and homes. At the beginning of the five-year term these goals must have seemed somewhat idealistic but one or two years later, in some areas, they began to look more and more realistic.

Local fields were challenged to create an 'aggressive plan of permanent and total evangelism'[60] and to train 20 per cent of church members to be soul winners and to organize a big evangelistic campaign in the largest city in that area.[61]

Local congregations were called upon to become centres of permanent evangelism and to 'make definite plans to achieve the best year in baptism in the

---

[54] 'A Bold Plan to Culminate Harvest 90', p. 2.

[55] Ibid., p. 2.

[56] Ibid., p. 4.

[57] Carlos E. Aeschlimann, *Harvest 90 Victory Special Edition*, Ministerial Association Bulletin Harvest 90 Number 11 (Washington DC, 1988), p. 7.

[58] Mark Finley, 'Soul winning experiences: Together with God in Reaping' (Third quarter, 1985), p. 5

[59] Carlos E.Aeschlimann, *Harvest 90*, p. 4.

[60] 'A Bold Plan to Culminate Harvest 90', pp. 3–4.

[61] Ibid., pp. 3–4.

history of the church.'[62] This meant total lay involvement as indicated in the following plan for division of labour:

'33% helping in evangelism and soul-winning;
33% helping to integrate the newly converted members;
33% helping with pastoral and administrative activities.'[63]

The expected result was that 'each church should hold monthly baptisms, make a call for decisions at each ceremony'.[64] The yearly goal for Harvest 90 baptisms for each division was set as follows:

'First year: 14% of total anticipated baptisms
Second year: 17% of the total
Third year: 20% of the total
Fourth year: 23% of the total
Fifth year: 26% of the total'[65]

Leaders recommended that every pastor should participate actively in evangelism.[66] Each pastor's task was to train at least 20% of church members to win souls. The rest should be trained in general missionary activities. Pastors were supposed to conduct at least two evangelistic events.[67] The goal for the whole Adventist church, in numerical terms, was to train a million lay people for direct soul winning annually.[68] According to the plan, each Adventist family should win one person for Christ and twenty-five per cent of church members' homes were supposed to become centres of evangelism. [69]

Harvest 90 was a plan for the quinquennium 1985-1990. In order to keep the motivation alive, subordinate targets for each year were established by the GC. For 1988 the subordinate theme was called 'Conquest Evangelism'. Every church was meant to organize a new congregation to double the possible results. The last year of Harvest 90 was dedicated specifically to decision-making evangelism, the aim being that by the end of the quinquennium every division's faith goals for baptism would have been reached. The plan for 1988 – 'Conquest Evangelism', reads as follows:

Penetration: enter and conquer new territories

---

[62] 'A Bold Plan to Culminate Harvest 90', pp. 3–4.

[63] Carlos E. Aeschlimann, *Harvest 90's First Anniversary*, Ministerial Association Bulletin Harvest 90 Number 3 (Washington, DC, 1986), p. 9.

[64] 'A Bold Plan to Culminate', p. 7.

[65] Kenneth Mittleider, and Carlos E. Aeschlimann, *'Harvest 90' Affirmation* (Nairobi, Kenya, 1988), p. 4.

[66] 'A Bold Plan to Culminate Harvest 90', pp. 3–4.

[67] Ibid., pp. 3–4.

[68] Ibid., pp. 3–4.

[69] Ibid., pp. 3–4.

Multiplication: 'mobilization of half a million laymen winning one soul each for Christ'
Division: 'Every church to form a new church'
Hold monthly baptisms, make call
Maintain 'permanent Evangelistic Training Program' for lay members
Maintain 'permanent program for consolidation of new converts'
Increase attendance at church meetings.[70]

Looking more closely at these special objectives, the language of superlatives is immediately obvious. 'Total participation' is the key phrase, though it was almost impossible to reach. This type of plan places excessive demands on people and when there is failure there is also discouragement.

The following year (1989-90) was given the sub-theme 'Global Evangelism'. The goal of this campaign was that at least twenty per cent of members should participate actively in soul winning Leaders 'set a faith goal of baptizing 2,000 souls per day or 180,000 during the last 90 days of Harvest 90'. On the last Sabbath of the quinquennium, 26 May 1990, the goal of 100,000 baptisms in one day was supposed to be reached worldwide.[71] An additional plan for the divisions was that every church should establish a new local congregation.[72]

Suggested methods and objectives for Harvest 90

As for the Harvest 90 vision, the methods and appropriate materials were designed at the church's headquarters. The methods promoted for mission were mainly linked to public evangelism and similar cognitive learning processes. Finley stated that the secret of rapid growth is in the method modelled by Christ.[73] However, for Finley this largely meant the truth-oriented approach carried out by means of public presentations or lectures. Leaders promoted five main methods as the most successful evangelistic strategies: holding public meetings, conducting Revelation seminars, opening houses of hope, establishing new local congregations in new areas, and offering baptismal classes.

The following steps were proposed for the organization of public evangelistic meetings:

1. 'Planning phase.

---

[70] Carlos E. Aeschlimann, *WorldWide Evangelistic Campaign, July 1989-June 1990: Total Participation*, Ministerial Association Bulletin Harvest 90 Number 13 (Washington D.C., 1988)

[71] Mark Finley, Trans-European Division Harvest 90 Report: Winter Meetings, November 14.-17, 1989 (St Albans, England, 1989), pp. 1–2.

[72] Carlos E. Aeschlimann, *The Inter-America Division reached One Million Church Members June 1987*, Ministerial Association Bulletin Harvest 90 Number 7 (Washington, DC,1987), p. 4.

[73] Finley, 'Harvest 90 – Administrative Slogan', p. 6.

Leaders and boards have to work out the process and approve it by committees, starting one year prior to the program. The communication of the plan has to reach all involved persons.

2. Previous preparations.

The program has to be prepared and the responsibilities finalized. The list of 'hundreds of interested persons who have received Bible studies and are ready to be brought to a decision for baptism' must be ready.

3. Conduct the public evangelistic meetings.

4. Reaping.

Teaching in baptismal classes and the 'baptism of well-prepared candidates'.

5. Follow-up work.

'The new converts are to be given careful attention.'[74]

Divisions and unions were encouraged to conduct national evangelistic campaigns to unite the country in evangelism and bring about major results. All levels of the church within the union had to be involved. Administrators, pastors and laity were expected to work together on the same campaign which would be conducted simultaneously in all the participating churches with the same topics being covered on the same dates and with the same materials. The advantages of a national campaign were described as:

> Creating a spirit of enthusiasm in the church and encouraging total mobilization. A large proportion of church members is active.
> Maintaining a feeling of unity. Church members work together with all pastors.
> While the church focuses on evangelism, problems will decrease.
> An impact upon the whole country and a great harvest of souls is possible.
> Through the large number of participating members and baptized converts it is easier to organize new local congregations.
> More members participate and they will present a more generous spirit in supporting the program financially. This will result in more funds for the program.
> The impact of the national evangelistic campaign will last longer, maintaining a general evangelistic spirit for years.[75]

The suggestions included the adoption of one main project for the whole country, possibly involving all members in order to do the work more effectively and obtain the best possible results.

Hungarian implementation of Harvest 90

In the life of the Seventh-day Adventist Church the year 1985 was the year of recovery and renewal in mission activities. Although the denomination in

---

[74] Carlos E. Aeschlimann, *Inter-America and its passion for Evangelism: Public Evangelism*, Ministerial Association Bulletin Harvest 90, Number 10 (Washington DC, 1988), p. 11.

[75] Carlos E. Aeschlimann, Annual Council: Harvest 90 Statement; Evangelistic Explosion in Africa; National Evangelistic Campaigns; Ministerial Association Annual Review, Ministerial Association Bulletin Harvest 90, Number 12 (Washington DC, 1988), pp. 10–14.

Hungary had not yet really participated in the Harvest 90 programme, its own activities showed strong similarities to those in the international plan. In its publications, articles and reports, Adventists directed their focus to mission activities and emphasized that the purpose of the church is to fulfil its missionary task. The Tisza conference report states that all sixteen pastors were deeply involved in conducting public lectures in the Eastern part of Hungary.

During the year they held meetings in more than fifty towns and villages,[76] almost 500 meetings in all, over the twelve-month period. The meetings were prepared for at prayer meetings and family worships, and the programme was often enriched with slide presentations and music.[77] According to the reports, about 8,140 visitors attended the meetings.[78] Some local congregations displayed extraordinary zeal. One article states that the members in Nyírpazony visited every home and invited everybody in the area to their meetings.[79]

The content of the evangelistic meetings was very often centred on the Second Coming of Christ, hope (provided by Christ's teachings) or the Book of Revelation. Some examples include the following: Árvai Henrik conducted meetings in Hidas, Nagydorog on hope in the Second Coming; Jenő Szigeti lectured in Budapest on the Book of Revelation; Dániel Farkas spoke about the history of salvation from Eden to Eden; the local congregation in Érd was given a presentation on the topic of Christ's second Advent, the Resurrection and a Hungarian youth meeting was conducted on the subject of the Second Coming of Christ.

Some preachers also spoke on topics such as 'Who am I?', peace, or the purpose of life. The strongly increasing number of public meetings shows that the denomination was trying to overcome past failures and to unite the church as well as to involve more and more members in its activities through one common missionary vision and through growing emphasis on eschatological urgency as justification for the growing intensity of mission activities. In many articles leaders describe the duty of the church, the call Adventists feel they have to fulfil before it is too late, and the expectations of God in relation to Adventists. The following methods were those mainly promoted for mission in church papers in 1985: conducting public evangelistic meetings, giving private Bible studies, friendship evangelism, caring for friends and maintaining good relationships and a habit of visitation.

---

[76] Detailed reports appeared regarding the following locations: Budapest Székely B. Church, Pestlőring, Rákocsaba, Nagy Ignác utca, Hidas, Nagydorog, Érd, Nemesvámos, Kiskunfélegyháza, Ócsa, Gyöngyös, Nyírmegyes, Fehérgyarmat, Medgyesegyháza, Hajdúböszörmény, Gönc, Kondoros, Nagyszénás, Orosháza.

[77] Report of Tisza Conference concerning the year 1985, presented to the Union executive comittee. HUC Archive Pécel, 1986.

[78] József Fegyverneki conducted meetings in the village of Kondoros where by the end of the series 140 people had attended the programme.

[79] 'Evangélizációs sorozat volt Nyírpazonyban' (1991), 14.

The numerical goals set by the General Conference for Hungary were published as early as 1985: 'The General Conference has decided that church membership should be doubled between 1985 and 1990.'[80] This statement was among the first that voiced the intentions of the international leadership for Hungary in clear terms and also indicated the expectations the church leaders had regarding Hungarian Adventists. The same article also described the steps Adventists must take as part of the preparations for the coming Harvest 90 programme: renewal of family spiritual life, the preparation of local congregations for evangelistic meetings, the activation of passive church members and planning of new activities – in readiness to reach the unreached.[81]

In 1986 the Hungarian Union Conference of the Seventh-day Adventist Church joined the Trans European Division and this step brought remarkable changes in its mission activities. Mark Finley was responsible for mission campaigns at the division level but at the same time he was also strongly involved in the Harvest 90 programme. The published statements of Hungarian denominational leaders reveal their attitude and the support they gave to the international programme. Vencel Pintér, the president of the Duna Conference, stated: 'We have received Harvest 90 with joy and made it our life's purpose. We conduct evangelistic meetings in many churches in our conference.'[82]

Szigeti, the president of the Hungarian Union stated in 1986 that Harvest 90 had reached all the church members. He reported that through training programmes for mission 200 qualified church workers are ready for the work. The Publishing House printed booklets to help form a personal library for people interested in Bible topics.[83] László Hangyás and Mark Finley published an article for Hungarians about the meaning of Harvest 90. In their message to the church a strong eschatological urgency is evident, making participation a duty for all church members:

'We have to put Harvesting into first place. It is our first priority in the next 5 years. [...] This is the call of the eternal gospel. We don't have time; people are waiting. [...] The only thing that has value for the kingdom of God is winning people for Christ. [...] Harvest 90 presents us with the most important challenge; it calls all church members to focus on the lost with all our energy.'[84]

They also presented the basic principles of the mission plan and emphasized that all were expected to participate:

---

[80] 'Aratás 90', *Lelkésztájékoztató* 19 (1985), p. 222.

[81] Ibid., p. 222.

[82] László Erdélyi, 'Események tükrében: A riport about the ministry of the executive committee', *Lelkésztájékoztató* (1986), 355–58 (pp. 355–56).

[83] Jenő Szigeti, 'A szolgálat Bázisa: A szolgáló gyülekezet', *Lelkésztájékoztató* (1986), 341–44 (pp. 341–44).

[84] My own translation. László Hangyás and Mark A. Finley, 'Aratás '90: Jelszó vagy bibliai motiváció?', *Lelkésztájékoztató* (1986), 169–74.

> Sending–The church would be unfaithful to her Lord if we did not participate in winning people
> Continuity – Harvest also needs sowing. Everybody has to make friendships first. An evangelist is supposed to care for the needs of people and become their friend.
> Unity–Harvest 90 is not based on just one spiritual gift but accepts the diversity of gifts. Members should work together, using all their gifts.
> Diversity – each harvest needs rain as well as sunshine. [...] Harvest 90 gives everybody the opportunity to choose a ministry. Some can invite people, others can offer hospitality, share food, do social work, show love towards neighbours, and carry out health ministry.
> Urgency – Harvest means urgency and needs to be our first priority.[85]

An article by József Szilvási also sets out the numerical expectations of the church leaders in regard to the Hungarian Union Conference. In each year a certain number of baptisms was to be achieved:

> In 1985/86 14% of the total baptisms were to be achieved: 156 baptisms
> In 1986/87 17% of the total baptisms were to be achieved: 191 baptisms
> In 1987/88 20% of the total baptisms were to be achieved: 226 baptisms
> In 1988/89 23% of the total baptisms were to be achieved: 259 baptisms
> In 1989/90 26% of the total baptisms were to be achieved: 283 baptisms
> Total: 1128 baptisms.[86]

Szilvási adds: 'These numbers are based on faith and will show what God can do for the church. We need supporting programmes and implementation.' He also explained what these supporting programmes might be and described activities that were strongly proclamation-oriented:

> - To motivate and train church members for mission
> - To conduct seminars, especially Revelation seminars, in the union and in the conferences
> - To train evangelists
> - To conduct workers' meetings and to present the unique characteristics of the European mission of the church
> - To provide supporting materials such as slides, pictures and videos for pastors.[87]

Szilvási concludes: 'Harvest 90 has a future only if it becomes a movement for the whole church'.[88]

The above statements and plans show that Hungarian Adventists had fully adopted Harvest 90 by the end of the year 1986 and that the denomination was prepared for the implementation of the programme. Leaders made Harvest 90

---

[85] My own translation. Hangyás and Finley, 'Aratás 90', pp. 169-74.
[86] My own translation. József Szilvási, 'Aratás '90', *Lelkésztájékoztató* (1986), 353–54.
[87] Szilvási, 'Aratás '90'.
[88] Ibid.

the top priority of the denomination, accepted the numerical goals set by for the country the General Conference and prepared members for the ministry. Eschatological urgency was also clearly presented as a strong motivational factor and the methods suggested by the worldwide leadership of the denomination determined most of the planned activities. Hungary became part of the international programme without much attention being paid to the local needs and the context in which Hungarian Adventists were living. The influence of the GC and TED leaders grew rapidly in Hungary. They were not only able to move Hungarian Adventists towards the implementation of Harvest 90 but also to lead the union session in 1989 and initiate major changes in church organization too.[89]

The relationship between the HUC and the division was limited to occasional conversations between officers prior to 1985. The political changes led to a further development in this relationship and Hungarian leaders agreed with division leaders to extend this association to more areas of church life. The division offered support to the Hungarian union in departmental work and in the training of pastors and church members. The divisional departments had a programme to use for most areas of church life.[90] From 19-22 April 1987 the TED offered a leadership seminar for 71 Hungarian leaders. These steps, in combination with the restructuring of the union into two conferences, lessened the influence of previous leaders of the old structure, loyal to the regime. Those were years characterized by inner struggles because different parties, especially József Szakács, the president of the Alliance of Free Churches, still tried to exercise influence on the denomination in order to keep the old system running.[91] In 1986 the TED leadership had put the exit from the Alliance of Free Churches on the Adventist agenda in order to lessen its influence on Adventists and to strengthen the relationship of the SDA church in Hungary to the international body of the denomination. Along with the process of decentralization, Hungarian Adventists introduced the international church manual in January 1988, establishing international and democratic standards. Besides the organizational actions, the leaders of the TED also took other steps. A number of church choirs and orchestras from the US and western European countries visited Hungary in the period from 1984 to 1989. This helped to reconnect ties of fellowship between the Hungarian members and the international body of Adventist church.[92] A survey among pastors and workers showed by the year 1988

---

[89] My own observation as a delegate at the union session in 1989. Rajki interviewed former leaders such as Jenő Szigeti, József Szilvási and Ferencz Rajki and came to the same conclusion. In: A.H. N. Rajki, Adventista Egyház, p.165.

[90] *Lelkésztájékoztató*, 2 (1989), pp. 81-89.

[91] Rajki, A H. N. 'Adventista Egyház', p.162.

[92] See reports about the event for example in: *Lelkésztájékoztató*, 5 (1985), 299; 3 (1986), 164.; 2 (1989), 91. 97.

measurable results because the majority of respondents supported the exit from the organisation in order to maintain church unity and mission.[93]

Hungarian Adventists faced a major challenge to their mission. The denomination was not the owner of about half of the church buildings and many local congregations did not have a building to meet in at all. The Duna Conference, for example, had 27 church properties but eight local congregations gathered in rented rooms and 22 in private homes.[94] That may have been one of the reasons why, when Harvest 90 began in Hungary, church leaders decided that their mission must be centred in the homes of church members.[95] The union president, Jenő Szigeti, was one of those who supported this initiative and he published an article in which he stated that mission is possible only if we talk to people on a personal level. Having a crowd to address at meetings makes mission impossible. Adventist mission is supposed to be based on personal conversations.[96] Later on an intensive church building programme was begun. Along with Hungarian Adventists' participation in Harvest 90, the church construction initiative was a clear demonstration of the generosity of these people and their exceptional performance in some areas.[97] However, it also diverted the church from this model of mission.

Although several publications in 1986 emphasized that the most important locations or situations for mission are homes, small groups, personal conversations and friendship,[98] the plans made by the union urged that meetings should also be organized in small churches. The suggestion was that one meeting should be conducted each week or three meetings held at the weekend as organized public events.[99] As a result, the number of converts grew steadily and in 1987 the denomination was able to reverse the decline and start growing again.[100]

The denomination also reorganized departmental work, following the plans set out in the Harvest 90 strategy and the instructions issued by the TED. The

---

[93] Letter from the union president to the pastors. 21 March 1988. Also the questionnaire is in the archive avaliable. Pécel, Archive of HUC of SDA. See also in Rajki, A H. N. 'Adventista Egyház', pp. 162-165.

[94] Report of the Duna Conference president at the conference session of 4-5 June 1987. Pécel, Archive of HUC of SDA.

[95] Protocol of the Tisza and Duna conference elections. Pécel, Archive of HUC of SDA. 1987.

[96] Ibid.

[97] See reports in: *Lelkésztájékoztató* (1988), 300-303.

[98] Several articles appeared in the magazine for pastors called *Lelkésztájékoztató* in 1986, concerning the best locations and settings for evangelism.

[99] Report on the work of the Tisza conference, 1987; Protocol of the Conference session of Tisza Conference 1987; Annual report of the Hungarian Union Conference 1988. Pécel, Archive of HUC of SDA.
The union worked on this concept in 1985. For a related article see: *Lelkésztájékoztató* 2 (1985), 90-91.

[100] Dániel Farkas, 'Evangélizációk', Lelkésztájékoztató 21 (1987), 363.

mission department and Sabbath school department increased their training activities in order to equip new workers, the health department developed new projects such as stop smoking programmes and weight loss courses in order to find new ways of making contact with the public. The communication department translated foreign materials for evangelistic meetings and duplicated slides for multimedia presentations. The radio studio increased its efforts to establish a presence in Hungarian radio broadcasting and the publishing house produced seven new booklets in tens of thousands of copies as its contribution to the Harvest programme.[101]

After the conference session elected new leaders in 1987, plans were made to double the number of church members involved in mission-related activities, to double the number of people using their talents for different kinds of ministries and to double the number of converts the conferences had achieved in the previous conference session.[102] In order to achieve this goal, leaders voted that each pastor must give full-time concentration to practical ministry in the church and that the conference administration should provide these ministers with materials for sermons and for training sessions.[103]

The plans for the year 1988 were set accordingly. GC leaders expressed their very high expectations for the year 1988 as it is also visible in the words of Aeschlimann: 'Strive to Reach the ighest Results in 1988: The exceptional results of this year, should be the basis for triumph in your field. Aim to make this the best year in baptisms.'[104]

The union started a special training course for church work and mission and 120 church members were enrolled. The following topics were on the curriculum: righteousness by faith, church organization and the church manual, Adventist history, how to teach doctrines, ministry and the life and work of Ellen G. White.[105]

The goals for evangelism were 'to carry the message to the farthest borders of our country', to turn church life from static to dynamic, from protection to action, from immobility to motion.[106] Three steps were considered essential to the success of this method:

- Entering new areas

---

[101] Jelentés a Magyar Unió 1987-es munkájáról, Pécel, Archive of HUC of SDA. 1987.

[102] The president of the General Conference urged leaders to double the efforts for more 'reaping'. Wilson, Neal C., 'Special Message: President, General Conference', in *Half-Way Point of Harvest 90*, ed. by Carlos E. Aeschlimann (Washington D.C., 1987), Ministerial Association Bulletin Harvest 90.

[103] Report about the conference session and plans. In: *Lelkésztájékoztató* (1987), 108.

[104] Carlos E. Aeschlimann, *Inter-America and it's passion for Evangelism: Public Evangelism*, Ministerial Association Bulletin Harvest 90 Number 10 (Washington D.C., 1988).

[105] Új első évfolyam a speciális tanfolyamon, *Lelkésztájékoztató*, 4 (1988), 220.

[106] Plan of the HUC concerning mission activities for 1988, as part of Harvest 90. Pécel, Archive of HUC of SDA.

- Growing through enrolling new church members in ministry,
- Multiplication of churches by establishing new local congregations.[107]

A special event in Budapest, planned by the leaders of the union in cooperation with representatives of the worldwide church, was intended to serve both needs with one major programme. The extraordinary project, 'Harvest Budapest', was supposed to involve not only all the congregations and church members in Budapest but also the members in the rest of the country.[108] It was part of the Harvest 90 closing initiatives. During the preparation year, Harvest Budapest was designed in such a way as to provide training for many volunteers on how to conduct public evangelism. However the event was a real one, with guest speaker Mark Finley, and there was the definite aim of baptizing as many people as possible. The preparation phase was begun under the supervision of Mark Finley in September 1988. As part of the plan, local congregations in Budapest were meant to run public meetings from December 1988 to January 1989 and baptize at least 100 people. Revelation seminars were supposed to be organized in the homes of 50 to 80 church members. Further attention was paid to the improvement of Sabbath school classes, to the involvement of the youth and to the proclamation of the 'health message' of the church.[109] All the departments of the church were urged to join the programme and describe how they could enrich it.

'Harvest Budapest' was the first and largest event the denomination organized that included the use of all the different types of media available at that time, including television and radio broadcasting. As part of the preparation, 100,000 invitation cards were distributed, public advertisements were taken out and personal effort was made on a huge scale. In 1988 the publishing house printed over 200,000 books and booklets, the health department increased its activity by establishing new connections to health programmes such as cancer prevention, and by carrying out social networking, telephone counselling and visitation in hospitals. A new type of ministry roused enthusiasm in large numbers of people. Because of the growing freedom, colporteurs went from house to house, freely selling thousands of books and contacting people.[110] 'Book evangelism' became one of the main channels of personal witnessing to the public about Adventist religious beliefs.

---

[107] Ibid.

[108] Jenő Szigeti, Report of the Hungarian Union Conference (TED Wintermeeting, 1989), 14/0. Archive material, HUC archive Pécel; Jenő Szigeti, 'Az 'Aratás '90' a Magyar Unióban', *Lelkésztájékoztató* (1990), 136–38.

[109] Plan of the HUC concerning mission activities for 1988, as part of Harvest 90. Pécel, Archive of HUC of SDA.

[110] János Rajki, 'Camp meeting for literature evangelists', Lelkésztájékoztató, 23 (1989), 285-286; Jenő Szigeti, *Report of the Hungarian Union Conference for the TED winter meetings – 1990*, archive material, HUC archive Pécel; Károlyné Rozmann, *Protocol of the executive comittee of the Hungarian Union Conference (1989)*, archive material, HUC archive.

The organization of 'Harvest Budapest' was directed by the TED, supervised by Mark Finley, and the entire apparatus of the church was united by this big event.[111] The six phases of the programme presented a very strong focus on proclamation orientation:

- Conducting church-growth seminars
- Team work for organizing health seminars, Daniel and revelations courses, projects for social care
- Conducting evangelistic meetings in the church on topics related to biblical archaeology and various Bible topics
- Maintaining personal contacts
- Organizing a big evangelistic campaign in Budapest from September to December 1989
- Organizing a closing worship service in the form of a major event that included the baptism of those interested.[112]

The final public lectures by Mark Finley attracted 6,758 visitors and 112 people made a decision for baptism.[113]

Analysis of the reports about mission activities from 1987 to 1990 shows clearly that the denomination's top priority was conducting public evangelism,[114] offering Revelation seminars and giving Bible studies, with the clear goal of motivating people to make decisions for baptism and church membership. Pastors and evangelists carefully reported in church magazines the numbers of baptismal candidates and baptisms. They seemed to play a crucial role. But as early as 1987 it was obvious that Hungarian Adventists would not be able to reach the numerical goals set by the GC.[115] The number of baptized people in 1986 and 1987 was less than half the number that had been expected for those years. Despite of the European challenges, Aeschlimann considered Harvest 90 successful: 'Until now (December 1988), Harvest 90 has been a success. It has united the world church in a common evangelistic thrust. It has inspired creativity for new effective methods to win souls. It has encouraged a spirit of

---

[111] István Fekete, 'Kezdj el Élni!', *Adventhírnök*, 1 (1990), 2–3.

[112] Fekete, 'Kezdj el Élni' pp. 2-3.; Finnley, Mark, *Trans-European Division Harvest 90 Report: Winter Meetings*, November 14.-17.1989 (St Albans, England, 1989).

[113] For a more detailed description of the event see: *Adventhírnök*, 1 (1990), 2-3.; Report about book evangelism. Pécel, Archive of HUC of SDA, 1988; Rajki, A H. N. 'Adventista Egyház', p 169.

[114] Archive documents report about public evangelistic meetings in Nyíregyháza, Nyírpazony, Hidas, Tiszaalpár, Kiskunfélegyháza, Kecskemét, Cegléd, Budapest, Boglárlelle, Rákoscsaba, Albertírsa, Kecskemét, Csenger, Békéscsaba, Gyömrő, Pestlőrinc, Újlengyel, Debrecen, Miskolc, Vecsés, Nagydorog and others.

[115] Report about the work of the Hungarian Union Conference in 1987 to the union session. Pécel, Archive of HUC of SDA.

revival. It has produced a tremendous mobilization, and above all, it has demonstrated the gigantic potential of using the laity to preach the gospel.'[116]

At the union sessions in 1989 leaders addressed the challenges Adventists faced in Hungary. Reporting on the previous five years, the president stated that one major problem lay in communication with the local churches. They seemed not to have worked completely according to the plans and directions that the leaders had initiated. Local congregations had not followed the national and international directions fully and they had not contributed enough of their resources to the fulfilment of the plans.[117]

A search of the archives did not reveal documents reporting evaluation, conducted by Hungarian leaders, of the SDA mission activities from 1986-1989 in Hungary. However, evidence can be found that the leaders discussed and analysed the situation and the reasons for failures and concluded that several factors played an important role. They requested more training in church growth and mission, recognized that 'success in mission' is often associated with evangelists who come from Western countries, and requested more such speakers.

The 'Harvest 90' programme in the denomination ended in 1989. Hungary could not meet the expectations which had been generated. Hungarian leaders pointed out in a survey that the possible reasons for their not having reached the goal for baptisms were: 'Because of the acute crisis in the HUC the missionary spirit of our fellow workers and church members weakened. The practical training for our ministers is not considered to have been satisfactory.'[118]

The coordinator of 'Harvest 90', Carlos Aeschlimann, came to the conclusion that 'There is no question that Europe is very secular and evangelism here is more difficult than in North America. But I believe there is a growing spiritual hunger on the part of the general population that is opening excellent doors of opportunity for our work here.'[119]

Another challenge was recognized but rarely addressed in the European field, including Hungary. The TED had to face a high number of apostasies, sometimes over fifty per cent of the baptismal rate. During my interviews in Hungary, Serbia and also in Prague, several leaders indicated that the rate of apostasy in some

---

[116] General Conference, *A Bold Plan to Culminate Harvest 90: An Interview with Carlos Aeschlimann, Coordinator of Harvest 90* (1988). In Nairoby, Kenya Kenneth together with Aeschlimann reported in 1988 that by March 1988 1.167.968 were baptised internationally. Mittleider, Kenneth, and Carlos Aeschlimann, *"Harvest 90" Affirmation* (Nairbo, Kenya, 1988).

[117] Presidential report. Jenő Szigeti, Unió választókonferencia Budapest, 1989 Ápr 19-21. Pécel, Archive of HUC of SDA.

[118] Carlos E. Aeschlimann, World Evangelism-Questionnaire: Ministerial Association GC – Evangelism and Harvest 90, p.2.

[119] Carlos E. Aeschlimann, *Worldwide Evangelistic Campaign, July 1989-June 1990: Total Participation*, Ministerial Association Bulletin Harvest 90 Number 13 (Washington DC, 1988), p.10.

parts of Eastern European countries was much higher– up to ninety per cent. This showed that while the church focused on gaining new converts, it lost many people from among the existing church members.

The International Action Plan 'Global strategy' and Its Implementation in Hungary after the Regime Change

'Global Strategy' for the world church

A new five-year period began in the Seventh-day Adventist Church in 1990 and the incoming leaders of the worldwide denomination also initiated a new programme for mission called 'Global Strategy'. It can be considered to have been, in part, a kind of continuation of 'Harvest 90', although it included some major changes in focus and methods. A thorough analysis of 'Harvest 90' could not be found but some interviews, reports and committee minutes reveal that leaders learned lessons and initiated changes because of their experiences with 'Harvest 90' and their reflections on that initiative. The following areas underwent recognizable changes, as well as developments in the strategic planning for 1990-1995 and in the methods applied to evangelistic campaigning.

'Reaching the unreached'

'Harvest 90' was an initiative for mission that involved local congregations. Consequently, growth usually occurred only in areas where an Adventist presence had already been established. 'Global Strategy', on the other hand, focused mainly on unreached territories with very little or no Adventist presence.

From geographical to anthropological understanding of the mission commission

For a long time Adventist mission had had the goal of establishing a presence in every country of the world. 'Global Strategy' derived its objectives from this traditional geographical goal-setting but, in a new interpretation of Revelation 14, shifted the focus to all 'nations, tribes, languages and people'. Robert Kloosterhuis had been a general vice president of the General Conference since 1985. He argued at the General Conference meeting in 1990 that the three angels' message of Revelation 14 is directed to every nation, tribe, language and people and that this is also intended to have consequences for Adventist mission.[120]

The Global Strategy Committee was now (in the 1990s) 'nudging the church away from the country concept in mission and toward the goal of reaching every

---

[120] General Conference minutes, 1990, HUC Archive, p.1.

person[121] on earth – every creature'.[122] The term 'people groups' was introduced and widely used in the denomination in relation to this new direction in mission. The anthropological understanding of 'mission commission' also forced the denomination to rethink the role of local churches, methods of conducting mission and the administrative process. The focus on ethnic groups required more understanding of them, greater professionalism and new approaches.

Changes in the understanding of the role of local churches in mission
Local congregations were previously considered to be responsible for certain missionary activities in order to reach people living in their locality. In contrast, 'Global Strategy' emphasized their regional and global responsibility for presenting God's love for the world.[123] More involvement by local churches was seen to be needed, not only in the work but also in setting the goals.[124]

A more holistic approach in mission
The new understanding and the responsibility to be taken by the local churches also required a new approach. Mission was considered to be more than just preaching. It was expected to be designed holistically. If local churches wanted to present God's love in their region, they needed to relate to the needs of the community holistically by adopting physical, mental, social and spiritual solutions. [125] 'Mission must include proclamation, service, and fellowship. Mission must meet the needs of human beings: whole mission to whole persons.'[126] 'The commitment of every church member and institution is to minister holistically to men and women by addressing their physical, mental, social, and spiritual needs.'[127]

Increased focus on urban mission
Denominational leaders came to the conclusion that many people groups in the cities should be considered as not yet having been reached. The General Conference president urged that special attention should be paid to the urban areas of the world: 'Global Mission must be redefined. We must not forget the part of Global Mission that is found in our own backyard. It is as close as our

---

[121] *Globale Mission – Von Mensch zu Mensch: Von Ernte 90 zur Globalen Mission*, p. 1; Michael Ryan, 'Into all the world: the meaning of Global Mission: The Seventh-day Adventist Church has launched the most arduous plan in the history of missions. An introduction', *Ministry Magazine*, 11 (1992), 5- (p. 8); Charles Taylor, 'Global Strategy: Simply having a presence in every nation is not enough. Global Strategy targets the kindreds, tongues, and people groups', *Ministry Magazine*, 8 (1990), 12- (p. 13).

[122] Taylor, 'Global Strategy', p. 12.

[123] General Conference Committee minutes, 1995, HUC Archive, p. 235.

[124] *Trans European Division – Global Mission*, 19 November 1990, p. 3.

[125] See: Global Strategy of the Seventh-day Adventist Church, 1990, A2: 14-36.

[126] Nancy Vyhmeister, 'Why world mission?: What is the mission of the Seventh-day Adventist Church? Must the mission be worldwide? And if so, why?', *Ministry Magazine*, 8 (1990), 8-10 (p. 8).

[127] General Conference of SDA Church, *Global Mission*, 1990, HUC Archive, pp. 3-4.

neighbour. Global Mission means planning to enter every community in every city. Global Mission means planning to enter every town in every conference.'[128]

Along with other world divisions, the TED became engaged in the initiative and designed projects what were specially tailored to the cities.[129]

Changes in the methods for mission
Since the denomination focused on working in new areas without much or any previous Adventist presence, methods and steps had to be developed that were suited to establishing an SDA presence in a short time.[130]

Two methods received growing attention: planting new churches and satellite evangelism. The first was significant as it assured long-lasting Adventist presence in new areas through the ministry of church members, while the second also made the Adventist message available in areas that had little or no Adventist presence. The General Conference included in its plan an estimate of how many new local congregations it would be feasible to plant.

In certain areas of the 'Global Strategy' plan, some recurring characteristics can be observed that reflect the American cultural background of the leaders of the worldwide denomination. The strong emphasis on numerical goal setting was not only maintained but was developed more specifically. Behind this was the firm belief that 'goals have the ability to lift the vision […] goals are statements of faith […] goals are inspired by God' and that they have to be specific, realistic and measurable.[131]

Leaders wanted to maintain a constant programme of evangelism[132] with a strong emphasis on achievement and urgency. One of the leading slogans for 'Global Strategy' expressed the eagerness and growth-oriented attitude behind the plans: 'The whole message to the whole world through the whole Church.'[133]

'Global Mission is an initiative to penetrate the unentered areas of the world with the gospel of Jesus. Every country of the world has 'unentered areas.'[…] Some have misunderstood the Global Mission initiative. They have thought that it was a program for some far-off distant land for which they were to contribute money.'[134]

The goal for the programme instituted in 1990 was 'to establish an Adventist presence in each' of the 'untouched groups of 1 million people before A.D.2000. That meant planting at least one new church every other day in these unreached

---

[128] Robert Folkenberg, General Conference Committee Minutes, 1992, EUD Archive, 92–106, p. 93.

[129] Mark Finley, Plans with Inter-Division Evangelists, 5 March 1990, HUC Archive.

[130] Folkenberg, EUD Archive, p. 93.

[131] *Trans-European Division – Global Mission: Programme and Agenda,* p. 10.

[132] Carlos E. Aeschlimann, *World Baptismal Day,* 1991, HUC Archive, p. 1.

[133] Global Mission Objectives, 1990, General Conference, Ref. #90-416, p. 1; see also: General Conference of SDA Church, HUC Archive, p. 1.

[134] Ryan, *The Meaning of Global Mission,* p. 8.

areas during the next 10 years'.[135] In several publications leaders explained what this meant for church members living in countries with a stronger Adventist presence: 'The Global Strategy Committee is nudging the church away from the country concept in missions and toward the goal of reaching every person on earth – every creature.'[136]

The General Conference chose three main objectives for 'Global Strategy' as leading principles for the work.

The first of these goals was to raise awareness through different programmes so that church members would recognize the need to become involved in all people groups, unentered areas and towns. Secondly, members were to participate in ministry to establish an Adventist presence in all these target groups. Thirdly, everybody must foster the expansion of the church by establishing baptismal goals and church growth objectives in all areas. 'Global Strategy' also included the nurture of members and reclaiming inactive members.[137]

Quality and quantity goals of 'Global Strategy'

An analysis of the specific goals shows that they can be divided into two groups: goals related to the quality of church life and numeric goals. The quality goals were linked to personal spirituality and motives for carrying out ministry. Some of them were associated with the recognized failures and shortcomings of 'Harvest 90':

The inner motivation of church members
Each person's motivation should be based on his or her own spirituality, not on pressure from outside. In order to become motivated, every church member should be led into a deep, fulfilling relationship with Jesus Christ.[138]

Participation by church members
Basic Christian values were also included in the plan, with more emphasis than previously: 'We envision every church member rich in love.'[139]

Church participation
In its description of the quality goals the General Conference emphasized a more holistic method for ministry: 'The church will witness in every neighbourhood, preaching the good news, serving mankind, developing disciples, and bringing people into meaningful church fellowship.'[140]

---

[135] Ted Wilson, in 'Global Mission: Person to Person', p. 3 (an insert in the *Adventist Review* of 5 July 1990).

[136] Taylor, Global Strategy, p. 13.

[137] Carlos E. Aeschlimann, *Global Mission's Challenges*, 1990, EUD Archive, pp. 2ff.

[138] General Conference, *Global Strategy of the Seventh-day Adventist Church*, 1989, HUC Archive, A3: 19-29; Aeschlimann, EUD Archive, p. 3.

[139] Aeschlimann, EUD Archive, p. 3.

[140] Ibid.

Recognizing the needs of young people and including them in ministry
Leaders and churches should give more attention to ministry for children aged
from ten to fifteen and should recognize the special needs of young people.
Ministry among college and university students has to receive priority.[141]

Quantity goals were intended to be landmarks in the development of the
church. These goals had three stages: annual goals, goals for the next
quinquennium and ambitions for the decade 1990-2000. 'The suggested faith
goal for 1991 is to baptize 600,000 well-prepared candidates. And at the same
time, we must aim to foster a strong program to keep these new members.'[142] At
the 1990Annual Council, the General Conference president suggested a basic
goal of baptizing one person per minute. 'That would be 2.6 million in the 1990-
1995 quinquennium.'[143] The goals of 'Global Strategy' for the following ten
years were to 'establish Adventist presence in every population segment by
2000',[144] working in 35 new languages Adventists have never worked with and
to enter a segment every other day for 10 years.[145]

On the European continent the plan focused on cities with 50,000 or more
inhabitants where Adventists did not yet have an organized Seventh-day
Adventist Church. The conferences had chosen some of these cities to start the
work and to establish SDA communities.[146]

The General Conference also divided the responsibilities worldwide. The
General Conference was willing to become financially involved and to work
towards the target population of over 20 million in areas with a below-average
SDA density. The GC was ready to take direct action, if no other administrative
entity (division or union) could take responsibility for the target population.
Divisions and unions were given responsibility for target groups of one to four
million people. Local conferences were asked to take on the task of reaching
target groups of 100,000 to 1 million and every church district was in charge of
reaching target groups of under 100,000.[147] The involvement of local churches
in responsibility and planning was intended to lead to quantitative results, as
Aeschlimann stated: 'Each church should hold monthly baptisms. This is a
perfect place to make calls, write down the names of the respondents and give
them Bible studies.'[148]

The Trans European Division also formulated its own specific goals for the
European field, including Hungary. The major objective for Europe was reaching

---

[141] Trans-European Division, pp. A11:40ff.

[142] Aeschlimann, *Global Mission's Challenges*, p. 4.

[143] Ibid. p. 2.

[144] General Conference of SDA Church, Global Mission, 1990, HUC Archive, p. 1.

[145] Ibid.

[146] General Conference, *Euro-Africa Division – Global Mission*, September 1990, EUD
Archive, p. 2.

[147] General Conference, Global Strategy of the Seventh-day Adventist Church, 1989, General
Conference, HUC Archive, A4:11-42.

[148] Aeschlimann, World Baptismal Day, 1991, HUC Archive, p. 1.

major cities for Christ.[149] The TED also stated clearly what concrete steps had been prepared to reach this goal. The division planned thirty major evangelistic campaigns with overseas evangelists from 1990 to 1995. It was planned that three of these projects would take place in Hungary.[150]

The 'how to' plans for the implementation of 'Global Strategy'

The General Conference also drew up strategic steps and devised methods for reaching the set goals of 'Global Strategy'. Three different levels of activity can be recognized in the plans.

Spiritual preparation and raising awareness

Church members should receive encouraging articles, including reports about personal experiences of sharing the gospel. The GC promised to provide articles in major denominational journals on a regular basis, produce leaflets and audio-visual materials about the global mission of the church and try to reach every family with information about 'Global Strategy'.[151]

Utilisation of membership resources

The denomination considered its own church members to be the greatest resource of the church for fulfilling the vision of 'Global Strategy'. Using their potential was especially important when starting new projects. The Church Ministries Department was established in order to support church members in their efforts to fulfil the mission of the church in general. 'The Church's greatest resources are its members: frail, fallible, and yet, under the guidance of the Holy Spirit, capable of unlimited potential. A careful utilization of their skills and talents, and a wider deployment of lay membership in outreach programs, offers scope for a speedier promulgation of our distinctive message.'[152]

The plan was to hold between six and ten training programmes each year for lay people in different fields. Each programme should last from seven to ten days and each field should receive training at least every second year.[153] It was also suggested in the plan that each Union should create centralized registers of members' skills, abilities and gifts. The main purpose of the registration was to motivate people: 'Members must feel their skills are wanted by church leadership. Those currently sidelined need involvement for personal growth.'[154] Past experiences also told leaders to encourage the creativity of their members

---

[149] Mark Finley, *Co-ordinated Public Evangelistic Plans with Inter-Division Evangelists*, 5 March 1990, HUC Archive, A36: 8-10.

[150] TED, *Global Strategy*, 24 April 1990, Trans-European Division. A40.; Finley, Co-ordinated Public Evangelistic Plans, A35:1ff.

[151] GC, Global Strategy of the Seventh-day Adventist Church, General Conference, HUC Archive, A4:50-A7:51.

[152] Martin L. Anthony, *Church Ministries Department: Lay Training Section: Global Strategy: 1990-2000* (St Albans, 1990) Rn. A2:1 – A4:12, A1:14ff.

[153] Anthony, Church Ministries, Rn. A2:1 – A4:12, A2: 1- A4:12.

[154] Ibid., A1: 39-40.

by inviting them to become involved in the projects: 'Members must be led to think creatively of how they can assist in the expansion of the gospel into new segments of their community; they must see how they, and their church, are to carry a burden for the sharing of the gospel with every person in their respective spheres.'[155]

The production of new 'outreach materials' also became a priority within the denomination. A *Witness Resource Training Manual* was produced, along with other source books dealing with philosophy, methods and strategies needed for success.[156] Various levels of the church organization also started producing training materials, sermons, media material, printed guidelines and books in order to support local pastors and church members in their ministry.

Ministry activities: 'seek, reap, keep'[157]

There were these three words that represented the steps that had been planned for mission: 'One of the objectives of the Global Mission program is to maintain a continual program of evangelism. The three key words are: Seek, Reap, and Keep. This means looking for interests among all people groups: instructing, baptizing, incorporating, and retaining them as faithful and active members.'[158]

Seeking stood for entering new people groups, catching the attention of the people by meeting their personal needs and designing pathways for target groups. Reaping indicated that evangelism was a type of harvesting with the definite purpose of baptizing people and leading them to Christ and into the fellowship in the church.[159] 'Keep' drew attention to nurturing members and reclaiming those who had become inactive.[160]

Analysis of the related literature about the methods designed to implement the strategy shows that the main focus was still directed towards preaching and teaching through public events. The Global Strategy Resolution states: '[The] primary mission of the SDA Church is to preach the gospel of Jesus Christ and teach the commandments of God to every nation, kindred, tongue and people.'[161]

The denomination started schools of evangelism and evangelistic workshops in order to foster proclamation of its message through public lectures.[162] 'Field schools of evangelism are flourishing with 125 campaigns run by national pastors and evangelists in progress. [...] Workers from outside the division will be holding 140 campaigns this year.'[163] Schools of evangelism and evangelistic

---

[155] Ibid., A1: 29-33.

[156] Ibid., A2: 1- A4:12.

[157] Global Mission Objectives, General Conference, Ref. #90-416, p. 1.

[158] Aeschlimann, World Baptismal Day, p. 1.

[159] *Planning process*, 1990, EUD Archive, pp. 10ff.

[160] Global Mission Objectives, General Conference, Ref. #90-416, p. 1.

[161] *Global Strategy*, 1990, EUD Archive, Ref. #90-1004, p. 1

[162] *Trans European Division – Global Mission*, 19 November 1990, p. 2.

[163] *Trans-European Division, Global Mission-Reports*, 1993, HUC Archive, Ref. #93-36, p. 2.

workshops were conducted in the TED countries[164] according to the instructions set out in the General Conference plans for national evangelistic campaigns. Aeschlimann had promoted these nationwide public lectures, held in many towns and villages with the involvement of the whole church body, as a 'powerful tool in soul winning as early as 1988 and he later gave them even more emphasis.' His arguments were that they

1. Unite a country in evangelism and achieve great results
2. Everyone is involved– administrators, pastors, laity
3. They create spirit of enthusiasm in the church
4. Encourage total mobilization
5. Promote a feeling of unity
6. Help in organizing new congregations
7. More involved members will also provide more financial support
8. Create a widespread evangelistic spirit for the years to come
9. Promote a feeling that something great is about to happen.[165]

He concluded in 1990 that traditional evangelism should be carried out in all parts of the world, because 'an increasing emphasis on mission is wanted'.[166] The Evangelism Council of the General Conference published the suggestions of leaders regarding which areas of public evangelism should be improved:

1. Evangelists need to make better presentations.
2. Fresh insights and new resources are needed.
3. Evangelists should be given better encouragement and support.
4. Because of the general interest in Bible lands, pastors must receive the opportunity to visit biblical archaeological sites.[167]

The content of public evangelistic meetings

The research conducted during the preparation of the present study did not reveal any major differences between the content of Adventist proclamation in 'Harvest 90' and 'Global Strategy'. Kloosterhuis states clearly that the vision of the General Conference 'that proclaiming Christ and his three Angels' Messages to every nation, kindred, tongue and people'[168] is the major objective of the church's work. The three angels' message recorded in Revelation 14.6 is the mission motivator for Adventists.[169]

---

[164] *Trans European Division – Global Mission,* 19 November 1990, p. 2.

[165] *Annual Council: Harvest 90 Statement; Evangelistic Explosion in Africa; National Evangelistic Campaigns; Ministerial Association Annual Review,* December 1988, Ministerial Association General Conference of Seventh-day Adventists, Number 12, pp. 10–14.

[166] Aeschlimann, *Global Mission's Challanges,* EUD Archive Friedensau, pp. 1–2.

[167] General Conference, *Evangelism Council,* 2 May 1991, EUD Archive, ADCC/lk, p. 1.

[168] Global Mission Objectives, General Conference, Ref. #90-416, p. 1.

[169] General Conference, A Global Strategy for a Global Mission, 1990, EUD Archive, p. 1.

Adventists proclaim the gospel of Jesus Christ. They have a special mission to inform the world about Christ's second coming and to restore lost truths (including the Sabbath and the Christian lifestyle). 'They follow Christ's example [of] giving witness to their faith in every part of the world to lead people […] into meaningful church fellowship.'[170]

Global Strategy also emphasizes eschatological urgency as a driving force behind the church's activities. Radical changes have given the impression that the end of the world is very near; the church must finish its task before Christ returns. 'Seventh-day Adventists are familiar with the signs of Jesus' coming. Every newspaper illustrates Matthew 24 and points to the nearness of His return.'[171]

The many major public events put the denomination under financial pressure. At the annual meeting of the General Conference in 1991 the issue was addressed but at the same time the attention the representatives of participating countries from all over the world was drawn to the statement, 'Financial pressures cause sober moments, but the Church wants to see the work finished!'[172]

Articles published worldwide, including words such as the following 1990 call to action by Nancy Vyhmeister, also contributed to the eschatological pressure that was put on the denomination: 'In the face of these changes, Global Strategy is a call to the Seventh-day Adventist Church worldwide to stop looking inward. It is a call to share and care. It corresponds approximately to what General Beckwith told the Waldenses in 1848 when their missionary zeal began to dwindle. He said, 'Voi sarete missionari o non sarete nulla' ('You will be missionaries, or you will not be at all').'[173]

One of the reasons for the eschatological urgency was the fact that 'Global Strategy' was being put into action in the last decade of the second millennium. Some statements included the idea that the world was 'ripe for the harvest' because the second coming of Jesus was going to happen soon. Adventists needed a new understanding of the time and the motivation to meet the needs of people in the world in order 'to prepare people for the soon coming of Christ'.[174]

'Christ's followers, those who have accepted the task He left them, cannot limit mission to their own environment. Their commission is to reach the ends of the earth. They dare not fail to satisfy the master's expectations.'[175]

---

[170] General Conference, Global Strategy, HUC Archive, A2: 14-36.

[171] Michael Ryan, 'Into all the world: the meaning of Global Mission: The Seveth-day Adventist Church has launched the most aruous plan in the history of missions. An introduction', *Ministry Magazine*, 11 (1992), 5-

[172] General Conference, Global Mission Report, *Ref. #91-257*, 1991, EUD Archive, p. 1.

[173] Nancy Vyhmeister, 'Why world mission?: What is the mission of the Seventh-day Adventist Church? Must the mission be worldwide? And if so, why?', *Ministry Magazine*, 8 (1990), 8–10.

[174] General Conference, *Von ernte 90 zur Globalen Mission*, 1990, EUD Archive, p. 1.

[175] Vyhmeister, 'Why world mission?', p. 9.

The plans of the General Conference and
Trans-European Division for Eastern Europe

Leaders of the denomination recognized the changes in Eastern-Europe and paid special attention to the work in those countries. Committee minutes reveal their high expectations and their eagerness to use the new opportunity for mission. Mark Finley stated in 1990: 'We are counting on God for an evangelistic explosion in Europe in the last decade of the 20th century.'[176] 'Europe is the most secularized part of the world. Hence Evangelism is hard, as people are not open to the gospel. But because of the recent political changes, especially in Eastern Europe, the situation has changed. People are now ready to listen to the message of the gospel. They wonder what the future holds. Change is in the air.'[177] 'A certain kind of religious competition can also be detected in his words: Already Jehovah Witnesses, Pentecostals and Mormons are sending thousands of missionaries to the Eastern Bloc countries in an attempt to win converts now! This is the time for Seventh-day Adventists to do something special for Europe.'[178]

The Euro-Africa Division also added its efforts to those of the General Conference and the TED. 'The Eastern European countries need our best attention. There are tremendous challenges to face for which financial help is needed from outside. The Euro-Africa Division tries to do its best, but the needs are beyond its means.'[179]

The Trans European Division drew up a strategic plan for its unions. The responsibilities were spread among various authorities and the duties were then determined. The unions were asked to prepare selected areas before conducting evangelistic campaigns. The preparation included the spiritual renewal of existing congregations, lay witness training, Bible studies, health outreach programmes and multi-faceted interest-building seminars.

The division's ministerial department was made responsible for providing overseas evangelists with information about the selected country: cultural and demographic information, suggestions for possible sermon sequences, etc. The same department was also responsible for allocating a budget of £10,000 for each location in order to supply the evangelist with accommodation, local transportation and a per diem allowance. Each campaign was planned to last for not less than eight weeks.[180]

'In co-operation with the General Conference North American Division, the Trans-European Division will plan thirty major evangelistic meetings/field schools of evangelism during the next five years in major European cities with

---

[176] Mark Finley, Co-ordinated Public Evangelistic Plans with Inter-Division Evangelists, Global Strategy (1990), HUC Archive Pécel, A39:3f.
[177] Finley, Co-ordinated Public Evangelistic Plans, A35: 7-A36:10.
[178] Ibid., A36:3ff.
[179] General Conference, Euro-Africa Division – Global Mission, EUD Archive, 1990, p. 7.
[180] Finley, Co-ordinated Public Evangelistic Plans, A36:19.

special emphasis on the three Eastern European countries within its territory (Poland, Hungary and Yugoslavia).'[181]

The major steps the division prepared for the work show that although the General Conference had promised changes in the objectives and methods of mission after the conclusion of 'Harvest 90', at the division level only very minor changes can be observed in terms of holistic ministry, cultural relevance and methods of mission. According to the strategic plan, evangelists from overseas had to be given training for the work in European countries but research has failed to find any evidence or information about the extent of the preparation, the content of the information evangelists received or how such information as was received influenced the work of these evangelists at the various locations. Reports on the meetings give the impression that most of the evangelists used the same methods everywhere, presenting the same topics with few adjustments, and that they followed a general plan for their missionary work.

Implementation of 'Global Strategy' in Hungary at leadership level

By the year 1990, when the programme 'Global Strategy' started, the work of the Trans European Division was highly appreciated by Hungarian Adventists. The wording of the Tisza Conference report indicates this: 'According to our recent experiences, the evangelizing carried out by the Division has been of great help in Harvest 90. Not only in Budapest, but in other towns too, the work started by Mark A. Finley was followed by good results. [...] We think it would be of great assistance in the Global Mission as well.'[182]

The new division programmes were accepted automatically and the conferences created their plans in accordance with these arrangements. The result was that, although the two conferences were quite different in terms of population, local church life and culture in general, the plans looked almost the same and the methods and materials supplied to the programme organizers were identical.

At the beginning the Duna Conference fully accepted the ambitious plans of the GC for unreached areas and set its own objectives accordingly. The focus was directed on planting new local congregations: 'According to our Global Mission programme, we intend to proclaim the gospel in 100 unreached or partly unreached settlements.[183] In the future we must address more than 3 million people living in places unreached up till now.'[184]

The TED expected very clear numeric goal-setting from the fields, as described in the document laying out 'Global Strategy' in 1990. Local churches were expected to set their own goals for seminars, evangelistic series, special visitors' days, the number of Bible studies and the number of baptisms.[185] In

---

[181] Finley, Co-ordinated Public Evangelistic Plans, A36:19

[182] *Global Mission Program*, 1990, HUC Archive, pp. 3–4.

[183] DET, *Global Mission Program 1990-1995*, 1990, HUC Archive, p. 1.

[184] Ibid. p. 3.

[185] Trans European Division – Global Mission, 19 November 1990, HUC Archive, pp. 1–2.

particular, numerical goal setting for baptism was explicitly emphasized: 'We will encourage each local church to set its own baptismal goal. The total of these goals will form the basis for the world church's goal.'[186]

While Hungarians did not seem to be in favour of numeric goal-setting according to the expectations of the TED, they set a baptism goal for the next five years, although it was not as strict as expected by the TED: 'The Conference hopes to win 500-1,000 new members during Global Mission and they want to be known in Hungary in a positive way.'[187]

Notably, in the same document, remarks had already been made to the effect that this ambitious goal was too high for the conference: 'The Duna Conference has 2,136 members in 58 churches. It may be too much work for them to reach 100 new places (with a great number of people who have never been touched by the Gospel).'[188]

Besides the numbers, the methods were also partly adjusted to the reality of life in the Hungarian conferences. Their church buildings were usually not suitable for public meetings and their standing in society was not strong enough for such an ambitious programme. Hungarian pastors had had less success than overseas evangelists in their missionary work. The methods Hungarians planned for mission matched this reality: 'We would do this work by distributing books and magazines, by offering health courses, Bible and cultural lectures and evangelistic campaigns to be held in cultural centres or other halls, and at the same time we would hold seminars based on what is possible in the current situation.'[189]

A closer look at the documents reveals hardly any intentions to try to enter new territories, or to plant churches in unreached towns.[190] Some reports present practical steps individuals took towards working in new territories but an overall concept for this new challenge was seemingly not available. Besides this, some Hungarian towns with an Adventist presence were considered 'unreached' because during the period of Communism Adventists were not able to run public meetings and engage with the public at large. This regulation helped Hungarian Adventists in their financial struggles to meet the criteria for receiving Global Mission funds from the General Conference: 'The general principle [...] is to reach unreached peoples who have not had an opportunity before to hear the message of Adventism.'[191]

The Tisza Conference evaluated the 'Harvest 90' programme in the Global Mission document and came to the following conclusion: 'The Harvest 90 goals

---

[186] Ibid., p. 3.

[187] Ibid., p. 4.

[188] DET, Global Mission Program 1990-1995, HUC Archive, p. 1.

[189] Ibid., 1990, pp. 1–2.

[190] Instead of planting churches in unreached towns, local congregations often focused more upon constracting, extending or renovating their own church buildings. 'Gyülekezeti házat avattunk Bucsán', *Adventhírnök*, 5 (1995), 14; Éva Csegedi-Nagy, 'A zalaegerszegi gyülekezet alapítása' (Seminar paper, Adventista Teológiai Főiskola, 2004).

[191] General Conference, pp. A33: 37-39.

were not fully accomplished, but they at least prevent the decline in membership and led to a constant growth.'[192]

This statement was true for the conference in general but when leaders looked at their local congregations in particular, they discovered challenging areas where the age structure, the situation and the development of local congregations in country towns indicated unsatisfactory situations: 'In three of our country towns […] the membership rate is extremely unfavourable. Our churches are declining. We would like to improve this situation by exchanging ministers and by holding evangelistic campaigns.'[193]

Hungarian Adventist leaders could not cope with some of the challenges by themselves and their predicament made them not only open to accept external solutions and advice but even dependent on Western methods as dominant directions. The only solution seemed to be to join the 'Global Strategy' initiative and participate in its projects fully. The Tisza conference and the Duna Conference accepted the TED programme and launched 'Global Strategy' in their territory.

The Practical Implementation of 'Global Strategy' in Hungary

From 'Harvest 90' to 'Global Strategy' in the praxis of the Hungarian context

The implementation of the new strategy in Hungary was strongly influenced by Hungarian Adventists' experiences with the previous international programme. The first year of 'Global Strategy' was simultaneously the first year of almost complete freedom after the regime change in Hungary in 1989. As a natural consequence, Adventists focused on previously blocked areas, rather than on devising plans for holistic ministry. The leaders of the Tisza Conference reported in 1990 that the goals of 'Harvest 90' could not be reached, and they presented a list of hindrances, circumstances that had stood in the way of progress. Some of these obstacles became central issues during the time when 'Global Strategy' was being conducted:

1. Using public communication channels
Before the regime change in 1989 the church's freedom to use public communication channels for advertising meetings was very limited. Church members mainly used personal friendship networks when they wanted to invite others to public meetings. However, from 1990 onwards, the denomination printed hundreds of thousands of invitation cards, handbills, placards, booklets and other materials in order to invite as many people as possible to evangelistic events.

---

[192] TET, Global Mission Program, 1990, HUC Archive, p. 1.
[193] Ibid., p. 3.

2. Conducting large meetings in public halls
Big outreach campaigns were not widespread before 1990 and the venues for meetings were usually limited to small halls or church buildings. From 1990 onwards, on the other hand, the denomination made plans to follow the 'Western paradigm' and conducted large meetings in prominent buildings, using foreign speakers.

3. Training and involving church members
Leaders considered the shortage of involvement by church members to be one of the main reasons why 'Harvest 90' failed. From 1990 onwards, church members, as well as pastors, were intended to receive education in conducting and supporting meetings. The training was meant to include how Adventists could contact new people, using newspaper articles, radio and television programmes, and invitation cards and how they could organize and run meetings.

4. Need-oriented service
Adventists recognized that they needed to offer more need-oriented service in order to reach more people. Besides religious programmes, health ministry, stop smoking courses, cooking clubs and social activities were also intended to be organized.[194]

Analysis of leading committee minutes, mission-related publications and articles in official Adventist magazines and newspapers in the period from 1990 to 1995 presents clearly what was being done in terms of the practical implementation of the plans. Hungarian Adventists were focusing on nine specific areas:
1. Major public evangelistic programmes with foreign speakers
2. Regular evangelism carried out by local pastors and church members
3. Literature evangelism by trained colporteurs, along with a publishing ministry
4. Child and youth evangelism through meetings, special camps and programmes
5. Church planting in new, unreached areas
6. Health evangelism
7. Social work (food banks, second hand clothing, support of large families…)
8. Media evangelism
9. Prison evangelism

These areas will be explored in the following sections.

Major public evangelistic programmes with foreign speakers

The denomination definitely established a new paradigm for mission in the period 1990–1995. The example set by Mark Finley in 1989 significantly

---

[194] See the presidential report of the Tisza Conference in: Elnöki beszámoló, *Lelkésztájékoztató* (1990), 136-137.

influenced the way in which Hungarian Adventists thought about mission. The programme was considered successful and set a new paradigm. The criteria for success seemed to be influenced by visible progress in previously neglected areas and the impact these advances had on the public. Success appeared to involve:

1. the presence of the denomination in various branches of the media and, because of that, in wider society too;
2. the high standard of rented facilities for the programmes (largest university halls, theatres, prestigious buildings…), corresponding to the strongly felt importance of the message Adventist wanted to spread;
3. the large number of attendees and the considerable number of baptismal candidates.

The leading paradigm for successful mission at this period of time involved the following stages:

1. a professionally organized event, supervised by successful Western evangelists
2. lengthy previous preparation and person-oriented follow-up work
3. public advertising of lectures by guest speakers from the West, using media events and the distribution of tens of thousands of invitation cards
4. growing awareness by the public about Adventists and their message
5. a Western evangelist conducting meetings in prominent halls for several weeks and the subsequent baptism of interested individuals at the close of the series of meetings.

This model targeted multitudes; it was aimed at attracting large numbers of people to the meetings. The numbers reported were very high at the beginning of the five-year period of 'Global Strategy' (1990–1995), as shown by the following examples:

During the preparations for the meetings to be held by Malcolm Pots from Australia in the university town of Szeged, 40,000 invitation cards were distributed, over 2,000 registered guests attended the meetings and 50 people made a decision for baptism.[195] When Hamilton Williams from England conducted his crusade in Békéscsaba and Gyula, 40,000 invitation cards were distributed and 150 people decided to be baptized.[196] In Nyiregyháza Adventists distributed 20,000 invitation cards and 498 attended the meetings.[197] Tony Campbell carried out intensive advertising on radio and television before he conducted his meetings in Zalaegerszeg. The Adventists there hired a large hall and Campbell had to offer his presentations twice each day because the auditorium was too small to accommodate everyone who wanted to attend the

---

[195] László Pócsi és László Csalami, 'Felfedezesek a bibliai földeken', *Adventhírnök* (1991), 11.

[196] András Szilvási, 'Hamilton J. Williams evangélizál Békés megyében', *Adventhírnök*, 1 (1991), 16.

[197] 'Válaszd az életet sorozat eredményei Nyíregyházán', *Adventhírnök*, 4 (1991), 14.

lectures. Over 1,000 people came to listen to him every day.[198] Adventists conducted large public meetings with foreign evangelists in many big and smaller towns in Hungary, following this paradigm. Reports are available about the campaigns in Gyula, Békéscsaba,[199] Nyiregyháza,[200] Orosháza,[201] Szeged,[202] Zalaegerszeg,[203] Miskolc,[204] Tatabánya,[205] Budapest,[206] Veszprém,[207] Pécs,[208] Debrecen,[209] Szekszárd,[210] Székesfehérvár,[211] Szolnok,[212] and other towns.[213]

Some feedback about the guest participants shows that the skills and the personalities of the presenters were less important to at least some members of the audience in the meetings than the atmosphere and the fellowship they experienced. One person who was interviewed even wondered why the guest speakers were regarded so highly, as key elements in the success of the meetings. He felt that the friendly atmosphere was the key component.[214]

On the other hand, leaders focusing on numerical results came to the conclusion in 1992, after three years' work in the post-communist era, that foreign evangelists had played the most important role in the growth of the church. Baptisms had taken place where they had worked.[215] Both conferences

---

[198] Árpád Szőllősi, 'Csodálatos felfedezések ókori országokban. Ilyen még nem volt'', *Adventhírnök*, 6 (1991), 10-11.

[199] Evangélizáció Békéscsabán és Gyulán, *Adventhírnök* 4 (1991), p. 16.

[200] Tamás Hock, 'Evangélizációs sorozat Nyiregyházán', *Adventhírnök*, 3 (1990), 3–4; Evangélizáció Nyiregyházán, *Adventhírnök* (1992), p. 10.

[201] Attila Rajki, 'Hogy örömötök teljes legyen', *Adventhírnök*, 5 (1990), 25; Tamás Balogh, 'A Biblia ma is beszél', *Adventhírnök*, 1 (1996), 16.

[202] László Csalami,'Szegeden is véget ért az evangélizáció', *Adventhírnök* (1992), 12; Panek József, 'Malcom Potts előadás sorozat', *Adventhírnök* (1991), 9.

[203] Tony Campbell előadás sorozat Zalaegerszegben (1991). In *Adventhírnök* (10), p. 8; Szőllősi Árpád, 'Csodálatos felfedezések ókori országokban: Ilyen még nem volt', *Adventhírnök* (1991), 10; Árpád Szőllősi, 'Újra Zalaegerszegen!', *Adventhírnök* (1992), 11.

[204] Éva Juhász, 'Evangélizáció Miskolcon', *Adventhírnök*, 3 (1992), 10.; 'Keresztség es hálaadó istentisztelet Miskolcon', *Adventhírnök*, 6 (1995), 12.

[205] Róbert Soós, 'Az ókor világáról', *Adventhírnök*, 3 (1996), 8.

[206] Árpád Szőllősi, 'Félelem-Remény-Öröm-Hálaadás', *Adventhírnök*, 1 (1996), 16; Imre, Tokics, 'Pesterzsébeten is hangzott az ige', *Adventhírnök* (1992), 10; Lajos Székely, 'Evangélizáció Sashalmon és Pesterzsébeten', *Adventhírnök* (1993), 12.

[207] István Agárdi, 'Evangelizációk Keresztségek', *Adventhírnök*, 11 (1992), 8; István, Agárdi, 'Felfedezések', *Adventhírnök* (1993), 8.

[208] Tibor Szilvási, 'Nem kell menned messzi útra', *Adventhírnök*, 5 (1994), 18.

[209] Zoltán Szilasi, 'Lépések egy új világrend felé', *Adventhírnök*, 5 (1994), 19; Zoltán, Szilasi, 'John Wesley Flower újabb látogatása a debreceni körzetben', *Adventhírnök*, 1 (1995), 30.

[210] 'Evangelizáció Szekszárdon', *Adventhírnök*, 6 (1994), 12.

[211] Tamás Hock, 'Evangelizaciok Keresztségek', *Adventhirnök* (1993), 10 (p. 10).

[212] 'Hamilton Williams ismét Szolnokon', *Adventhírnök*, 3 (1993), 8.

[213] Ferenc Rajki, 'Gépkocsiból hívogattak az evangélizációra', *Adventhírnök* (1990), 36; Simon, Ágnes, 'A lélek esője Mogyoródon is hullik', *Adventhírnök, 19-12* (1990), 39

[214] 'Új Arcok', *Adventhírnök* (1990), 7.

[215] 'Tiszavidéki Egyházterület Választókonferenciája', *Adventhírnök* (1993), 11.

were in agreement in reaching this assessment. However, at the meeting of the plenary session of the Hungarian union on 7 March 1993, the reports submitted by the two conferences revealed a significant difference in the number of conversions. The Tisza Conference had baptized twice as many people as the Duna Conference was able to do. Leaders came to the conclusion that two factors had played important roles in the growth of the Tisza Conference. Firstly, the larger number of public events with foreign evangelists was clearly recognizable. Secondly, Tisza Conference pastors spent considerably more time visiting interested parties (potential converts) in their homes than they spent on administration.[216] The Duna Conference argued at the meeting that they needed more support from outside and wanted to have more foreign evangelists come to help them in the future.[217]

Analysis of how leaders and pastors wrote about public evangelism run by foreigners from 1990 to 1995 leads to the impression that this paradigm for mission reached its peak in 1992. Although leaders were still promoting it at the beginning of 1993, various publications show that by the first half of 1993 some leaders had already started to analyse this leading paradigm critically and to address several problem areas.

Changes in the paradigm after 1993
As union president, Szigeti was deeply involved in the implementation of the 'Global Strategy' initiative by the General Conference and he promoted it at the beginning of the programme. As early as 1993 a clear change could be recognized in his focus regarding mission and what he advocated. Without criticizing the leading model for evangelism, Szigeti addressed two areas that he believed could actually lead to a paradigm change:
1. He emphasized that the spiritual renewal of local congregations was vital because this was one secret of success when it came to outreach campaigns. This statement indicates that local congregations were often not prepared for the programmes that were planned for them as part of the worldwide strategy. He seemed to be admitting that top-down planning had failed to recognize local realities.
2. Szigeti urged Hungarian Adventists to start small-group ministry as the leading new paradigm for mission because this was what people really needed. He also stated that this was the specific way in which growth would be possible in the future.[218]

Promoting small-group ministry meant that local people needed to become involved as leaders of smaller groups of people. Indeed, more people needed to

---

[216] See the Minutes of the plenary session of the Hungarian Union Conference of 7 March 1993. HUC Archive, Pécel.
[217] Beszámoló és tervek, *Adventhírnök*, 2 (1993), 4-5.
[218] Jenő Szigeti, *Adventhírnök* 3 (1993), 3.

participate in ministry and it should be carried out in a holistic way.[219] These concerns appeared to identify the problem areas affecting Hungarian Adventists in regard to the leading pattern for mission at that time.

The difficulty with financial challenges
Inviting guest speakers from Western countries, renting large halls, distributing tens of thousands of invitation cards and organizing big events involved too much expense for the small Hungarian Union Conference of around 3,500 members at a time of serious economic shortage. Funds from the division or the General Conference were mostly what made the large events possible. Hungarian Adventists often received fairly large amounts from outside sources such as the GC or the Trans-European Division for the specific purpose of financing public evangelistic meetings. [220] However, the number of these sponsored events was much smaller than Hungarians had hoped. More contributions were needed but the conferences had only limited financial resources. The Hungarian leadership turned towards church members for more money. In order to be able to pay the bills, the Tisza Conference leaders urged local congregations to set aside a budget to support public meetings.[221] One idea was that if a local church had enough funds, it would also be possible to invite foreign speakers. These directions from the conference leadership passed on financial responsibility to the local congregations. There is no evidence on record about what this meant for the church members, who were mostly financially challenged, but the facts reveal clearly that inviting Western evangelists depended almost entirely on external resources.

Problem with reliability of foreign evangelists
One or two months later, another difficulty was added to the above concerns. The preparation of major events took months and needed large sums of money. The Tisza Conference reported that on many occasions the evangelists were unable to come, for a variety of reasons.[222] The resulting failure to conduct programmes that had been announced led to disappointment and brought discredit to the church. These negative side effects of dependence on external resources caused dissatisfaction, not only among the public but also among church members. Not only had the absence of guest speakers created considerable inconvenience but also sometimes the content of the

---

[219] Trainings were organized, networking was initiated and publications supported the participation of church members in ministry. See Zoltán Szilasi, 'Ifjú gyülekezeti munkások találkozója', *Adventhírnök*, 1 (1994), 5; József Szilvási, 'Az evangéliumi szolgálat hű betöltése', *Adventhírnök*, 6 (1995), 2; Tibor Szilvási, 'Nem kell menned messzi útra', *Adventhírnök*, 5 (1994), 18.

[220] One example is the donation of 20,000 USD received from the General Conference in 1991 for Nyíregyháza, Nemesvámos and Rákoscaba. In 'A Generál Konferencia evangélizációs adománya', *Adventhírnök*, 3 (1991), 14.

[221] Beszámoló, tervek, *Adventhírnök* 2 (1993), 13-14.

[222] Árpád Szőllősi, 'A Dunamelléki Egyházterület terve az 1994-es esztendőre', Adventhírnök 6 (1993), 10.

lectures that were given in place of those that had been expected was considered to be second-rate. Some lecturers presented archaeological and historical topics without having had professional training in these areas. University students from these disciplines listened to the presentations and complained about the inadequate content of the lectures.[223] Afterwards, local church members had to face critics because of such issues.

Despite the challenges, Hungarian Adventists continued to run public meetings with Western speakers. One of the last such large meetings was conducted in Debrecen in 1994, with John Fowler as the main speaker. Sadly, the results, in terms of numbers, were considerably lower than might have been expected previously. Despite the huge number of invitation cards –80,000 – the number of audience members did not rise above 350 and there were just 27 converts baptised. From 1994 onwards, the number of such big events with foreign speakers and large numbers of people in attendance dropped significantly. The denomination learned to focus more and more on activities carried out by locally trained pastors and lay members of the church.[224]

Regular evangelism by local pastors and church members

Hungarian church leaders had expected pastors to conduct evangelistic meetings before the regime change but these meetings had usually been held in church buildings or in small halls and the expectations had been far more modest than the later possibilities presented in relation to larger projects run by foreign evangelists. The pressure of expectation placed on pastors grew substantially after the regime change, without significant increase in human resources, personal and financial support for the expected work. Local pastors, such as Ferenc Rajki, had to work in quite primitive conditions. When Rajki conducted his lectures in Medgyesegyháza, there was a lack of invitation cards so church members drove around in cars and invited people to the meetings personally.

---

[223] I have received the information in personal interviews with pastors about the program. They used to be involved in the organization of these events and cared for the later follow up programs.

[224] See reports: Béla Szőllősi, 'Evangélizáció Csengerben', *Adventhírnök*, 3 (1994), 15; Szilvia Zágonyiné Nagy, 'Gyülekezeti Ifjúsági csopportok ötletbörzéje', *Adventhírnök*, 4 (1994), 9, 14; Zagyva, László, 'Televíziós műsor Karcagon', *Adventhírnök*, 2 (1995), 8; 'Lezárult a Magyar Unió történetének egy fontos szakasza', *Adventhírnök*, 2 (1994), 1; 'Munkátok nem hiábavaló az Úrban: Beszámoló az 1994-ben végzett szolgálatunkról', *Adventhírnök*, 3 (1995), 4–5; Farkas, Dániel, 'Dohányzás leszoktató tanfolyam Szegeden', *Adventhírnök*, 1 (1994), 16; Robert S. Folkenberg, 'Meghatározni a gyülekezet misszióját', *Adventhírnök*, 4 (1994), 2; *Global Mission Progam: Tisza Conference, Report to the plenary session of the executive committee of HUC (1995),* Archive material, HUC Archive Pécel, 1-4; Gyűrűs, Istvánné, 'Hírek a Bács-Kiskun megyei körzet életéből', *Adventhírnök*, 2 (1995), 15; Ócsai, Sándor, *Titkári beszámoló (Secretary report)*, 1 March 1995, Archive of HUC of SDA church Pecel, UBXII/7.

Despite the difficulties, the number of people who attended the lectures in this small town of about 3,600 inhabitants ranged between 80 and 140.[225]

Church leaders recognized the need for more support and from 1991 onwards they took definite steps to empower local Hungarian pastors to succeed in the kind of ministry that was expected. In 1991 Adventists from the USA donated twenty slide projectors to the Hungarian union, along with twenty-nine pre-written sermons illustrated with slides.[226] This was the start of the use of media in public preaching.

Both Hungarian conferences also formulated their expectations in relation to local pastors in no uncertain terms. Each pastor was expected to conduct at least two series of public evangelistic events per year.[227] From 1990 onwards, more and more plans and reports could be found in committee minutes about pastors not only working in their own church buildings but stepping out of their comfort zones and conducting series of meetings in public halls, rented facilities and school buildings. Some Hungarian pastors developed skills for delivering public presentations and even travelled across the country, conducting meetings. These pastors included: József Fegyverneky,[228] Zoltán Mayor,[229] Jenő Szigeti,[230] József Szilvási,[231] and Árpád Szőllősi.[232]

The reports show a particular kind of development in the activities of Hungarian pastors. Instead of following Western models they developed creative and need-oriented ideas for the ministry, such as meetings with married couples, cooking programmes, a 'helping hands' programme offering practical support to

---

[225] Ferenc Rajki, 'Gékocsiból hívogattak az evangélizációra', *Adventhírnök* (1990), 36.

[226] 'Vetítőgépek diasorozatok az evangélium szolgálatában', *Adventhírnök* (1991), 16.

[227] 'Dunamélleki egyházterület választókonferenciájának határozatai', *Adventhirnök* (1993), 9–10; Árpád Szőllősi 'A Dunamelléki Egyházterület 1993 évi terve', *Adventhírnök*, 12 (1992), 8; Sándor Ócsai, 'A Tiszavidéki Egyházterület terve az 1993-as évre', *Adventhírnök*, 12 (1992), 9.; András Szilvási, 'A Tiszavidéki Egyházterület terve az 1994-es esztendőre', *Adventhírnök*, 12 (1993), 11; Tiszavidéki Egyházterület, 'A növekedés iránya', *Adventhírnök*, 2 (1993), 13.

[228] 'Evangelizáció a csongrádi körzetben', *Adventhírnök* (1991), 16; 'Evangélizációs sorozat volt Nyírpazonyban', *Adventhírnök* (1991), 14; Hilda Beres, 'Evangelizácios sorozat Nyírturán', *Adventhírnök* (1991), 15; Imre Labanc, 'A lélek esője Hajduszoboszlón is hullik', *Adventhírnök* (1991), 9; 'Elmenvén azért tegyetek tanitványokká minden népeket', *Adventhírnök* (1992), 10; Antal Molnár, 'Evangélizáció Hajduböszörményben', *Adventhírnök* (1992), 19; Tivadar Kormos, 'Adventista keresztelő Lentiben', *Adventhírnök*, 3 (1994), 15; József Fegyverneky, 'Evangélizációs sorozatok', *Adventhírnök*, 2 (1995), 11. Fegyverneky, József, 'Evangélizációs sorozatok', *Adventhírnök*, 2 (1995), 11.

[229] Sándorné Nagy, 'Evangelizáció Várpalotán', *Adventhírnök* (1992), 12; Laszlone Figus, 'Keresztség ünnepélyek Csengerben', *Adventhírnök* (1993), 16.

[230] László Zagyva, 'Evangelizació Karcagon', *Adventhírnök*, 3 (1996), 12; János Sztán, 'Evangelizációk és bibliaklubok a csongrádi körzetben', *Adventhírnök* (1992), 10; Zoltán Hoffer, 'Kecskeméten', *Adventhírnök*, 1 (1994), 14; Dániel Farkas, 'Gyülekezeti hír az Óbudai körzetből', *Adventhírnök* (1993), 15.

[231] János Sztán, 'Evangelizációk es bibliaklubok a csongrádi körzetben', *Adventhírnök* (1992), 10.

[232] László Simon, 'Sopronban várják az adventista fiatalokat', *Adventhírnök* (1993), 12.

people in need,[233] evangelistic pathfinder camps for young people[234] and a programme for children about God.[235]

The main focus was still on evangelism in the official communication published by the denomination. 'This is the key to our effective ministry,' stated leaders in 1992 and they urged pastors and church members to demonstrate more enthusiasm in this regard.[236] During the five years of the quinquennium, a slight shift in focus can be observed in statements by the leaders regarding evangelism. They placed strong emphasis on conducting large-scale meetings with guest speakers from abroad. Two years later an increasing emphasis on the ministry of local pastors as the key element of mission could be observed. Then, while importance continued to be given to this second element, the focus shifted increasingly towards a third one — the training of church members and their involvement in ministry.[237] Because of the previous reorganization of the structure of ministries, the department of home missionary increasingly received and took on responsibility for the training and equipping of church members.

The year 1995 became a landmark in Hungary, in the development of the denomination from within. At a workers' meeting in Parád pastors expressed their disappointment in the foreign models used in evangelism.[238] They were especially critical of how large public meetings had been run with foreign evangelists. The pastors urged their leaders to change direction and to adopt and implement new models for maintaining church life and mission. Some pastors also noted that they were no longer content to simply wait for instructions to come from across the borders; they wanted to be involved in the evaluation of the situation and in planning future strategies. They also expressed their frustration with the emphasis on numerical goal-setting. A strong desire was voiced for more stress to be given to growing quality in church life, for national cooperation by pastors according to their talents and expertise and for national networking. Young pastors, in particular, made it clear that they wanted to be involved in designing the development of the denomination. They wanted to

---

[233] István Gyűrűs, 'Beszámoló a Bács-Kiskun megyében 1994-ben végzett munkáról', *Adventhírnök*, 3 (1994), 18 (p. 18).

[234] Tibor Háló, 'Kihivás – Elhivás', *Adventhírnök*, 2 (1990), 7.

[235] István Podina, 'Gyermekekkel az Úrért Izsofalván', *Adventhírnök*, 1 (1995), 29.

[236] *Adventhírnök*, 1 (1992), 8.

[237] See the plans and strategies of the union in *Adventhírnök* 6 (1993), 7.

[238] Different kinds of regular meetings of Hungarian pastors and workers contributed strongly to a maturing process and growing networking activities. See reports: 'Lelkészek táborozása', *Adventhírnök*, 4 (1994), 5; 'Parádi találkozó', *Adventhírnök*, 1 (1995), 4–5; 'Parádi találkozó', *Adventhírnök*, 6 (1995), 4; Szilasi, Zoltán, 'Ifjú gyülekezeti munkások találkozója', *Adventhírnök*, 1 (1994), 5. See also a summary of the development in Vilmos Kovács, 'Az Adventista Egyház misszói fejlődése 1985 és 1995 között Magyarországon' (Adventista Teológiai Főiskola, 2004); Olivér Krisán, 'Stratégiai tervek, célkitűzések, evangélizációk, keresztségek, eredmények az 1985-1995-ös években' (Adventista Teológiai Főiskola, 2003).

write history.[239] This meeting of Hungarian pastors became a landmark and signalled the end of the era of domination by models of Western culture. Frustratingly, however, although pastors were able to set the agenda for the meeting in Parád, later interviews with participating ministers showed that the leaders were not yet ready to abandon the top-down style of administration and embrace the idea of designing ministry according to the plans developed in Parád in cooperation with the Hungarian pastors.

Conclusion

The foregoing list of focus areas in mission and the description of ´Harvest 90´and ´Global Strategy´, along with the account of how they were implemented, present a picture of the struggle that Hungarian Adventists experienced during a key period in the history of their country.

The struggle took place between, on the one hand, traditional ways of doing mission, based on a 'truth-oriented' approach and, on the other hand, ministries focusing on the needs expressed by people.

There was also tension in Hungary between using evangelistic or other outreach activities that had been forbidden during Communism and developing new, creative and relevant ways of conducting ministry.

The Adventist Church in Hungary needed to choose between models promoted by western evangelists and mission methods better suited to the budget, skills and abilities of Hungarian pastors and local churches. Evangelists and pastors who came to Hungary from western countries, especially those leaders from the higher levels of the denominational structure, presented a kind of dominant culture in very decisive terms and expressed high expectations of Hungarian Adventists. Within a few years the influence of that dominant culture had vanished and Hungarians demonstrated growing maturity in evaluating, designing and implementing their own mission theory.

---

[239] Magyar Unió, 'Parádi Találkozó', *Adventhírnök*, 1 (1995), 4–5.

Final Conclusions

Religious Openness in Society Needs to Be Properly Understood

The time of regime change was a turbulent period for Hungary but also for all the other Central and East European countries. This historical overview of the process leading to regime change and the study of the political, socio-economic and religious developments has presented the dramatic challenges millions experienced and has provided insights concerning the demanding setting Adventists were placed in, along with all the other Christian denominations in Hungary during those years. However, before concluding comments are offered, the limitations of the findings must be noted. The complex historical development of the nation and, within it, of the denomination – including its particular theological, structural and cultural backgrounds – makes it unreasonable to generalize too broadly. Besides major trends in society and also in the Seventh-day Adventist Church, many differing interests, initiatives and activities were observed.

Enough has been discovered about Adventist missionary thinking and actions, and about the development of Hungarian society as the context of that outlook and activity at the time of the regime change, to permit some tentative conclusions to be offered here. As additional, necessarily empirical studies of various aspects of Adventist mission in Hungary are completed in the future and as the impact on the society the denomination is serving in is assessed, more insight will be available and then, perhaps, the findings can be declared normative.

The foregoing analysis of the strategic steps taken by Adventists gives the impression that the Adventist church was not prepared to evaluate the specific Hungarian situation analytically and that, as a consequence, it failed to accurately understand the reactions and the changing attitudes of the public. The complex development undergone by Hungarian society and its openness towards religious matters apparently led to the hasty and simplistic conclusion that a religious renaissance had begun. The openness of the Hungarian public was a kind of curiosity or a need-driven search for alternative solutions and answers to life's challenges. It provided a unique opportunity for religious organizations to try to share religious values, beliefs and alternative lifestyles that had been mostly suppressed during the Communist era and to respond, when appropriate, to the needs expressed by people.

Because the openness in the community was not accompanied by any marked increase in appreciation of the church or by a significantly raised level of faith among the population,[1] the conclusion can be drawn that that established Christian denominations, including the Adventist church, had a very limited understanding of the nature of the new openness and that they failed to use it to increase the effectiveness of Christian faith.

Although interest in religious matters remained at a fairly high level throughout the country, church attendance fell by almost 30% between 1991 and 1996 and the downward trend in public self-assessment as being religious[2] indicates the diminishing prestige of the churches in Hungarian society. This became obvious in reference to Seventh-day Adventists in Hungary because of falling attendance at public programmes conducted by the denomination and also because of the growing number of newly baptized people who were leaving the church.

The membership survey designed by Zoltán Rajki and carried out by the Hungarian Union Conference in 2006 reveals the religious background of those church members who joined the Adventist churches in Hungary after the regime change and remained in the denomination for more than ten years after they were baptized.

Figure 6. Background of baptized SDA people in Hungary 1989-1993

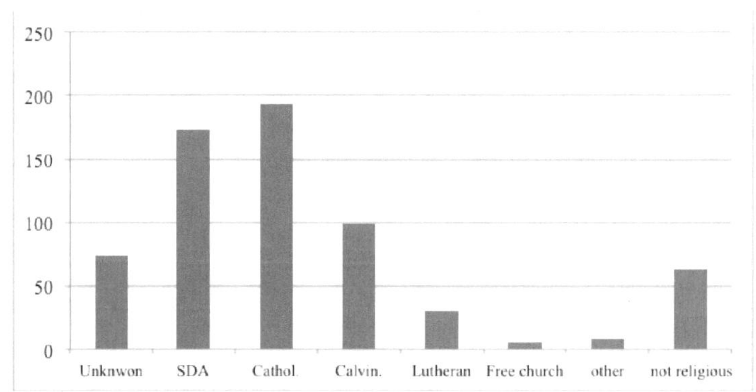

Source: Survey of the Hungarian Union of the
Seventh-day Adventist Church in 2006

The chart makes it clear that Adventist mission activities, in the main, reached members of other churches and their children. Very few people joined the denomination from an atheistic, non-religious background. It can be stated with confidence that, despite intensive missionary efforts and a mobilized membership, Hungarian Adventists found it difficult to reach secular people.

---

[1] Fischer, A vallásosság és a médiumok világa', Slide 6.
[2] See: Pollack, 'Modifications in the Religious Field'.

SDA evangelists benefited mainly from their apologetic approach and had some success in converting other Christians to Adventism.

Moreover, it is significant that the number of dropouts was very high during the years after the regime change. It is possible that the denomination reached more secular people than is indicated by the number of baptisms, but the survey carried out in 2006 shows that, regardless of the actual number of people from secular backgrounds who were baptized during the period of intensive evangelism following the regime change, only a very few of them remained in the Adventist church.

Inappropriate or Varying Mission Theology
Leads to Crises in Missionary Praxis

This study highlights the importance of mission theology. One of the key questions asked during the research was, 'How did the mission theology and the global strategy of the Seventh-day Adventist Church affect the life and missionary activities of the church in Hungary and to what extent was the SDA Church able to meet to the needs of the public in the context of the regime change?'

The section of the development of the missionary thinking of Seventh-day Adventists presented the changing nature, justification and aims of Adventist mission theology throughout the history of the denomination. These developments led to recurring crises long before the time of regime change in Hungary. Despite an honest search (involving efforts that consumed both time and resources) for ways to build a healthy church and a ministry that would be relevant to the circumstances of the world in which it was located, Adventists had to reflect from time to time on the fundamental principles of mission and on the consequences of their work in terms of missionary praxis. This work was carried out mainly by individuals who had the passion or the expertise for mission, during both the initial phases of denominational development and also during the years of regime change in Hungary.

The findings of this study regarding Adventist mission theology can be divided in three areas: the biblical foundation of mission, the relationship of this mission theology to the society or population that is the context of the mission, and the impact of mission theology on the church as a faith community.

Mission theology needs a holistic biblical foundation

Seventh-day Adventism arose within an apocalyptic movement, out of eschatological expectations. People with this Christian heritage focused on the nearness of the second coming of Jesus Christ. During the time of regime change in Hungary this theological background also encouraged a sense of urgency. The increase in the focus on urgency in Adventist mission because of the eschatological character of proclamation-oriented missionary thinking during the period of time under examination often occurred at the expense of holistic service. Howard Snyder's words indicate what happens if the focus deviates: 'Kingdom people seek first the Kingdom of God and its justice; church people often put church work above concerns of justice, mercy and truth. Church people think about how to get people into the church; Kingdom people think about how to get the church into the world. Church people worry that the world might change the church; Kingdom people work to see the church change the world.'[3]

Adventist scholars and pastors promoted adjustments in mission theology and indicated that the biblical foundations of mission activities had to be reviewed. However a healthy process and a forum for theological reflection proved virtually impossible to bring into being. This study has highlighted the influence on mission activities brought to bear by the various theological points of view. There is clearly a need for a biblically relevant and holistic mission theology and for its communication throughout the denomination.

Mission theology needs to relate to the given context of mission activities

Mission theology is supposed to lead to an incarnational process and make Christian activities contextually appropriate and meaningful. The church in Hungary, with its limitations in terms of life and activities, was simply not able to meet the sometimes unreasonably high expectations of the people at the time of the regime change. Modern-day needs challenged local congregations and the new openness of society seemingly urged them to do something more than they were prepared for. They longed for orientation, and opted to use outreach methods and content that came from the Western divisions of the denomination, which dominated the church's design of Adventist missionary materials and programmes. The difference between methods developed in a Western context and the real-life Hungarian situation created a growing tension in the life of already overburdened communities.

Hungarian Seventh-day Adventists turned with enthusiasm towards the public in their country during the period of time covered by this thesis. The willingness of these church members to serve – and their self-sacrificing attitude – is clearly recognizable in the reports about their plans and activities. In their attitude, and in the friendly ways in which they tried to tackle the needs of the public in various areas involving young people, adults and senior citizens, they came very close to meeting the expectations of many potential Adventists in Hungary. On the other hand, the strong emphasis placed by church leaders on quantitative growth and on the methods suggested by western evangelists for reaching numerical and quantitative goals hindered the inculturation of the ministry of Hungarian Adventists within their own country. The message was rather inward-oriented, presenting answers to questions that were not necessarily urgent or related to the

---

[3] Howard A Snyder, *Liberating the Church: The ecology of Church and kingdom* (Downers Grove IL.: InterVarsity Press, 1983), p. 11.

needs experienced by the people. There was a focus on the 'truth' and this was delivered by a proclamation-oriented method. Many members of the public who attended evangelistic meetings very often heard one lecture and left without coming back again. The method and the content failed to meet their expectations and rarely offered people any meaningful alternative lifestyle.

The ministry of Jesus gives the theology of mission an incarnational nature and always relates to a specific time and place.[4] From 1985 on, this incarnational nature was not clear in the official outreach programmes conducted by the church in Hungary. However, through experience, Hungarian Adventists increasingly adjusted their methods and the content of their evangelistic material and activity to the milieu in which they worked. A consciously designed process for a contextually relevant ministry would have helped the denomination to set priorities and to use resources more meaningfully for the ministry.

Mission theology needs to relate to the particular faith community and is supposed to move them towards action starting from their standpoint

Because of the particular structure of the Adventist faith community in Hungary it was difficult for the local churches in the country to make a significant contribution to the rebuilding of the nation by presenting a distinctive lifestyle and worldview as a worthwhile alternative to what they saw around them. Their below-average social status meant that Adventists tended to avoid involvement in public life or in mainstream social life. As Tomka suggests, only a small proportion of religious people were to be found in socially advantaged groups and this hindered the churches from representing themselves properly to the non-religious segment of the population.[5]

Further study of the age structure of the denomination reveals that there was also a lack of a healthy gender balance among the church members. The number of female members was almost double that of the male members at the time of the regime change. Moreover, records show that 58.4 % of church members were aged sixty or over and that 43.9% of the total membership was made up of women over the age of sixty.

In contrast to the age structure of the denomination in Hungary, the average age of people baptized between 1984 and 1988 was very young; 71.63% of them were under 40. Comparing this statistic with the average age of church members, a huge difference can be seen. This may have been responsible for generational conflicts within the denomination in Hungary.

---

[4] Engen, *Mission on the way,* pp. 17-31.
[5] See: Tomka, *Church, state, and society in Eastern Europe*, p. 54.

Figure 7. Age structure of HUC in 1988 (proportional)

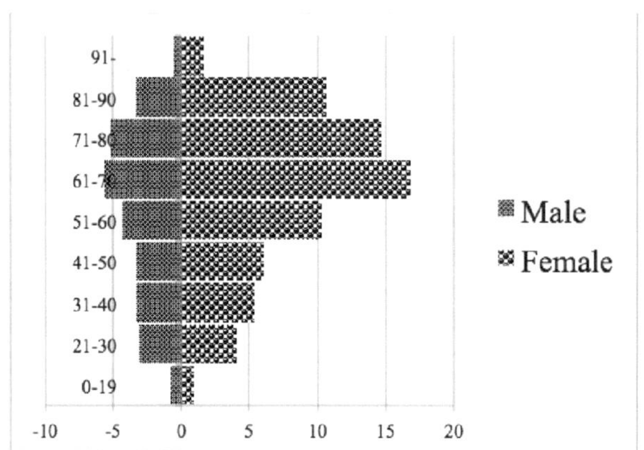

Source: Statistical reports of HUC, Archive Pécel

Statistics from the years that followed indicate the same tendency; young people formed the majority of those who joined the Adventist church in Hungary. The average age of baptized members rose a little after 1994 but it still differed considerably from the average age of church members in general.

Figure 8. Membership development of HUC 1984-1998

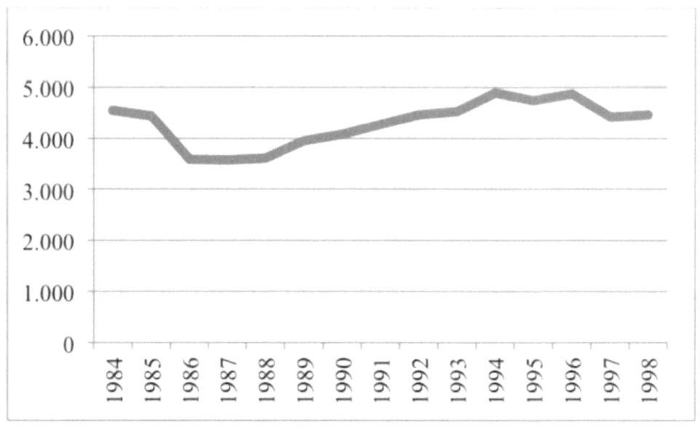

Source: Office of Archives, Statistics and Research,
General Conference of SDA Church[6]

Data available in the archive of the Hungarian Union Conference and at the statistical office of the General Conference show constant membership growth during the period of time under examination. After many years of decreasing

---

[6] Office of Archives, Statistics and Research, General Conference of SDA Church, *Statistical reports* (2014) <http://www.adventiststatistics.org> [accessed 16 December 2014].

membership, a clear shift can be recognized in the development of the denomination in Hungary.

The Adventist community in Hungary began growing in 1988, reaching a plateau in terms of membership in 1994. The steady growth did not depend entirely on new people joining the denomination through baptism; in fact, the pattern of baptisms appears somewhat erratic. Besides baptism, two other factors influenced the growth of the church significantly. One of these was immigration to Hungary, mainly from Romania. The other factor was accession to the church by baptized Christians who joined the denomination by profession of faith rather than by further baptism.

Figure 9. Development of Baptisms 1985-1995

Source: Office of Archives, Statistics and Research,
General Conference of SDA Church[7]

Analysis of the statistical development helps to explain why the president of the Hungarian Union of Seventh-day Adventists complained in 1990 about growing tensions within the denomination, about weakening or even dying congregations, despite the unique change Christians had experienced in the post-communist era: 'The majority of the members clung to the status quo, preserving legalistic traditions. As a result, the church found it almost impossible to cope with young people and the congregations became old and weak [...]. Because of that, about a hundred or a hundred and twenty church groups, both large and small, have died out in the past fifty years.'[8]

---

[7] Statistics and Research, General Conference of SDA Church.
[8] Jenő Szigeti, Report of the Hungarian Union Conference for the TED winter meetings in 1990, HUC Archive Pécel.

Study of this historical and statistical development leads to the conclusion that mission theology at the time of the regime change in Hungary was not able to meet challenges or provide answers to the questions with which Adventists were struggling. Actions prevailed over reflection throughout the period of time examined in this study. The lack of proper interweaving of reflection and action made actual missionary engagement more and more demanding and resulted in growing questions and struggles. Missionary participation declined over the years.

Mission theology, by its very nature, calls for participation and action. Leaders have a responsibility, not only to outline a biblically grounded and informed mission theology leading to contextually appropriate missional action, but also to take into account the faith community in its particular context. This study has led to the recognition of necessity of an integrating theme or type of ministry, which has a solid foundation in Scripture, appears appropriate in the context and corresponds to the possibilities and potential of the faith community. With these characteristics, mission means that church strategies, methods and actions always develop within a context and lead Christians to witnessing engagement and meaningful praxis in that particular setting.

Although Adventists showed enthusiasm for the work for Hungary and in Hungary, just as they also did in other East European countries, the dedication of resources and energy brought challenges as well as blessings for the church at that time which did not stem from external pressures of the kind experienced during the Communist years. Instead they were a consequence of the missionary methods and theology applied by the church leaders. Those leaders, in their positions within the hierarchical structure of the Seventh-day Adventist Church, often chose a top-down way of suggesting strategies, methods and actions for mission and frequently failed in terms of cultural sensitivity, East European reality and the specific characteristics of the Hungarian Adventist faith community.

Concluding Comments on Adventist Mission Theology and Theory

Some challenges which arose because of the international character of the denomination and its specific structure still need to be addressed. While leaders of the worldwide denomination search for ways of maintaining and celebrating unity, what points should they consider when they are trying to form, harmonize and communicate the mission theology of the denomination so that it can become biblically grounded, appropriate in its multi-cultural, international context and also sensitive with regard to the local characteristics of its multitude of very different Adventist faith communities?

While international exchange is a natural process in the special structure of the worldwide Adventist church, the denomination must ask what preventive steps ought to be taken in order to avoid introducing, along with the gospel, a type of dominant culture that offers people deceptive concepts and raises unrealistic expectations and hopes.

Adventists are losing ground in the European and American fields. A common problem is decreasing participation in ministry by church members – a difficulty which may be linked to growing consumerism within the denomination. The use of modern media in the proclamation of the Christian 'Good News' often seems to compensate for the growing passivity of church members. Adventists invest tremendous amounts of resources in radio and television programmes, printed materials, attractive internet platforms and smartphone apps in order to allow the gospel to be heard globally, but if Adventist mission theology is not leading people to action and participation, mission has lost its calling. Proclamation of God's message by a few people, even if it is widely distributed through modern media, can never be a substitute for personal participation by all those who call themselves members of the church. In face of current reality, it is time to start renewed reflection and communication about the biblical basis of Adventist mission theology in order to recognize what contextually appropriate missional action must be entered into at the present time.

Bibliography

A Bold Plan to Culminate Harvest 90: An Interview with Carlos Aeschlimann, Coordinator of Harvest 90 (1988), handouts to TED executive committee meetings, archive material, HUC Archive Pécel

A Bold Plan To Culminate Harvest 90: Worldwide Evangelistic Campaign, General Conference of SDA (1988), Archive material, HUC Archive Pécel

A Bucsa-i Gyülekezet, 'Gyülekezeti házat avattunk Bucsán', *Adventhírnök*, 5 (1995), 14

A Comparison of Baptisms/Professions of Faith for 18 quarters of "Harvest 90": Trans-European Division (1990), a report to the executive committee meeting of TED, archive material, HUC Archive Pécel

'A divízió titkárának látogatása a Művelődési és Közoktatási Minisztériumban', *Adventhírnök*, 6 (1995), 9

'A Dunamelléki Egyházterület globális missziói terve az 1990-1995-ös években', *Adventhírnök*, 9-12 (1990), 18

'A Dunamelléki Egyházterület Választókonferenciájának határozatai', *Adventhírnök*, 2 (1993) 9-10

'A Generál Konferencia evangélizációs adománya', *Adventhírnök*, 2 (1991), 14

A III. Magyar Földrajzi Konferencia tudományos közleményei, Conference procedeing (Budapest: MTA Földrajztudományi Kutatóintézet, 2006) CD ROM, [accessed 6 February 2011]

'A Kommunkiációs Osztály beszámolója a magyarországi nyilvános evangélizációról' *Adventhírnök*, 3 (1991), 5–7

'A Nemzetközi Vallászabadsági Társaság magyarországi szervezetének alapítása', Adventhírnök, 4 (1993), 3

'A növekedés iránya', *Adventhírnök*, 2 (1993), 13

A Szerkesztőség, 'Bibliaolvasó Mozgalom', *Adventhírnök*, 5 (1995), 1

'A Tiszavidéki Egyházterület Globális Misszió Terve', *Adventhírnök* (1995). 10

'A TV programok keresztségi eredménye, *Adventhírnök*, 1 (1991), 14

Abilene, Jason Locke, 'Contextualizing the Christian Message for the Czech Republic', *Journal of Applied Missiology*, 04.2 (1993) [accessed 22 November 2010]

Adeney, Frances S, 'Why Biography? Contributions of Narrative Studies to Mission Theology and Mission Theory', *Mission Studies*, 26.2 (2009), 153–72

'ADRA Híradó', *Adventhírnök*, 3 (1992), 15

'ADRA Hírek', *Adventhírnök*, 4 (1992), 13

'ADRA-Híradó', *Adventhírnök*, 1 (1994), 9

'ADRA-Tájékoztató, *Adventhírnök*, 2 (1992), 14

'Advent utca Földeákon', *Adventhírnök*, 1 (1994), 15

'Adventista rádiófélóra', *Adventhírnök*, 2 (1992), 16

Aeschlimann, Carlos E., *World Evangelism-Questionaire: Ministerial Association GC – Evangelism and Harvest 90* (Washington D.C.: General Conference of SDA, 1988)

______. *Annual Council: Harvest 90 Statement; Evangelistic Explosion in Africa; National Evangelistic Campaigns; Ministerial Association Annual Review*, Ministerial Association Bulletin Harvest 90 Number 12 (Washington D.C.: General Conferene of SDA, 1988)

______. *Global Mission's challenges 1990-1995* (Washington D.C.: Gereral Conference of SDA, 1990)

______. *Half-Way Point of Harvest 90*, Ministerial Association Bulletin Harvest 90 Number 8 (Washington D.C.: General Conference of SDA 1987)

______. *Harvest 90 Stretagy for Victory: Baptismal Classes, Baptisms and Retaining Members*, Ministerial Association Bulletin Harvest 90 Number 14 (Washington D.C.:Gereral Conference of SDA, 1989)

______. *Harvest 90's First Anniversary*, Ministerial Association Bulletin Harvest 90 Number 3 (Washington D.C.: Gereral Conference of SDA, 1986)

______. *Inter-America and it's passion for Evangelism: Public Evangelism*, Ministerial Association Bulletin Harvest 90 Number 10 (Washington D.C.: Gereral Conference of SDA, 1988)

______. *World Baptismal Day* (Washington D.C.: General Conference of SDA, 1992), EUD Achive Friedensau

______. *Harvest 90 Victory Final Report: based on the report of the General Conference Office of Archives and Statistics*(Washington D.C.: Gereral Conference of SDA, 1990)

______. *Harvest 90 Victory Special Edition*, Ministerial Association Bulletin Harvest 90 Number 11 (Washington D.C.:Gereral Conference of SDA, 1988)

______. *The Inter-America Division reached One Million Church Members June 1987*, Ministerial Association Bulletin Harvest 90 Number 7 (Washington D.C.: Gereral Conference of SDA, 1987)

______. *WorldWide Evangelistic Campaign, July 1989-June 1990: Total Participation*, Ministerial Association Bulletin Harvest 90 Number 13 (Washington D.C.: Gereral Conference of SDA, 1988)

Agárdi, István, 'Evangelizációk, Keresztségek', *Adventhírnök* (1992), 8

______. 'Felfedezések ókori országokban és a Bibliában', *Adventhírnök,* 1 (1993), 8

Ahlstrom, Sydney E., *A religious history of the American people* (New Haven, CT: Yale University Press, 1972)

Allen, M.J, 'Revelation Seminars in Australia', in *The Inter-America Division Reached One Million Church Members June 1987*, ed. by Carlos E. Aeschlimann (Washington D.C., 1987), Ministerial Association Bulletin Harvest 90, 9

Altschuler, Glenn C., and Jan M. Saltzgaber, *Revivalism, social conscience, and community in the Burned-over District: The trial of Rhoda Bement* (Ithaca, NY: Cornell University Press, 1983)

Ambrus, András, 'Cserkésztábor 1990', *Adventhírnök* (1990), 31

Anderson, Gerald H., *Theology of the Christian Mission* (Nashville, TN: Abingdon Press, 1961)

Andorka, Rudolf, 'A Magyarországi Evangelikus Egyház és az evangélikusok helyzete és problémái 1941-től', *Valóság*, 5 (1994), 32–44

______. 'A Társadalmi Egyenlőtlenségek Növekedése a Rendszerváltás Óta', *Szociológiai Szemle*, 1 (1996) <http://www.szociologia.hu/dynamic/9601andorka.htm> [accessed 4 April 2012]

Andorka, Rudolf and Spéder, Zsolt, 'Poverty in Hungary in 1992-1995', *Szociologiai szemle*, 1996, pp. 126–59

______. 'Social changes and social problems in Hungary Since in 1930s. Economic, Social and Political causes of the domise of state socialism', in *The Transition from*

state socialism in Eastern Europe: The Case of Hungary, ed. by Adam B. Seligman (Greenwich, CT: JAI Press, 1994), 49–96

András, Imre S. J., 'A Kalot Mozgalom Megújulása és a Társadalmi Változások', in *Tomka Miklós 60. Szociológus a Társadalom és az Egyház Szolgálatában*, ed. by András Máté-Tóth (Szeged, 2003)

András, Imre, and Julias Morel, *Hungarian catholicism: A handbook* (Vienna: The Hungarian Inst. for Sociology in Religion, 1983), 1983: UKI-Berichte über Ungarn

André, Károlyné, 'Hírek Dorogról' *Adventhírnök*, 2 (1991), 8

Andrews University Seminary Studies, 42 vols (Berrien Springs, MI: Andrews University Press, 2005)

Andrews, J. N., 'Cause in Switzerland', *Review and Herald* 35.3 (1870) 21-22

_____. 'Our Arrival in Switzerland', *Review and Herald* 44.21 (1874) 166

_____. 'The Seventh-day Adventists of Europe', *Review and Herald* (Nov. 30,1869) 181

Anthony, Martin L., *Church Ministries Department: Lay Training Section: Global Strategy: 1990-2000* (St Albans, 1990) Archive document, HUC Archive Pécel

Appels, A., 'The Year Before Myocardial Infarction', in *Biobehavioural Bases of Coronary Heart Disease*, ed. by TM Dembroski, H Smidt and G Blumchen (Basel: Karger, 1983), 204

Arthur, W. J., *Proposed Contribution by Adra* (St Albans, 1990) Archive document, HUC Archive Pécel

'Az üdvösség reménysége', *Adventhírnök*, 4 (1992), 1–3

Balia, Daryl M., and Kirsteen Kim, *Edinburgh 2010 Volume II: Witnessing to Christ today* (Oxford: Regnum Books International, 2010), Edinburgh 2010 Series

Balogh, Margit: 'Egyház és egyházpolitika a Kádár-korszakban' *Eszmélet, 34* (1997), 69-79

Banyán, Magdolna, 'Krisna Társadalma: Max Weber Hinduizmus Koncepciójának Társadalomtörténeti alkalmazása' (Történelemtudományok Doktori Iskola, 2011)

Barrett, David B., *World Christian Encyclopaedia: A Comparative Survey of Chruches and Religions in the Modern World A.D. 1900-2000* (Oxford: Oxford University Press, 1982)

Bates, Joseph, 'From Bro. Bates', *Review and Herald*, 6.30 (1855), 182

Bauer, Bruce L., 'Congregational and Mission Structures and How the Seventh-day Adventist Church Related to them' (doctoral dissertation, Berrien Springs: Andrews University, 1982)

Bavinck, J.H, and D.H Freeman, *An Introduction to the Science of Missions* (Phillipsburg, NJ: Presbyterian & Reformed Publishing Company, 1992)

Becker, Jürgen, *Jesus of Nazareth* (New York: De Gruyter, 1998)

_____. *Jesus von Nazaret* (Berlin: W. de Gruyter, 1996)

Bereczki, Lajos, *"Krisztusért járva követségben": Tanulmányok a magyar baptista misszió 150 éves történetéből* (Budapest: Baptista Kiadó, 1996)

Beres, Hilda, 'Evangélizációsorozat Nyírturán 1991. február 1-17', *Adventhírnök, 2* (1991), 15

Berhens, Lyn, B., 'Egyek az Ő együttérzésében', *Adventhírnök*, 4 (1995), 22–23

Bevans, Stephen B., *Models of contextual theology* (Maryknoll, N.Y.: Orbis Books, 1992), Faith and cultures series

_____. The Mission has a church: Perspectives of a Roman Catholic Theologian, *in:* Kirsteen Kim and Andrew Anderson, *Edinburgh 2010: Mission Today and Tomorrow* (Oxford: Regnum Books International, 2011), pp. 201-108

'Biblia Levelező Iskola', *Adventhírnök*, 6 (1995), 9

Bicskei, Róbert, 'Felmérés a HNA Egyházból kimaradt, illetve kizárt személyek okairól és körülményeiről' (seminary paper, Pécel: Adventista Teológiai Főiskola, 2000)

Bietz, Gordon, 'Egyek az Ő üdvösségében', *Adventhírnök*, 4 (1995), 7

Billington, James H., 'The Crisis of Communism and the Future of Freedom', *Ethics & International Affairs*, 5.1 (1991), 87–97

Bliss, Sylvester, *Memoirs of William Miller: With Appendices Containing Three Other Contemporary Biographical Sketches* (Berrien Spring, MI: Andrews University Press, 2005), Adventist classic library

Bocola, V. F., 'Editorial: It Is Harvest Time', in *WorldWide Evangelistic Campaign, July 1989-June 1990: Total Participation*, ed. by Carlos E. Aeschlimann (Washington D.C., 1988), Ministerial Association Bulletin Harvest 90

Bócz, Edit Köpeczi, Az állami Egyházügyi Hivatal tevékenysége (Budapest: Akadémiai

Edit Köpeczi Bócz, *Az Állami Egyházügyi Hivatal tevékenysége* (Budapest: Akadémiai Kiadó, 2004).

Bogárdi Szabó, István, *Egyházvezetés és teológia a Magyarországi Református Egyházban 1948 és 1989 között: Teológiai doktori értekezés / Bogárdi Szabó István* (Debrecen: Ethnica, 1995), 3: Societas et ecclesia

Bognár, István, 'Külmisszióban Kréta szigetén', *Adventhírnök,* 6 (1993), 14

Bogomilova, Nonka, 'Reflections on the contemporary religious "revival" religion, secularization, globalization', *Religion in Eastern Europe*, XXIV.4 (2004) <http://www.georgefox.edu/academics/undergrad/departments/soc-swk/ree/2004/Bogomilova.pdf> [accessed 5 April 2012]

_____. 'Reflections on the contemporary relitious "revival" religion, secularization, globalization', *Religion in Eastern Europe*, XXIV.4 (2004), 1–1

Bögre, Zsuzsa, 'Társadalmi – politikai változások hatása a vallásos identitás alakulására Magyarországon (1948-1990) – különös tekintettel 1948-1964 közötti időszakra' (Doctoral Dissertation, Budapest: University of Economic Sciences and Public Administration, 2002)

Bonnell, Victoria E., *Identities in transition: Eastern Europe and Russia after the collapse of communism* (Berkeley, CA: Center for Slavic and East European Studies, University of California at Berkeley, 1996), Research series

Booth, Carlton, 'Evangélizáció az Egyházban', *Lelkésztájékoztató* (1986), 392–400

Borowik, Irena, and Tomka, Miklós, *Religion and Social Change in Post-Communist Europe* (Kraków: "Nomos", 2001)

Bosch, J. David, 'The Structure of Mission: An Exposition of Matthew 28:16-20', in *Exploring church growth*, ed. by Wilbert R. Shenk (Grand Rapids, MI: Wm B Eerdmans, 1983), 218–48

_____. *Transforming mission: Paradigm shifts in theology of mission / David J. Bosch* (Maryknoll, N.Y.: Orbis Books, 1991), no. 16: American Society of Missiology series

_____. *Witness to the World: The Christian mission in theological perspective* (London: Marshall Morgan & Scott, 1980)

Botomani, F.A, 'Guest Editorial', in *The Inter-America Division reached One Million Church Members June 1987*, ed. by Carlos E. Aeschlimann (Washington D.C.: General Conference of SDA, 1987), Ministerial Association Bulletin Harvest 90, 2–3

Boyd, Gregory A., 'God at War', in *Perspectives on the World Christian Movement: A reader*, ed. by Ralph D. Winter and others, 4th edn (Pasadena Calif: William Carey Library, 2009), pp. 100–11

Bremer, Thomas S., *Religion and the Conceptual Boundary in Central and Eastern Europe: Encounters of faiths* (Basingstoke England, New York: Palgrave Macmillan, 2008), Studies in Central and Eastern Europe

Bresee, Floyd, 'Training Ministerial Interns', in *The Inter-America Division reached One Million Church Members June 1987*, ed. by Carlos E. Aeschlimann (Washington D.C., 1987), Ministerial Association Bulletin Harvest 90, 20

Bristish Union Conference, *Process Report for First Ten Months of 1989: Harvest 90* (1990), archive material, HUC Archive Pécel

British Council of Churches. Study Commission on Trinitarian Doctrine Today., *The forgotten Trinity. 1, The report of the BCC Study Commission on Trinitarian Doctrine Today* (London: British Council of Churches, 1989)

Brown, Archie, *The Rise and fall of Communism*, 1st edn (New York: Ecco, 2009)

Brown, Georg, 'Membership Conservation And Authentic Church Growth', in *Harvest 90 Strategy for Victory: Baptismal Classes, Baptisms and Retaining Members*, ed. by Carlos E. Aeschlimann (Washington D.C., 1989), Ministerial Association Bulletin Harvest 90, pp. 21–22

Brown, James F., *Hopes and shadows Eastern Europe after Communism* (Durham, NC: Duke University Press, 1994)

——. *Surge to freedom: The end of communist rule in Eastern Europe* (Durham, NC: Duke University Press, 1991)

Bull, Malcolm, and Keith Lockhart, *Seeking a sanctuary: Seventh-day Adventism and the American dream*, 2nd edn (Bloomington, IN: Indiana University Press, 2007)

——. 'The Intellectual World of Adventist Theologians', *Spectrum*, October (1987), 32–37

Burrill, Russell *Recovering an Adventist Approach to the Life and Mission of the Local Church* (Fallbrook, CA: Hart Research Center, 1996)

——. *Radical Disciples for Revolutionary Churches* (Fallbrook, CA: Hart Research Center, 1996)

——. *Radical Disciples for Revolutionary Churches* (Fallbrook, CA: Hart Research Center, 1996)

Bush, Lennon, *Effective church planting: A Qualitative Analysis of Selected Church Planting Models* (Lousiville: Southern Baptist Theological Seminary, 1999)

Canright, Dudley M., 'Present Condition of the World', *Review and Herald* (April 16, 1872), 137-138.

Casanovas, José, *Public Religions in the Modern World* (Chicago, IL: The University of Chicago Press, op. 1994)

Chaney, Charles L., *The Birth of Bissions in America* (Pasadena, CA: William Carey Library, 1976)

Cho, Paul H., 'Between Edinburgh 1910-2010: changing theological views of mission', *Modern Believing*, 51.3 (2010), 16–24 <http://search.ebscohost.com/login.aspx?direct=true&db=rfh&AN=ATLA00017936 86&site=ehost-live>[accessed 28 February 2012]

Cipkowski, Peter, *Revolution in Eastern Europe understanding the collapse of communism in Poland, Hungary, East Germany, Czechoslovakia, Romania, and the Soviet Union* (New York: Wiley, 1991)

Co-ordinated Public Evangelistic Plans with Inter-Division Evangelists, Global Strategy (1990) Archive material, HUC Archive Pécel

Costas, Orlando E., *Theology of the crossroads in contemporary Latin America: Missiology in mainline Protestantism, 1969-1974* (Amsterdam [Keizersgracht 302-304]: Rodopi, 1976)

Courtois, Stéphane, and Mark Kramer, *The black book of communism crimes, terror, repression* (Cambridge, MA, London, England: Harvard University Press, 1999)

Courtois, Stéphane, *The black book of communism: Crimes, Terror, Repression*, 5th edn (Cambridge, MA, London, England: Harvard University Press, 2004)

Crampton, R. J., *Eastern Europe in the Twentieth Century*, 2nd edn (London, New York: Routledge, 1997)

Criteria for Disbursement of Global Strategy funds: including application form. General Conference of SDA (Washington D. C.: *Ministerial Association*of SDA, 1990)

Cross, Whitney R., *The Burned-over District: The social and intellectual history of enthusiastic religion in western New York, 1800-1850* (Ithaca, NY: Cornell University Press, 1950)

Csalami, László, 'Szegeden is véget ért az evangélizáció', *Adventhírnök,* 1 (1992), 12

Csegedi-Nagy, Éva, 'A zalaegerszegi gyülekezet alapítása' (Seminary paper, Pécel: Adventista Teológiai Főiskola, 2004)

Csite, András, and Kovách, Imre, 'Posztszocialista Átalakulás Közép- és Kelet-Európa Rurális társadalmaiban', *Szociológiai szemle*, 2 (1995), 49–72

Csizmadia, Andor, *A magyar állam és az egyházak jogi kapcsolatainak kialakulása és gyakorlata a Horthy-korszakban* (Budpest: Akadémiai Kiadó, 1966)

Currie, David, *Models of Christian Witness*, 1993 – TED Winter Meetings (1994) Archive material, HUC Archive, Pécel

Czakó, Gábor, *Indulatos jelentések* (Budapest: Magvető Könyvkiadó, 1973)

Czékmán, János, 'Könyevangélista munka', *Adventhírnök,* 4 (1994), 20

______. 'Könyvevangélista munka: Szekcióülés', *Adventhírnök,* 4 (1994), 20

Dąbrowski, Rajmund Ł., and Beach, Bert B., *Michał Belina Czechowski, 1818-1876: Rezultaty sympozjum naukowego o jego życiu i działalności, które odbyło się w Warszawie, 17-23 maja 1976 roku, z okazji setnej rocznicy jego śmierci*, 1st edn (Warzawa: Wydawn. "Znaki czasu", 1979)

______. *Harvest 90 – Interview with Mark Finley* (1985), Archive material, HUC Archive, Pécel

Damsteegt, P. G., *Foundations of the Seventh-Day Adventist message and mission* (Grand Rapids, MI: Eerdmans, 1977)

Daniells, Arthur G, *Christ Our Righteousness: A Study of the Principles of Righteousness by Faith as Set Forth in the Word of God and the Writings of the Spirit of Prophecy* (Review and Herald Pub. Association, 1941)

______. 'General Conference Session 1901-1902.', in *General Conference Bulletins*, 4 (Battle Creek, Mich., 1895-1922)

Dembroski, TM, H Smidt, and G Blumchen, *Biobehavioural bases of coronary heart disease* (Basel: Karger, 1983)

Dick, Everett N., *Founders of the Message* (Takoma Park, Washington D.C: Review and Herald Publishing Association, 1938)

'Dohányzásleszoktató tanfolyam Szegeden', *Adventhírnök,* 1 (1993), 12

Doss, Gorden R., 'Structural Models for World Mission in the Twenty-first Century: An Adventist Perspective', in *Andrews University Seminary Studies*, 43/2 (Berrien Springs, MI: Andrews University Press, 2005), 301–13

Douglas, Herbert E., *Messenger of the Lord: Chapter 44: The Shut Door—A Case Study* (Berrien Spring, MI: 1999) <http://www.whiteestate.org/books/mol/Chapt44.html#The%20Shut%20Door%E2%80%94A%20Case%20Study> [accessed 5 January 2011]

______. *Messenger of the Lord: The prophetic ministry of Ellen G. White* (Nampa, ID: Pacific Press Pub. Association, 1998), <http://www.whiteestate.org/books/mol/TOC.html#The%20Shut%20Door-A%20Case%20Study> [accessed 5 January 2011]

Duraisingh, Christopher, 'From church-shaped mission to mission-shaped church', *Anglican Theological Review*, 92.1 (2010), 7–28

Dyrness, W.A and others, *Global Dictionary of Theology: A Resource for the Worldwide Church*(Downers Grove, IL: Intervarsity Press, 2008)

East, Roger, and Pontin, Jolyon, *Revolution and change in Central and Eastern Europe* (London, New York: Pinter, 1997)

Eberts, Mirella, and Peter Török, 'The Catholic Church and Post-Communist Elections: Hungary and Poland Compared', in *Religion and social change in post-communist Europe*, ed. by Irena Borowik and Miklós Tomka (Kraków: "Nomos", 2001), 125–47

'Egyek Krisztusban – Parancsoló szükségszerűség', *Adventhírnök*, 4 (1995), 3–6

'Elmenvén azért tegyetek tanítványokká minden népeket"', *Adventhírnök*, 5 (1992), 10

Endrőczi, E., 'Stress és az immunrendszer', *Psychiatria Hungarica*, 1989.2 (4), 107–18

Engelsviken, Tormod, 'Missio Dei: The Understanding and Misundersanding of a Theological Concept in European Churches and Missiology', *International Review of Mission*, 92.367 (2003), 481–97

Engen, Charles E. v., 'Mission Theology in the Light of Postmodern Critique', *International Review of Mission*, 86 (1997), 437–61 [accessed 1 February 2011]

_____. 'What Is Theology of Mission', *Teología y cultura,*, 1.1 (2004) <http://www.teologiaycultura.com.ar/arch_rev/van_engen_theology_of_mission.pdf >[accessed 28 February 2012]

_____. *Mission on the Way: Issues in Mission Theology* (Grand Rapids, MI: Baker Books, 1996)

'Énvelem cselekedtétek meg...", *Adventhírnök*, 1 (1991), 15

Emmerich, András, „Basic Characteristics of Hungarian Church Politics" *Occasional Papers on Religion in Eastern Europe*, 4/1 (1984), Article 4

Erdélyi, László, '"Aki nékem szolgál"', *Adventhírnök*, 6 (1994), 13

_____. 'Advent kiadó', *Adventhírnök*, 2 (1994), 12

_____. 'Események tükrében: A Report about the Ministry of the Executive Committee', *Lelkésztájékoztató* (1986), 355–58

_____. 'Evangélizáció a Tiszavidéken', *Adventhírnök*, 6 (1994), 13

_____. 'Könyvevangélista értekezlet', *Lelkésztájékoztató*, 2 (1990), 74–75

_____. 'Sajátos könyvevangélizáció', *Adventhírnök*, 2 (1995), 9

_____. 'Tapasztalatok története' (1991), 9

Erdélyiné, H. Edit, 'Az ADRA Hungary tevékenysége', *Adventhírnök*, 2 (1994), 11

_____. 'Az ADRA-HUNGARY tevékenysége', *Adventhírnök*, 2 (1994), 11

_____. 'Küldetésben Sopronban', *Adventhírnök,* 5 (1993), 14

_____. 'Megkezdte működését az ADRA Hungary alapítvány', *Adventhírnök,* 3 (1991), 16

_____. 'Segélyt kapott az ADRA', *Adventhírnök, 4* (1993), 11

Euro-Africa Division – Global Mission: A Global Strategy for a Global Mission (Silver Spring, 1990) Archive material, EUD archive Friedensau

European and World Values Surveys four Wave integrated data file, 1981-2004, v.20060423, 2006. Surveys designed and executed by the European Value Study Group and World Value Study Association. (File producers: ASEP/JDS, Madrid Spain and Tilburg University, Tilburg; the Netherlands, 2006)

Evangelism Council: May 13 – 24, 1992 (Washington D.C.: Ministerial Association of SDA), archive material, HUC Archive Pécel, ADCC/lk

Evangelistic Video Set (Ministerial Association, 1991), archive material, HUC Archive Pécel,

'Evangélizáció a Csongrádi Körzetben' *Adventhírnök*, 3 (1991), 16

'Evangélizáció Nyírturán', *Adventhírnök,* 3 (1992), 10

'Evangélizáció Szekszárdon', *Adventhírnök*, 6 (1994), 12

'Evangélizációk', *Lelkésztájékoztató* (1986), 221-224

'Evangélizációs segítség Kárpátalján' *Adventhírnök,* 1 (1991), 15

'Evangélizációs sorozat volt Nyírpazonyban' *Adventhírnök,* 2 (1991), 14

Evans, M., J. Kelley, and T. Kollosi, 'Images of Class: public Perceptions in Hungary and Australia', *Ameriacn Sociological Review*, 57 (1992), 461–82

Executive committee of the Hungarian Union Conference, 'A magyar Unió tervkészítő ülése 1990. november 29-30.', *Adventhírnök,* 1 (1991), 9–11

Executive committee of the Hungarian Union Conference, 'Határozatok', *Lelkésztájékoztató*, 18 (1984)

Executive committee of the Hungarian Union Conference, *Report on the Work of the Hungarian Union 1988* (1989) Archive material, HUC Archive Pécel

Fábián, Zoltán, *Review of the main research on poverty* (Budapest: TÁRKI, 1994) <http://www.tarki.hu/adatbank-h/panelcd/pub/wbp/povrev.html> [accessed 4 April 2012]

Fabinyi, Tibor, 'Bishop Lajos Ordass and the Hungarian Lutheran Church', *Hungarian Studies*, 10.1 (1995), 65–98

Falger, P, and A Appels, 'Psychological risk factors over the life course of myocardial infarction patients', *Advances in Cardiology*, 29 (19˙2), 132–39

Faris, Tommy L., *A Common Sense Life* (Medellin, Colombia: Columbia University, 2007)

Farkas, Dániel, 'A véradómozgalom sem tétlenkedik', *Adventhírnök*, 1 (1994), 9

_____. 'Cegléd', *Adventhírnök*, 2 (1988), 83

_____. 'Dohányzás leszoktató tanfolyam Szegeden', *Adventhírnök*, 1 (1994), 16

_____. 'Evangélizáció Dorogon', *Adventhírnök*, 5 (1992), 10

_____. 'Gyülekezeti hír az óbudai körzetből', *Adventhírnök,* 3 (1993), 15

_____. 'Hírek az óbudai körzetből', *Adventhírnök,* 4 (1993), 12

_____. 'Pestlőrinc', *Adventhírnök,* 2 (1988), 83

_____. 'Vecsés', *Adventhírnök,* 2 (1988), 83

Fazekas, Csaba, *Kisegyházak és szektakérdés a Horthy-korszakban* (Budapest: Teljes Evangéliumi Diák- és Ifjúsági Szövetség; Szent Pál Akadémia, 1996)

Fegyverneky, József, 'Evangélizációs sorozatok', *Adventhírnök*, 2 (1995), 11

Fehér, Ágnes, 'A szabadegyházak', in *Egyházak és vallások a mai Magyarországon*, ed. by Tamás Gesztelyi and Elek Bartha, 1st edn (Budapest: Akadémiai Kiadó, 1991) 121-141

_____. Adventista Házasságok (Adventis marriages): Egy szabadegyházi közösség vallási endogámiájának vizsgálata', *Világosság*, 25.2 (1984), 115–22

Fekete, István, 'A Főzőtanfolyamtól a Bibliakörig', *Adventhírnök* (1990), 29

_____. 'Kezdj el élni!', *Adventhírnök*, 1 (1990), 2–3

Ferge, Zsuzsa, *A Society in the Making: Hungarian Social and Societal Policy, 1945-1975* (Harmondsworth: Penguin Books, 1979)

Figus, Lászlóné, 'Keresztség, ünnepélyek Csengerben', *Adventhírnök,* 6 (1993), 16

Finley, Mark, 'Goals: Man-made or God inspired?', in *Harvest 90's First Anniversary*, ed. by Carlos E. Aeschlimann (Washington D.C., 1986), Ministerial Association Bulletin Harvest 90, 10

_____. 'Hogyan lehetünk eredményes evangélisták?', *Lelkésztájékoztató* (1988), 67–72

_____. *Harvest 90 – Administrative slogan or Compelling Biblical Motivation*, 1985, archive material, HUC archive Pécel

_____. *Harvest 90,* Plans (1986), project document for TED executive committee, archive material, HUC archive Pécel

_____. 'Kulcsok a modern vallási irányzatok megítéléséhez', *Adventhírnök*, 2 (1990), 1

_____. 'Lelkiismereti kérdes-e adventistának vallani magunkat?', *Adventhírnök*, 2 (1990), 6–7

_____. *Soul winning experiences: Together with God in Reaping* (Third quarter, 1985)

_____. *Trans-European Division Harvest 90 Report: Winter Meetings, November 14.-17.1989* (St Albans, England, 1989)

First Meeting of the Euro-Africa Division (Indianapolis, USA, 1990), Archive material, EUD Archive Friedensau

Fischer, György, *A vallásosság és a médiumok világa (Religiosity and the world of media): (Nem elsősorban a közvélemény-kutató szemével)* (Budapest: Gallup, 2000)

_____. 'A "közszolgálati" médiumok és a vallásos közönség', *Vigília*, 3 (1997), 192–98

_____. *A vallásosság és a médiumok világa.* (Budapest: Gallup 2000.)

Fodor, József, *Vallási kisközösségek Magyarországon* ([Budapest: Magyarországi Szabadegyházak Tanácsa, 1986)

Földvári, Mónika, 'A vallásosság típusai a mai Magyar társadalom generációiban', *Szociologiai Szemle*, 4 (2003), 20–33

Folkenberg, Robert S., 'A Generál Konferencia Elnökének véleménye a független mozgalmakról', *Adventhírnök*, 3 (1992), 2–3

_____. 'Meghatározni a gyülekezet misszióját', *Adventhírnök*, 4 (1994), 2

Förster, Michael F., and István G. Tóth, 'Child Poverty and Family Transfers in the Czech Republic, Hungary and Poland', *Journal of European Social Policy*, 11 (2001), 324–41 <http://esp.sagepub.com/content/11/4/324.full.pdf> [accessed 4 April 2012]

Förster, Michael and G. Tóth, István, *Szegénység és Egyenlőtlenségek Magyarországon és a Többi Visegrádi Országban* (Budapest, 1997), TÁRKI Társadalompolitikai Tanulmányok 1.

Förster, Michael and d'Ercole, Mira Marco, *Income Distribution and Poverty in OECD Countries in the Second Half of the 1990s* (2005) <http://www.oecd.org/dataoecd/48/9/34483698.pdf>[accessed 15 April 2012]

Fowkes, Ben, *The Rise and fall of Communism in Eastern Europe* (Houndmills, Basingstoke, Hampshire, New York: Macmillan Press; St. Martin's Press, 1993)

Furet, François, *The passing of an illusion: The idea of Communism in the Twentieth Century* (Chicago, IL: University of Chicago Press, 1999)

Fürtös, László, and Szakolcai Árpád, 'Kontinuitás és Diszkontinuitás az Értékpreferenciákban (1977-1998)', *Szociológiai Szemle*, 3 (1999) <http://www.szociologia.hu/dynamic/9903fustos.htm> [accessed 4 April 2012]

Galasi, Péter, and Nagy, Gyula, 'Are children being left behind in the transition in Hungary?: The paper has been prepared for UNICEF International Child Development Centre.', *Budapest Working Papers on the Labour Market*, 1 (2000) <http://www.econ.core.hu/doc/bwp/bwp/bwp001.pdf> [accessed 4 April 2012]

Gattman, Heinz-Ewald, 'The Understanding of Mission among Seventh-day Adventists in Germany, with Special Reference to the Years 1992-2005: Ph.D. Dissertation' (University of South Africa, 2008)

Gautier, Mary L., 'Church Attendance and Religious Belief in Postcommunist Societies', *Journal for the Scientific Study of Religion*, 36.2 (1997), 289–96

General Conferenc Session 1990, 5 July 1990, General Conferenc of SDA, Archive material, HUC Archive Pécel

General Conference Bulletins, 8 vols (Battle Creek, Mich., 1895-1922)

General Conference of SDA Annual Council, *Report about Church Ministries* (1990), Archive material, HUC Archive Pécel

General Conference of Seventh-Day Adventists, *The Channel: Communication for Biblical, Theological, and Related Studies* (Washington, DC: General Conference of Seventh-Day Adventists, 1978)

General Conference Office Staff Christmas gift to Eastern Europe (1990), Archive material, HUC Archive Pécel

'General Conference Proceedings: Seventeenth Meeting', *General Conference Bulletin* (1889) 141-142

'General Conference Report', *Review and Herald* (1869) General Conrerence of Seventh-day Adventist Church, *World Church Structure and Governance*<http://www.adventist.org/world-church/facts-and-figures/structure/index.html>[accessed 4 April 2012]

Gergely, Jenő, *A Katolikus Egyház Magyarországon, 1944-1971* ([Budapest]: Kossuth, 1985)

Gergely, Jenő, Kardos, József and Rottler, Ferenc, *Az egyházak Magyarországon: Szent Istvántól napjainkig* (Budapest: Korona, 1997)

Gesztelyi, Tamás, and Elek Bartha, *Egyházak és vallások a mai Magyarországon*, 1st edn (Budapest: Akadémiai Kiadó, 1991)

Glatz, Ferenc, and Kálmán Kulcsár, *Magyar tudománytár*, 1st edn (Budapest: MTA Társadalomkutató Központ [u.a.], 2003)

Glatz, Ferenc, *MTA Stratégiai Kutatások, Népegészség, orvos, társadalom* (Budapest: MTA Földrajztudományi Kutatóintézet, 1998)

Global Mission Objectives, HUC document for the executive committee (1990), Archive material, HUC Archive Pécel

Global Mission Progam: Tisza Conference, Report to the plenary session of the executive committee of HUC (1995), Archive material, HUC Archive Pécel, 1-4

Global Mission Program 1990-1995: Duna Conference, Report to the plenary session of the executive committee of HUC (1995), Archive material, HUC Archive Pécel, 5-8

Global Mission Report by Michael L Ryan, Executive Secretary for Global Mission (1991), archive material, EUD Archive Friedensau, *Ref. #91-147*

Global Strategy of the Seventh-Day Adventist Church, General Conference of SDA (1989), Proposal for the meeting, Archive material, HUC Archive Pécel, 1–51

Globale Mission – Von Mensch zu Mensch: Von ernte 90 zur Globalen Mission, General Conference of SDA (1990), Archive material, EUD Archive Friedensau

'God's Free-men', *The Review and Herald*, 22.1 (1863)

Goerner, Martin G., *Die Kirche als Problem der SED: Strukturen Kommunistischer Herrschaftsausübung Gegenüber der Evangelischen Kirche, 1945 bis 1958* (Berlin: Akademie, 1997), Studien des Forschungsverbundes SED-Staat an der Freien Universität Berlin

Goldman, Minton F., *Revolution and change in Central and Eastern Europe Political, Economic, and Social challenges* (Armonk, N.Y.: M.E. Sharpe, 1997)

Golovin, Sergei, 'Worldview: The missing Dimension of Evangelism in Postcommunist Society.', *Religion in Eastern Europe*, XXVIII.3 (2008), 27/64 <http://www.georgefox.edu/academics/undergrad/departments/soc-swk/ree/08index.html>[accessed 4 April 2012]

Greeley, Andrew, 'Religious Revivals in Eastern Europe', *Society*, 1 (2002), 76–77
______. 'A Religious Revival in Russia', *Journal for the Scientific Study of Religion*, 33.3 (1994), 253–727

Gutierrez, Gustavo, *A Theology of Liberation: History, Politics, and Salvation* (Maryknoll, N.Y: Orbis Books, 1988)

Gyetvainé, Gerlay Krisztina, 'Egészségügyi misszió Békés megyében', *Adventhírnök*, 5 (1996), 11

Gyűrűs, István, 'Beszámoló a Bács-Kiskun megyében 1994-ben végzett munkáról', *Adventhírnök*, 3 (1994), 18

Gyűrűs, Istvánné, 'Evangélizáció Kiskunhalason', *Adventhírnök*, 5 (1993), 10

______. 'Hírek a Bács-Kiskun megyei körzet életéből', *Adventhírnök*, 2 (1995), 15

______. 'Táborozások, könyvtáborok', *Adventhírnök*, 5 (1995), 16

______. 'Táborozás Várgesztesen', *Adventhírnök*, 5 (1992), 13

H. N. Adventist Egyház Unióbizottsága, *Jegyzőkönyv*, Protocol of the meeting (1989)

H. N. Adventista Egyház, 'Állásfoglalás a H. N. Adventista Egyház megbízatásáról', *Adventhírnök*, 4 (1994), 2

'Hadd hirdessem nevedet atyámfiainak', *Adventhírnök*, 1 (1990), 3

Hahn, Ferdinand, *Das Verständnis der Mission im Neuen Testament*, 2nd edn (Neukirchen-Vluyn: Neukirchener Verl, 1965), 13: Wissenschaftliche Monographien zum Alten und Neuen Testament

______. *Probleme Japanischer und Deutscher Missionstheologie: [Vorträge und Aufsätze]* (Heidelberg: Geschäftsstelle der Dt. Ostasienmission, 1972)

Halász, Edit, 'Adra-Hiradó', *Adventhírnök*, 2 (1993), 2

Háló, Tibor, 'Kihívás – elhívás', *Adventhírnök*, 2 (1990), 7

'Hamilton Williams ismét Szolnokon', *Adventhírnök*, 1 (1993), 8

Hangyás, László, 'Az evangélista felelőssége a döntsére hívásban', *Lelkésztájékoztató* (1986), 328–30

______. 'Ifjúság és belmisszió', *Lelkésztájékoztató* (1986), 18–21

______. 'Ifjúság és belmisszió', *Lelkésztájékoztató*, 1 (1988), 25–27

______. 'Ifjúság és belmisszió', *Lelkésztájékoztató*, 4 (1988), 227–28

______. 'James Huzzey testvér látogatása', *Lelkésztájékoztató* (1986), 18–21

Hangyás, László, and Mark A. Finley, 'Aratás '90: Jelszó vagy Bibliai motiváció?', *Lelkésztájékoztató* (1986), 169–74

Hankiss, Elemér, *East European Alternatives* (Oxford: Clarendon Press, 1990)

Harkness, Reuben E. E., 'Social Origins of the Millerite Movement' (Ph. D. Thesis, University of Chicago, 1927)

Harvest '90, 31 March 1988, Minutes of the HUC executive committee, Archive material, HUC Archive Pécel, 1

Harvest '90 – July 1 1985 to March 31.1989 Euro Africa Division, 15 quarters (1989) Archive material, EUD archive Friedensau

Harvest '90 report, General Conferenc of SDA (1989), Archive material, HUC Archive Pécel

Haskell, S. N., 'Session 1901-1902.', in *General Conference Bulletins*, 4 (Battle Creek, Mich., 1895-1922)

Havasy, Gyula, *A magyar katolikusok szenvedései, 1944-1989* (Budapest: Havasy Gyula magánkiadás, 1990)

Hegedűs, Rita, 'A vallásosság alakulása Magyarországon a kilencvenes évek kutatásainak türkében' (Ph.D. thesis, Budapest: University of Economic Sciences and Public Administration, 2000)

______. 'A Vallásosság Kérdése Magyarországon a Nemzetközi és Magyar Kutatások eredményeinek tükrében', *Szociologiai szemle*, 1 (1998), 113–26

Heiland, H. G., and L. Shelley, *Civilization, Modernization and the Development of Crime and Control: A paper prepared for the 50th Annual Meeting the American Society of Criminology* (San Francisco, CA: 1991)

Heinz, Daniel *L. R. Conradi: A Hetednapi Adventista Egyház misszionáriusa, evangélistája és szervezője Európában* (Budapest: Élet és Egészség Könyvk., 2004), Adventtörténelem

______. 'Exklusivität und Kontextualisierung: Geschichte und Selbstverständnis der Siebenten – Tags – Adventisten in Deutschland', in *Spes Christiana: A Journal of Theology*, 12 (2001), 121–39

______. 'L. R. Conradis missionarischer Durchbruch: Ein Modell für die Zukunft?', in *Die Adventisten und Hamburg: Von der Ortsgemeinde zur internationalen Bewegung / Baldur Ed. Pfeiffer, Lothar E. Träder, George R. Knight (Hrsg.)*, ed. by Baldur E. Pfeiffer, Lothar E. Träder and George R. Knight (Frankfurt am Main: Lang, 1992), 4: Archives of international Adventist history, 146–70

Hengel, Martin, 'Die Ursprünge der Christlichen Mission', *New Test. Stud.*, 18.01 (1971), 15

Heppenstall, Edward, *In touch with God* (Washington, DC: Review and Herald Pub. Association, 1975)

______. *Our High Priest Jesus Christ in the Heavenly Sanctuary* (Washington, DC: Review and Herald Pub. Association, 1972)

______. *Salvation unlimited: Perspectives in Righteousness by Faith* (Washington, DC: Review and Herald Pub. Association, 1974)

______. *The Man Who is God: A Study of the Person and Nature of Jesus, Son of God and Son of Man* (Washington, DC: Review and Herald Pub. Association, 1977)

Herbert, David, 'Christianity, Democratisation and Secularisation in Central and Eastern Europe', *Religion, State and Society*, 27.3-4 (1999), 277–93

Heron, Alasdair I. C., *The Forgotten Trinity. 3, A Selection of Papers Presented to the BCC Study Commission on Trinitarian Doctrine Today* (London: BCC/CCBI, 1991)

'Hiányzanak-e darabok élete puzzlejából?, *Adventhírnök*, 2 (1992), 10

Hiebert, Paul G., Tite T., *Missional Theology* (2005) <http://www.globalmissiology.org/cms/images/stories/hiebert/Heibert_Tienou_Missi onal_Theology.pdf> [accessed 28 February 2012]

Himes, Joshua, 'Camp-Meeting Notice', in *The Signs of the Times and Expositor of Prophecy*, 3, ed. by Ellen G. White Estate (Silver Spring, 1841-1844)

______. 'Christ's Kingdom at Hand: Reply to the above', *Signs of the Times* (July 15, 1840) 6

______. 'Fall of the Ottoman Empire', *Signs of the Times*, 21 (1841) 162

______. 'The Lord is at Hand.', *Signs of the Times* (October 16, 1844) 85

______. 'The ten Virgins', *Signs of the Times* (1844) 77

Historical Sketches of the Foreign Missions of the Seventh-day Adventists (Berrien Springs, MI: Andrews University Press, 2005)

Hock, Tamás, 'Evangélizációs sorozat Nyíregyházán', *Adventhírnök*, 3-5 (1990), 3

______. 'Evangélizációk és keresztségek', *Adventhírnök*, 5 (1993), 10

______. 'Kezdj el főzni', *Adventhírnök* (1990), 4

Hoekendijk, Johannes C., and Erich-Walter Pollmann, *Kirche und Volk in der deutschen Missionswissenschaft* (München: Chr. Kaiser, 1967), 35: Theologische Bücherei

Hoffer, Zoltán, 'A boldog eet a lelekmentes szolgalataban' (1991), 16

______. 'Bibliakör Kecskeméten', *Adventhírnök*, 6 (1992), 18

______. 'Hogyan árusítsuk könyveinket és a Boldog Életet?', *Adventhírnök*, 1 (1994), 14

______. 'Ifjúsági Tábor', *Adventhírnök*, 1 (1990), 32

______. 'Ifjúsági tábor', *Adventhírnök*, 5 (1991), 7

______. 'Kecskeméten', *Adventhírnök*, 1 (1994), 14

Holmes, Raymond, and Douglas R. Kilcher, *The Adventist minister* (Berrien Springs, MI: Andrews University Press, 1991)

Horányi, Özséb, *Az egyház mozgástereiről a mai Magyarországon.* (Budapest: Vigília, 1997)

Horváth, Tibor, 'Religions, Churches in Modern Hungary and METEM Research', *Hungarian Studies*, 10/1 (1995), 131–37

Horváth, Zsuzsa, 'Az egyház kovásza: a bázisközösségi mozgalmak Magyarországon', in *Hitek és emberek*, ed. by Zsuzsa Horváth (Budapest: ELTE, 1995), pp. 243–82

_____. *Hitek és emberek* (Budapest: ELTE, 1995)

Höschele, Stefan, *From the End of the World to the Ends of the Earth: The Development of Seventh-day Adventist Missiology* (Zomba, Malawi: Kachere Series, 2004)

HUC Executive Committee Minutes, 5 November 1989., archive material, HUC archive Pécel

HUC Plan for Evangelism – TED minutes, *Evangelistic Workshop*, 4 October 1989, Archive material, HUC Archive Pécel

HUC Report for the XII. Union Session about Church Growth (1994. május 12-13.), Archive material, HUC Archive Pécel

'Ifjúsági kongresszus', *Adventhírnök,* 1 (1992), 13

Intézőbizottsági jegyzőkönyv (Executive committee Minutes), Oct. 3. 1983, Archive material, HUC archive Pécel

Irk, Ferenc, *Social Transformation and Crime: Hungarian-German Criminological Symposium: 20–25 August 1995 Budapest, 1995. augusztus 20 – 25* (Budapest: Országos Kriminológiai és Kriminalisztikai Intézet, 1997)

'Isten és a zene', *Adventhírnök*, 5 (1995), 6

Ivan Szelényi, and Donald J. Treiman, *Social Stratification in Eastern Europe After 1989: General Population Survey*<http://archiv.soc.cas.cz/SSEE/SSEE.intro.html>[accessed 22 November 2010]

Ivan, Szelényi, *Social Stratification in Eastern Europe After 1989 (general population, Slovak Republic)* (1993) <http://sasd.sav.sk/en/data_katalog_abs.php?id=sasd_1993001>

James, White, 'Leading doctrines', *The Review and Herald,*6.1 (1854) 1-4

'Járatlan útra vezetett az Úr', *Adventhírnök*, 3-5 (1990), 8

*Javaslat a konyvevangelista munka megszervezesere, Proposal for HUC executive committee,*Archive material, HUC Archive Pécel, 13

Jenkins, Philip, *The Next Christendom: The Coming of Global Christianity / Philip Jenkins* (Oxford: Oxford University Press, 2002)

Job description of pastors, Leadership meeting on the 6 May 1988, Seventh-day Adventist –Archive material, HUC Archive Pécel, HNAE 4314, 2

Johnson, Nigel, and Paddy Moloney, *The Light of the Nations: Lumen gentium the Dogmatic Constitution on the Church of the 2nd Vatican Council* (Harare: Catholic Students Chaplaincy, between 1996 and 2002), booklet no. 2: The thinking Christian

'Jótékonysági hangverseny Békésen', *Adventhírnök,* 2 (1992), 11

'Jótékonysági koncert a Békéscsabai Gyülekezetben', *Adventhírnök,* 1 (1991), 16

Jovanovic, Mladen, *New Evangelistic Opportunities in Eastern Europe*, 01th edn (1990) <http://www.bible.acu.edu/ministry/centers_institutes/missions/page.asp?ID=304> [accessed 22 November 2010]

Józan, Péter, 'Epidemiológiai válság Magyarországan a kilencvenes években II.', *Statisztikai Szemle*, 2 (1994), 101–13 [accessed 3 July 2012]

_____. 'Epidemiológiai Válság Magyarországon a Kilencvenes Években I.', *Statisztikai Szemle*, 1 (1994) <http://www.ksh.hu/statszemle_archive/viewer.html?ev=1994&szam=01&old=7&lap=16> [accessed 4 April 2012]

Juhasz, Éva, 'Evangélizáció Miskolcon', *Adventhírnök,* 3 (1992), 10

Juhasz, Zsuzsanna, 'A lapmisszió', *Adventhírnök,* 2 (1994), 15

Kääriäinen, Kimmo, Religion in Russia after the collapse of communism religious renaissance or secular state (Lewiston, NY: E. Mellen Press, 1998), Symposium series

Kähler, Martin, and Heinzgünter Frohnes, Schriften zu Christologie und Mission: Gesamtausgabe der Schriften zur Mission; mit einer Bibliographie (München: Kaiser, 1971), 42: Theologische Bücherei

Kalosa, Eszter, 'Fiataloknak', Adventhírnök, 4 (1994), 21

Kamarás, István, *Krisnások Magyarországon* (Budapest: Iskolakultúra, 1998)

______. 'Tendencies of Religious Changes in Modern Hungary', Hungarian Studies, 10.1 (1995), 121–30

______. Lelkierőmű Nagymaroson: Religiográfia (Budapest: Vita, 1989)

'Kárpátaljai gyerekek üdültetése Nyárlőricen', Adventhírnök, 5 (1993), 14

Kasdorf, Hans, Current State of Missiology: Reflections on Twenty-five Years 1968-1993 (1994) <http://www.directionjournal.org/article/?823> [accessed 24 November 2010]

'Kelet-európai adventista rádiós szeminárium', *Adventhírnök,* 5 (1991), 16

Keller, Tamás, 'Trendek az életszínvonallal való elégettséget magyarázó tényezők hatásának időbeli alakulásában 1992 és 2007 között', *Társadalmi Riport* (2008), 415–28 <http://www.tarsadalomkutatas.hu/kkk.php?TPUBL-A-824/publikaciok/tpubl_a_824.pdf> [accessed 4 April 2012]

Kennedy, Michael D., *Envisioning Eastern Europe: Postcommunist Cultural Studies* (Ann Arbor, MI: University of Michigan Press, 1994)

Kerekasztal beszélgetések, 'Növekszik-e a vallás befolyása Magyarországon?', *Népszabadság* (9 July 1988) 4

'Keresztség és hálaadó istentisztelet Miskolcon', *Adventhírnök,* 6 (1995), 12

'Keresztség Rákoscsabán', *Adventhírnök,* 5 (1992), 11

'Keresztségek a Dunamelléki Egyházterületen', *Lelkésztájékoztató* (1986), 162

Kerr, David A., and Kenneth R. Ross, *Edinburgh 2010 mission then and now* (Oxford: Regnum, 2009), Regnum Studies in Mission

Kertelge, Karl, *Mission im Neuen Testament,* Norbert Brox (Freiburg im Breisgau: Herder, 1982), 93: Quaestiones disputatae

'Kiadó', *Adventhírnök,* 1 (1994), 14

Kirk, J. A., *What is Mission?: Theological Explorations* (Minneapolis, Minn: Fortress Press, 2000)

Kischkowsky, Alexander, *Die sowjetische Religionspolitik und die Russisch Orthodoxe Kirche,* 2nd edn (München: Inst. zur Erforschung d. UdSSR, 1960), 58: Serie 1

Kiszely, Gábor, *Állambiztonság, 1956-1990* (Budapest: Korona, 2001)

______. *ÁVH: Egy terrorszervezet története / Kiszely Gábor* (Budapest: Korona Kiadó, 2000)

Klingeberg, Heidemarie, 'Globál Stratégia', *Lelkésztájékoztató,* 4 (1990), 201

Knight, George R., "Historical Introduction", in *Historical sketches of the Foreign Missions of the Seventh-day Adventists* (Berrien Springs, MI: Andrews University Press, 2005)

______. *1844 and the rise of Sabbatarian Adventism* (Hagerstown, MD: Review and Herald Pub. Association, 1994)

______. *Anticipating the Advent: A brief History of Seventh-Day Adventists* (Bois, ID: Pacific Press Pub. Association, 1993)

______. *Es war nicht immer so: Die Entwicklung Adventistischer Glaubensüberzeugungen* (Lüneburg: Advent-Verl., 2002)

_____. *Millennial Fever and the End of the World: A study of Millerite Adventism* (Boise, ID: Pacific Press, 1993)

Kolosi, Tamás, and Vukovics G. Tóth István György, *Társadalmi Riport 2002* (Tárki, Budapest 2002)

Kolosi, Tamás and Róbert, Péter, 'A magyar társadalom szerkezeti átalakulásának és mobilitásának főbb folyamatai a rendszerváltás óta idősoros illetve longitudinális nézőpontból', in *Stabilizálódó társadalomszerkezet: TÁRKI MONITOR JELENTÉSEK 2003*, ed. by Péter Szívós and István György Tóth (Budapest, 2004), pp. 10–22

Koning, D.T, *Importing God: The Mission of the Ghanaian Adventist Church and other Immigrant Churches in the Netherlands* (Amsterdam: Vrije Universiteit, 2011)

Kool, Anne-Marie, 'The Church in Hungary and Central and Eastern Europe: Trends and Challenges', *The Princeton Seminary Bulletin*, 28 (2007), 146–64

_____. 'Trends and Challenges in Mission and Missiology in "Post-Communist" Europe', in *Mission Studies: Journal of the International Association for Mission Studies*, 25 (2008), 21–36

Kopp, Mária, and Árpád Skrabski, 'Magyar lelkiállapot – 1997', *Távlatok*, 2 (1997), 157–67

_____. 'MAGYAR LELKIÁLLAPOT AZ EZREDFORDULÓ UTÁN', *Távlatok*, 4 (2000) <http://www.tavlatok.hu/86/86kopp_skrabski.pdf> [accessed 24 November 2010]

Kopp, Mária, Árpád Skrabski, and Sándor Szedmák, 'A szociális kohézió jelentõsége a magyarországi morbiditás és mortalitás alakulásában', in *MTA Stratégiai Kutatások, Népegészség, orvos, társadalom*, ed. by Ferenc Glatz (Budapest: MTA Földrajtudományi Kutatóintézet, 1998), 15–37

Kopp, Mária, Csilla Csoboth, and György Purebl, 'Fiatal nők egészségi állapota', in *Szerepváltozások. Jelentés a nők és férfiak helyzetéről*, ed. by Tiborné Pongrácz and István G. Tóth (Budapest: TÁRKI Társadalomkutatási Intézet Rt., 1999), 239–59

Kopp, Mária, *Magyar lelkiállipot 2008: Esélyerősités és életminőség a mai magyar társadalomban* (Budapest: Semmelweis K, 2008)

Kopstein, J. S, and J Wittenberg, 'Beyond Dictatorship and Democracy: Rethinking National Minority Inclusion and Regime Type in Interwar Eastern Europe', *Comparative Political Studies*, 43.8-9 (2010), 1089–118

Korinek, László, 'Békés egymás mellett félés, avagy félelem a bûnözéstõl Közép-Kelet-Európában', in *Social Transformation and Crime: Hungarian-German Criminological Symposium: 20–25 August 1995 Budapest, 1995. augusztus 20 – 25*, ed. by Ferenc Irk (Budapest: Országos Kriminológiai és Kriminalisztikai Intézet, 1997), pp. 145–50

Kormos, Tivadar, 'Adventista keresztelő Lentiben', *Adventhírnök*, 3 (1994), 15

_____. 'Akik új eletet kezdtek', *Adventhírnök*, 1 (1994), 16

_____. 'Keresztség a Kerka patakban', *Adventhírnök*, 5 (1992), 11

_____. 'Keresztség Balatonlellén', *Adventhírnök*, 5 (1993), 11

_____. 'Két keresztség Rákoscsabán', *Adventhírnök*, 5 (1993), 11

_____. 'Missziós örömök Gyömrőn', *Adventhírnök*, 2 (1988), 72

_____. 'Öröm van a mennyben egy bűnös felett', *Adventhírnök*, 5 (1994), 21

_____. 'Segítség Háza Alapítvány', *Adventhírnök*, 3 (1991), 14

Kornai, János, 'Transformational Recession: The Main Causes', *Journal of Comparative Economics*, 19 (1994), 39–63 <http://www.irisprojects.umd.edu/ppc_ideas/Revolutionizing_Aid/Resources/typology_pdf/transformational_recession.pdf> [accessed 12 July 2012]

Kostov, Viktor, 'Christian Mission in Post-Communism:
    MissiologicalImplicationsandthe BulgarianContext, *Religion in Eastern Europe*,
    29.2 (2009), 26–37
    <http://search.ebscohost.com/login.aspx?direct=true&db=a9h&AN=43365468&site
    =ehost-live&scope=site>[accessed 14 July 2012]
Kovács, Vilmos, 'Az Adventista Egyház misszói fejlődése 1985 és 1995 között
    Magyarországon' Seminary paper (Adventista Teológiai Főiskola, 2004)
Köbel, Szilvia, 'Az Egyházügyi Hivatal működése az újjászervezéstől a megszűnésig
    1959–1989' *Magyar Közigazgatás*, 10 (2001)
_____. 'Vallásfelekezetek törvényes elismerése a Kádár-Korszakban', *Jogtudományi
    Közlöny*, 56.6 (2001), 287–97
Köpeczi-Bócz, Editl, *Az Állami Egyházügyi Hivatal tevékenysége* (Budapest, Akadémiai
    Kiadó, 2004).
Központi Statisztikai Hivatal, *2001. évi népszámlálás* (Budapest, 2001)
Kraaykamp, G. e. a., 'Parental Background and Lifestyle Differentiation in Eastern
    Europe: Social, Political, and Cultural Intergenerational Transmission in Five
    Former Socialist Societies', *Social Science Research*, 29 (2000), 92–122
    <http://gerbertkraaykamp.ruhosting.nl/Pdf_files/2000_SSR.pdf> [accessed 10 July
    2012]
Kraaykamp, Gerbert, and Paul Nieuwbeerta, *Cultural and Material Life-Style
    Differentiationin Eastern Europe: A Study on the Intergenerational Transmission of
    Inequalities in Five Former Socialist Societies* (NWO, 1997)
Kraemer, Hendrik, *The Christian message in a Non-Christian World* (New York:
    Harper, 1938)
Krisán, Olivér, 'Stratégiai tervek, célkitűzések, evangélizációk, keresztségek,
    eredmények az 1985-1995-ös években' (Adventista Teológiai Főiskola, 2003)
Kulcsár, Kálmán, and Bayer,József 'Társadalom, politika, jogrend', *Magyar
    tudománytár* (2003)
Labanc, Imre, 'A lélek esője Hajdúszoboszlón is hullik', *Adventhírnök,* 3 (1991), 9
Ladd, George E., 'The Gospelof the Kingdom', in *Perspectives on the world Christian
    movement: A reader*, ed. by Ralph D. Winter and others, 4th edn (Pasadena, CA:
    William Carey Library, 2009), pp. 83–95
Lakatos, János, 'Menj el, ezzel a te erőddel!', *Adventhírnök*, 5 (1995), 8
Lakatos, Judit, *Keskeny utak: Tanulmányok a Magyarországi Metodista Egyház
    történetéről* (Budapest: Mo. Metodista Egyh, 2005)
Laki, László, 'A magyar fejlődés sajátszerűségégnek néhány vonása', *Szociologiai
    szemle*, 3 (1997), 67–91
Lamont, Christopher, 'Contested Sovereignty: The International Politics of Regime
    Change in the Federal Republic of Yugoslavia', *J. of Communist Stud. & Transition
    Politics*, 25.2 (2009), 181–98
László, Péter, 'Church-state Relationship and civil Society in Hungary: a Historical
    Perspective', *Hungarian Studies*, 1995.1 (10), 3–33
    <http://epa.oszk.hu/01400/01462/00016/pdf/003-033.pdf>
Latourette, Kenneth S., *Christianity in a Revolutionary Age: A History of Christianity in
    the Nineteenth and Twentieth Centuries*, 1st edn (New York: Harper, 195862), III.
Lázár, István, and Albert Tezla, *Hungary: A brief history* (Budapest: Corvina, 1989)
'Leading doctrines', *The Review and Herald* 01- 18. (1854), a series of articles
Le Froom, Roy E., *The Prophetic Faith of our Fathers: The Historical Development of
    Prophetic Interpretation*, 4 v. (Washington, DC: Review and Herald, 1950)

Lelkes, Orsolya, *Tasting freedom: Happiness, religion and economic transition*, 59th
  edn (Londón, 2002) <http://www.euro.centre.org/data/1196258294_82387.pdf>
  [accessed 4 April 2012]

'Lelkészek táborozása', *Adventhírnök*, 4 (1994), 5

Lendvai, L. F., *A Magyar protestantizmus, 1918-1948: Tanulmányok* ([Budapest]:
  Kossuth, 1987, c1986)

Lévai, Miklós, 'Social Changes and Rising Crime Rates: The Case of Central and
  Eastern Europe: Revised version of the paper presented at the Plenary Session II-2 of
  the 12th International Congress on Criminology (24–29 August 1998 Seoul, Korea)',
  European Journal of Crime, Criminal Law and Criminal Justice, 8.1 (2000)
  [accessed 14 December 2011]

'Lezárult a Magyar Unió történetének egy fontos szakasza', *Adventhírnök*, 2 (1994), 1

Liberation theology – Wikipedia, the Free Encyclopedia (2010)
  <http://en.wikipedia.org/wiki/Liberation_theology> [accessed 10 November 2010]

Lienemann-Perrin, Christine, *Contextuality in reformed Europe: The Mission of the
  Church in the Transformation of European Culture* (Amsterdam [u.a.]: Rodopi,
  2004)

Lindén, Ingemar, *1844 and the Shut door Problem* (Uppsala, Stockholm Sweden:
  [Uppsala University]; distributor Almqvist & Wiksell International, 1982), 35: Acta
  Universitatis Upsaliensis

_____. *The Last trump: An Historico-Genetical Study of Some Important Chapters in
  the making and Development of the Seventh-day Adventist Church* (Frankfurt am
  Main, Bern, Las Vegas: Lang, 1978), 17: Studien zur interkulturellen Geschichte des
  Christentums

Loughborough, John N., *Last Day Tokens* (Mountain View, CA: Pacific Press, 1904)

Lukátsi, Vilma, *Élő kövek: Dr. Kiss Ferenc orvosprofesszor dokumentum jellegű
  életrajza* (Budapest: Primo Evangéliumi Kiadó, 1990)

Luxmoore, Jonathan, 'Eastern Europe 1997-2000: a Review of Church Life', *Religion,
  State and Society*, 29.4 (2001), 305–30 [accessed 11 July 2012]

Madarász Ivett, 'Zergék a gyülekezeten', *Adventhírnök*, 3 (1995), 10

'Magyar diákmisszionárius Mikronéziában', *Adventhírnök*, 6 (1991), 14

'Magyar könyvvásár', *Adventhírnök*, 5 (1993), 12

Márffy Csaba, 'Az Úr csodásan működik Lentiben is!', *Adventhírnök*, 3 (1992), 11

Marian Hillar, *Liberation Theology* (2003) <http://www.socinian.org/liberty.html>
  [accessed 10 November 2010]

Marosán, György, 'A rendszerváltás "pszichológiája" avagy a siker útja', *Valóság*, 37.2
  (1994), 27–40

Martin, David, *A General Theory of Secularization* (New York: Harper & Row, 1978)

Mason, David S., *Revolution and transition in East-Central Europe*, 2nd edn (Boulder,
  CO: Westview Press, 1996), Dilemmas in world politics

Máté-Tóth, András, 'Transzcendencia hit Magyarországon: -hozzászólás a "Vallásosság
  szindróma és polgári társadalom" eszmecseréhez', in *Tomka Miklós 60. Szociológus
  a társadalom és az egyház szolgálatában*, ed. by András Máté-Tóth (Szeged, 2003)

Máté-Tóth, András, and Csaba M. Sarnyai, *Egyházak a rendszerváltó Kelet-Közép-
  Európában: Egy nemzetközi vizsgálat tapasztalatai, különös tekintettel
  Magyarországra, Szlovákiára és Ukrajnára* (2008)
  <http://www.mtatk.hu/interreg/kotet2/17_mate_toth.pdf> [accessed 15 April 2012]

Máté-Tóth, András, *Tomka Miklós 60. Szociológus a társadalom és az egyház
  szolgálatában* (Szeged, 2003)

Mátetelki, 'Lelkész a börtönlakók között', *Adventhírnök*, 1 (1994), 5

Maxwell, C. M., *Tell it to the world: The Story of Seventh-day Adventists* (Nampa, ID: Pacific Press Pub. Association, 2011], 1977)

Mayor, Zoltán, '"Jól gondoljátok hát meg e naptól fogva az elmúltakat is…"', *Adventhírnök*, 2 (1994), 8

_____. 'Országos lelkészértekezlet Balatonlellén', *Lelkésztájékoztató* (1986), 285–86

_____. 'Tanácsok a szavazásról', *Adventhírnök*, 2 (1994), 7–8

_____. 'Világkeresztségi nap', *Lelkésztájékoztató*, 1 (1992)

Medgyessy, László, 'Mission or proselytism? Temptations, tensions and missiological perspectives in Eastern European Christianity. A case study of Hungary.', in *Contextuality in reformed Europe: The mission of the Church in the Transformation of European culture*, ed. by Christine Lienemann-Perrin (Amsterdam [u.a.]: Rodopi, 2004), 99–120

'Megalakult a Magyar Adventista Feljesztési és Segély Alapítvány', *Adventhírnök*, 4 (1991), 15

'Megalakult a Szabadegyházak Tanácsának utódszervezete', *Adventhírnök*, 2 (1995), 8

Mészáros, István, … *Kimaradt tananyag.*, 2nd edn (Budapest: Márton, 1994)

Goheen, W. Michael '"As the Father Has Sent Me, I Am Sending You": J. E. Lesslie Newbigin's Missionary Ecclesiology' (2002)

Midyear Meeting of The Euro-Africa Division (Berlin, Germany, 1992, June 15-19)

Mihalec, Gábor, 'Magyarországon is beindult a Bibliai Levelező Iskola', *Adventhírnök*, 3 (1995), 15

Milei, Sándor, 'Keresztség Nyíregyházán', *Adventhírnök*, 2 (1988), 79–80

_____. 'Nyíregyháza', *Adventhírnök*, 4 (1988), 212

_____. 'Hamilton J. Williams előadásai Szolnokon', *Adventhírnök*, 3 (1991), 2

Miller, William, 'A Lecture on the Signs of the Present Times', *Signs of the Times*, 20 March 1840, 4

_____. 'Address to Second Advent Believers', *Signs of the Times*, VI.144 (1844), 196

_____. *Apology and Defence* (Boston, MA: J. V. Himes, August 1, 1845)

_____. *Evidence from Scripture and History of the Second Coming of Christ about the Year 1843: Exhibited in a course of lectures* (Boston: Publisched by Joshua V. Himes, 1842)

'Minden népeket', *Adventhírnök*, 1 (1992), 11

Minutes of meeting of XI/9. UB, 5 November 1989, HUC Executive Committee (1989) Archive material, HUC Archive Pécel

'Misszió', *Adventhírnök*, 9-12 (1990), 6

Mittleider, Kenneth, 'Editorial: Harvest 90', in *Harvest 90's First Anniversary*, ed. by Carlos E. Aeschlimann (Washington D.C., 1986), Ministerial Association Bulletin Harvest 90, 1-2

_____. 'Special Message: Chairman, Harvest 90 Advisory Committee', in *Half-Way Point of Harvest 90*, ed. by Carlos E. Aeschlimann (Washington D.C., 1987), Ministerial Association, Bulletin Harvest 90, 3

Mittleider, Kenneth, and Aeschlimann, Carlos, *"Harvest 90" Affirmation* (Nairobi, Kenya, 1988)

'Modellkísérlet a vallás- és Bibliaismeret oktatására', *Adventhírnök*, 2 (1991), 15

Moksony, Ferenc, 'A fejlődés ára, vagy az elmaradottság átka?: Az öngyilkosság alakulása Magyarország községeiben', *Szociologiai szemle*, 2 (1995), 73–84 <http://www.szociologia.hu/dynamic/9502moksony.htm> [accessed 4 April 2012]

_____. 'Társadalmi Mobilitás és Öngyilkosság', *Demográfia*, 48.1 (2005), 7–22 <http://www.demografia.hu/letoltes/kiadvanyok/Demografia/2005_1/Moksony%20Ferenc_tan.pdf> [accessed 4 April 2012]

Molnár Antal, 'Evangélizáció Hajdúböszörményben', *Adventhírnök*, 6 (1992), 19

______. 'Hírek Hajdúságból', *Adventhírnök,* 6 (1992), 19

Molnár, Adrienn, and Tomka, Miklós, 'Ifjúság és vallás', *Világosság*, XXX.4 (1989), 246–56

Mueller, Konrad F., *Die Frühgeschichte der Siebenten-Tags-Adventisten: Bis zur Gemeindegründung 1863 und ihre Bedeutung für die moderne Irenik*, 3rd edn (Berlin: Sigma, 1991)

'Munkátok nem hiábavaló az Úrban": Beszámoló az 1994-ben végzett szolgálatunkról', *Adventhírnök*, 3 (1995), 4–5

Mustard, Andrew G., 'The Church and Society', 1–18 <https://adventistbiblicalresearch.org/sites/default/files/pdf/AMustard-SDA%20polity.pdf> [accessed 12 June 2014]

______. *James White and the Seventh-day Adventist Organization: Historical Development, 1844-1881* (Berrien Springs, MI: Andrews University Press, 1988)

Musvosvi, Joel N., 'Egyek az Ő szavában', *Adventhírnök*, 4 (1995), 14

Nagy-Ajtai, Erzsébet, Zoltán Rajki, and József Telegdi, *Tanulmányok a magyarországi újprotestáns egyházak múltjából, jelenéből és teológiájából* (Budapest: Kisegyházkutató Egyesület, 2010)

Nagy, Lajos, *A szekták és az ellenük való védekezés* (Komárno, 1870)

Nagy, Sándorné, 'Beszámoló a börtönmisszióról', *Adventhírnök,* 3 (1993), 7

______. 'Börtönmisszió munkaterve', *Adventhírnök,* 6 (1992), 12

______. 'Börtönmisszió Veszprémben', *Adventhírnök,* 3-5 (1990), 8

______. 'Egyházzenei koncert az aulában', *Adventhírnök* (1990), 23

______. 'Evangélizáció Várpalotán', *Adventhírnök,* 1 (1992), 12

______. 'Lobogjon a lang az Úr oltárán', *Adventhírnök*, 5 (1994), 22

______. 'Ötödik év a börtönben', *Adventhírnök*, 2 (1994), 9

'Négy hét missziómunka', *Adventhírnök,* 9-12 (1990), 40

Neill, Stephen, Gerald H. Anderson, and John Goodwin, *Concise dictionary of the Christian world mission* (Nashville, TN: Abingdon Press, 1971)

'Nem kérnek állami támogatást', *Adventhírnök,* 4 (1992), 5

Némedi, Dénes, and Róbert, Péter, *Sociology – Hungary* (2012) <http://www.gesis.org/knowledgebase/archive/sociology/hungary/report1.html?no=no3_12> [accessed 4 April 2012]

Newbigin, Lesslie, 'The Kingdom of God in the Life of the World', in *Perspectives on the world Christian movement: A reader*, ed. by Ralph D. Winter and others, 4th edn (Pasadena, CA: William Carey Library, 2009), pp. 98–99

______. *The Open Secret: Sketches for a Missionary Theology* (Grand Rapids, MI: W.B. Eerdmans, 1981)

______. *The Relevance of Trinitarian Doctrine for Today's Mission* (Edinburgh House Press: London, 1963), [C.W.M.E. Study Pamphlets. no. 2.]

______. *Trinitarian Doctrine for Today's mission* (Carlisle: Paternoster Press, 1998), Biblical classics library

Newman, David J., 'Folkenberg three years later: Has the president changed his views since the publication of his article on church structure three years ago?', *Ministry*, 6 (1992) 12–14

______. 'Global Mission, my mission: Is our church growth flawed? Are we preaching the pure gospel? Should we revise the 27 fundamental beliefs?', *Ministry Magazine*, 4 (1992), 5-

Nielsen, Niels C., *Revolutions in Eastern Europe the religious roots* (Maryknoll, N.Y.: Orbis Books, 1991)

North American Bible Conference 1974, Printed materials from theBiblical Research
     Committee of the General Conference of Seventh-day Adventists (Silver Spring:
     Biblical Research Committee, 1974)
'Növekvő keresztségi számadatok', *Adventhírnök,* 3 (1992), 15
Nyisztor, Zoltán, *Adventisták* (Budapest: Szent István társulat, 1927)
______. *Baptisták* (Budapest: Szent István társulat, 1927)
______. *Baptisták és Adventisták* (Budapest: Szent István társulat, 1925)
O'Neil, Patrick H., *Revolution from within the Hungarian Socialist Workers' Party and
     the collapse of communism* (Cheltenham, UK, Northampton, MA: E. Elgar, 1998),
     Studies of communism in transition
Ócsai, József, 'Keresztség Szolnokon', *Adventhírnök,* 5 (1995), 14
______. 'A Tiszavidéki Egyházterület beszámolója és terve az 1992. évre', *Adventhírnök,*
     1 (1992), 9
______. 'A Tiszavidéki Egyházterület elnöki beszámolója az 1987-1990 konferenciai
     időszak munkájáról', *Adventhírnök,* 9-12 (1990), 3–6
______. 'A Tiszavidéki Egyházterület terve az 1993-as évre', *Adventhírnök,* 6 (1992), 9
______. 'A Tiszavidéki Egyházterület terve az 1993-as évre', *Adventhírnök,* 6 (1992), 9
______. 'Missziómunka', *Adventhírnök,* 9-12 (1990), 5–6
______. *Titkári beszámoló (Secretary report),* 1 March 1995, Archive of HUC of SDA
     church Pecel, UBXII/7
Office of Archives, Statistics and Research, *Statistical reports* (2014)
     <http://www.adventiststatistics.org> [accessed 16 December 2014]
Oliver, Barry David, 'Principles for Reorganization of the Seventh-day Adventist
     Administrative Structure, 1888-1903: Implications for an International Church'
     (doctoral dissertation, Andrews University, 1989)
Ömböli, Gyula, '"Hála Istennek, betegek voltak..."', *Adventhírnök,* 3 (1993), 14
Oossannen, Karel C. v., *Secretary's Report January 1986-December 1990,* December
     1990, Archive of HUC of SDA church Pecel
Oosterwal, Gottfried ... Firth, Robert E, ed, *Servants for Christ the Adventist Church
     facing the '80s* (Berrien Springs, MI: Andrews University Press, 1980)
______. 'Training for Missions Tomorrow', in *Adventist Missions facing the 21st
     century: A Reader,* ed. by Baldur Pfeiffer (Frankfurt am Main, New York: P. Lang,
     1990), Bd. 3: Archives of international Adventist history, 78–91
______. *Mission possible: The challenge of mission today* (Nashville, TN: Southern Pub.
     Association, 1972)
______. *Misszió egy megváltozott világban* (Budapest: H. N. Adventista Egyház, 1982)
______. *Misszió egy megváltozott világban* (Budapest: Boldog Élet Alapítvány, 2006)
______. *Patterns of SDA Church Growth on North America: A Preliminary Report on
     the Findings of a Series of Pilot Studies on the Factors of Church Growth in Selected
     Churches of the Lake Union Conference of Seventh-day-Adventists* (Berrien Springs,
     MI: Andrews University Press, 1976)
'Összejöveteli helyiség Hévízen', *Adventhírnök,* 1 (1993), 12
Ott, Craig, Stephen J. Strauss, and Timothy C. Tennent, *Encountering Theology of
     Mission: Biblical Foundations, Historical Developments, and Contemporary Issues /
     Craig Ott and Stephen J. Strauss, with Timothy C. Tennent* (Grand Rapids, MI:
     BakerAcademic; Oxford Lion [distributor], 2010)
Ottati, Frank, 'Hadd kongajanak a szabadság harangjai', *Adventhírnök,* 4 (1995), 18–20
'Our European Missions', *Review and Herald,* 7 (1877), 181
*Our Firm Foundation: A Report of the Seventh-day Adventist Bible Conference Held
     September 1-13, 1952, in The Sligo Seventh-day Adventist Church Takoma Park,
     Maryland* (Washington D.C.: Review and Herald Pub. Association, 1953)

Pachuau, Lalsangkima, *Missiology in a Pluralistic World: The Place of Mission Study in Theological Education* (2000) <http://www.religion-online.org/showarticle.asp?title=1177> [accessed 5 March 2012]

Palotay, Sándor, and Szigeti, Jenő, *A Nazarénusok* (Budapest: [s.n.], 1969)

Panek, József, 'Malcolm Potts előadás-sorozata; A kezdetek titka', *Adventhírnök*, 5 (1991), 9

Papp, Zsolt, '40 Év – Avagy a szocialista Magyar út és néhány sajátossága', *Szociológiai Szemle*, 3 (1992), 103–26

'Parádi találkozó', *Adventhírnök*, 1 (1995), 4–5

Partington, Gary, 'Qualitative Research interviews: Identifying Problems in Technique', *Issues In Educational Research*, 2001, 32–44

Froese, Paul, 'Hungary for Religon: A Supply-Side Interpretation of the Hungarian Religious Revival', *Journal for the Scientific Study of Religion*, 40.2 (2002), 251–68

Paulsen, Jan, 'Egymáshoz vagyunk kötve', *Adventhírnök*, 3 (1991), 4–5

______. 'Lassítsunk?', *Adventhírnök*, 1 (1991), 6–7

______. 'Tegyünk valami rendkívülit Krisztusért 1990-ben', *Adventhírnök*, 1 (1990), 4–5

Pavlik, Mikulás, 'Reasons for membership dropout from the Seventh-day Adventist Church in the Slovak Conference' (A Project presented in Partial Fulfilment of the Requirements for the Degree Master of Leadership, Andrews University, 2000)

Pažitná, Žofia, '"Experiencing the Closeness of God": Mediated Religious Experience and the Role of Authority in the Faith Church in Budapest' (Master Thesis, Central European University, 2008)

Penner, Péter, 'Critical Evaluation of Recent Developments in the CIS', in *Mission in the former USSR*, ed. by Walter Sawatsky, Peter Penner and and International Baptist Theological Seminary (Schwarzenfeld: Neufeld, 2005), 120–63

Pesch, Rudolf, 'Voraussetzungen und Anfänge der urchristlichen Mission', in *Mission im Neuen Testament*, ed. by Karl Kertelge (Freiburg im Breisgau: Herder, 1982), 93: Quaestiones disputatae, pp. 11–70

Pew Research Center, *Two Decades After the Wall's Fall: End of Communism Cheered but Now with More Reservations: Overview – Pew Global Attitudes Project* (NOVEMBER 2, 2009.) <http://pewglobal.org/reports/display.php?ReportID=267> [accessed 3 November 2009]

Pfeiffer, Baldur E., Lothar E. Träder, and George R. Knight, *Die Adventisten und Hamburg: Von der Ortsgemeinde zur internationalen Bewegung / Baldur Ed. Pfeiffer, Lothar E. Träder, George R. Knight (Hrsg.)* (Frankfurt am Main: Lang, 1992), 4: Archives of international Adventist history

______. *Adventist Missions Facing the 21st century: A Reader* (Frankfurt am Main, New York: P. Lang, 1990), Bd. 3: Archives of international Adventist history

Pintér Vencel, 'De akik az Úrban bíznak…', *Adventhírnök*, 2 (1992), 13

Pócsi, László and Csalami, László, 'Felfedezések bibliai földeken', *Adventhírnök*, 6 (1991), 11

Podina, István, 'Átadás egy életre', *Adventhírnök*, 1 (1995), 28

______. 'Gyermekekkel az Úrért Izsófalván', *Adventhírnök*, 1 (1995), 29

______. 'Jézus és a fiatalok', *Adventhírnök*, 5 (1995), 7–8

Pöhler, Rolf J., " … And the Door was Shut": Seventh-day Adventists and the Shut-door Doctrine in the Decade After the Great Disappointment (Andrews University, 1978)

Pollack, Detlef, 'Modifications in the Religious Field of Central and Eastern Europe', *European Societies*, 3.2 (2001), 135–65 <http://www.tandfonline.com/doi/pdf/10.1080/14616690120054302>

______. 'Religiousness Inside and Outside the Church in Selected Post-Communist Countries of Central and Eastern Europe', *Social Compass*, 50.3 (2003), 321–34

Pollack, Detlef, *Religiöser Wandel in den postkommunistischen Ländern Ost- und Mitteleuropas* (Würzburg: Ergon-Verl, 1998), 6: Religion in der Gesellschaft

Pongrácz, Tiborné, and István G. Tóth, *Szerepváltozások. Jelentés a nők és férfiak helyzetéről* (Budapest: TÁRKI Társadalomkutatási Intézet Rt., 1999)

Rácz, Sándor Béla, 'Ifjúsági evangélizáció Hajdúhadházon', *Adventhírnök*, 4 (1993), 13

Rady, Martyn C., *Causes and consequences of the collapse of communism in Eastern Europe* (Austin, Tex.: Raintree Steck-Vaughn, 1996), Causes and consequences

Rajki, Attila, 'Hogy örömötök teljes legyen', *Adventhírnök* (1990), 25

Rajki, Ferenc, 'Gépkocsiból hívogattak az evangélizációra', *Adventhírnök* (1990), 36

Rajki, János, 'Evangélizációk', *Lelkésztájékoztató* (1986), 221–23

Rajki, Zoltán, 'A Hetednapi Adventista Egyház missziója Magyarországon a rendszerváltás után a statisztika tükrében', *Theológiai Szemle*, 1 (2009) pp. 45-53

______. 'A Hetednapi Adventista Egyház tagsága családi megoszlása a 2006. évi felmérés szerint', *ATF Szemle*, 2 (2008) 43-73

______. 'Az adventista misszió társadalmi bázisának alakulása Magyarországon 1945 és 1989 között', *Egyháztörténeti szemle*, 2 (2008), 67–85

______. 'Az Evangéiumi Pünkösdi Közösség kialakulása és története 1989-ig', *Egyháztörténeti szemle*, 3 (2009), 21–42

______. 'Az Evangéliumi Pünkösdi Közösség a rendszerváltozás után', in *Tanulmányok a magyarországi újprotestáns egyházak múltjából, jelenébõl és teológiájából*, ed. by Erzsében Nagy-Ajtai, Zoltán Rajki and József Telegdi (Budapest: Kisegyházkutató Egyesület, 2010), 43–62

______. *A H. N. Adventista Egyház története 1945 és 1989 között Magyarországon* (Budapest: Advent, 2003)

______. *A pünkösdi mozgalom története Magyarországon 1945 és 1961 között* (Budapest: Gondolat Könyvkiadó, 2011), Universitas Pannonica 2062-5073 8

______. *Az Egervári-mozgalom: A Keresztény Advent Közösség kialakulása és vallásszabadsági küzdelmei a Kádár-korszak második felében (1975-1990)* (Budapest: Gondolat Könyvkiadó, 2012)

______. *Egy államilag manipulált kisegyházi választás. Az 1958. évi unióválasztás története a Hetednapi Adventisták Felekezete életében* (2012)

Rajki, Zoltán, and Szigeti, Jenő, *Szabadegyházak Története Magyarországon 1989-ig* (Budapest: Gondolat Könyvkiadó, 2012)

'Rendkívüli Uniókonferencia – Budapest, 1996. december 6.', *Adventhírnök*, 6 (1996), 2–3

Report of the Duna Conference (1988), Achrive document, HUC Arcive Pécel, 1

Report, 1971, Inner Mission department of the Hungarian Union Conference of SDA church, Archive material, HUC archive Pécel

Report, 1972, Inner Mission department of the Hungarian Union Conference of SDA church, Archive material, HUC archive Pécel

Report, 1978, Inner Mission department of the Hungarian Union Conference of SDA church, Archive material, HUC archive Pécel

'Report', *Lelkésztájékoztató*, 2 (1983), 12

'Report', *Lelkésztájékoztató*, 2 (1984), 24–25

'Report', *Lelkésztájékoztató*, 6 (1981), 7

Restás, László, 'Gyerek sportnap Kisvárdán', *Adventhírnök*, 4 (1993), 12

______. 'Mit várhatunk a FILEK-től?', *Adventhírnök*, 4 (1993), 6

______. 'Utóhang egy utcai evangélizációról', *Adventhírnök*, 2 (1995), 11

Révai, József, 'A klerikális reakció elleni harc feladatairól', *Magyar Nemzet*, Június 7. (1950), 3

Riches, Rex, *The Establishment of the British Mission of the Seventh-day Adventist Church, 1863-1887* (Seventh-day Adventist – BUC Historical Archive, 1995) <http://www.adventisthistory.org.uk/documents/rexriches/index.php> [accessed 5 January 2011]

Ricoeur, Paul, and John B. Thompson, *Hermeneutics and the Human Sciences: Essays on Language, Action and Interpretation / edited, Translated and Introduced by John B. Thompson* (Cambridge: Cambridge University Press, 1981)

Ringer, Wesley, *The Shut Door and the Sanctuary: Historical and Theological Problems* (Southern California Conference of Seventh-day Adventists, 1982)

Róbert, Péter, 'Social Determination of Living Conditions in Post-Communist Societies', *Czech sociological Review*, 5.2 (1997), 197–216 <http://sreview.soc.cas.cz/uploads/5012c60b1e99f0ed53fa02d36510e32313150031_431_197ROBER.pdf> [accessed 5 April 2012]

Rokeach, M., *The Nature of human values* (New York: Free Press, 1973)

Rose, Otis, 'A közösség Isten Szeretadománya', *Adventhírnök*, 4 (1995), 16–17

Rose, Richard, and Christian Haerpfer, *New democracies barometer III.: Studies in public policy* (Glasgow: Univeristy of Strathclyde, 1994)

Rose, Richard, William Mishler, and Christian Haerpfer, *Democracy and its alternatives: Understanding post-communist societies* (Cambridge, UK: Polity Press in association with Blackwell Publishers, 1998)

Ross, Kenneth R, *Edinburgh 2010 New directions for church in mission* (Pasadena, Calif.: William Carey International University Press, 2010)

_____. *Edinburgh 2010 springboard for mission* (Pasadena, CA: William Carey International University Press, 2009)

Rowe, David L., *God's Strange Work: William Miller and the End of the World* (Grand Rapids, MI: William B. Eerdmans Pub. Co, 2008), Library of religious biography

Rozmann, Károlyné, 'Visszatekintés a gyermekiskolai munkára', *Adventhírnök*, 2 (1994), 10

_____. *Protokoll of the Executive Comittee of the Hugnarian Union Conference* (1989)

Rózsa, Elemér, 'Rövid bezsámoló az elmúlt negyven év illegális lelkigyakorlatairól', *Távlatok*, 11.3 (1993), 356–73

Ryan, Michael, 'Into all the world: the Meaning of Global Mission: The Seventh-day Adventist Church has Launched the Most Ambitious Plan in the History of missions. An introduction.', *Ministry Magazine*, 11 (1992), 5-

Sack, Fritz, 'Társadalmi átalakulás és kriminalitás', in *Social Transformation and Crime: Hungarian-German Criminological Symposium: 20–25 August 1995 Budapest, 1995. augusztus 20 – 25*, ed. by Ferenc Irk (Budapest: Országos Kriminológiai és Kriminalisztikai Intézet, 1997), pp. 95–132

Sági, Matild, 'Elégedettség, jövedelmi feszültség', in *Társadalmi Riport 2002*, ed. by Tamás Kolosi and Vukovics G. Tóth István György (Budapest, 2002), pp. 75-92.

_____. 'Hogyan legyünk pesszimisták? Viszonyítsunk a sokkal jobbhoz!', *Századvég*, 17 (2000), 41–66 <http://www.c3.hu/scripta/szazadveg/17/sagi.htm> [accessed 4 April 2012]

Sandeen, R. E., *The Roots of Fundamentalism: British and American Millenarianism 1800-1930* (Grand Rapids, MI: Baker, 1978)

Sawatsky, Walter, Peter Penner, and and International Baptist Theological Seminary, *Mission in the former USSR* (Schwarzenfeld: Neufeld, 2005)

Schantz, Borge, *The Development of Seventh-Day Adventist Missionary Thought:
     Contemporary Appraisal: Fuller Theological Seminary, School of World Mission*
     (UMI Dissertation Services, 1983)
Scherer, James A., and Stephen B. Bevans, *New directions in mission and
     evangelization* (Maryknoll, N.Y.: Orbis Books, 1992)
______. *Theological Foundations* (Maryknoll, N.Y: Orbis Books, 1994), / edited by
     James A. Scherer, Stephen B. Bevans; 2: New directions in mission and
     evangelization
Schoen, Valentin, *Istennek emberekre vvan szüksége* (Budapest: Advent Kiadó, 1993)
Schöpflin, George, *Politics in Eastern Europe, 1945-1992* (Oxford, UK, Cambridge,
     MA, USA: Blackwell, 1993)
Schütz, Paul, *Zwischen Nil und Kaukasus: Ein Reisebericht zur religionspolitischen
     Lage im Orient*, 3rd edn (Kassel: Stauda, 1953)
Schwarz, Richard W., and Floyd Greenleaf, *Light bearers: AHistory of the Seventh-day
     Adventist Church* (Nampa, Idaho: Pacific press publishing association, 2000)
Scott, Waldron, *Karl Barth's Theology of Mission* (Downers Grove, IL: InterVarsity
     Press, 1978), no. 1: Outreach and identity
Sears, Clara E., *Days of Delusion: A Strange Bit of History* (Boston, MA: Houghton
     Mifflin Co., 1924)
'Segítő kezek Albániáért', *Adventhírnök*, 6 (1991), 15
Seligman, Adam B., *The Transition from State Socialism in Eastern Europe: The Case
     of Hungary* (Greenwich, CT: JAI Press, 1994)
Senior, Donald, and Carroll Stuhlmueller, *The Biblical foundations for mission*
     (Maryknoll, NY: Orbis Books, 1983)
Session actions: Role and Function of Denominational Organizations – Commission
     report, *Adventist Review*, 7 (1985), 9
Seventh-day Adventist Encyclopedia, 2nd edn (Hagerstown MD: Review & Herald Pub.
     Association, 1996), 10-11: Commentary reference series
Shearer, Gary,*The Shut Door Controversy: Bibliography* (2005)
     <http://library.puc.edu/heritage/bib-ShutDoCon.html> [accessed 14 June 2012]
Shenk, Wilbert R., *Exploring church growth* (Grand Rapids, MI: Wm B Eerdmans,
     1983)
______. *Mission focus: Current issues* (1980)
______. *The Priority of Mission for Renewal of the Church*, 28th edn (1999)
     <http://www.directionjournal.org/article/?1005> [accessed 24 November 2010]
______. *The Priority of Mission for Renewal of the Church* (2010)
     <http://www.directionjournal.org/article/?1005> [accessed 24 November 2010]
______. *Write the Vision: The Church Renewed / Wilbert R. Shenk* (Leominster:
     Gracewing, 1995), Christian Mission and Modern Culture
Shuler, John L., *Public Evangelism its Approach and Problems* (Washington, D.C.:
     Review and Herald Pub. Association, 1939)
Sík, Endre, and G. Tóth, István, *Magyar Háztartás Panel Műhelytanulmányok: Jelentés
     a Magyar Háztartás Panel 6. hullámának eredményeiről* (Budapest: TÁRKI
     Társadalomkutatási Intézet Rt., 1998)
Simon, Ágnes, 'A lélek esője Mogyoródon is hullik', *Adventhírnök, 19-12* (1990), 39
Simon, László, 'Egy nyitott könyv', *Adventhírnök,* 3 (1992), 12
______. 'Keresztség a soproni Tómalom fürdőn', *Adventhírnök*, 5 (1994), 21
______. 'Kezdj el élni!', *Adventhírnök,* 3 (1991), 3
______. 'Oroszlányban', *Adventhírnök*, 1 (1994), 14
______. 'Sopronban várják az adventista fiatalokat', *Adventhírnök,* 3 (1993), 12
Sitkei, Zoltán, 'Kereszténység és a Zene', *Adventhírnök*, 5 (1995), 6

Sklar, L, and H Anisman, 'Stress and Coping Factors Influence Tumour Growth', *Science*, 205 (1979), 513–15

Skrzypaszek, John, 'Conversion and identity in the context of the Seventh-day Adventist faith tradition', *Melanesian Journal of Theology*, 28.1 (2012), 61–77

Smith, H. S., *American Christianity: An Historical Interpretation with Representative Documents*, 2 vols (New York: Scribner, 1963), 2

Snook, B.F, 'The Great Missionary Society', *Review and Herald*, XXII.6 (1863)

———. 'The Great Missionary Society', *Review and Herald*, 6 (July 1863), 46

Snyder, Howard A., *New wineskins: Changing the Man-Made structures of the Church* (Basingstoke: Marshall Pickering, 1987)

———. *Kingdom lifestyle: Calling the Church to live under God's reign* (Basingstoke: Marshall Pickering, 1986)

———. *Liberating the Church: The ecology of Church and kingdom* (Downers Grove, IL: InterVarsity Press, 1983)

———. *Problem of Wineskins: Church Renewal in a Technological Age* (Downers Grove, IL: Inter Varsity Press, 1975)

Soós, Róbert, 'Mily boldog nap', *Adventhírnök*, 5 (1995), 15

Spicer, William A., *Our Story of Missions* (California: Pacific Press Publishing Association, 1921), 11

Spieker, Manfred, *Katholische Kirche und Zivilgesellschaft in Osteuropa: Postkommunistische Transformationsprozesse in Polen, Tschechien, der Slowakei und Litauen* (Paderborn: Schöningh, 2003), 22: Politik- und kommunikationswissenschaftliche Veröffentlichungen der Görres-Gesellschaft

Staples, Russell L., *Community of Faith the Seventh-day Adventist Church and the contemporary world* (Hagerstown, MD: Review and Herald Pub. Association, 1999)

Stark, David, 'Path Dependence and Privatization Strategies in East Central Europe', *East European Politics & Societies*, 6.1 (1991), 17–54

Symposium on Mission and Social Action: The Role of Social Ministry in the Sevent-day Adventist Church (Silver Spring, MD: Adventist Development and Relief Agency, 1997)

Szabó, Ágnes Kapitány-Gábor Kapitány: Theses about "Kádárism" or "Kádárism" and the Future', *Eszmélet*, 18-19 (1993) <http://www.freeweb.hu/eszmelet/angol1/kapitanyang1.html> [accessed 19 January 2011]

Szabó, László, 'A szocializmus hatása az egyházi misszióra', *ATF Szemle*, 2 (2005), 48–56 <http://atf.adventista.hu/kiadvanyok/atf_szemle/2005_2.pdf> [accessed 15 April 2012]

Szabó, Ottó, 'Farmoson is hirdettük az evangéliumot', *Adventhírnök*, 3 (1993), 12

Szántó, János, *Vallásos családok társadalmi-gazdasági helyzete Magyarországon* (Budapest: TÁRKI Társadalomkutatási Intézet Rt., 1994)

Szántó, Konrád, *A Kommunizmusnak sem Sikerült: A Magyar Katolikus Egyház Története 1945-1991 / Szántó Konrád* (Miskolc: Új Misszió Alapítvány, 1992), 2: Új Misszió könyvek

Szántó, Konrád, *A meggyilkolt katolikus Papok Kálváriája*, 2nd edn (Budapest: Mécses Kiadó, 1992)

———. *Az Egyházügyi Hivatal Titkai* ([Budapest]: Mécses, 1990)

Szaszi, Tamás, 'Keresztség Csengerben', *Adventhírnök*, 3 (1994), 16

Szebeni, Olivér, *Német baptisták Magyarországon* (Jánoshalma: BMA-Könyvek, 2010)

Szegedi, Kovács György, 'Ahogyan fogadtak bennünket', *Adventhírnök*, 1 (1993), 15

———. 'Gondolatok egy evangélizáció kapcsán', *Adventhírnök*, 2 (1992), 11

———. 'Sárbogárd ismerkedik az igazsággal', *Adventhírnök*, 1 (1992), 10

Székely, Lajos, 'Evangélizáció Sashalmon és Pesterzsébeten', *Adventhírnök,* 3 (1993), 12

Szigeti, Jenő, '"Ne félj, hanem szólj, ne hallgass!"', *Adventhírnök,* 1 (1990), 2

______. 'A félamatőrök országa: Elnöki beszámoló', *Adventhírnök,* 6 (1993), 6–7

______. 'A kisebb magyarországi egyházak', in *A Magyar protestantizmus, 1918-1948: Tanulmányok,* ed. by L. F. Lendvai ([Budapest]: Kossuth, 1987, c1986)

______. 'A Lélek esője már hullik', *Adventhírnök,* 3-5 (1990), 1

______. 'A szolgálat bázisa: a szolgáló gyülekezet', *Lelkésztájékoztató* (1986), 341–44

______. 'A találkozások éve: Jelentés a TED év végi ülésére', *Lelkésztájékoztató,* 4 (1992), 4

______. 'A Transzeuropai Divizió tavaszi ülése', *Adventhírnök,* 3 (1994), 8

______. 'Az 'Aratás '90' a Magyar Unióban', *Lelkésztájékoztató* (1990), 136–38

______. 'Bátran előre az új kihívások között: A Trans-Európai Divízió téli ülése – Skodsborg, 1990. nov. 19-23.', *Adventhírnök,* 1 (1991), 5

______. 'Beszámoló ülés 1993. március 7.; „Hálát adok érettetek Istennek…"', *Adventhírnök,* 2 (1993), 3

______. 'Hadd hirdessem nevedet atyámfiainak', *Adventhírnök,* 1 (1990), 3

______. 'Hogyan lehet missziómunkára serkenteni a gyülekezetet?', *Lelkésztájékoztató,* 2 (1988), 122–28

______. 'Jelentés a Magyar Unió 1992. évi tervkészítő üléséről: Vajon elérjük-e az el nem értet?', *Adventhírnök,* 6 (1992), 5–6

______. 'Jelentés a Trans-európai Divízió évvégi üléséről', *Adventhírnök,* 6 (1991), 3–4

______. 'Mi vagyunk Isten keze, hogy elérjük az egész világot: A Globál Misszióról az 1992-es generál konferenciai ülés fényében', *Lelkésztájékoztató,* 4 (1992), 45–53

______. *"És emlékezzél meg az útról": Tanulmányok a magyarországi szabadegyházak történetéből* (Budapest: Szabadegyházak Tanácsa, 1981)

______. *Fejezetek a H. N. Adventista Egyház magyarországi történetéből* (Budapest: Hetednapi Adventista Egyház, 1985)

______. *Report of the Hungarian Union Conference* (1989), archive material, HUC archive Pécel

______. *Report of the Hungarian Union Conference for the TED Winter Meetings – 1990* (1990), archive material, HUC archive Pécel

______. *Report on the work of the Hungarian Union Conference December 1987 – April 1988* (1988), archive material, HUC archive Pécel

Szigeti, Jenő, and Kardos, László, *Boldog emberek közössége: A magyarországi nazarénusok* (Budapest: Magvető, 1988)

Szigeti, László, 'Az egészségügyi és mértékletességi osztály 1993. évi munkaterve', *Adventhírnök,* 6 (1992), 12

______. 'Egészségnevelés, mértékletesség', *Adventhírnök,* 2 (1994), 9

______. 'Felhívás!', *Adventhírnök,* 1 (1993), 12

Szilasi, Zoltán, 'Az egészségnevelés lehetőségei az iskolában', *Adventhírnök,* 6 (1993), 14

Szilvási, András, '"Jöjjetek és lássátok az Isten dolgait" Elnöki jelentés', *Adventhírnök,* 2 (1996), 4–6

______. 'A Tiszavidéki Egyházterület 1995. évi terve', *Adventhírnök,* 6 (1994), 10

______. 'A Tiszavidéki Egyházterület terve az 1994-es esztendőre', *Adventhírnök,* 6 (1993), 11

______. 'Evangélizációs tanácskozás', *Adventhírnök,* 5 (1992), 9

______. 'Hammilton J. Williams evangélizál Békés megyében', *Adventhírnök,* 1 (1991), 16

______. 'Keresztség Békéscsabán', *Adventhírnök,* 3 (1988), 155

______. 'Válaszd az életet!', *Adventhírnök,* 3 (1991), 8
Szilvási, József, 'A jót tartsátok meg!', *Adventhírnök,* 2 (1996), 15
______. 'A lélekmentésről', *Adventhírnök,* 6 (1992), 6–7
______. 'A remény jegyében tartották meg a divizió téli ülését', *Adventhírnök,* 6 (1994), 6
______. 'Állhatatossággal fussuk meg az előttünk lévő pályát!', *Adventhírnök,* 6 (1992), 6–7
______. 'Aratás '90', *Lelkésztájékoztató* (1986), 353–54
______. 'Az adventista katonák vallásszabadsága', *Adventhírnök,* 9-12 (1990), 40
______. 'Az evangéliumi szolgálat hű betöltése', *Adventhírnök,* 6 (1995), 2
______. 'Bátran hozzáfogtak a jó munkához', *Adventhírnök,* 6 (1991), 6-7
______. 'Csendüljenek fel az Úr igaz tettei', *Adventhírnök,* 2 (1994), 4
______. 'Egyházunk jelentős lépésre szánta el magát a vallásszabadsági munkában', *Adventhírnök* (1993), 8–9
______. 'Egység Krisztusban', *Adventhírnök,* 5 (1995), 2
______. 'Éljetek békességben', *Adventhírnök,* 2 (1995), 2–3
______. 'Ezek a népek félték az Urat, és tiszteték bálványaikat is', *Adventhírnök,* 5 (1991), 3
______. 'Folyamatos evangélizáció a Budapest "B" gyülekezetben', *Lelkésztájékoztató* (1988), 28
______. 'Irányelvek az osztályok munkájáról', *Adventhírnök,* 6 (1993), 7–9
______. 'Isten titkainak sáfárai: Titkári jelentés 1992-ről', *Adventhírnök,* 2 (1993), 4–5
______. 'Járjunk az Úr világosságában!', *Adventhírnök,* 1 (1990), 4
______. 'Lelki egyház: Minden itt kezdődik és itt ér véget', *Adventhírnök,* 6 (1994), 4
______. 'Magyarországon is százak nézik George Vandeman műsorait', *Adventhírnök,* 9-12 (1990), 28
______. 'Mi van a kezedben?', *Adventhírnök,* 2 (1992), 7
______. 'Növekedés' *Adventhírnök,* 3 (1991), 2
______. 'Számvetés – toronyépítés előtt', *Adventhírnök,* 4 (1994), 3–5
______. *Százéves a Hetednapi Adventista Egyház Magyarországon (The Seventh-day Adventist Church is One Hundred Years old in Hungary): Ünnepi Beszéd (Ceremonial speech)* (Budapest, 1998)
Szilvási, Józsefné, 'A Biblia és a lelki növekedés', *Adventhírnök,* 6 (1993), 18
Szilvási, Tibor, 'A Reménység Hangja Stúdió 1992. évi beszámolója', *Adventhírnök* (1992), 7
______. 'A Reménység Hangja Stúdió 1993. évi munkaterve', *Adventhírnök,* 6 (1992), 15
______. 'Hang, mely előtt nincsenek határok', *Adventhírnök,* 4 (1993), 7
______. 'Nem kell menned messzi útra', *Adventhírnök,* 5 (1994), 18
______. 'Reménység Hangja Stúdió', *Adventhírnök,* 2 (1994), 13
Szilvási, Zoltán, 'Ifjú gyülekezeti munkások találkozója', *Adventhírnök,* 1 (1994), 5
______. 'John Wesley Flower újabb látogatása a debreceni körzetben', *Adventhírnök,* 1 (1995), 30
______. 'Kapcsolat vagy programkozpotú ifjúság?', *Adventhírnök,* 1 (1995), 30
______. 'Lépések egy új világrend felé', *Adventhírnök,* 5 (1994), 19
Szivós, Péter and Tóth, István György ed., *Stabilizálódó társadalomszerkezet: TÁRKI MONITOR JELENTÉSEK 2003* (Budapest:TÁRKI, 2004), *http://www.tarki.hu/hu/research/issp/*<http://www.tarki.hu/hu/research/issp/> [accessed 17 December 2009]
Szívós, Péter, and István G. Tóth, *Feketén, fehéren: Tárki Monitor Jelentések 2006* (Budapest: TÁRKI Társadalomkutatási Intézet Rt., 2006)

______. *Monitor 1999: Tárki Háztartásmonitor* (Budapest: TÁRKI Társadalomkutatási Intézet Rt., 1999)

______. *Növekedés alulnézetben* (Budapest, 2000) <http://www.tarki.hu/adatbank-h/kutjel/pdf/a316.pdf> [accessed 5 April 2012]

______. *Tíz év: Tárki Monitor Jelentések* (Budapest, 2001. december), Tárki Háztartásmonitor

Szőllősi, Árpád id., 'Az evangélizálás', *Adventhírnök*, 2 (1990), 2

______. 'A nyírpazonyi kápolna felszentelése', *Adventhírnök*, 1 (1991), 14

______. 'A Dunamelléki Egyházterület 1993. évi terve', *Adventhírnök*, 6 (1992), 8

______. 'A Dunamelléki Egyházterület beszámolója és terve az 1992. évre', *Adventhírnök*, 1 (1992)

______. 'A Dunamelléki Egyházterület elnöki beszámolója az 1987-1990 konferenciai időszak munkájáról', *Adventhírnök*, 9-12 (1990) 11-14

______. 'A Dunamelléki Egyházterület terve az 1994-es esztendőre', *Adventhírnök*, 6 (1993), 10

______. 'A Dunamelléki Egyházterület terve az 1995-ös évre', *Adventhírnök*, 8 (1994), 8

______. 'Gyülekezetszervezés Szekszárdon' *Adventhírnök*, 1 (1995), 27

______. 'Csodálatos felfedezések ókori országokban, Ilyen még nem volt', *Adventhírnök*, 6 (1991), 10

______. 'Debrecen', *Adventhírnök*, 4 (1988), 212

______. 'Dunamelléki Egyházterület beszámolója és terve az 1992. évre', *Adventhírnök*, 1 (1992), 8

______. 'Elnöki jelentés az 1993 és 1995 között eltelt konferenciai időszakról' Dunamelléki egyházterület', *Adventhírnök*, 2 (1996), 2–3

______. 'Evangélizációs sorozat Nyíregyházán 1990. Február 3-17-ig', *Adventhírnök*, 3-5 (1990), 3

______. 'Félelem-Remény-Öröm-Hálaadás', *Adventhírnök*, 1 (1996), 16

______. 'Keresztség Debrecenben', *Lelkésztájékoztató*, 3 (1988), 159

______. 'Keresztségek: Budapest', *Lelkésztájékoztató*, 1 (1988), 12

______. 'Lelkészcsaládok közös üdülése', *Lelkésztájékoztató*, 4 (1988), 210

______. 'Országos lelkészértekezlet Boglárlellén', *Lelkésztájékoztató*, 4 (1988), 208

______. 'Újra Zalaegerszegen!', *Adventhírnök*, 3 (1992), 11

Szőllősi, Béla, 'Evangélizáció Csengerben', *Adventhírnök*, 3 (1994), 15

______. 'Keresztség a Tiszában', *Adventhírnök*, 4 (1996), 17

Sztán János, 'Evangelizációk es bibliaklubok a csongrádi körzetben', *Adventhírnök* (1992), 10

______. 'Könyveink a városi könyvtárban', *Adventhírnök*, 3 (1994), 15

Tabajdi, Gábor; Ungvári, Krisztián, *,Elhallgatott múlt. A pártállam és a belügy. A politikai rendőrség működése Magyarországon 1956-1990.'* (Budapest, Corvina Kiado-1956-os Intézet, 2008)

Tamás Andrásné, 'A kábeltévé közvetítése a szabadkígyósi gyülekezetből', *Adventhírnök*, 5 (1995), 15

Tamási, Pál, 'Egyházi mozgásterek a társadalomban', in *Az egyház mozgástereiről a mai Magyarországon.*, ed. by Özséb Horányi (Budapest: Vigília, 1997), p. 49

Tanok és szövetségek Tanok és szövetségek és az egyház története (Belgium: Az Utolsó Napok Szentjeinek Jézus Krisztus Egyháza, 2002)

TÁRKI, *Social Structure, Social Mobility*<http://www.tarki.hu/en/projects/social/index.html> [accessed 30 November 2012]

'Tavaszi Divízióülés: Az elvilágiasodott európai ember evangélizálásáról', *Adventhírnök*, 3 (1996), 4–5

Taylor, Charles, 'Global Strategy: Simply Having a Presence in every Nation is Not Enough. Global Strategy Targets the Kindreds, Tongues, and People Groups.', *Ministry Magazine*, 8 (1990), 12-

Taylor, R. C., 'Globális missziói eredmények', *Adventhírnök*, 2 (1995), 2

TED, *World Church Survey, Six Focus Areas*, Started 1993

'Teljes odaszentelődés', *Adventhírnök*, 5 (1996), 5–7

'Tervkészítő ülés', *Adventhírnök*, 6 (1993), 6

TET leaders, 'A Tiszavidéki Egyházterület globális missziói terve', *Adventhírnök*, 9-12 (1990), 10

The "Shut Door" Documents: Statements Relating to the "Shut Door," the Door of Mercy, and the Salvation of Souls by Ellen G. White and Other Early Adventists, Compiled with Occasional Commentary by Robert W. Olson (Washington, D.C.: White Estate, 1982) <http://www.whiteestate.org/issues/shutdoor.html> [accessed 5 January 2011]

The Signs of the Times and Expositor of Prophecy, 6 vols (Ellen G. White Estate, Silver Spring, 1841-1844)

Thomas, Norman E., 'World mission conferences: What impact do they have?', *International Bulletin of Missionary Research*, 20.4 (1996), 146

Thompson, G. Ralph, 'Nem mesterkélt mesék', *Adventhírnök*, 4 (1995), 10–12

______. 'The Role of the New Missionary: From Pioneer and Parent to Partner and Participant', in *Adventist missions facing the 21st century: A reader*, ed. by Baldur Pfeiffer (Frankfurt am Main, New York: P. Lang, 1990), Bd. 3: Archives of international Adventist history, 65–77

______. 'A globális missziói stratégia', *Adventhírnök*, 6-8 (1990), 7

Thun, Éva, *Women in Hungary in Times of social and Cultural Transition* (1999) <http://epa.oszk.hu/00000/00010/00002/thun.htm> [accessed 29 November 2010]

Tillemann, Tomicah, 'How to end an empire: The refugee crisis of 1989 and the collapse of the Eastern Bloc' (Doctoral Thesis, The John Hopkins University, 2009)

'Tiszavidéki Egyházterület Választókonferenciája', *Adventhírnök*, 2 (1993), 11

Tiszavidéki Egyházterület, 'A növekedés iránya', *Adventhírnök*, 2 (1993), 13

'Tisztelt Advent Kiadó', *Adventhírnök*, 1 (1994), 15

Tőkés, Rudolf, *A kialkudott forradalom gazdasági reform, társadalmi átalakulás és politikai hatalomutódlás 1957-1990* (Budapest: Kossuth, 1998)

Tokics, Imre, 'Pesterzsébeten is hangzott az Ige', *Adventhírnök*, 5 (1992), 10

Tomka, Ferenc, 'A Befogadó Közösség', in *Tomka Miklós 60. Szociológus a társadalom és az egyház szolgálatában*, ed. by András Máté-Tóth (Szeged, 2003)

______. 'Közösség és "Megtérés"', in *Tomka Miklós 60. Szociológus a társadalom és az egyház szolgálatában*, ed. by András Máté-Tóth (Szeged, 2003)

Tomka, Miklós, 'A felekezeti struktúra változása Kelet- és Közép-Európában', *Sociológia*, 1 (1996), 157–73 <http://www.mtapti.hu/mszt/19961/tomka.htm> [accessed 4 April 2012]

______. 'A Magyar Vallási Helyzet öt dimenziója', *Magyar Tudomány*, 5 (1999), 549–59 <http://nyitottegyetem.phil-inst.hu/vallas/tm_magy.htm>

______. 'A vallás mint változó rendszer (Religion as a System – and its Changes)', *Szociológiai Szemle*, 3-4 (1990), 155–84

______. 'A vallásosság változása – egy és több dimenzióban.', *Kultúra és Közösség*, 5 (1985), 3–16

______. 'Az egyházak az ezredfordulón', *Theológiai Szemle*, 38.2 (1995), 78–82

______. 'Changes in the Structure of Denominations in East and Central Europe', *Review of Sociology*, 1 (1996), 88–103 <http://www.mtapti.hu/mszt/a1996/tomka.htm> [accessed 29 November 2010]

_____. 'Felekezeti Szerkezet, Felekezeti Reprodukció', *Statisztikai Szemle*, 4-5 (1994), 329–43 <http://www.ksh.hu/statszemle_archive/viewer.html?ev=1994&szam=04-05&old=51&lap=15> [accessed 4 April 2012]

_____. 'Religiosity in Central and Eastern Europe. Facts and Interpretations', *Religion and Society in Central and Eastern Europe*, 3.1 (2010) <http://www.rascee.net/index.php/rascee/issue/view/3>[accessed 4 November 2010]

_____. 'Religious identity and the gospel or reconciliation', *Religion in Eastern Europe*, XXIX.1 (2009), 20–28 [accessed 4 November 2010]

_____. 'Secularization or Anomy? Interpreting Religious Change in Communist Societies', *Social Compass*, 38.1 (1991), 93–102

_____. 'The Changing Social Role of Religion in Eastern and Central Europe: Religion's Revival and its Contradictions', *Social Compass*, 42 (1995), 17–26

_____. 'The Religious – Non-Religious Dichotomy as A Social Problem', *The Annual Review of the Social Sciences of Religion*, 3 (1979), 105–37

_____. 'Vallás a rendszerváltás után – kelet-közép európai realitások', *Egyházfórum*, 3 (1993), 17–37

_____. 'Vallás és társadalom Magyarországon: Gyakorlait teológiai és vallásszociológiai megközelítések' (Habilitation, Evangélikus Hittudományi Egyetem, 2001)

_____. 'Vallási változások Kelet-Közép-Európában, különös tekintettel Magyarországra.', *Confessio*, 2 (2001), 24–52

_____. *Church, State, and Society in Eastern Europe* (Washington, D.C: Council for Research in Values and Philosophy, 2005), 28: Cultural Heritage and Contemporary Change Series IVA

_____. *Expanding religion: Religious revival in post-communist central and eastern europe* (Berlin: De Gruyter, 2011), 47: Religion and Society

_____. *Magyar katolicizmus 1991* (Budapest: Országos Lelkipásztori Intézet Katolikus Társadalomtudományi Akadémia, 1991)

'Tony Campbell előadás-sorozata Zalaegerszegen', *Adventhírnök,* 5 (1991), 8

Török, Péter, 'A magyarországi bejegyzett kisegyházak tagságának alakulása 1990 és 1997 között', *Távlatok*, 48 (2000), 290–300

_____. 'Hungarian Church State Relationships: A Social Historical Analysis' (unpublished doctoral thesis, University of Toronto, 2000)

_____. *Hungarian Church-State Relationships: A Socio-Historical Analysis* (Budapest: Hungarian Institute for Sociologie of Religion, 2003)

_____. *Magyarországi Vallási Kalauz: 2004* (Budapest: Akadémiai Kiadó, 2004)

Tóth, István György, 'Jövedelemelosztás', in *Stabilizálódó társadalomszerkezet: TÁRKI MONITOR JELENTÉSEK 2003*, ed. by Péter Szívós and István György Tóth (Budapest, 2004), 30–38

Tóth, László, *A Pünkösdi Mozgalom Magyarországon* (Budapest: Evangéliumi Pünkösdi Közösség, 1998)

Trans European Division – Global Mission: Programme and Agenda, Winter Meetings (Skodsborg Sanitarium, Denmark, 1990)

Trans-European Division Executive Comittee, *Mission Statement of the Seventh-day Adventist church* (1993), archive material, HUC archive Pécel

Trans-European Division Ministerial Department, *A Vision of the Future 1990-1995: A Report of the Ministerial Department Presented to TED Spring Meetings*, 22 April 1990, A22-A26

Trans-European Division, *Global Strategy and Youth Ministry* (1990), archive material, HUC archive Pécel

Trans-European Division, *Global Strategy: Master Evangelistic Schedule for Overseas Evangelists* (1990), archive material, HUC archive Pécel
'Új Arcok', *Adventhírnök* (1990), 7
'Új életforma', *Adventhírnök*, 3 (1995), 14
'Új testvéreink Pilisszántón', *Adventhírnök*, 5 (1992), 11
Újlaki, Béla, 'Beszámoló a FILEK munkájáról', *Adventhírnök*, 3 (1993), 10
_____. 'Keresztség és őrsegváltás Nyíregyházán', *Adventhírnök*, 4 (1993), 12
Utterbaeck, Bertil, *Report from the Swedish Union Conference for the Trans-European Division Comittee*, TED Executive Committee (1990)
Uzzoli, Annamária, 'A hazai egészségi állapot változásai 1990 után', in *A III. Magyar Földrajzi Konferencia tudományos közleményei* (MTA Földrajztudományi Kutatóintézet, 2006), 1–10
'Vakok is olvashatják a „Jézushoz vezető út"-at', *Adventhírnök*, 1 (1993), 12
Varga, Iván, 'Post communist dilemmas of Hungarian churches', *Hungarian Studies*, 10.1 (1990), 139–47
Várhegyi, Asztrid, 'Magyar egyház a fordulat után', *Egyházfórum*, 3 (1995), 91–94
Várhelyi, Zoltán, '"…és lesztek nékem tanúim…"', *Adventhírnök*, 5 (1993), 12
_____. 'Apokalipszis', *Adventhírnök*, 3 (1996), 9
'Várod-e a Királyt', *Adventhírnök*, 1 (1993), 12
Vas, Vince, *Baptisták, Nazarénusok, Methodisták, Adventisták, Üdvhadsereg, Nemzetközi Bibliatanulók* (Budapest: Sylvester nyomda, 1926)
Verkuyl, Johannes, *Contemporary missiology: An introduction* (Grand Rapids, MI: Eerdmans, 1978)
'Vetítőgépek, diasorozatok az evangélium szolgálatában', *Adventhírnök*, 5 (1991), 16
Vyhmeister, Nancy, 'Why world mission?: What is the mission of the Seventh-day Adventist Church? Must the mission be worldwide? And if so, why?', *Ministry Magazine*, 8 (1990), 8–10
Warneck, Johannes G., *The Living Christ and Dying Heathenism: The Experiences of a Missionary in Animistic Heathendom* (Grand Rapids, MI: Baker, 1954)
Webster, E.C., 'Milyen lelkület tesz bennünket adventistává?', *Adventhírnök*, 6 (1991), 1–2
Weigel, George, *The final revolution the resistance church and the collapse of communism* (New York: Oxford University Press, 1992)
Welfare Department of Seventh-day Adventist Church, *Annual Report*, 1978, Archive material, HUC archive Pécel
White, Arthur, *Ellen G. White and the Shut Door Question: A Review of the The Experience of Early Seventh-day Adventist Believers in its Historical Context* (1982) <http://www.whiteestate.org/issues/shut-alw.html> [accessed 5 January 2011]
White, Ellen G, *Life Sketches* (Mountain View, CA: Pacific Press Publishing Association, 1915)
_____. *Selected Messages From The Writings Of Ellen G. White: Significant and Ever-Timely Counsels Gathered From Periodical Articles, Manuscript Statements, and Certain Valuable Pamphlets and Tracts Long out Of Print* (Washington, DC: Review and Herald Pub. Association, 1958), Christian home library
_____. *Manuscript Releases: The Shut door; Ellen White's labro for Sinners, 1845-1850*, 5th edn (1990), 91
_____. *Counsels to Parents, Teachers, and Students Regarding Christian Education* (Mountain View, CA: Pacific Press Publishing Association, 1913)
_____. *Education* (Mountain View, CA: Pacific Press Publishing Association, 1952)
_____. *Testimonies to the Church*, Volume 3 (Mountain View, CA: Pacific Press Publishing Association, 1948)

______. *Testimonies for the church,* Volume 8 (Mountain View, CA: Pacific Press Publishing Association, 1948)

______. *Testimonies for the church,* Volume 9 (Mountain View, CA: Pacific Press Publishing Association, 1948)

White, James, 'Call at the Harbinger Office', *Review and Herald*, 17 February 1852, 95

______. 'The Present Work', *The Advent Review and Sabbath Herald*, 3 (1852), 5-6

______. 'Publications in other Languages', *Review and Herald*, XI.25 (1858), 200

______. 'The Shut Door', *The Advent Review and Sabbath Herald*, 3 (1853), 188

______. 'The light of the World', *Review and Herald*, 8 (1863), 165

______. 'Repairing the Breach in the Law of God', *The Present Truth* (September 1849), 25–29

______. 'The Shut Door', *Review and Herald* (1853), 188

______. 'The Third Angel's Message', *Review and Herald*, 8.18 (1856), 141

White, James, and Sylvester Bliss, *Sketches of the Christian life and public labors of William Miller* (New York: AMS Press, 1972)

Widmer, Miros, 'Adventista Világrádió', *Adventhírnök,* 5 (1991), 11

Williams, Colin C., 'Beyond Marketization: Rethinking Economic Development Trajectories in Central and Eastern Europe', *Journal of Contemporary European Studies*, 14.2 (2006), 241–54 [accessed 11 July 2012]

Wilson Price, Frank, *Christian Presuppositions for the Encounter with Communism*, 158-167

Wilson, Neal C., 'Special Message: President, General Conference', in *Half-Way Point of Harvest 90*, ed. by Carlos E. Aeschlimann (Washington D.C., 1987), Ministerial Association Bulletin Harvest 90

______. 'Global Mission: Person to Person', *Adventist Review* (1990), 3

______. 'Globális missziói stratégia', *Adventhírnök*, 6-8 (1990), 8

Winter, Ralph D. and others, *Perspectives on the world Christian movement: A reader*, 4th edn (Pasadena, CA: William Carey Library, 2009)

Wood, Kenneth H., 'The role of the Seventh-day Adventist church in the great controversy in the end time', in *North American Bible Conference 1974*, ed. by General Conference of Seventh-day Adventists Biblical Research Committee (Silver Spring: Biblical Research Committee, 1974)

Woolsey, Raymond H., *Evangelism handbook* (Washington, D.C.: Review and Herald Pub. Association, 1972)

World Council of Churches., *Come Holy Spirit: Heal and reconcile Athens 2005* (2005)

World Values Survey Association, *Values Change the World: World Values Survey* (2011) <http://www.worldvaluessurvey.org/wvs/articles/folder_published/article_base_110/files/WVSbrochure6-2008_11.pdf> [accessed 27 June 2012]

World Values Survey I. 1980-1983<http://www.tarsadalomkutatas.hu/termek.php?termek=TDATA-B50> [accessed 4 April 2012]

World Values Survey<http://www.wvsevsdb.com/wvs/WVSDocumentation.jsp?Idioma=I> [accessed 4 April 2012]

Wright, N.T, 'Building for the Kingdom: Our Work is Not in Vain', in *Perspectives on the world Christian movement: A Reader*, ed. by Ralph D. Winter and others, 4th edn (Pasadena, CA: William Carey Library, 2009), 96–97

Youth Survey 1990, General Conrefence of SDA (1990), Archive material, HUC Archive Pécel

Zágonyiné, Nagy, Szilvia, 'Gyülekezeti Ifjúsági csopportok ötletbörzéje', *Adventhírnök*, 4 (1994), 9, 14
Zagyva, László, 'Televíziós evangélizáció', *Adventhírnök*, 3 (1995), 7
_____. 'Televíziós műsor Karcagon', *Adventhírnök*, 2 (1995), 8
'Zalai hírek', *Adventhírnök*, 1 (1995), 31
Zarka, Péter, 'A gyülekezeti szolgálatok osztályának 1993-as munkaterve', *Adventhírnök*, 6 (1992), 10
_____. 'Ifjúsági evangélizációs tábor', *Adventhírnök*, 5 (1993), 6
_____. 'Ifjusági nap Nemesvámoson', *Lelkésztájékoztató*, 3 (1988), 157
_____. 'Külmisszió munka ifjúságunknak!', *Adventhírnök*, 1 (1994), 4
_____. 'Változatosabb lett gyülekezeteink élete', *Adventhírnök*, 2 (1994), 6
Zarkáné Teremy Krisztina, and Ócsai Tamás, 'Szünidei bibliai tábor Balatonlellén', *Adventhírnök*, 4 (1993), 11
Zsilinszki Mihály, 'Tanácsok könyvevangélistáknak', *Adventhírnök*, 1 (1993), 15
Zulehner, Paul and Others, *Religion und Kirchen in Ost(Mittel)Europa: Tschechien, Kroatien, Polen* (Schwabenverlag, 2001)

Archival Sources

Archive of the Tzech-Slovak Union of the Seventh-day Adventist Church, Prague
Archive of the Euro-Afrika Divison of the Seventh-day Adventist Church, Friedensau
Archive of the Hungarian Union of the Seventh-day Adventist Church, Pécel
Collection of Jenő Szigeti, Budapest